A Manager's
Guide to
Software
Engineering

Other McGraw-Hill Books of Interest

0-07-002604-1	AYER	*Documenting the Software Development Process: A Handbook of Structured Techniques*
0-07-002603-3	AYER	*Software Configuration Management: Identification, Accounting, Control, and Management*
0-07-016622-6	BERK, DEVLIN	*Hypertest/Hypermedia Handbook*
0-07-010912-5	CHARETTE	*Application Strategies for Risk Analysis*
0-07-010645-2	CHARETTE	*Software Engineering Environments: Concepts and Technologies*
0-07-010661-4	CHARETTE	*Software Engineering Risk Analysis and Management*
0-07-016803-2	DICKINSON	*Developing Quality Systems*
0-07-015788-2	DIXON	*Winning with CASE*
0-07-023165-6	GENERAL ELECTRIC CO., STAFF	*Software Engineering Handbook*
0-07-032813-7	JONES	*Applied Software Measurement*
0-07-911366-4	KEYES (ED.)	*Software Engineering Productivity Handbook*
0-07-036964-X	LECARME, PELLISIER, GART	*Software Portability*
0-07-040235-3	MARCA, MCGOWAN	*Structural Analysis and Design Structures*
0-07-042632-5	MODELL	*A Professional's Guide to Systems Analysis*
0-07-042634-1	MODELL	*Data Analysis, Data Modeling, and Classification*
0-07-042633-3	MODELL	*Data-Directed Systems Design*
0-07-043198-1	MORRIS, BRANDON	*Relational Diagramming: Enhancing the Software Development Process*
0-07-044118-9	MURPHY, BALKE	*Software Diagramming*
0-07-044119-7	MUSA ET AL.	*Software Reliability*
0-07-050783-X	PRESSMAN	*Software Engineering: A Practitioner's Approach, Third Edition*
0-07-055663-6	SCHULMEYER	*Zero Defect Software*
0-07-059177-6	SMITH	*Concepts of Object-Oriented Programming*
0-07-157879-X	SODHI	*Software Requirements Analysis and Specification*
0-07-061716-3	STONE	*Inside ADW and IEF: The Promise and Reality of CASE*
0-07-068484-7	WATSON	*Portable GUI Development with C^{++}*

A Manager's Guide to Software Engineering

Roger S. Pressman, Ph.D.

McGraw-Hill, Inc.

New York   St. Louis   San Francisco   Auckland   Bogotá
Caracas   Lisbon   London   Madrid   Mexico   Milan
Montreal   New Delhi   Paris   San Juan   São Paulo
Singapore   Sydney   Tokyo   Toronto

Library of Congress Cataloging-in-Publication Data

Pressman, Roger S.
  A manager's guide to software engineering / Roger S. Pressman.
      p.   cm. -- (McGraw-Hill systems design & implementation series)
  Includes bibliographical references and index.
  ISBN 0-07-050820-8
  1. Software engineering. I. Title. II. Series.
QA76.758P73   1993
005.1—dc20   92-13456
                                                                  CIP

1 2 3 4 5 6 7 8 9 0 DOC/DOC 9 8 7 6 5 4 3 2

ISBN 0-07-050820-8

The sponsoring editor for this book was Jeanne Glasser, the editing supervisor was Frank Kotowski, Jr., and the production supervisor was Donald F. Schmidt. It was set in Century Schoolbook by McGraw-Hill's Professional Book Group composition unit.

Printed and bound by R. R. Donnelley & Sons Company.

To Matt and Mike,
Boys $_2$ Men

Credits

Information obtained from the following references has been used with the permission of the publisher:

In Chapter 3: Jones, Capers, *International Software Productivity and Quality Levels, Preliminary Report*, SPR Inc., September 1991, 69 pages. Reprinted by permission of Software Productivity Research, Inc., Burlington, MA.

In Chapter 3: Fenton, N. E., *Software Metrics: A Rigorous Approach*, Chapman and Hall, 1991, p. 44. Reprinted by permission of Chapman and Hall, London, England.

In Chapter 3: Dreger, B. J., *Function Point Analysis*, Prentice-Hall, Inc., 1989, p. 15. Reprinted by permission of Prentice-Hall, Inc., Englewood Cliffs, NJ.

In Chapters 1, 2, 4, and 13: Pressman, R. S., and S. R. Herron, *Software Shock: The Danger and The Opportunity*, Dorset House Publishing, 1991, pp. 115, 118–121, 160–161, 167. Reprinted by permission of Dorset House Publishing, New York, NY.

In Chapter 13: DeMarco, T., and T. Lister, *Peopleware: Productive Projects and Teams*, Dorset House Publishing, 1987, p. 123. Reprinted by permission of Dorset House Publishing, New York, NY.

In Chapter 14: Freedman, D. P., and G. M. Weinberg, *Handbook of Walkthroughs, Inspections, and Technical Reviews*, Dorset House Publishing, 1990, pp. 7–8. Reprinted by permission of Dorset House Publishing, New York, NY.

Contents

Preface

Like many projects in the business world, this book began with a single comment. A software project manager for a large computer company called me after he received a copy of the new edition of my book, *Software Engineering: A Practitioner's Approach.*

"You know," he said, "this is good stuff, but it's just too much. I'm sure the information in here is necessary for students and techies, but I don't have the time to go through almost 800 pages on software engineering. What you ought to do is boil this material down to the topics that are of immediate interest to managers."

My immediate reaction (recalling it with hindsight) was defensive. *Dammit*, I thought, *if he's responsible for managing the technology, he should take the time to read about software engineering. This guy is simply lazy.* I dismissed the comment and went about my daily tasks.

But the manager's words kept creeping into my thoughts, and after some reflection, I began to agree with him. I decided to develop an outline for a manager's book on software engineering. Deciding on the content was relatively easy, but determining an effective format for communicating the information was another story.

I spend a significant portion of my time consulting with managers who have software responsibility. Whether I'm meeting with a single individual or speaking to a large group at a technical conference, good questions invariably arise. I try to provide meaningful answers. A question-and-answer format is an especially effective way to communicate information, and for that reason I decided to use it for this work. The result is the book that you're holding right now.

A Manager's Guide to Software Engineering has been written for managers who have direct or indirect responsibility for the development or maintenance of computer-based systems. If you're a member of this diverse group, you need answers to these questions:

- What is software engineering and how does it impact my business?

- How should I manage the cultural changes that result as software engineering technology is introduced?

- What are the critical management activities that occur during a successful software project?

- What is the underlying technology and how does it result in high-quality computer-based systems?

A Manager's Guide to Software Engineering is designed for those who must answer these questions, but don't have the time or the inclination to read four or five different textbooks to cull out the necessary information.

The book has been organized into four parts. Part 1—*The Product and the Process*—provides a reasonable introduction to software and software engineering. It is intended to define the technology while at the same time raising issues that are relevant to managers at many different levels of responsibility. Part 1 also presents a chapter on measurement—an activity that calibrates the product and the process and is missing in most software development organizations. Part 2—*Instituting Effective Software Engineering Practices*—presents what I believe is the most important topic of all: how to make software engineering happen within a company. In my experience, understanding and managing the technology are relatively easy when compared to understanding and managing cultural problems associated with the introduction of new technology. Part 3—*Project Management*—presents each of the key activities that is required to plan and manage the development and maintenance of computer software. More often than not, software projects get into trouble because of a failing in project management, not a failing in technology. Part 4—*The Underlying Technology*—provides an overview of the methods and tools that are used in modern software engineering work. Every manager should have a conversational knowledge of key technology components, if for no other reason than he or she may someday have to spend large sums of money to acquire training and tools to support these components.

At the end of each chapter I have included a *Manager's Checklist*. The checklist contains a set of actions that you might take and questions that you might ask to better understand the topic presented in the chapter. If you read the chapter and then follow the checklist, you'll gain a working knowledge of the process and the product and how they relate to your situation. I've also included a *Further Readings* section for each chapter. If you need even more information on a particular topic, the books that I've suggested are a good place to begin.

Because readers of this book will have different backgrounds and knowledge levels, the book has been designed as a random access volume. That is, you don't necessarily have to start at the beginning. If you're a senior manager who has been chartered with the responsibility for instituting the technology, start with Parts 1 and 2. If you have a good understanding of software engineering, but can't seem to make it work within your organization, Part 2 is for you. If you already understand the technology, but need help with project management, start with Part 3. If all you need is an overview of the technology, Parts 1 and 4 are your choices. And if you're like me, you'll pick and choose among the chapters finding those morsels that tempt your intellectual pallet and nourish your organizational needs.

A book is always a joint effort. It is shaped by the literature the author has read, students (at the university and industry level) who have asked the right questions, colleagues who have often provided intriguing answers, clients from around the world who have stubbornly insisted that real-life problems deserve pragmatic solutions, and loved ones who add balance to a hectic life. All, in their own inimitable way, have contributed to this book.

Special thanks also goes to McGraw-Hill for allowing me to adapt portions of *Software Engineering: A Practitioner's Approach* for use in this book.

Finally, my love and thanks to Barbara, Mathew, and Michael, who above all else, help me to keep things in perspective.

Roger S. Pressman

A Manager's
Guide to
Software
Engineering

The Product
and the Process

The Product:
A Business
Perspective

If you're reading this book, it's likely that you already know that software has a direct impact on your business. You may be a software "player," that is, a person with direct project responsibility for the creation of new software or the maintenance and support of existing programs. Or you may sit passively on the sidelines, contributing information, requirements, and criticism as new computer-based systems evolve.

You've seen the impact of software in the quality of the products, systems, or services that your company brings to the marketplace, the timeliness with which they are delivered, and the cost effectiveness with which they are produced.

Your market is becoming increasingly competitive. Your customers are demanding rapid response to their requests for new products, new systems, and new services. And yet, the following statement may still come as a shock: *You work for a "software company."*

That's a hard statement to buy...my management views software as a support activity, something that buttresses other, more important parts of our business. How can we be a "software company"?

If your company sells software as a product, you'll have no problem with the above statement, but if it doesn't, if you work for a bank, an aerospace company, a food processing giant, a drug company, an automobile manufacturer, an insurance company, or any of the thousands of businesses that thrive in our high-technology culture, I can understand your skepticism. After all, software is never mentioned in your company's sales brochures, it is not listed in the price book, your salespeople rarely, if ever, mention it to a customer. And yet, software always seems to be there.

Software might be embedded inside the products that you sell; it may process the information necessary to serve your customers; it assists engineers in designing new products and controlling manufacturing processes; it is used to collect raw business data and produce management information.

Sure, Lotus, Microsoft, Oracle, and others like them are the obvious software companies, but is yours? In reality, every company that builds high-technology products or uses high-technology systems is a software company.

Still not convinced? Your reaction is reasonable and predictable. In fact, the vast majority of technical and business managers, and virtually all of the senior management team in companies such as yours might react in the same way.

"We use software," they say, "but we're certainly not a software company."

Unfortunately, the problems that many companies have with software have much to do with a prevailing attitude that views software as a low-level support activity—something to be built, acquired, or maintained so that other business functions can proceed. In this chapter, I'll make the argument that software is a strategic business issue that is pivotal to the long-term success of your business.

But why is software business strategic? What makes it so important?

Software is, above all else, a *differentiator*. When it is embedded inside consumer or industrial products, it makes them unique by providing an extended function that differentiates an otherwise similar product from its competitors. When software forms the basis of a service (e.g., an automatic teller machine at a bank or an airline reservation system[1]), its capabilities offer features and functions that provide benefit to the customer. When software lies at the kernel of a system (e.g., insurance claims processing, computer-integrated manufacturing, telecommunications), its impact on the behavior, performance, efficiency, and integrity of the system makes it a key factor in differentiating the

---

[1]It is interesting to note that a major airline currently makes a larger profit and attains significantly better margins from its widely used flight-reservation system than it attains from its overall airline operations. Software that was originally developed to support the business has become a business!

system from others that perform similar functions. In essence, software is a key component of competitive advantage—and competitive advantage is a strategic business issue.

If you agree that software is a differentiator, that it is, in fact, business-strategic, you will begin to understand why every company that uses computers as an integral part of its business can be characterized as a software company. Directly or indirectly, the capability and quality of the software that you acquire or build can be traced to the bottom line. Software technology should not be considered as an afterthought. It must be managed using a disciplined approach that provides a clear path for the achievement of current needs, and more importantly, establishes a foundation from which future changes to products, systems, and services can be readily accommodated.

You keep using the term "software," but you haven't really defined it. Is there an accepted definition?

Twenty years ago, less than 1 percent of the public could have intelligently described what the term *computer software* meant. Today, most professionals and many members of the public at large feel that they understand software. But do they?

A textbook description of software might take the following form: *Software is (1) instructions (computer programs) that when executed provide desired function and performance, (2) data structures that enable the instructions to adequately manipulate information, and (3) documents that describe the operation and use of the instructions.*

To gain an understanding of software (and ultimately an understanding of software engineering), it is important to examine the characteristics of software that make it different from other things that human beings build. When hardware is built, the human creative process (analysis, design, construction, testing) is ultimately translated into a physical form. If we build a new computer, our initial sketches, formal design drawings, and breadboarded prototype evolve into a physical product [VLSI (very-large-scale-integration) chips, circuit boards, power supplies, etc.].

Software is different. It captures information, it produces information, and it is itself information. Software is a logical rather than a physical system element.

That helps, but only a little. What approach do I take when software development is to be managed? I've read about "software factories." Can I treat software development like a manufacturing activity?

Software is developed or engineered; it is *not* manufactured in the classical sense. Although some similarities exist between software development and hardware manufacture, the two activities are fundamentally different. In both activities, high quality is achieved through good design, but the manufacturing phase for hardware can introduce quality problems that are nonexistent (or easily corrected) for software. Both activities are dependent on people, but the relationship between people applied and work accomplished is entirely different (see Chapter 10). Both activities require the construction of a "product," but the approaches are different.

Software costs are concentrated in engineering (prior to delivery) and support (after delivery). This means that software projects cannot be managed as if they were manufacturing projects.

To illustrate, assume that you're a manager of a hardware manufacturer that builds "widgets." You receive a major order and commit to an aggressive delivery schedule. Before long, you realize that you're not producing enough widgets to make your dates. What should you do?

First, you'd examine your manufacturing process in an effort to find and remove inefficiencies, thereby increasing productivity with the same work force. If that doesn't work, you'll buy additional widget-making machines, hire more widget makers, and put them to work in parallel with existing staff in an effort to produce more output per unit time. If all goes well, you just might succeed. Adding additional resources in a manufacturing environment is a relatively easy way to increase productivity. But is the same true for software?

To find out, let's assume that you're a manager responsible for software development. You receive a major order and commit to an aggressive delivery date. Before long, you realize that you're way behind schedule. What should you do?

If you apply a manufacturing mind set (and why not; software is a labor-intensive activity, isn't it?), your first reaction is to add additional people, thereby producing more software per unit time.

In 1974, Frederick Brooks [1] wrote *The Mythical Man-Month,* a landmark book about software development, in which he states: "Adding [people] to a late software project makes it later." If you find this statement counterintuitive, think about it for a moment. Because software is complex information, every person who is added to a late project must be trained to understand the existing software. This in itself would be no problem, if the newcomers could go off by themselves and learn. But who must do the training? The same people who were doing the work before the newcomers arrived. While training is conducted, less work is accomplished and schedules slip even more. By the time everyone is ready to begin working again, schedules have slipped so much that even more people must be added and the vicious cycle begins anew.

Although I'll discuss this phenomenon in greater detail later in the book, it's important to note that people can be added to a software project, but only if the software and the process through which it is to be built are well designed.

One of the things I don't completely understand is why a software application seems to become more troublesome as it ages; after all, software doesn't wear out, does it?

Software is not susceptible to the environmental maladies that cause hardware to wear out. Dust, vibration, physical abuse, and temperature extremes work on hardware components and cause them to fail as time passes. This phenomenon is illustrated in Figure 1.1. The relationship between failure rate and time, often called the "bathtub curve," indicates that hardware exhibits relatively high failure rates early in its life (these failures are often attributable to design or manufacturing defects); defects are corrected and failure rate drops to a steady-state level (hopefully, quite low) for some period of time. As time passes, however, the failure rate rises again as hardware begins to wear out.

In theory, the failure-rate curve for software should take the form of the "idealized" curve for software shown in Figure 1.2. Undiscovered defects will cause high failure rates early in the life of a program. However, these are corrected (ideally, without introducing other er-

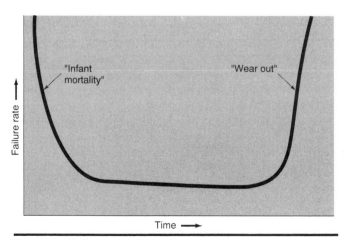

Figure 1.1   Failure curve for hardware.

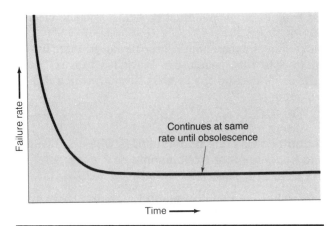

Figure 1.2 Failure curve for software (idealized).

rors) and the curve flattens as shown. The implication is clear—*software doesn't wear out. But it does deteriorate!*

This seeming contradiction can best be explained by considering the "actual" curve for software shown in Figure 1.3. During its life, software will undergo change. As changes are made, it is likely that some new defects will be introduced, causing the failure-rate curve to spike as shown in Figure 1.3. Before the curve can return to the original steady-state failure rate, another change is requested, causing the curve to spike again. Slowly, the minimum failure-rate level begins to rise—the software is deteriorating because of change.

Another aspect of wear illustrates the difference between hardware and software. When a hardware component wears out, it is replaced by a "spare part." There are no software spare parts. Every software

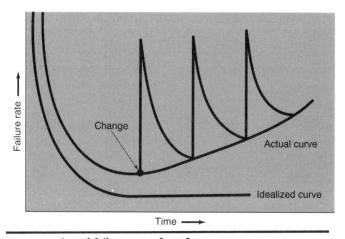

Figure 1.3 Actual failure curve for software.

failure indicates an error in design or in the process through which design was translated into machine-executable code. Therefore, software maintenance involves considerably more complexity than hardware maintenance.

You said that software spare parts don't exist. Yet, people are talking about building software from "reusable" parts. Is there reason to expect that this will happen?

Business efficiency is achieved through reuse. A banker reuses standard forms, documents, and procedures to make her interaction with the customer as systematic and efficient as possible. A furniture maker reuses designs that may have been created 50 years ago, making only small changes to conform to modern needs. At the same time, he reduces design and construction errors. A design engineer reuses existing engineering building blocks by drawing a simple schematic of digital circuitry, doing some fundamental analysis to ensure that proper function will be achieved, and then going to the shelf where catalogs of digital components exist. Each integrated circuit (an engineering building block that is called an "IC" or a "chip") has a part number, a defined and validated function, a well-defined interface, and a standard set of integration guidelines. After each component is selected, it can be ordered off-the-shelf.

Software developers are only beginning to recognize the importance of reuse. To date, there are few catalogs that list reusable software components. It is possible to order off-the-shelf software, but only as a complete unit, not as components that can be reassembled into new programs.[2] Although much has been written about "software reusability" [2], we are only beginning to see the first successful implementations of the concept.

The more software my company creates, the more software that must be supported over the long term. Like every company, our costs for software maintenance continue to increase, but something else troubles me. Some of the programs we maintain are older than the people doing the maintaining! I have an uneasy feeling about all of this. Are my concerns justified?

In the 1950s and 1960s many commentators criticized the steel industry in the United States for lack of investment in its physical plant. Factories had begun to deteriorate, modern methods were rarely ap-

---

[2]This situation is changing rapidly. The widespread use of object-oriented programming has resulted in the creation of "software ICs." These are discussed in Chapter 17.

plied, the quality and cost of the end product suffered, and competition began to win substantial market share. Management in these industries decided against making the capital investment that was required to remain competitive in their core business. Over time, the steel industry suffered, losing significant market share to foreign competition—competition had newer plants, used more modern technology, and was provided with government subsidies to make them extremely cost-competitive.

During that period, many of us in the fledgling computer industry looked at the steel industry with contempt. "If they're unwilling to invest in their own business," we said, "they deserve to lose market share." Those words may come back to haunt the software industry.

At the risk of sounding melodramatic, the software industry today is in a position that is quite similar to the steel industry of the 1950s and 1960s. Across companies large and small, we have an aging "software plant"—there are thousands of critical software-based applications that are in dramatic need of refurbishing:

- Information system applications written 20 years ago have undergone 40 generations of changes and are now virtually unmaintainable. Even the smallest modification can cause the entire system to fail.

- Engineering applications are used to produce critical design data, and yet, because of their age and state of repair, no one really understands the internal workings of the program.

- Real-time systems (used to control power plants, air traffic, and factories, among thousands of applications) exhibit strange and sometimes unexplained behavior, but cannot be taken out of service because there's nothing available to replace them.

It will not be enough to "patch" what is broken and give these applications a modern look. Many components of the software plant require significant reengineering, or they will not be competitive during the 1990s and beyond. Unfortunately, many business managers are unwilling to commit the resources to undertake this reengineering effort. "The applications still work," they say, and it is "uneconomic" to commit the resources to make them better.

I'm not sure that your analogy with the steel industry is appropriate. Who is the competition and where will it come from?

The fact is that competition is forming right now. It will be intense, it will be competent, and it will be here sooner than many think. Countries in the Far East (Japan, Korea, Singapore, Taiwan), Asia (India, China), and eastern Europe all offer a large pool of highly motivated, competently educated, and relatively low-cost professionals. This work force will move rapidly to adopt state-of-the-art software engineering methods and tools and may very well become a force to be reckoned with during the late 1990s. Bill Gates, the CEO of Microsoft, summarizes the situation well when he states: "Most of the U.S. software companies are spoiled. There's this notion that the Japanese [and other Pacific rim competitors] can't write software, and it's not true. They're a first class competitor [3]."

Has "the competition" made any inroads as yet?

Some companies have already decided to throw in the towel and have begun "outsourcing." A company cuts its information systems staff to the bone and contracts all new software development, much of its ongoing system maintenance, and all of its computer operations to a third party. To date, outsourcing is generally restricted to local service bureaus. But because this trend has one primary goal—to save money—it won't be long before outsourcing goes off-shore. Recall that in the 1960s, companies such as RCA and Motorola attempted to cut television manufacturing costs by outsourcing only a few electronic components to off-shore manufacturers. The core industry would remain in the United States, they said. Today, there are no television manufacturing facilities left in the United States.

In their book on the impact of information services on the United States and the world, Feigenbaum and McCorduck [4] state the following:

> Knowledge is power, and the computer is an amplifier of that power.... The American computer industry has been innovative, vital, successful. It is, in a way, the ideal industry. It creates value by transforming the brainpower of knowledge workers, with little consumption of energy and raw materials. Today [1983], we dominate the world's ideas and markets in this most important of all modern technologies. But what about tomorrow?

Indeed, what about tomorrow? Already, computer hardware is becoming a commodity, available from many sources. But software remains an industry where the United States has been "innovative, vital, and successful." Will we maintain our place at the top?

Feigenbaum and McCorduck may be closer to the mark than many of us want to believe. There are economic, political, technological, and national security reasons why the United States cannot afford to lose its leadership in software development technologies. Yet, we do nothing about our aging software plant. There may come a time when it will be less costly to "outsource" software development and maintenance to third parties located halfway around the world. These third parties will be supported by their government, will be extremely competent, and, therefore, very competitive. Software is not steel, but foreign competition may make them look very much alike.

It seems that you can't read an article on computer software without encountering the word *crisis*. Yet we do build software and some of it works pretty well. Isn't the "crisis" characterization a bit melodramatic?

Many industry observers (including myself) have characterized the problems associated with software development as a "crisis." Yet, what we really have may be something rather different.

The word *crisis* is defined in *Webster's Dictionary* as "a turning point in the course of anything; decisive or crucial time, stage, or event." Yet, for software there has been no "turning point" or "decisive time," only slow, evolutionary change. In the software industry, we have had a "crisis" that has been with us for close to 30 years, and that is a contradiction in terms.

Anyone who looks up the word *crisis* in the dictionary will find another definition: "the turning point in the course of a disease, when it becomes clear whether the patient will live or die." This definition may give us a clue about the real nature of the problems that have plagued software development.

We have yet to reach the stage of crisis in computer software. What we really have is a *chronic affliction*.[3] The word *affliction* is defined as "anything causing pain or distress." But it is the definition of the adjective *chronic* that is the key to our argument: "lasting a long time or recurring often; continuing indefinitely." It is far more accurate to describe what we have endured for the past three decades as a chronic affliction, rather than a crisis. There are no miracle cures, but there are many ways that we can reduce the pain as we strive to discover a cure.

Regardless of what we call this situation, what are the problems associated with it?

The problems that afflict software development can be characterized from a number of different perspectives, but as a manager responsible

---

[3]This terminology was suggested by Professor Daniel Tiechrow of the University of Michigan in a talk presented in Geneva, Switzerland, in April 1989.

for software development, you should concentrate on "bottom line" issues: (1) schedule and cost estimates that are often grossly inaccurate, (2) "productivity" of software people that hasn't kept pace with the demand for their services, and (3) software quality that is sometimes less than adequate. These problems are the most visible manifestation of other software difficulties:

- We haven't taken the time to collect data on the software development process. With little historical data as a guide, estimation has been "seat of the pants" with predictably poor results. With no solid indication of productivity, we can't accurately evaluate the efficacy of new tools, methods, or standards.

- Customer dissatisfaction with the "completed" system is encountered too frequently. Software development projects are frequently undertaken with only a vague indication of customer requirements. Communication between customer and software developer is often poor.

- Software quality is often suspect. We have only recently begun to understand the importance of systematic, technically complete software testing. Solid quantitative concepts of software reliability and quality assurance do exist, but are not applied widely in the industry.

- Existing software can be very difficult to correct, adapt, and enhance, a set of activities that is often referred to as *software maintenance*. The software maintenance task devours the majority of all software dollars. Software maintainability has not been emphasized as an important criterion for software acceptance.

One final problem (I could call it a fact of life) remains. Software will absorb a larger and larger percentage of the overall development cost for computer-based systems. In the United States, we spend close to 100 billion dollars each year on the development, purchase, and maintenance of computer software. We had better take the problems associated with software technology seriously.

I have presented the bad news first. Now for some good news. Each of the problems described above can be corrected. An engineering approach to the development of software, coupled with continuing improvement of techniques and tools, provides the key.

Why do the problems that you've just described exist in companies that apply high-technology solutions? What are the underlying causes?

Problems associated with software have been caused by the character of software itself and by the failings of the people charged with software development responsibility. It is possible, however, that we have expected too much in too short a period of time. After all, our experience spans little more than 40 years.

The character of computer software was discussed briefly earlier in this chapter. To review, software is a logical rather than a physical system element; therefore, success is measured by the quality of a single entity, rather than the quality of many manufactured entities. Software does not wear out. If faults are encountered, there is a high probability that each was inadvertently introduced during development and went undetected during testing. We replace "defective parts" during software maintenance, but we have few, if any, spare parts; that is, maintenance often includes correction or modification to design.

The logical nature of software provides a challenge to the people who develop it. For the first time we have accepted the task of communicating with an alien intelligence—a machine. The intellectual challenge of software development is certainly one cause of the affliction that affects software, but the problems discussed above have been caused by more mundane human failings.

Middle- and upper-level managers with no background in software are often given responsibility for software development. There is an old management axiom that states: "A good manager can manage any project." The following qualification should be added: "if he or she is willing to learn the milestones that can be used to measure progress, apply effective methods of control, disregard mythology, and become conversant in a rapidly changing technology." The manager must communicate with all constituencies involved with software development—customers, software developers, support staff, and others. Communication can break down because the special characteristics of software and the problems associated with its development are misunderstood. When this occurs, the problems associated with software are exacerbated.

Software practitioners have had little formal training in new techniques for software development. In many organizations a mild form of anarchy reigns. Each individual approaches the task of "writing programs" with experience derived from past efforts. Some people develop an orderly and efficient approach to software development by trial and error, but many others develop bad habits that result in poor software quality and maintainability.

We all resist change. It is truly ironic, however, that while computing potential (hardware) experiences enormous change, the software people responsible for tapping that potential often oppose change when it is discussed and resist change when it is introduced. Maybe that's the real cause of the software affliction.

The implication of some of the things that you're saying is a bit unsettling. In fact, it's causing me to examine some of the "conventional wisdom" that seems to dictate the way managers look at software. Is the conventional wisdom worth questioning?

Managers with software responsibility, like managers in most disciplines, are often under pressure to maintain budgets, keep schedules from slipping, and improve quality. Like a drowning person who grasps at a straw, a software manager often grasps at belief in a software myth, if that belief will lessen the pressure (even temporarily). In some cases the myth is characterized as "conventional wisdom." In others, it's simply a "fact." Let's examine a few:

Myth. We already have a book that's full of standards and procedures for building software. Won't that provide my people with everything they need to know?

Reality. The book of standards may very well exist, but is it used? Are software practitioners aware of its existence? Does it reflect modern software development practice? Is it complete? Does it lead to faster software development? In many cases, the answer to all of these questions is "no."

Myth. My people do have state-of-the-art software development tools. After all, we buy them the newest computers.

Reality. It takes much more than the latest-model mainframe, workstation, or PC to do high-quality software development. Computer-aided software engineering (CASE) tools are more important than hardware for achieving good software quality and productivity, yet the majority of software developers still do not use them.

Myth. A general statement of objectives is sufficient to begin writing programs. We can fill in the details later.

Reality. Poor up-front definition is the major cause of failed software efforts. A formal and detailed description of information domain, function, performance, interfaces, design constraints, and validation criteria is essential. These characteristics can be determined only after thorough communication between customer and developer.

Myth. Sure, quality is important, but doing all the things required to build high-quality software will cause delivery dates to slip and costs to rise.

Reality. Quality is free! If you build software correctly the first time; if you meet customer requirements, if you apply good methods and competent tools, if you review your work—the time you spend on the process will be paid back. You'll manage software projects that require less testing and debugging time, demand less iteration prior to release, and produce fewer defects encountered in the field. You'll save money and time.

So where do we go from here? Is there a way that the myths can be debunked? Is there a technology structure that will help me to improve the process that we use to build computer software?

The answers to your questions lie in a systematic, disciplined framework that demands an engineering approach. It is called *software engineering*. Pressman and Herron [5] draw an analogy between the tasks required to design and build a factory and the tasks that are the essence of software engineering:

> Before a manufacturing engineer can worry about the design and creation of a single machine, he or she must understand the overall function and flow of the entire factory. The engineer should learn how each of the machines interacts with the others and define the modes of coordination that will allow raw materials to become an end product. Then, after the big picture is understood, the engineer can begin to focus on the discrete parts (the machines).
>
> You don't need an engineering degree to recognize that this approach has merit—it's simply common sense. The construction of any complex system (the factory is a system) begins with the big-picture view and proceeds through a series of iterations toward the nuts and bolts.
>
> Some software builders, deeply entrenched in the hacker's culture, begin by focusing all of their attention and energies on a single "machine." That is, rather than expending the effort to understand the specific requirements of a problem and laying out a complete design for the entire system, these programmers feel more comfortable writing the programming language source code that will enable them to create a program component. Often, they do a reasonably good job of building the program components, but problems surface when components must be combined to form a system, when the system is tested, and when changes to the system are required. No one spent any time considering the big picture.
>
> Software engineering suggests that a computer-based system should be built from the top down. That is, before worrying about all the components, a software engineer should understand overall requirements and establish an architecture for the system. The role of each individual component is then defined in terms of both the requirements and the architecture. Once this is done, design for each of the components can be accomplished with some certainty that each will integrate properly with others. This approach represents good software engineering practice (supported by centuries of practical application in other disciplines) and, more importantly, good common sense. It is encouraging that more and more organizations are using the software engineering approach and we are beginning to realize the benefits of higher quality products with greater functionality.

The essence of software engineering lies in its holistic approach. A software engineer solves a set of problems that begins with a recognition of need and terminate with the creation of machine-executable instructions. Using an early definition [6], software engineering can be defined as "The establishment and use of sound engineering principles in order to obtain economically software that is reliable and works efficiently on real machines."

Although many more comprehensive definitions have been proposed, all reinforce the requirement for engineering discipline in software work.

Software engineering is an outgrowth of hardware and system engineering. It encompasses a set of three key components—procedures, methods, and tools—that enable the manager to control the process of software development and provide the practitioner with a foundation for building high-quality software in a productive manner.

I presume that when you talk about software engineering in an industry context, the "components" are what make the technology work. Can you discuss these components in more detail?

All software engineering components must be applied in concert to achieve our primary objective of obtaining "software that is reliable and works efficiently on real machines." Software engineering *procedures* are the glue that holds the methods and tools together and enable rational and timely development of computer software. Procedures define the sequence in which methods will be applied, the deliverables (documents, reports, forms, etc.) that are required, the controls that help ensure quality and coordinate change, and the milestones that enable software managers to assess progress. In essence, procedures provide the framework that supports all other aspects of the engineering discipline.

Software engineering *methods* provide the technical "how to's" for building software. Methods encompass a broad array of tasks that include project planning and estimation, system and software requirements analysis, design of data structure, program architecture and algorithmic procedure, coding, testing, and maintenance. Methods for software engineering often introduce a special language-oriented or graphical notation and introduce a set of criteria for software quality.

Software engineering *tools* provide automated or semiautomated support for methods. Today, tools exist to support each of the methods noted above. When tools are integrated so that information created by one tool can be used by another, a system for the support of software development, called *computer-aided software engineering* (CASE), is established. CASE combines software, hardware, and a software engineering database (a data structure containing important information about software projects and technical information about analysis, design, code, and testing) to create a software engineering environment that is analogous to CAD/CAE (computer-aided design/engineering) for hardware.

OK, now for the big question: How should we manage these procedures, methods, and tools in a way that will enable us to build and maintain high-quality software?

The product that is created as a consequence of the software engineering process has been notoriously difficult to manage. Part of the problem is the process itself. In many companies it is ill-defined, making it hard to specify a manageable set of tasks that can be planned in advance, executed with confidence, controlled during their execution, and tracked to completion. Another part of the problem is technological. Software engineers create high-technology products, systems, and services, but they often do this using outmoded or underpowered methods and tools. Part of the problem is cultural. The echo of a freewheeling "hacker's" culture that evolved throughout the 1960s and 1970s still exists in many companies, making technology transition difficult to achieve.

Throughout the remainder of this book, we'll examine each of these problem areas and suggest a framework of solutions that will enable you to do a better job of managing the development of computer software.

A Manager's Checklist

Understanding the true nature of computer software is a prerequisite to an understanding of software engineering. The "product"—as we have called software in this chapter—can be as simple as a word processing program on your personal computer or as complex as a high-performance, real-time flight-control system for a commercial airliner. Interestingly, software at both ends of the complexity spectrum has many characteristics in common.

The checklist that follows should help you to explore the nature of software within your work environment. If you take the time to address each checklist item, you'll have a better understanding of software within your company and lay a solid foundation for the discussions of software engineering that follow.

Actions

- Make a list of all programs that you use regularly on your PC or workstation. Estimate the number of hours each day that you spend using these computer programs.
- Make a list of all business information that you receive that is gen-

erated directly by software. Estimate the worth of this information relative to your job on a scale of 0 (useless, should be eliminated) to 10 (critical to job function).

- List your company's revenue-producing products, systems, and services. Indicate how software has an impact on each.

Questions

- Does software clearly differentiate your company's products, systems, and services? Does it provide competitive advantage? How?

- Within your company, is software perceived as a bottleneck in the creation of new products, systems, and services? Is the perception justified?

- Have you heard any of the management myths stated as fact? Why do you think that myth and reality weren't differentiated?

- Have you encountered software that is deteriorating? How is this manifested, and what are the reasons?

- Does your organization reuse software? At the design level? At the program level? At the component level?

- Are you aware of programs that are candidates for reengineering? How should the management decision for reengineering be made?

- Does your company have a defined policy for achieving high-quality software? Can you define what *software quality* is?

Further Readings

The role of computers and software in a broader societal context is discussed by Stoll (*The Cuckoo's Egg,* Doubleday, 1989) and Toffler (*Powershift,* Bantam Publishers, 1990). Pressman and Herron (*Software Shock,* Dorset House, 1991) consider software and its impact on individuals, businesses, and government. Yourdon (*The Decline and Fall of the American Programmer*, Yourdon Press, 1992) presents a provocative discussion of software competitiveness on a worldwide scale. Gelernter (*Mirror Worlds,* Oxford University Press, 1991) presents a thought-provoking image of how software may evolve in the new millennium.

Robert Glass (*Software Conflict,* Yourdon Press, 1991) presents a wry overview of the product and the process in a series of short essays. Walsh (*Productivity Sand Traps and Tar Pits,* Dorset House, 1991) considers techniques that enable managers to improve the productivity of those who produce computer software.

References

[1] Brooks, F., *The Mythical Man-Month*, Addison-Wesley, 1975.
[2] Tracz, W., *Software Reuse: Emerging Technology*, IEEE Computer Society Press, 1988.
[3] Rogers, M., "The Whiz They Love to Hate," *Newsweek*, June 24, 1991, pp. 38–39.
[4] Feigenbaum, E.A., and P. McCorduck, *The Fifth Generation*, Addison-Wesley, 1983.
[5] Pressman, R.S., and S.R. Herron, *Software Shock*, Dorset House, 1991, pp. 159–161 (reproduced with permission).
[6] Naur, P., and B. Randell (eds.), *Software Engineering: A Report on a Conference Sponsored by the NATO Science Committee*, NATO, 1969.

2

The Process:
Software Engineering

Software engineering brings discipline to the process of software development. The nature of the discipline requires customers, practitioners, and managers to each become involved; therefore, software engineering makes demands of each. The customer must be willing to spend time to state the requirements of a new system (or a modification to an existing system) in an unambiguous and relatively complete manner. The practitioner must be willing to learn technical methods and apply CASE tools to create models that will ultimately be translated into a high-quality, executable program that meets all customer requirements. The manager must understand the process for what it is—a *framework* that can be used to guide all constituencies in their attempt to build high-quality systems.

But there must be many different ways to build high-quality systems and many different and acceptable approaches to software engineering. Is there a way to describe the process generically, using actions that will always occur?

The software engineering process can be described using three generic phases: *definition, development,* and *maintenance.* The phases are encountered in all software work, regardless of application area, project size, or complexity.

The definition phase focuses on *what.* That is, during definition, the software developer and the customer attempt to identify what information is to be processed, what function and performance are desired, what interfaces are to be established, what design constraints exist, and what validation criteria are required to define a successful system. The key requirements of the system and the software are identified. Although the methods applied during the definition phase will vary depending on the software engineering paradigm that is applied, three specific steps will occur in some form:

Customer contact.   A research and consultation activity, customer contact defines the role of each element in a computer-based system, and focuses on the role that software will play.

Project planning.   Once the scope of the software is established, risks are analyzed, resources are allocated, costs are estimated, and work tasks and schedule are defined.

Requirements analysis.   The scope defined for the software provides direction, but a more detailed definition of the information, behavior, and function of the software is necessary before work can begin.

The development phase focuses on *how*. That is, during definition the software developer attempts to define how data structure and software architecture are to be designed, how procedural details are to be implemented, how the design will be translated into a programming language (or nonprocedural language), and how testing will be performed. The methods applied during the development phase will vary, but three specific steps will always occur in some form:

Design.   Design translates the requirements for the software into a set of representations (some graphical, others tabular or language-based) that describe data structure, architecture, and algorithmic procedure as well as the nature of the human–computer interface.

Coding.   Design representations must be translated into an artificial language (the language may be a conventional programming language or a nonprocedural language) that results in instructions that can be executed by the computer. The coding step performs this translation.

Testing.   Once the software is implemented in machine-executable form, it must be tested to uncover errors in function, logic, and implementation.

The maintenance phase focuses on *change* that is associated with error correction, adaptations required as the software's environment evolves, and changes due to enhancements brought about by changing customer requirements. The maintenance phase reapplies the steps of the definition and development phases, but does so in the context of existing software. Four types of change are encountered during the maintenance phase:

Correction.   Even with the best quality assurance activities, it is likely that the customer will uncover defects in the software. *Corrective maintenance* changes the software to correct defects.

Adaptation.   Over time, the original environment (e.g., CPU, operating system, peripherals) for which the software was developed is likely to change. *Adaptive maintenance* results in modification to the software to accommodate changes to its external environment.

Enhancement.   As software is used, the customer or user will recognize additional functions that will provide benefit. Perfective maintenance extends the software beyond its original functional requirements.

Reengineering.   Using a specialized set of CASE tools, old software is reengineered so that its internal workings can be understood and improved (see Chapters 17 and 18).

The phases and related steps described in a generic view of software engineering are complemented by a number of *umbrella activities* that occur throughout the software engineering process.

Quality assurance.   Reviews are conducted to ensure that quality is maintained as each step is completed. Documentation is developed and controlled to ensure that complete information about the system and software will be available for later use.

Configuration management.   All information created as part of the definition, development, and maintenance phases should be uniquely identified and controlled. Change control is instituted so that changes can be approved and tracked.

Project monitoring.   The software engineering process defines a set of milestones that provides an indication of progress. These must be monitored to ensure that schedule and cost are under control.

Measurement.   The software engineering process and the product that is produced as a result of it can be measured. Direct and indirect measures of quality and productivity can be determined.

The manner in which the generic phases and related umbrella activities are applied will vary across different software development organizations. Yet, definition, development, and maintenance will always exist in some form. You can conduct the phases in a disciplined manner, or you can muddle through the phases haphazardly. But you will perform them nonetheless.

So I was right in assuming that software engineering can be implemented in different ways, even though generic phases always exist. What are the characteristics of frameworks that are used to implement software engineering?

In practice, the generic software development phases discussed above are manifested as a *software engineering paradigm*. A paradigm is a template, pattern, or framework that defines the process through which software is created. It establishes the procedural context for a software project, implying the milestones and deliverables that are created, the quality assurance activities that are to be imposed, and the management oversight that will be required.

Sequentiality, iteration, and parallelism are important characteristics of a software engineering *paradigm*. Certain definition and development activities are performed in a step-by-step manner. The output of one activity becomes the input of the next and software is developed in a sequence of predictable steps. For example, software can be derived from a statement of customer requirements using a sequence of technical steps that are called analysis, design, coding, and testing. Once the software has been delivered to the customer, support and maintenance activities begin.

Yet, a purely sequential approach to software development is rarely encountered in the real world. The uncertainty that is inherent in the development of most computer-based systems causes the definition and development phases to be iterative in nature. A version of the software is created, reviewed by the customer and then re-created based on changing perceptions of what is required. The iterative cycle continues over weeks or months until the computer-based system evolves toward a stable implementation.

In addition to sequentiality and iteration, software engineering paradigms impose varying degrees of parallelism as technical activities occur. It is often possible to compartmentalize software work so that technical tasks occur concurrently. For example, analysis activities (the definition of what is required) can occur at the same time that design activities (the specification of how the system will be implemented) are being conducted for another part of a system. The asynchronous nature of each task demands careful management and monitoring so that progress can be tracked and controlled.

A software engineering paradigm defines a framework for building the product. It identifies the overall development philosophy; establishes the amount of sequentiality, iteration, and parallelism; specifies the distinct technical steps that will be required to produce the software; and, by implication, suggests the milestones and deliverables that will be required to manage a software project. In essence, a software engineering paradigm defines the process and, in so doing, becomes the driving force behind all software engineering work conducted within your organization.

Are the paradigms identified by different names, and if so, can you describe each one?

Software engineering paradigms are discussed in detail in Chapter 16. For now, I'll present an overview of some of the more common paradigms.

A sequential paradigm—the classic life cycle. This, the oldest and most widely used paradigm for software engineering, defines a sequential approach to software development. Requirements are defined, software is developed using a sequence of design, coding, and testing steps, and the finished product is supported throughout a maintenance phase. The classic life-cycle paradigm for software engineering has both advantages and disadvantages (discussed in Chapter 16) and has been the focus of much debate over the past decade. Although its influence and importance are waning, it remains the backbone of software development at many companies.

A modeling paradigm—prototyping. This iterative model for software development relies on close communication between the customer and the software developer. Requirements are defined through the creation of progressively more detailed models (prototypes) of the software. The developer discusses requirements with the customer, who attempts to define the current vision of the system. A mock-up of the system is created for the customer to evaluate, and changes are suggested. A new mock-up is developed, further evaluation occurs, and still more change is suggested and implemented. Over a number of iterations, an accurate model of customer requirements begins to evolve. Depending on the prototyping approach, one of two different options may be chosen: (1) the model (prototype) may be discarded and the final system rebuilt using the classic life cycle or some other paradigm, or (2) the prototype may be further extended and engineered to become the final system. Regardless of which option has been chosen, prototyping demands close communication between developer and customer and thoughtful management to ensure that progress is being made and schedules are being maintained.

An evolutionary paradigm—the spiral model. Combining elements of both sequential and iterative software engineering, the spiral model melds some elements of the classic life cycle with other characteristics of prototyping and produces an *evolutionary* approach to software engineering. The spiral model defines an iterative process that incorporates four major components: management planning, risk analysis, engineering, and customer evaluation. Management planning identifies basic customer requirements and establishes a plan that reflects the time, effort, and resources required to implement those requirements. Risk analysis is a formal, statistical activity that can help the developer and the customer understand and avoid key project risks. Engineering applies a set of methods that are used to create the software, and customer evaluation allows the customer to make requests for change. These four phases are applied iteratively, and with each iteration the software becomes more complete.

A reuse paradigm—object-oriented development. This approach to software engineering assumes that new software can be constructed from a library of reusable software components. Iterative in nature, the object-oriented paradigm begins with a definition phase that is similar in many ways to each of the preceding paradigms. The primary difference in the object-oriented approach is that an attempt is made to identify key *classes* and *objects* (see Chapter 17) that are part of the problem domain. Once these classes and objects have been identified, the software engineer attempts to find them in a library of existing, reusable classes and objects. If they can be found, the software is created by assembling new systems from preexisting components. If the classes and objects cannot be found, it may be possible to adapt them from other similar components. If all else fails, new components will have to be built. Like prototyping and the spiral model, the object-oriented paradigm is iterative in nature. The definition of classes and objects begins at a high level of abstraction and through a series of iterations ultimately evolves into more detailed definition and development. The key to the success of this paradigm is the existence of a comprehensive program component library that is organized and classified in a way that will enable a software engineer to find existing components when they are needed.

A formal methods paradigm—the cleanroom model. Many researchers believe that the only way to produce high-quality computer software is to specify requirements using the language of mathematics. The formal methods paradigm incorporates this approach by translating customer requirements into a mathematical specification of program data, function, and behavior using a combination of set theory and predicate calculus; the mathematical representation of requirements is then evaluated for completeness and consistency. Once the requirements have been validated against customer needs, the formal model is translated into an appropriate programming language representation. Because a formal model exists, the resultant source code can be "proved" to correspond to the requirements model. In this way, the implemented software can be directly validated against requirements of the system that themselves have been formally specified using a mathematical approach. Although the formal methods paradigm is not as yet widely used, it has gained a number of enthusiastic supporters. With the advent of CASE tools that make application of formal modeling more straightforward, this paradigm may grow in importance during the latter half of the 1990s.

Fourth-generation techniques. The application of fourth-generation techniques (4GTs) is not so much a single software engineering paradigm as it is a collection of tools that can be applied to complement a process for software development. The fourth-generation techniques paradigm must call on one or more of the other paradigms discussed above to form a framework in which nonprocedural languages, code generators, database query systems, and other "fourth generation" approaches are applied. It is still necessary to identify requirements, to create an overall design, to implement the design (using 4GTs) and to test it. The use of fourth-generation techniques raises the level of abstraction with which a software engineer needs to specify a system. In theory, the primary work of software engineering (when 4GTs are used) focuses on specifying what must be accomplished. Fourth-generation tools then automatically translate the specification of *what* into an executable system. Although great strides have been made in the breath and efficiency of fourth-generation techniques, the use of 4GTs still tends to be application-domain-specific.

The paradigms that you've just described seem reasonable enough, but somebody technical has to get inside the paradigm and build computer software. Is that where methods come in?

The software engineering paradigms that we just discussed imply the use of distinct technical methods for defining requirements and designing, implementing, and testing solutions. A more detailed discussion of software engineering methods is presented in Chapter 17. In this chapter, I'll discuss the philosophy that underlies all software engineering methods and describe how these methods combine with paradigms to create a framework for software engineering.

Software engineering is a modeling activity. From the moment that the customer makes a request for a new system, the software engineer begins to create models of what is desired. At first, the models may be nothing more than a set of notes scribbled on a few sheets of paper during a preliminary meeting. Over time, these notes are translated into a more structured representation that can be transformed into executable software. When we discuss software engineering methods, what we actually consider is a set of structured modeling activities. Software requirements (initially defined by the customer) can be modeled using a standardized graphical notation that enables the software engineer to represent data, function, and behavior in an unambiguous manner. The graphical symbology and associated modeling heuristics define a particular method (e.g., structured analysis) for requirements analysis and specification.

The benefit of creating models using standardized methods is that we create representations of software that are *transformable*. An analysis model that has been created using a well-established analysis method can be transformed into a design model using a set of rules that are part of a complementary design method. The transformation leads to a design model of the software that moves us closer to the executable system. The design model, unlike the requirements model, focuses on implementation detail and represents specific characteristics of the software that has to be built by the software engineer. Progressive transformations ultimately lead to executable code that can be validated against customer requirements.

But why should we bother with models? Why not just get down to the nitty gritty and write code?

There are many reasons to build models: (1) the problem can be approached in a stepwise fashion, reducing the likelihood that major features will be missed or misinterpreted; (2) the customer is better able to review a model and can help to eliminate areas of ambiguity; (3) models are layered in a way that enables development to progress in a rational and manageable fashion; (4) developers create a shorthand notation (other than English-language narrative) for describing system data, function, and behavior. Each of these reasons is sufficient to justify the use of models in the software engineering process, but the most important reason of all is: the use of models enables a software engineer to assess the *quality* of the system to be built before it is actually built.

As progressively more detailed models of a system are created, a set of quality criteria can be established at each step. Models are reviewed against these criteria and errors are uncovered at the earliest possible time. In the days when we just wrote code, there was no way to assess the quality of a computer program until it was "up and running." Those errors that were uncovered at this late stage created major management and technical problems. Worse, many other defects remained undetected and were discovered only once the software was put into operation. Embarrassment, frustration, and economic loss were often the result.

Software engineering paradigms provide a basic framework for building computer-based applications. But it is the software engineering methods that are applied within this framework that establish an effective approach from which quality will be built.

Building models appears to have merit, but it also seems to be a time-consuming activity that can lead to lots of paper and more than a little confusion. Is there help on the way?

Paradigms provide the procedural framework for software engineering. Methods define a symbology and specify heuristics that enable a software engineer to create models of the software at different levels of detail. *Automation* facilitates the model building process, and, more importantly, provides a mechanism that affects transformability.

In the context of software engineering, automation occurs through the use of computer-aided software engineering (CASE) tools. These tools, described in detail in Chapter 18, support the model building process as well as other related technical and management activities.

Pressman and Herron [1] discuss the use of automation in software engineering in the following way:

> The best workshops have three primary components, a collection of useful tools that will help in every step of building a product; an organized layout that enables tools to be found quickly and used efficiently; and a skilled craftsman who understands how to use the tools in an effective manner. Software engineers now recognize that they need more and varied tools (hand tools alone just won't meet the demands of modern sys-

tems development). They need an organized and efficient workshop in which to place the tools.

The workshop for software engineering uses an array of *computer-aided software engineering* (CASE) tools. CASE adds tools to the software engineer's tool box.... It provides the software engineer with the ability to automate manual activities and to improve engineering insight. Yet to have significant impact, CASE must do much more. It must form the building blocks of a *workshop* for software development.

CASE is a "workshop" for both the software practitioner and the manager. It provides direct automation for the modeling activities that we call software engineering methods.

You've talked about methods (and CASE support for them) as if they're the only things that are happening as software is being built. Earlier, you mentioned other activities that occur throughout the process. Can you provide some details on them?

It is always easiest to discuss a process by describing a sequence of technical steps that are linear, predictable, and systematic. However, many software engineering activities occur concurrently and are applied in parallel with tasks that are defined by the paradigm(s) that have been adopted. These *umbrella activities* focus on quality assurance, project management, and configuration control. Each is essential to successful software development.

Every company has a "focus on quality." It's become a primary philosophy worldwide. But I don't think we emphasize this umbrella activity that you're calling software quality assurance. Just what is it?

Software quality assurance encompasses both management and technical activities with one primary objective: to implement "a planned and systematic pattern of actions necessary to provide adequate confidence that the item or product conforms to established technical requirements" [2]. The management activities associated with this objective focus on the creation of standards that describe the framework defined as part of the paradigm(s). The framework is adopted by an organization and control activities are used to ensure that technical activities conform to those standards that have been created. The technical activities normally performed as part of software quality assurance include the conduct of *formal technical reviews* (FTRs) that are conducted at the culmination of each modeling activity, and software testing.

A focus on quality should dominate the software engineering process, just as it dominates other areas of your business. For this reason, it is your job (as a manager) to ensure that quality activities are being conducted. In some companies, software quality assurance (SQA) is the primary responsibility of an independent SQA group who (paraphrasing from Joseph Juran) "provides all concerned with evidence needed to establish confidence that the quality function is being performed adequately" [3]. When the role of an SQA group is defined in this way, a subtle and important implication follows: The job of implementing software quality resides with the technical practitioners and managers who are responsible for the day-to-day development of computer software. That is, software engineers are as responsible for quality assurance as any independent software quality assurance group would be.

As we have already noted, technical practitioners achieve quality by applying a set of well-defined methods. The methods result in transformable models that allow the representation of software to progress from a statement of requirements to implemented code. To ensure quality as these transformations are made, the following SQA activities must occur:

- The sequence of transformations must be predictable and defined as part of a standard framework for software engineering.

- Each model that is created must be documented in a manner that is standardized and predictable.

- One or more formal technical reviews (for details on formal technical reviews, see Chapter 14) should be conducted after a particular model has been completed and documented.

- The types of errors uncovered during reviews should be recorded and categorized for later analysis in an attempt to improve the overall software engineering process.

- A definitive strategy for software testing, beginning with the testing of small program components and progressing through to the testing of the entire system, should be established as part of the framework for software development.

- Test case design methods should be instituted so that tests that are conducted have the highest possible likelihood of uncovering errors in the software.

In my experience, changes have a significant impact on quality. Yet you haven't really mentioned changes in your discussion of SQA. Isn't something missing?

As we will see in Chapter 15, change is an inherent part of any software project. The activities that are required to control change are collectively called *software configuration management* (SCM) and are another of the umbrella activities that must be performed as part of the software engineering process. To effectively manage change, a set of umbrella tasks is initiated with the very first customer meeting. Once basic requirements have been defined, a basis for change is established and the need for change control becomes apparent. Subsequent changes can occur as a result of new customer requirements, technological innovation or constraints, or the demands placed on software by other system components. Regardless of its origin, change should be controlled. Software configuration management encompasses a set of technical and management activities for controlling change.

When considered as a whole, SCM enables a software engineering organization to identify those components of data, documents, and programs that will undergo change; establish a strict procedure for specifying, evaluating, and approving change; report changes that are made to "those who have a need to know"; audit changes that are made to ensure that quality has been maintained; and reconstruct the software to accommodate the changes that have been implemented.

You've spent time talking about paradigms, methods, tools, and selected umbrella activities. What ties all of this together?

Software project management is an umbrella activity that ties paradigms, methods, tools, SQA, and SCM together. It encompasses a collection of tasks that are applied throughout the software engineering process and is considered in detail in Part 3 of this book. For now, a simple statement of objectives will serve to illustrate the nature of this important umbrella activity.

The goal of software project management is to establish an effective software project plan and then monitor software engineering activities against milestones established in the plan. The plan contains estimates of the effort, duration, and complementary resources that will be required to build a computer-based system. It delineates the technical and management risks associated with the project to be undertaken, and develops a strategy for managing those risks. The plan presents a detailed project schedule based on a work breakdown structure that defines all important tasks, milestones, and deliverables throughout the software process.

Project monitoring tasks track progress using the milestones that have been defined as part of the project schedule. Using the plan as a guide, people who will be responsible for each of the project tasks are managed and communication among staff members and customers is coordinated as the project proceeds. The primary objective is to ensure that a concern for quality permeates the organization and the project.

Measurement is an increasingly important (and controversial) umbrella activity. If the process and the product are measured (Chapter 3), it is possible to enhance estimates for new projects, establish a baseline for process improvement, and determine whether new methods and/or tools are effective.

Wouldn't it be easier to implement software engineering by choosing, say, only tools, and forgetting about umbrella activities, paradigms, and methods for now?

The procedures, methods, tools, and umbrella activities that collectively define software engineering have a synergistic relationship with one another. In fact, the whole (software engineering) is greater than the sum of its parts. A well-defined procedure will be of little value if effective methods are not employed. Well-defined methods will prove to be drudgery if meaningful automation has not been acquired to assist in the implementation of the method. The overall process will spin out of control unless the umbrella activities occur in parallel with the methods, procedures, and tools implied by an effective process framework. All must work together, and an effective software project manager must serve as an agent to ensure that this happens.

A Manager's Checklist

The software engineering process is elegant in its simplicity. But at the same time it can be intimidating in its complexity. If this sounds like a contradiction, consider that the discipline of software engineering actually defines a process for doing only three things: defining what you need, representing how you'll achieve it, and then implementing and supporting it. Yet, within this simple three-phase approach lies a bewildering array of procedures, methods, tools, and umbrella activities that must all be coordinated. It is important to note that we'll spend considerably more time on the software process in

Parts 3 and 4 of this book. But you can take some actions and ask some questions right now.

Actions

- Using only the brief descriptions of paradigms presented in this chapter, select the paradigm or paradigms that you feel would be most appropriate for your organization. After you have completed Chapter 16, return to your choice to determine whether you still agree with it.

- Getting help from technical staff where appropriate, select the software engineering paradigm that most closely approximates the process that your organization uses. You may find that no definable process exists.

- Getting help from technical staff where appropriate, make a list of all software engineering methods that are currently in use within your organization.

- Getting help from technical staff where appropriate, make a list of all CASE tools that are currently in use within your organization.

Questions

- If your organization has already adopted a paradigm for software engineering, which of the paradigms presented in this chapter has been chosen?

- If your organization is currently using technical methods, which method is used most effectively by your technical staff? Which of the methods has been embraced by your technical staff? Are the methods used consistently across all software projects? Is there tools support for these methods?

- Does your organization have a short- and long-range CASE strategy?

- Have you begun planning for an integrated CASE environment? How many people within your organization currently use CASE tools on a regular basis?

- Does your organization have a defined SQA function? Is it independent of the software engineering group?

- Of the umbrella activities described in this chapter, which does your organization perform on a regular basis?

Further Readings

DeGrace and Stahl (*Wicked Problems, Righteous Solutions,* Yourdon Press, 1990) have written an informative and somewhat irreverent book that presents the strengths and weaknesses of each of the major software engineering paradigms.

References

[1] Pressman, R.S., and S.R. Herron, *Software Shock,* Dorset House, 1991, pp. 164–165. Reproduced with permission.
[2] Software Engineering Technical Committee of the IEEE Computer Society, *IEEE Standard Glossary of Software Engineering Terminology,* IEEE-STD-729-1983, IEEE, 1983.
[3] Juran, J.M., "Basic Concepts," in *Quality Control Handbook,* 3d ed., McGraw-Hill, 1979.

3

Measurement: Establishing a Point of Departure

Measurement is fundamental to any engineering discipline. Lord Kelvin once said:

> When you can measure what you are speaking about and express it in numbers, you know something about it; but when you cannot measure, when you cannot express it in numbers, your knowledge is of a meager and unsatisfactory kind: it may be the beginning of knowledge, but you have scarcely, in your thoughts, advanced to the stage of a science.

Over the past decade, the software engineering community has begun to take Lord Kelvin's words to heart. But not without frustration and more than a little controversy. Managers and practitioners argue about the efficacy of specific metrics, about the use of measures within the corporate environment, about the costs of measurement and how they compare to the benefits, about "fairness," about practicality.

What does measurement mean in the context of software engineering?

Measurement is ubiquitous in the engineering world. We measure power consumption, weight, physical dimensions, temperature, voltage, signal-to-noise ratio...the list is almost endless. Fenton [1] suggests that measurement "is concerned with capturing information about the attributes of entities." In the context of measurement, an *entity* can be a real-world object or a process that creates the object. An *attribute* is some feature or characteristic that enables us to better understand the entity.

Unfortunately, measurement is far from commonplace in the software engineering world. We have trouble agreeing on the proper set of entities and attributes to measure and trouble evaluating measurements that are collected.

Software is measured for many reasons: (1) to indicate the quality of the product, (2) to assess the productivity of the people who produce the product, (3) to assess the benefits (in terms of quality and productivity) derived from new software engineering methods and tools, (4) to form a baseline for estimation, and (5) to help justify requests for new tools or additional training.

What are the entities that we must measure?

It's likely that you'll have an interest in measuring each of the following entities:

- Processes—software engineering tasks (e.g., analysis modeling, design, testing) that are required to produce computer software.

- Products—artifacts (e.g., design documentation, source code, test suites) produced as a consequence of the application of software engineering tasks.

- Resources—items (e.g., people, computers, dollars) that enable the processes or are input to them.

Each of these entities can be measured by defining either internal or external attributes [1]. An *internal attribute* is measured in terms of the entity itself and is often referred to as a direct measure of the entity. For example, an internal measure of source code is size as measured by lines of code. The number of lines of code can be counted directly (once conventions for counting have been established) by examining the source listing. An *external attribute* is a measure of the entity with a relationship to some external need defined by the environment in which the entity is produced or used. For example, the *maintainability* of source code (an external measure) represents the ability of a specific product entity (source code) to achieve the requirement that it accommodate change in a facile manner. While internal measures can generally be determined directly, an external measure can be determined only indirectly. Examples of the relationship between entities and attributes are shown in Table 3.1.

Referring to Table 3.1, you'll note that internal attributes combine both direct and indirect measures. External attributes are always determined using indirect measures.

TABLE 3.1   Components of Software Measurement [1]. (Reproduced with permission.)

	Attributes	
Entities	Internal	External
Products		
Specifications	Size, reuse, modularity, redundancy, functionality, syntactic correctness	Comprehensibility, maintainability
Designs	Size, reuse, modularity, coupling, cohesiveness, functionality	Quality, complexity, maintainability
Code	Size, reuse, modularity, coupling, functionality, algorithmic complexity, control-flow structuredness	Reliability, usability, maintainability
Test data	Size, coverage level	Quality
Processes		
Constructing specification	Time, effort, number of requirement changes	Quality, cost, stability
Detailed design	Time, effort, number of specification faults found	Cost-effectiveness, cost
Testing	Time, effort, number of bugs found	Cost-effectiveness, stability, cost
Resources		
Personnel	Years of experience, labor rate	Productivity, experience, intelligence
Teams	Size, communication level, structuredness	Productivity, quality
Software	Price, size	Usability, reliability
Hardware	Price, speed, memory size	Reliability
Offices	Size, temperature, light	Comfort, quality

Direct measures in software engineering focus on attributes that can be measured directly by examining the process,[1] the product, or the resources applied. *Indirect measures* are determined by establishing an empirical relationship between the measure desired and other countable (directly measurable) attributes of the entity.

To illustrate, consider measurements made during the procedural design task (a process entity). The *effort* attribute can be determined directly by counting the number of person-days applied to the task. A *module complexity* attribute for the procedural design can be determined only indirectly by measuring other countable characteristics of the design logic (e.g., the number of simple decisions made in the algorithm). The empirical relationship might be as follows:

Complexity = (number of simple decisions) + 1

As another example, program *size* can be measured directly (by counting the number of lines of code), but program *functionality* can be determined only by computing the function point value using other related direct measures. We'll discuss this in more detail later.

All of this talk about external and internal attributes, direct and indirect measures can be a bit confusing. Going to the bottom line, what are some of the things that we should measure when we first start?

Although the set of potential direct and indirect measures for software engineering is quite large, your first attempts at measurement will probably focus on a relatively small set of direct measures. For the process these include the cost and effort expended throughout a project and the calendar time required to complete a project; for the product, lines of code (LOC) or function points (FP)[2] produced, pages of documentation written, program execution speed, memory size, and defects reported over some set period of time; and for resources, the number of people involved, team size and experience level, tool cost, and availability.

The cost and effort required to build software, the number of lines of code produced, and other direct measures are relatively easy to collect, as long as specific conventions for measurement are established in advance. However, indirect measures such as the quality and function-

---

[1]In this context, measurements of the process are made on a project-by-project and task-by-task basis. We collect hard data about the cost, effort, and time expended on a specific project and from this data derive average results for the process as a whole.

[2]The method for deriving function points is discussed later in this chapter.

ality of software, or its efficiency or maintainability are more difficult to assess and can be measured only indirectly.

Is there a way to characterize metrics that can be related directly to quality, productivity, and technology?

We can further categorize the software metrics domain as shown in Figure 3.1. *Productivity metrics* focus on the output of the software engineering process, *quality metrics* provide an indication of how closely software conforms to implicit and explicit customer requirements (software's fitness for use), and *technical metrics* focus on the character of the software (e.g., logical complexity, degree of modularity) rather than the process through which the software was developed.

Referring again to Figure 3.1, we note that a second categorization can also be developed. *Size-oriented metrics* are used to normalize direct measures of software engineering output and quality. *Function-oriented metrics* provide indirect measures of the functionality delivered by a computer program, and human-oriented measures collect information about the manner in which people develop computer software and human perceptions about the effectiveness of tools and methods.

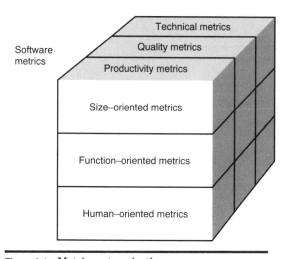

Figure 3.1   Metrics categorization.

Maybe it's because I can easily visualize it, but size seems like a reasonable measure for software. How do we use size in the context of software measurement?

Size-oriented software metrics are computed using direct measures of the process, the product, and the resources applied. These data are normalized by computing ratios that are determined by dividing each direct measure by the size of the software, measured in lines of code. If a software organization maintains simple records, a table of size-oriented data, such as the one shown in Figure 3.2, can be created. The table lists each software development project that has been completed over the past few years and corresponding size-oriented data for that project. Referring to the table entry (Figure 3.2) for project aaa-01: 12.1 KLOC (thousand lines of code) were developed with 24 person-months of effort at a cost of $168,000. It should be noted that the effort and cost recorded in the table represent all software engineering activities (analysis, design, code, and test), not just coding. Further information for project aaa-01 indicates that 365 pages of documentation were developed, 29 defects were encountered after release to the customer within the first year of operation. Three people worked on the development of software for project aaa-01.

From the rudimentary data contained in the table, a set of simple size-oriented productivity and quality metrics can be developed for each project. Averages can be computed for all projects. From Figure 3.2, we obtain

$$\text{Productivity} = \frac{\text{KLOC}}{\text{person-month}}$$

project	effort	$ (000)	KLOC	pgs. doc.	defects	people
aaa–01	24	168	12.1	365	29	3
ccc–04	62	440	27.2	1224	86	5
fff–03	43	314	20.2	1050	64	6
.	.	.	.	.		
.	.	.	.	.		
.	.	.	.	.		

Figure 3.2 Size-oriented metrics.

$$\text{Quality} = \frac{\text{defects}}{\text{KLOC}}$$

In addition, other interesting metrics may be computed:

$$\text{Cost} = \frac{\$}{\text{LOC}}$$

$$\text{Documentation} = \frac{\text{pages of documentation}}{\text{KLOC}}$$

Size-oriented metrics are controversial and are not universally accepted as the best way to measure the process of software development. Most of the controversy swirls around the use of LOC as a key measure. Proponents of the LOC measure claim that LOC is an "artifact" of all software development projects that can be easily counted, that many existing software estimation models use LOC or KLOC as a key input, and that a large body of literature and data predicated on LOC already exists. On the other hand, opponents claim that LOC measures are programming language–dependent; that they penalize well-designed but shorter programs; that they cannot easily accommodate nonprocedural languages; and that their use in estimation requires a level of detail that may be difficult to achieve (i.e., the planner must estimate the LOC to be produced long before analysis and design have been completed).

It seems that size-oriented measures are workable, if somewhat problematic. Function-oriented metrics are a mystery to me. How do you measure functionality?

Function-oriented software metrics are computed using direct measures of the process and the product and the resources applied, but then normalizing these measures with an indirect value that indicates program "functionality" or "utility." Function-oriented metrics were first proposed by Albrecht [2], who suggested a productivity measurement approach called the *function-point* method. Function points are derived using an empirical relationship based on countable measures of software's information domain and assessments of software complexity.

Just how does one compute a function point?

Function points are computed by completing the table shown in Figure 3.3. Five information domain characteristics are determined and

Measurement parameter	Count	Weighting factor		
		Simple	Average	Complex
Number of user inputs	☐	× 3	4	6 =	☐
Number of user outputs	☐	× 4	5	7 =	☐
Number of user inquiries	☐	× 3	4	6 =	☐
Number of files	☐	× 7	10	15 =	☐
Number of external interfaces	☐	× 5	7	10 =	☐
Count - total				→	☐

Figure 3.3 Computing function-point metrics.

counts are provided in the appropriate table location. Only those information domain characteristics that are visible at the application boundary[3] are counted. Information that is passed between program components (modules) is not considered. Information domain values are defined in the following manner:

Number of unique outputs. Each unique output that provides application-oriented information to the end user or to other applications and their users is counted. To be counted, an output must encompass encapsulated information that can be referenced with a specific name (e.g., bill of materials or robot status report). Individual data items within a report are not counted separately. If encapsulated information is produced in different formats, each separate format is considered unique if it represents similar data but in a different form (e.g., a tabular report and a histogram presenting the same data would be considered to be two unique outputs).

Number of unique inputs. Each input that provides distinct application-oriented data to the software is counted. In most cases, inputs are identified by listing each of the input devices for an application [e.g., mouse, OCR (optical character recognition), bar code, analog-to-

---

[3]Those readers familiar with structured analysis (Chapter 17) should note that the "context diagram" provides a good indication of the unique outputs and inputs for a system.

digital sensors, voice, pen, keyboard, disk] and then specifying the unique inputs that originate from each. Inputs should be distinguished from inquiries which are counted separately.

Number of user inquiries. An *inquiry* is defined as an on-line input that directs a search through existing information (e.g., a file, a database) and results in the generation of some immediate software response in the form of an on-line output that is retrieved as a consequence of the input. To distinguish the query for separate and individually counted inputs and outputs, it should be noted that the query does not add, modify, or delete information, it results merely in retrieval and immediate display. The input/output combination is counted as one unique query.

Number of files. Each logical master file, that is, a logical grouping of data that may be one part of a large database or a separate file, is counted.

Number of external interfaces. All machine-readable interfaces (e.g., data files on tape or disk) that are used to transmit information to another system are counted.

Although I can see some possibility for ambiguity, it appears that establishing these counts is relatively straightforward. But not all programs are created equal. How do we account for differing levels of complexity among otherwise similar programs?

Once the preceding data have been collected, a complexity value is associated with each count. Organizations that use function-point methods develop criteria for determining whether a particular entry is simple, average, or complex. For example, Dreger [3] suggests the criteria shown in Table 3.2 to determine the complexity weighting for outputs.

TABLE 3.2   Criteria for Complexity of Outputs [3]. (Reproduced with permission.)

	1–5 data items referenced	6–19 data items referenced	≥20 data items referenced
0 or 1 file referenced	Simple (4)	Simple (4)	Average (5)
2 or 3 files referenced	Simple (4)	Average (5)	Complex (7)
4 or more files referenced	Average (5)	Complex (7)	Complex (7)

To compute function points (FP), the following relationship is used:

$$FP = \text{count-total} \times [0.65 + 0.01 \times \text{SUM}(F_i)] \qquad (3\text{-}1)$$

where count-total is the sum of all FP entries obtained from Figure 3.3 and F_i (i = 1 to 14) are "complexity adjustment values" based on responses to questions [4] noted in Figure 3.4. The constant values in equation (3-1) and the weighting factors that are applied to information domain counts are determined empirically.

Once function points have been calculated, they are used in a manner analogous to LOC as a measure of software productivity, quality, and other attributes:

$$\text{Productivity} = \frac{FP}{\text{person-month}}$$

$$\text{Quality} = \frac{\text{defects}}{FP}$$

$$\text{Cost} = \frac{\$}{FP}$$

$$\text{Documentation} = \frac{\text{pages of documentation}}{FP}$$

The terminology, counts, and weights associated with function-point computation seem to have a definite information systems feel. Can the function-point measure be used effectively for engineering and other technical applications?

The function-point measure was originally designed to be applied to business information systems applications. However, extensions proposed by Jones [5], called *feature points,* enable this measure to be applied to systems and engineering software applications. The feature-point measure accommodates applications in which algorithmic complexity is high. Real-time, process control, and embedded software applications tend to have high algorithmic complexity and are therefore amenable to the feature point.

To compute the feature point, information domain values are again counted and weighted as described earlier. In addition, the feature-point metric counts a new software characteristic, *algorithms*. An algorithm is defined as "a bounded computational problem that is included within a specific computer program" [5]. Inverting a matrix, decoding a bit string, or handling an interrupt are all examples of algorithms.

To compute feature points, the table shown in Figure 3.5 is used. A

Rate each factor on a scale of 0 to 5:

0	1	2	3	4	5
No influence	Incidental	Moderate	Average	Significant	Essential

F_i:

1. Does the system require reliable backup and recovery?
2. Are data communications required?
3. Are there distributed processing functions?
4. Is performance critical?
5. Will the system run in an existing, heavily utilized operational environment?
6. Does the system require on-line data entry?
7. Does the on-line data entry require the input transaction to be built over multiple screens or operations?
8. Are the master files updated on-line?
9. Are the inputs, outputs, files, or inquiries complex?
10. Is the internal processing complex?
11. Is the code designed to be reusable?
12. Are conversion and installation included in the design?
13. Is the system designed for multiple installations in different organizations?
14. Is the application designed to facilitate change and ease of use by the user?

Figure 3.4   Determining complexity adjustment values.

Measurement parameter	Count		Weight		
Number of user inputs	☐	×	4	=	☐
Number of user outputs	☐	×	5	=	☐
Number of user inquiries	☐	×	4	=	☐
Number of files	☐	×	7	=	☐
Number of external interfaces	☐	×	7	=	☐
Algorithms	☐	×	3	=	☐
Count - total				→	☐

Figure 3.5   Computing feature-point metrics.

single weight value is used for each of the measurement parameters and the overall feature-point value is computed using equation (3-1).

It should be noted that feature points and function points represent the same thing—"functionality" or "utility" delivered by software. In fact, both measures result in the same value of FP for conventional engineering computation or information systems applications. For more complex real-time systems, the feature-point count is often between 20 and 35 percent higher than the count determined using function points alone.

I think that I understand both normalization approaches, but which should we use, function-oriented or size-oriented normalization?

There is no doubt that the LOC measure has been the most widely used approach in past years. LOC is relatively easy to measure and can be collected in a consistent manner. A reasonably large collection of industry studies have used LOC normalization, enabling you to examine the literature and find metrics that conform to LOC measures collected by your company. But the arguments against LOC that were discussed earlier are compelling: How do we accommodate mixed-language applications? How are fourth-generation languages (4GLs) and other fourth-generation techniques factored into the measurement mix? How do we account for excessively long programs (that look good when the LOC metric is used) but in reality are inefficient and difficult to maintain? How do we use the LOC metric for estimation, when our ability to estimate LOC easily in a project is highly questionable? Each of these questions causes concern, and when taken together, they present a reasonably compelling argument against size-oriented normalization.

The function-point (or feature-point) metric, like LOC, is controversial. Proponents argue that FP is programming language–independent, making it ideal for applications using conventional and nonprocedural languages; that it is based on data that are more likely to be known early in the evolution of a project, making FP more attractive as an estimation approach; that FP does not penalize implementations of a system that use few lines of code; and that the measure makes it easier to reward program component reuse. Opponents claim that the method requires some "sleight of hand" in that computation is based on indirect measurement, that information domain information can be difficult to collect after-the-fact, and that FP has no direct physical meaning—it's just a number.

On balance, I believe that the function-point metric is a more effective approach (than size-oriented measures) for normalization of process, product, and resource attributes. It is true that subtle differences in function-point computation can occur because of natural ambiguities in the definition of information domain values and complexity adjustments. However, your organization can develop conventions that will lead to consistent computation of FP. Variations among trained analysts are small enough to be statistically insignificant.

I also believe that either normalization approach is better than none. Use the function-point normalization approach if you can. It's a better choice. But use LOC if that's your only option. The insight gained through consistent collection and evaluation of normalized metrics outweighs the vagaries of either normalization approach. Both can provide managers and technical staff with useful insight into the quality of the product and the productivity of the people who produce it.

Is there an empirical relationship between LOC and function points?

The relationship between lines of code and function points depends on the programming language that is used to implement the software and the quality of the design. A number of studies have attempted to relate FP and LOC measures. To quote Albrecht and Gaffney [6]:

> The thesis of this work is that the amount of function to be provided by the application (program) can be estimated from the itemization of the major components of data to be used or provided by it. Furthermore, this

estimate of function should be correlated to both the amount of LOC to be developed and the development effort needed.

The following table [6, 7] provides rough estimates of the average number of lines of code required to build one function point in various programming languages:

Programming language	LOC/FP (average)
Assembly language	300
C	120
COBOL	100
FORTRAN	100
Pascal	90
Ada	70
Object-oriented languages	30
Fourth-generation languages (4GL)	20
Code generators	15

A review of the data presented above indicates that one LOC of Ada provides approximately 1.4 times the "functionality" (on average) as one LOC of FORTRAN. Furthermore, one LOC of a 4GL provides between 3 and 5 times the functionality of a LOC for a conventional programming language.

Is it possible to use these relationships (or ones like them) to "reverse compute" function points if LOC are known?

More precise data on the relationship between FP and LOC are presented in Jones [7] and can be used to "backfire" (i.e., to compute the number of function points when the number of delivered LOC are known) existing programs to determine the FP measure for each.

Backfiring [7] can be used when an organization decides that it must establish an historical baseline using data collected from past software projects. Ideally, FP values for each application should be computed using the guidelines presented earlier. However, resource and time constraints may dictate a "quick and dirty" approach that enables you to determine FP with only a small fraction of the work. Jones [7] recommends adjusting the LOC/FP data (see the above table) based on code, problem, and data complexity. Highly complex programs require more LOC/FP than relatively simple code. As an approximation, we can compute a *backfiring adjustment factor* (BAF) that can be applied to the LOC count. The following table [7] summarizes key values for BAF:

Complexity	BAF
Very simple	0.70
Simple	0.85
Average	1.00
Moderately complex	1.20
Complex	1.30

Once application complexity has been determined, the following relationship is used to compute FP:

$$FP = \frac{LOC_{appl}}{[(LOC/FP) \times BAF]}$$

where LOC_{appl} is the number of LOC required to implement the application. For applications that have been implemented using two or more different programming languages, the computation noted above is performed for each programming language separately.

As an example, consider an engineering analysis application that was developed in 1982. The application contains 34,000 lines of FORTRAN, 3650 lines of assembler language (for specialized device drivers), and an enhancement (completed in 1987) of 18,500 lines of C. The FORTRAN code and the data structures that it implements are judged to be simple, the assembler language portion is complex, and the C portion is moderately complex. Backfiring this application, we obtain

$$\text{FORTRAN: } FP_{FORT} = \frac{34,000}{100 \times 0.85} = 400$$

$$\text{Assembly: } FP_{assem} = \frac{3650}{300 \times 1.30} = 9$$

$$\text{C: } FP_C = \frac{18,500}{120 \times 1.2} = 128$$

The total estimated number of function points for this application is the sum of the FP values for each of the languages:

$$FP_{backfire} = FP_{FORT} + FP_{assem} + FP_C$$

$$= 400 + 9 + 128 = 537$$

To be most effective, backfiring should be calibrated. That is, a sample of all applications that are backfired should be selected. FP computation, resulting in a value FP_{actual}, should be performed using the standard approach described earlier. The percent difference between FP_{actual} and $FP_{backfire}$ should be noted. If possible, a correction factor should be computed to adjust $FP_{backfire}$ to conform the actual FP values. Once calibrated FP values are computed for past applications, process, product, and resource attributes for each application can be normalized and simple statistical analysis (e.g., computation of averages, mean, standard deviation) can be performed.

Let's assume that we've collected external and internal attributes for the product and the process; that we've normalized and acquired quality and productivity metrics. How do we then interpret and use the data that's been collected?

Any discussion of software quality or productivity measurement invariably leads to a debate about the use of such data. Should the LOC/person-month (or FP/person-month) of one group be compared to similar data from another? Should managers appraise the performance of individuals by using these metrics? The answer to these questions is an emphatic "*No!*" The reason for this response is that many factors influence productivity, making for "apples and oranges" comparisons that can be easily misinterpreted.

Basili and Zelkowitz [8] define five important factors that influence software productivity:

People factors.   The size and expertise of the development organization.

Problem factors.   The complexity of the problem to be solved and the number of changes in design constraints or requirements.

Process factors.   Analysis and design techniques that are used, languages and CASE tools available, and review techniques.

Product factors.   Reliability and performance of the computer-based system.

Resource factors.   Availability of CASE tools and hardware and software resources.

The effects of these and other factors are illustrated by the results of a landmark study conducted by Walston and Felix [9]. If one of the above factors is highly favorable for a given project, software development productivity will be significantly higher than if the same factor is unfavorable. For the five factors noted above, changes from highly favorable to unfavorable conditions will affect productivity in the following manner:[4]

Factor	Approximate variation, %
People factors	90
Problem factors	40
Process factors	50
Product factors	140
Resource factors	40

To understand the meaning of these numbers, assume that two software engineering teams have people with equal skills who use the same resources and process. One of the teams is working on a relatively simple problem with average reliability and performance requirements. The other team is working on a complex problem with extremely high reliability and performance goals. On the basis of the numbers in the table above, the first team might exhibit software development productivity that is between 40 and 140 percent better than that of the second team. Problem and product factors make a productivity comparison between the two teams meaningless.

Function points and LOC have been found to be relatively accurate predictors of software development effort and cost. However, in order to use LOC and FP in the estimation techniques described in Chapter 10, an historical baseline of information must be established.

What are some of the issues that we'll need to take into account if we try to integrate metrics into our software engineering process?

Most software developers do not measure, and sadly, most have little desire to begin. The problem is cultural. Attempting to collect measures where none had been collected in the past often precipitates resistance. "Why do we need to do this?" asks a harried project manager. "I don't see the point," complains an overworked practitioner.

Some words of wisdom have been suggested by Grady and Caswell [10]:

> Some of the things we describe here will sound quite easy. Realistically, though, establishing a successful company-wide software metrics pro-

---

[4]The factors noted by Walston and Felix have been placed into one of the five categories specified by Basili and Zelkowitz and average variation has been computed. This is done to illustrate the relative impact of variations in people, problem, process, product, and resources.

gram is hard work. When we say that you must wait at least three years before broad organizational trends are available, you get some idea of the scope of such an effort.

This caveat is well worth heeding, but the benefits of measurement are so compelling that the hard work is worth it.

What are some arguments for software metrics? Why is it so important to measure process, product (software), and resources?

The primary answer is relatively obvious. If you don't measure, there is no real way of determining whether you are improving. And if you're not improving, you're lost.

Measurement is one of a number of medications that may help cure the "software affliction" described in Chapter 1. It provides benefits at the strategic level, at the project level, and at the technical level.

By requesting and evaluating productivity and quality measures, senior management can establish meaningful goals for improvement of the software engineering process. In Chapter 1 we noted that software is a strategic business issue for many companies. If the process through which it is developed can be improved, a direct impact on the bottom line can result. But to establish goals for improvement, the current status of software development must be understood. Hence, measurement is used to establish a process baseline from which improvements can be assessed.

The day-to-day rigors of software project work leave little time for strategic thinking. Software project managers are concerned with more mundane (but equally important) issues, such as developing meaningful project estimates, producing higher-quality systems, and getting the product out the door on time. By using measurement to establish a project baseline, each of these issues becomes more manageable. We have already noted that the baseline serves as a basis for estimation. Additionally, the collection of quality metrics enables an organization to "tune" its software engineering process to remove the "vital few" causes of defects that have the greatest impact on software development.[5]

At the technical level (in the trenches), software metrics, when they are applied to the product, provide immediate benefit. As the software design is completed, most developers would be anxious to obtain answers to questions such as the following:

---

[5]These ideas have been formalized into an approach called *statistical software quality assurance* and are discussed in detail in Chapter 14.

- Which user requirements are most likely to change?
- Which modules in this system are most error-prone?
- How much testing should be planned for each module?
- How many errors (of specific types) can I expect when testing commences?

Answers to these questions can be determined if metrics have been collected and used as a technical guide. In later chapters we will examine how this is done.

You've used the word *baseline* a few times. What does this term mean in a metrics context?

The baseline consists of data collected from previous software development projects and can be as simple as the table presented in Figure 3.2 or as complex as the template illustrated in Figure 3.6.

By establishing a metrics baseline, benefits can be obtained at the strategic, project, and technical levels. Yet, the information that is collected need not be fundamentally different to satisfy each of the different constituencies discussed earlier. The manner in which the information is presented will be different, but the metrics themselves can serve many masters.

To be an effective aid in strategic planning and/or cost and effort estimation, baseline data must have the following attributes: (1) data must be reasonably accurate—"guestimates" about past projects are to be avoided; (2) data should be collected for as many projects as possible; (3) measurements must be consistent—for example, a line of code must be interpreted consistently across all projects for which data are collected or FP must be computed or backfired in a predictable manner; and (4) applications should be similar to work that is to be estimated—it makes little sense to use a baseline for batch information systems work to estimate a real-time microprocessor application.

You talked earlier about some of the issues that we'll need to take into account if we try to integrate metrics into our software engineering process. But what about some pragmatic guidance on metrics collection, computation, and evaluation?

The process for establishing a baseline is illustrated in Figure 3.7. Ideally, data needed to establish a baseline has been collected in an ongoing manner. Sadly, this is rarely the case. Therefore, *data collection* requires an historical investigation of past projects to reconstruct required data. Once data have been collected (unquestionably the most

```
COST DATA INPUT

                                                            Example
DESCRIPTION                             UNITS                  Data

labor cost                              $/person-month       $7,744
labor year                              hrs/year               1560

DATA FOR METRICS COMPUTATION

                                                            Example
DESCRIPTION                             UNITS                  Data

project name or identifier              alphanumeric         Proj#1
release type (development/maint)        alphanumeric    maintenance
number of project staff                 people                    3
effort                                  person-hours           4800
effort, computed                        person-months          36.9
elapsed time to completion              months                 13.0
source lines newly developed            KLOC                   11.5
source lines modified (existing code)   KLOC                    0.4
source lines delivered (includes existing LOC)  KLOC          33.4
source lines reused (from other programs/libraries)  KLOC      0.8
number of separate programs             programs                  1
technical documentation                 pages                   265
user documentation                      pages                   122
number of errors (1st year after release)   errors             26
maintenance effort-modifications (1st year)  person-hours     3550
maintenance effort-errors (1st year)    person-hours           1970

PROJECT DATA
Percentage of total project time spent on:
  problem analysis & specification      %                      18%
  design                                %                      20%
  coding                                %                      23%
  testing                               %                      25%
  other_describe                        %                      14%

FUNCTION-ORIENTED DATA INPUT

DESCRIPTION                             UNITS                  DATA

Information Domain
  1. no. user inputs                    inputs                   24
  2. no. user outputs                   outputs                  46
  3. no. use inquiries                  inquiries                 8
  4. no. files                          files                     4
  5. no. external interfaces            interfaces                2

Weighting Values
Use first number for simple, second for
average, and last for complex
  1. input weights                      3, 4, 6                   4
  2. outputs                            4, 5, 7                   4
  3. inquiries                          3, 4, 6                   6
  4. files                              7, 10, 15                10
  5. interfaces                         5, 7, 10                  5

Processing Complexity Factors
Factors rated from 0 to 5 where:
no influence (0); incidental (1); moderate (2);
average (3); significant (4); essential (5)
  1. backup and recovery required       0,1,2,3,4,5               4
  2. data communication required        0,1,2,3,4,5               1
```

Figure 3.6 Software metrics: collection, computation, and evaluation.

	0,1,2,3,4,5	
3. distributed processing function	0,1,2,3,4,5	0
4. performance critical	0,1,2,3,4,5	3
5. heavily utilized operating environment	0,1,2,3,4,5	3
6. online data entry	0,1,2,3,4,5	5
7. input transcation with multiple screens	0,1,2,3,4,5	4
8. master files updated online	0,1,2,3,4,5	4
9. input, output, files, inquiries complex	0,1,2,3,4,5	3
10. internal processing complex	0,1,2,3,4,5	3
11. code designed to be reusable	0,1,2,3,4,5	2
12. conv./installation included in design	0,1,2,3,4,5	2
13.system design for multiple installations	0,1,2,3,4,5	4
14. maintainability/ease of use	0,1,2,3,4,5	5

SIZE-ORIENTED METRICS

DESCRIPTION	UNITS	DATA
Productivity and Cost Metrics:		
project name	alphanumeric	Proj #1
output	KLOC/p-m	0.905
cost-all maintained code	$/KLOC	$22,514
cost excluding reused	$/KLOC	$24,028
elapsed time	months/KLOC	1.0
documentation	pages/KLOC	30
documentation	pages/p-m	10
documentation	$/page	$739
Quality Metrics:		
defects	errors/KLOC	2.0
cost of errors	$/error	$376
maint. errors/total maint.	ratio	0.36
maint. mods./total maint.	ratio	0.64
maint. effort/dev.effort	ratio	1.15

Note: Size oriented metrics computed above use "KLOC maintained," that is, source lines newly developed, modified and reused only.

FUNCTION-ORIENTED METRICS

DESCRIPTION	UNITS	DATA
Function-Point Computations		
unadjusted function points		378
total degree of influence		43
complexity adjustment		1.08
function points (FP)		408
Productivity and Cost Metrics FP		
project name	alphanumeric	Proj # 1
output	FP/p-m	11.1
cost	$/FP	$700
elapsed time	FP/month	31.4
documentation	pages/FP	0.9
Functionality		
program size	FP/program	408
function to size	FP/KLOC-maintained	32
Quality Metrics		
defects	errors/FP	0.064
maint. effort-errors	person-days/FP	0.817
maint. effort-mods.	person-days/FP	1.472

Figure 3.6 (*Continued*)

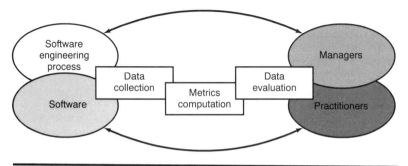

Figure 3.7   Software metrics collection process.

difficult step), *metrics computation* is possible. Depending on the breadth of data collected, metrics can span a broad range of LOC or FP measures. Finally, computed data must be evaluated and applied in estimation. *Data evaluation* focuses on the underlying reasons for the results obtained. Are the computed averages relevant to the project at hand? What extenuating circumstances invalidate certain data for use in this estimate? These and other questions must be addressed so that metrics data are not used blindly.

Figure 3.6 presents a spreadsheet model for collection and computation of historical software baseline data. Note that the model includes cost data, size-oriented data, and function-oriented data, enabling computation of both LOC- and FP-oriented metrics. It should be noted that it is not always possible to collect all data requested in this model. If you apply such a model to a number of completed projects, a software metrics baseline will have been established.

What things can go wrong? What are some of the problems associated with metrics collection in an industry setting?

No one ever said that metrics collection would be easy. In fact, a number of things can go wrong and create problems during software metrics work [11]. Among many potential problems are the following:

Inadequate and/or out-of-date data. It is sometimes difficult to reconstruct project data. In some cases, necessary information is missing or erroneous.

Faulty data. In some cases project accounting is inaccurate. For example, people "charge" one project while working on another.

Improper analysis. The data that are collected are used incorrectly, resulting in erroneous conclusions.

Inappropriate presentation. Data that are presented to management are too detailed or too technical. The meaning of the information is buried in a morass of numbers.

Time lag. The data are no longer representative of the current software development organization because so much time has lapsed between completion of a project and collection of the data.

To overcome these problems, you must institute a strategy for metrics collection and evaluation that is both systematic and realistic (see Chapter 5).

If metrics are being collected, one would assume that overall industry averages for LOC and/or function-point measures are readily available. Can you provide us with some indication of what they are?

Although there have been dozens of studies published over the years, global metrics data are still spotty. Determining meaningful averages for LOC (across many companies and industry segments) is hampered by a variety of factors:

1. Many different programming languages.
2. Inconsistency in the way LOC are measured.
3. Many, many different application areas.
4. No consistent standard of quality for a particular measure of productivity.

For this reason, LOC averages must be taken with a grain of salt. If a variety of published and unpublished studies are taken into account, the following average ranges for productivity and quality are reasonable for conventional third-generation programming languages (e.g., FORTRAN, COBOL, C):

Application area	Average productivity range, LOC/person-month
Information system applications	800–3200
System applications	400–1000
Real-time embedded system	100–600
Human-rated systems	30–400

It is important to note that the upper-range values indicated above can be easily exceeded, if (1) good CASE tools are used to generate code, (2) reusable code components are built into a system, and (3) expertise in a particular application area is high. Regrettably, the lower bound may not be achieved if poor software development practices are the norm.

Quality data is less common than productivity data (a sad commentary our the industry emphasis). However, a variety of published and unpublished studies provides us with some averages:

Application area	Average quality range, defects/KLOC
Information system applications	5–30
System applications	0.8–10
Real-time embedded system	0.5–5
Human-rated systems	0.01–0.1

It's interesting to note that even though the complexity of software increases as we move downward in the quality table, the reported quality tends to improve. This has more to do with damage avoidance (and the perceived impact of an error) than anything else. Stated simply, people who work on complex applications tend to take quality more seriously because the impact of an error is perceived to be greater. Not surprisingly, however, the cost to produce a LOC increases dramatically. For example, the cost of one LOC of human-rated software can be 10 times the cost of a LOC in a conventional information system (IS) application.

Capers Jones [7] has published extensive data that provides industry averages for function-point data. Figures 3.8 and 3.9 provide a summary of some of his findings. For further information, I'd suggest that you obtain a copy of his book.

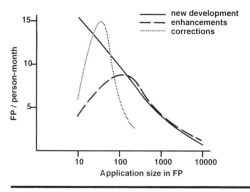

Figure 3.8   Productivity averages [7].

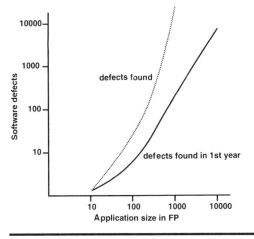

Figure 3.9   Quality averages [7].

How does the United States compare to other countries?

Metrics data collected on an international scale have been even more sparse than U.S. data for reasons that are similar to those noted above. In fact, there are few published studies that compare LOC or FP normalized metrics on an international basis. Data collected by researchers at the University of Maryland and NASA [12] compare software development practices in the United States and Japan. These are summarized in Table 3.3. The authors of the study examine some of

TABLE 3.3   Comparison of U.S. and Japanese Software Practices

Qualitative (Japan)			
No closed, individual workspace; 70–120 staff and managers in a room, 2–3 programmers per terminal			
Relatively little emphasis on state-of-the-art SE technology			
Long working hours, paid overtime, few secretaries			

Quantitative			
	Japanese	U.S.	Units
Turnover	<1%	10%	Per year
Training budget	6–8%	1–2%	Of total budget
Quality management	10%	2%	Of development cost
Development productivity	20–50	10–25	LOC/day
Maintenance productivity	100	25–50	LOC/person
Quality assurance	>10%	2%	Use an independent SQA group
Reported defect rate	0.008	1–3	Defects/KLOC
		0.01–0.1	Defects/KLOC (critical applications)

the reasons for the differences indicated in the figure and conclude that the Japanese:

- Focus on proven technologies and work hard to customize and optimize those that are chosen.
- Focus on quality and/or reliability rather than productivity.
- Focus on management and people, rather than technology.
- Focus on long-term improvement and investment, but also identify well-defined short-term improvement goals.
- Make meticulous use of metrics, which should be routinely collected, analyzed, and fed back.

These characteristics are well worth emulating.

Software Productivity Research, Inc., a consultancy specializing in software metrics [13], has studied companies in many industrialized nations and has developed a "software effectiveness questionnaire" that allows consistent rating. Based on responses to the questionnaire, the software effectiveness of many countries has been compared to the United States. Using a five-point scale in which 1 is excellent, 2 is good, 3 is the U.S. average, 4 is below average, and 5 is poor, ratings for each of the effectiveness levels noted in Table 3.4 have been developed. It should be noted that all effectiveness levels for the United States get a grade of 3, resulting in a total of 24.00.

Finally, the Software Engineering Institute (SEI) in the United States has been collecting data that leads to a maturity rating for companies within the U.S. The SEI assessment approach will be discussed in greater detail in Part 2 of this book.

TABLE 3.4   Effectiveness of Software Development [13]*

	Japan	England	Germany	France	India
Management	2.75	2.80	3.05	3.00	3.05
Technical staff	2.95	3.00	3.10	3.00	3.00
Methodology	2.65	2.85	3.05	2.90	3.05
Tool usage	3.05	3.00	3.00	3.00	3.10
Quality assurance	2.50	3.05	2.95	3.05	3.00
Reuse	2.50	3.00	3.00	3.00	3.05
Maintenance	3.10	2.90	3.00	3.00	3.00
Work ethic	2.75	3.10	3.20	3.20	2.95
Total	22.25	23.60	24.35	24.15	24.20

*Scale: 1—excellent, 2—good, 3—U.S. average, 4—below average, 5—poor.
NOTE: All effectiveness levels for the United States get a grade of 3; total of 24.00.

A Manager's Checklist

If your company is typical, you've spent little time collecting data about the software engineering process, the product that is produced, and the resources that are applied. Your predecessors may have debated the efficacy of metrics and found them wanting; they may have given software metrics a half-hearted attempt, but never really followed through; they may have been unaware of the potential benefits of measurement. At this point, it's all water under the bridge. Here are some things you can do right now.

Actions

- Create a table like the one shown in Figure 3.2 (keep it simple). Select 10 projects that your organization has completed over the past few years and fill in the table.
- Compute function points for each of the projects that you've just studied. If possible, compute FP using the approach described in this book. If necessary, use the backfiring technique, but don't forget to calibrate your results.
- Normalize using LOC and/or FP and compute appropriate averages.
- Compute the cost of producing an FP or a LOC.

Questions

- How do your quality and productivity averages compare with the ranges presented in this chapter?
- What problems did you have when you began to collect metrics data?
- What is the prevailing attitude regarding metrics within your organization? How can you change it if it's negative? How can you change it if it's ambivalent? How can you reinforce it if it's positive?

Further Readings

A number of good books have been published on software metrics over the past few years. Fenton [1] presents the most academically rigorous approach to the subject published to date. Jones [7] presents a more pragmatic treatment with a heavy emphasis on the FP measure. The book also reports on a wide array of industry averages. Dreger [3] is an excellent guidebook for those who must learn to compute function points as a normalization measure. Grady and Caswell [10] remains the definitive guide for those who must institute a metrics program in an industry setting. Putnam and Myers (*Measures for Excellence,* Yourdon Press, 1992) present a thorough treatment of metrics with an emphasis on project estimation.

Software metrics can be used not only to tune existing software development processes, but also to assist an organization in implementing new software engineering practices. Bouldin (*Agents of Change,* Yourdon Press, 1989), Humphrey (*Managing the Software Process,* Addison-Wesley, 1989), and Pressman (*Making Software Engineering Happen,* Prentice-Hall, 1988) have written books that discuss the use of software metrics as a catalyst for change.

A quasi-expert system for software project planning is described by Capers Jones. The tool, called CHECKPOINT [7], may be used for metrics evaluation as well as project estimation. Books on productivity by Arthur (*Programmer Productivity,* Wiley, 1983) and Parikh (*Programmer Productivity,* Reston, 1984) treat aspects of this broad subject. Schulmeyer and McManus (*Handbook of Software Quality Assurance,* Van Nostrand-Reinhold, 1987) present useful information on quality metrics and the statistical methods that result in an improved process.

A major source for software productivity data is a large database maintained by the Rome Air Development Center (RADC) at Griffiss Air Force Base in New York. Data from hundreds of software development projects have been entered in the database. Software metrics data has also been collected by the *Software Engineering Institute* at Carnegie-Mellon University and the *Software Productivity Consortium,* an industry-sponsored software engineering think tank located in Herndon, Virginia.

Software metrics has become a popular research topic and many papers contained in major technical publications focus on the subject. A special issue of *IEEE Software* (March 1990) is dedicated to software metrics and contains seven worthwhile papers on both management and technical measurement.

References

[1] Fenton, N.E., *Software Metrics—A Rigorous Approach,* Chapman & Hall, 1991, p. 2.
[2] Albrecht, A.J., "Measuring Application Development Productivity," *Proc. Joint SHARE/GUIDE/IBM Application Development Symposium,* October 1979, pp. 83–92.
[3] Dreger, J.B., *Function Point Analysis,* Prentice-Hall, 1989.
[4] Arthur, L.J., *Measuring Programmer Productivity and Software Quality,* Wiley-Interscience, 1985.

[5] Jones, C., "A Short History of Function Points and Feature Points," Software Productivity Research, Inc., Burlington, MA, June 1986.

[6] Albrecht, A.J., and J.E. Gaffney, "Software Function, Source Lines of Code and Development Effort Prediction: A Software Science Validation," *IEEE Trans. Software Engineering*, November 1983, pp. 639–648.

[7] Jones, C., *Applied Software Measurement*, McGraw-Hill, 1991.

[8] Basili, V., and M. Zelkowitz, "Analyzing Medium Scale Software Development," *Proc. 3d Intl. Conf. Software Engineering*, IEEE, 1978, pp. 116–123.

[9] Walston, C., and C. Felix, "A Method for Programming Measurement and Estimation," *IBM Systems J.* 16(1), 54–73 (1977).

[10] Grady, R.B., and Caswell, D.L., *Software Metrics: Establishing a Company-Wide Program*, Prentice-Hall, 1987.

[11] Fenick, S., "Implementing Management Metrics: An Army Program," *IEEE Software* (March), 65–72 (1990).

[12] McGarry, F., and V. Basili, "Software Technology in Japan" (an unpublished presentation).

[13] Jones, C., Software Productivity Research, Inc., Burlington, MA.

Instituting Effective Software Engineering Practices

Technology Transition: A Management Challenge[1]

Human beings adopt traditions that rapidly become institutionalized. Once these traditions are cemented into place, they are defended regardless of their intelligence, efficiency, or effectiveness. Change to these traditions is often a jolting experience.

In the technologies, change occurs rapidly, but the traditions that have been established by technologists change at a much slower pace. Over the past 40 years, people who have worked with software technologies have established a set of traditions—a culture—that has become deeply entrenched. Changes to the culture are often resisted by managers and practitioners alike.

Over the past two decades, significant changes have occurred in the software world. To take advantage of new software engineering paradigms, methods, and CASE tools, your organization must manage technology transition and the cultural change that goes along with it.

What is the real challenge of technology transition?

The real challenge for you as a manager is not technical, it's cultural. Most companies have little difficulty in understanding software engineering technologies. Yet they have trouble integrating these technologies into their day-to-day operations.

---

[1]Portions of this chapter have been adapted from: Pressman, R.S., "Managing the Transition to a Software Engineering Environment," *Software Engineering*, Auerbach Publishers, pp. 27–40, copyright 1990 by Warren, Gorham & Lamont. Used with permission.

Why has a culture become so deeply entrenched, and why is it so difficult to change?

To answer your question, it is necessary to travel back in time to understand the software development culture that was established during the "golden years" of computing—the 1960s and 1970s. During that era, programming (as it was then called) was viewed as a mystical art form performed by an unusual collection of technical and nontechnical people who somehow established a rapport with the computer. From the very beginning, programmers were different from other technologists. To quote Pressman and Herron [1]:

> In the early days of computing, programmers were viewed as the strangers in the back room. Few people really understood what they did and fewer cared to find out. Yet, one thing was obvious. These "strangers" were quite unlike their colleagues who worked in the front office. Front-office people worked normal business hours. Programmers often came into work at 3:00 pm, remained at their desk until 3:00 am, then left for two days only to return and work 36 hours straight. The front-office folks had degrees in conventional fields of study—marketing, finance, accounting, engineering, even physics, chemistry, or math. Some of the strangers had degrees that appeared to have no relationship to the work that they did—degrees in English literature, psychology or music. Others had migrated from the fields of science, engineering, or business and were now "computer types." A few were trained in a new discipline that was even more mysterious—computer science. Front-office people dressed alike and spoke a language that was understandable to all of their contemporaries. From the very beginning, many programmers came to work wearing jeans and a flannel shirt, when a jacket and tie were viewed as *de riguer*. They spoke the arcane language of computing, peppering every sentence with terms such as "asynchronous multiprocessing," "nibbles," or "IEEE 488 interfacing protocol."

It is important to note that the early programming culture was not ineffective. Many outstanding applications were developed during the early days of computing and some continue to be used today.

Since successes were achieved using the early programming culture, why do we need to change the culture?

In the early days, software work was often conducted by a single person (the software "artist") who had almost dictatorial control over an entire project. The artist's informal, often undisciplined, approach to software development worked reasonably well when (1) problems were relatively simple, (2) customers made relatively few demands, and (3) the impact of software was peripheral to overall business strategy. Today, the role of software has changed dramatically. Software has now become business strategic.

Sophisticated hardware architectures (e.g., parallel processors, client-server networks, distributed systems) place new and significant demands on software developers. Business and individuals now rely on software and the information that it produces to a far greater extent than they did two decades ago. Sophisticated technologies and requirements demand large, complex projects that involve many people. The current business climate demands rapid time to market. Software quality has become paramount because defects in system or application software can propagate to many locations, causing frustration and economic or even human loss. For all of these reasons, our approach to software development must change.

Why do practitioners and technical managers tend to resist changes in technical cultures?

Although there are many reasons—some emotional, some technical, and a few that are difficult to label—it appears that the primary resistance to change occurs because everyone is concerned about "rocking the boat." Technical managers are concerned that changing the procedures, methods, and tools that are used to create computer software will introduce a "learning curve" that will cause projects to fall behind schedule and budgets to be exceeded. Technical people are concerned that new tools and techniques will slow them down and may provide relatively little advantage over existing practices. Senior managers are concerned about the inherent cost and projected return of the new technology.

But aren't the concerns that you've noted reasonable?

Realistically, concern about rocking the boat is reasonable. It is a legitimate reason to proceed with caution when technology transition is undertaken. The lesson to be learned is this: Technological change must be made, but the change should be made in a manner that causes small ripples rather than large waves. There is no doubt that the boat will rock, but rocking will be gentle and the journey will proceed with few ill effects.

As an organization, we're very set in our ways. Is change really possible?

The modus operandi of every software development organization appears to be cast in concrete. The fact is that organizations change regularly: new tools, new people, new policies, new products and applications, and even new organizational structures are commonplace in the software development community. Even if your organization is "set in its ways," a move toward a software engineering culture (and the changes it portends) is essential for the continued production of high-quality systems. Change is certainly possible, but only if both managers and technical staff take a systematic approach to it.

But with all of our work, it often seems like we're going a million miles an hour, how can we make the time?

This question is often asked by managers of young, high-technology companies that are growing at a precipitous rate, or in large, well-established companies that are experiencing a significant growth in software demand. It is true that rapid growth stretches resources to their limit. But it is also true that rapid growth exacerbates any underlying software development problems that do exist. The need for change becomes more important.

To make the time, you should treat technological change as you'd treat any technical project—it must be prioritized, budgeted, scheduled, and executed with a sense of controlled urgency. Software engineering technology transition cannot be a spare-time activity. You should develop a transition plan (Chapter 6) that defines the responsibilities, tasks, milestones, and deliverables for the technology transition project. Most important, you should be sure that one person has control—that you've found a "champion" for technology transition.

Over the past few years we've worked hard to develop internal standards and procedures for software engineering, isn't that enough?

Although standards and procedures can help guide technological change, they are not enough. Many software development organizations have fallen into an "S&P (standards and procedures) trap." That is, they have expended time and resources developing voluminous standards and procedures documents that few staff members understand or use. Just because an approach to software development has been codified, there is no guarantee that it will be followed.

Should technological change be driven from the top down or from the bottom up?

When successful technological change occurs, it usually occurs in a way that might best be called a "sandwich." Senior management establishes goals and provides resources, driving the process from the top down. At the same time, technical management and staff implement a series of transition activities (to be discussed later) that drives the process from the bottom up. Both meet in the middle.

What about project managers, won't they resist?

If software engineering is viewed as a destabilizing influence, project managers will resist it, and, frankly, their reaction is not unreasonable. To gain the support of project managers, we must look at software engineering from their point of view and ask the question: "What's in it for me?" The answer is simple—*control*. Software engineering procedures, methods, and tools will improve the manager's ability to control a project, something that every manager desires. Once the project manager recognizes this benefit, resistance will disappear.

Money is always tight; how do I get resource commitment from management?

Too many requests for resources (to be allocated to software engineering transition) continue to use the "trust me" school of justification. That is, a request for resources attempts to sell middle and senior management on the overall qualitative benefits of new software engineering technology, without translating these benefits to the bottom line. Although this approach sometimes works, it is often viewed with skepticism by senior managers. For this reason, it is necessary to develop concrete measures of the software development process and establish an historical baseline that will enable quantitative justification to be made.

Why can't we just buy some good CASE tools and leave the rest alone?

Any power tool can be a wonderful thing. Whether you are cutting wood, washing dishes, or building computer software, a power tool can improve the quality of your work and the productivity with which you do it. But this is true only if you understand the methods and procedures that must be applied to properly use the tool. If a power tool is used without an understanding of underlying procedures and methods, it can be unproductive and even dangerous. Most of us wouldn't use a large chainsaw without first understanding the procedures and methods that guide its use. Few people would attempt to wash socks in a dishwasher. Yet, many software developers attempt to use sophisticated CASE tools with little more than a passing understanding of software engineering methods and procedures. Then, they wonder why "these tools don't work for us."

Let's assume that we decide to improve the state of software engineering practice within our organization. How do we begin?

The first thing has already been done—you've recognized that change is required. Once the decision to change has been made, many managers and most technical people feel that immediate action is necessary. Although a "bias for action" is commendable, the road to a new software engineering culture must be viewed as a journey with many steps.

Before the journey can begin, you must recognize that people, not technology, will enable you to reach your destination. You must select a person who will act as your guide and task master throughout the journey.

Who is this person and what does he or she do?

An organization must have a single individual—a person I call the *champion*—who will drive the process and ensure that it succeeds. Although technological change can be guided by a committee (e.g., an advisory group for software engineering), it cannot be instituted by a committee. The champion must have the authority and the resources to make software engineering happen within your company. It is important to note that the champion does not do all the work, but acts as the catalyst for getting the work done.

How does the champion get things started?

The champion works with other staff members to implement a software engineering implementation life cycle. The life cycle, discussed in greater detail later in this chapter, incorporates six distinct steps: assessment, education, selection, justification, installation, and evaluation. As a consequence of these activities, the champion and colleagues develop a software engineering *transition plan*.[2] The transition plan identifies the key tasks, deliverables, milestones, and resources that will be required to make the transition to software engineering. The transition plan provides a framework for all activities that will be required to cause cultural change and improve software practice.

Like any good project plan, the transition plan for software engineering provides a roadmap from which technical people can follow the tasks required to develop an effective technology. Management can track and coordinate the execution of those tasks in an efficient manner.

Do we really need to go through the effort of creating a written transition plan?

Without a plan, there is a tendency to defocus effort by moving in many directions at one time. In such situations, progress, if it can be measured at all, is painfully slow and enthusiasm often wanes over time.

The creation of a transition plan also enables management to prioritize transition tasks (those tasks required to improve practice). Task prioritization will help managers understand the time and effort that will be required to accomplish comprehensive changes in practice and the limitations to change that will occur if resources for making changes are severely limited.

Is the champion the only "job description" that we need to think about?

No, there's one more "job" that must be in place regardless of the transition strategy that you choose. As your transition plan is executed, new procedures, methods, and tools will be introduced into your organization. In many cases, this new technology will cause substantial changes in the way work is conducted. These changes may cause confusion and frustration among technical staff.

It is essential that your organization establish a strategy for dealing with confusion and frustration prior to its occurrence. One way to do this is to establish the role of the *systant*.

What is a systant?

The systant is a member of your technical staff who has received special training and access to detailed information concerning the proce-

---

[2]Transition planning is discussed in greater detail in Chapter 6.

dures, methods, and tools that are implemented as part of changes in software engineering practice. Part of the systant's job function is to provide assistance to any staff members who have begun to use any component of software engineering practice. A practitioner who is confused by a specific design notation should be able to contact the systant who would explain its intricacies. If a technical manager is having difficulty with a project planning tool, a systant would provide the necessary backup to be sure that the tool was being used effectively and that the manager would not become frustrated with its use.

There are, of course, other sources of information that a manager or practitioner could use when a new procedure, method, or tool is introduced. But experience indicates that nothing beats a colleague who can explain the problem quickly and directly and provide guidance in overcoming it. The role of the systant is to alleviate frustration, and if this role is performed effectively, the resistance to technological change will be greatly reduced.

How do companies and their management react when the issues that we've discussed come to the surface?

Every software development organization has options when it comes to software engineering. The following represent the most common responses:

Do nothing: After recognizing that change is required, management and technical staff may decide to do nothing—hoping that problems will fix themselves or that "we can continue like this for a few more years." In the software business, problems rarely cure themselves; in fact, problems (e.g., on-time delivery, questionable quality, poor maintainability) tend to become amplified as time passes.

Dictate change: Management has seen the light and then decides that the "techies will get on board or else." This dictatorial approach rarely works because technical staff must make the technology happen. Unless practitioners support software engineering, they will not apply it enthusiastically and can (in extreme circumstances) work to subvert it.

Push from the bottom: Practitioners often recognize the benefits of software engineering methods, procedures, and tools, and attempt to make the technology happen by trying to convince management that money should be spent. This is a reasonable approach if practitioners' efforts raise management consciousness, but it results in frustration if management provides no support or if dollars are spent with little planning.

Be systematic: The most successful adopters of software engineering establish a game plan for cultural and technological change and then execute it. They recognize that the plan must be revisited frequently, that changes and iteration are likely, and that small failures will accompany successes. But through it all, a systematic approach is maintained.

Companies often begin the process of software engineering technology transition by starting in the wrong place; they iterate endlessly, become frustrated, and stop, only to restart with a new team of people who repeat the mistakes of their predecessors. Sometimes, management will become frustrated and stop, never to restart, and thereby lose the benefits of software engineering technology. Many companies run into trouble because they take a relatively disorganized approach to the integration of software engineering. An organized, systematic approach is the only viable alternative.

O.K., I'll accept that we need a systematic approach to technology transition. Can you suggest one?

A systematic approach to software engineering transition begins not with a selection of new tools or methods, but rather with process assessment. It proceeds through a series of steps that you can use to integrate software engineering and CASE effectively within your company. These steps form a *software engineering implementation life cycle.* The six steps that constitute this life cycle, illustrated in Figure 4.1, can be summarized in the following way:

1. *Look in the mirror:*   Understand your current software development strengths and weaknesses.

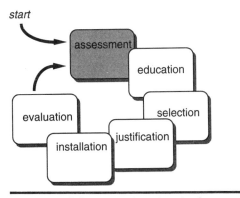

Figure 4.1   Software engineering implementation life cycle.

2. *Get smarter:*   Raise the level of software engineering knowledge among both managers and practitioners.

3. *Make choices:*   Once you understand your software development strengths and weaknesses and have raised the level of knowledge, you're ready to begin selecting procedures, methods, and tools that are appropriate for your situation.

4. *Justify your choices:*   Technology transition leads to technology acquisition, and acquisition leads to requests for expenditures that must be justified.

5. *Install the technology:*   A systematic transition plan for installing the technology must be developed and executed.

6. *Evaluate what you've done:*   After change begins, it must be continuously evaluated and tuned.

It is important to note that the six steps discussed above should be viewed as a cycle. Arrival at step 6 puts you back at the beginning of the cycle and prepares your organization for another iteration. Also, the steps are often concurrent. For example, education, selection justification, and installation may all be happening at the same time.

You suggest that we begin by "looking in the mirror." Can you summarize the assessment activity?[3]

In many software development organizations, managers and technical staff are all too anxious to make technical decisions—to select technical methods and/or new CASE tools and then proceed at a rapid rate toward "modern" software development practice. The problem is that many of these same managers and technical people have a weak understanding of procedures, methods, and tools that are currently being applied within their organizations. Because of this they proceed without a good foundation—without understanding what needs to be changed and what can be left alone. To paraphrase Waterman and Peters in their book *In Search of Excellence,* these individuals take a "ready, fire, aim" approach!

The term *assessment* refers to both qualitative and quantitative information gathering about the process used to develop software. A process assessment considers the methods and procedures that are applied, the tools that are used, the modes of communication between customers and software developers, the amount of training that is pro-

---

[3]Process assessment is considered in more detail in Chapter 5.

vided to both technical practitioners and management staff, and many other issues. The understanding gained from this portion of an assessment establishes a qualitative foundation for decision making that must occur as culture transition takes place.

In addition to qualitative information, it is important to gather quantitative data—metrics that measure software productivity and quality on past projects. This provides support for the justification of expenditures for software engineering and CASE and provides a baseline for comparison once change has been initiated.

Why do you suggest that education is the second step in the implementation life cycle? Wouldn't it make more sense to select first and then educate?

Most software developers know relatively little about software engineering. Although developers build software every day, they often use an ad hoc approach that has changed little since the 1970s. Detailed knowledge of modern methods, software engineering paradigms, and tools (including CASE) is inadequate.

But why educate first? If you attempt to make choices without a solid understanding of the technology and the context into which the technology fits, you'll likely be led astray by "flash" instead of content. Education is, of course, a continuing activity. You'll educate during each of the implementation life-cycle steps. But education must occur before you begin making decisions that will have a lasting impact on your organization.

We never seem to provide our people with the right training at the right time. Why do you think that is?

Some managers view software engineering education as a perquisite. Rather than being viewed as a necessary activity that must be conducted to support the development staff, education is viewed as a reward to be offered only when workload is light, times are good, and projects are on schedule. The irony is that we often fall behind schedule on projects because people don't have an understanding of software engineering methods that might keep them on schedule. And because the project is behind schedule, staff members "don't have the time" to obtain training. In too many companies, software development staff receive fewer than three days of software engineering methods training per year. Although educational needs vary, a good rule of thumb is that software engineering staff should receive at least 3, and as many as 6 weeks of methods education during the time required to achieve technology transition.

Is classroom training the only worthwhile approach?

It is important to understand that education can take many forms. The most common is classroom instruction, conducted on site or through public course offerings. However, other modes of education are also valuable. For example, video-based education in software engineering can prove especially useful when tight project schedules do not allow staff members to spend long periods of time away from the office or when new staff are being hired over a rather long period of time. Although video-based education does not contain the interactive element that is particularly beneficial in classroom work, it still provides a useful mode of information transfer.

In addition to formal modes of education delivery, a software engineering library should be established within the software development organization. For an expenditure of 5 to 10 thousand dollars, an organization can establish a reasonably comprehensive collection of textbooks and periodicals that serves to supplement formal education.

All education mechanisms send a set of important signals to practitioners. First, education tells them that software engineering is deemed important by management and that management is willing to commit resources to improve their technical capabilities. Second, it provides all staff members with a consistent source of information that can be translated into practical use. Third, it provides a foundation from which methods, procedures, and CASE can be selected and effectively applied. Last, it helps to "sell" the change of culture that comes as a result of greater knowledge.

So the next time you hear the complaint, "we don't have the time to educate," remember that a lack of education has likely caused the situation that doesn't allow you the time. If you think education is expensive (in time and dollars), consider the cost of ignorance!

At some point, we're going to have to begin making choices. How do we select procedures, methods, and tools systematically when so many options are available?

In the context of the software implementation life cycle, the selection step is three things: (1) an understanding of available procedures, methods, and tools for software engineering practice; (2) the definition of goals and criteria for selection of procedures, methods, and tools;

and (3) a rational mechanism for choosing, justifying, and acquiring procedures, methods, and tools.

The selection process is often confusing. A vast array of procedures, methods, and tools are available to the industry, and the differences between them are often subtle. However, once the assessment and education steps have been conducted, the specific criteria required to make appropriate choices can be more easily targeted.

Technical criteria for selection of software engineering and CASE are important (these are discussed in Chapter 7), but overall management goals are even more important. These goals are always the same: *quality* and *productivity*. Each technical criterion that is developed for the selection of a method, procedure, or tool should be traceable to one or both of these goals. If it is not, it should be rejected.

Let's assume that we've been systematic and have chosen technology that has a high likelihood of improving our product quality and process productivity. How do we convince management to spend the money?

As the selection step proceeds, it will become necessary to present management with a detailed justification for the tools to be acquired and the expenses to be associated with implementation of methods and procedures. To develop a believable justification, it is necessary to collect data from past projects to establish a baseline from which productivity and quality projections can be made. Using the baseline as a starting point, quantitative cost justification (see Chapter 7) can be accomplished.

Too many managers attempt to justify CASE tools and software engineering methods using only qualitative benefits. Few people would argue that implementation of these new technologies results in improved product quality, better project control, improved product documentation, and overall improvements in specification, design, and testing. But senior managers also want to understand justification of software engineering technology in bottom-line terms—that is, using return on investment as motivation for expenditures on new technology.

What problems occur as choices are made?

Many organizations attempt to install software engineering technology by forcing a square peg into a round hole. Overly complex procedures are chosen, creating difficulty and frustration when installation commences. Inappropriate methods are designated, leading to confusion over how and when they should be applied. Powerful tools are selected, but they address either the wrong aspects of software development or they are applied to the wrong problems by the wrong people.

How should we approach the activities that are required to install the technology within our organization?

In order to achieve successful installation, it is necessary to proceed incrementally. Some organizations attempt to install CASE and software engineering in one dramatic stroke, but such an approach is doomed to failure. A "big bang" approach introduces too much risk and overly complicates the introduction of new technology. It is better to install CASE tools, software engineering methods, and procedures in small steps, using each success as a stepping stone to the next installation activity. Transition planning and the installation step are discussed in detail in Chapters 6 and 8.

I'm sure that there are missteps as installation begins. What are some of the most common mistakes?

Too many companies begin the installation step by developing a voluminous set of standards and procedures. Unless your company must use software engineering standards that are mandated by regulatory control (e.g., defense contractors), it is a mistake to write a standards document that is 400 pages long. Stated bluntly, it is unlikely that very many people will read the document. Would you?

At the early stages of installation it is better to write a "skinny" set of software engineering/CASE guidelines and have these guidelines evolve slowly into more formal standards and procedures. By developing guidelines first, practitioners can contribute to evolution of a standards document and will ultimately have greater ownership in the end result.

When practitioners learn a new method, frustration is the most dangerous enemy. Lack of experience with a tool or method can often turn a trivial problem into a major source of frustration. Finding the answer (using vendor-supplied manuals or an 800 customer assistance number) is often a lengthy and confusing process that leaves the practitioner with a feeling that "all this isn't worth the effort." In order to overcome this situation, one or more staff members should be given the role of a systant. The systant was discussed earlier in this chapter.

You suggested that evaluation closes the cycle, preparing us to start anew with another iteration. Are evaluation and assessment really the same thing?

There is sometimes a tendency to play ostrich when software engineering and CASE are installed. Some managers select and install the technology and then stick their heads in the sand, not spending nearly enough time evaluating whether the technology is working. The evaluation step performs an ongoing assessment of the CASE/software engineering installation process. We ask the same questions that were asked during the assessment step and perform both quantitative and qualitative data collection. In essence, we attempt to answer a single question: Is the technology working?

During evaluation, both qualitative and quantitative data are collected. In fact, the guidelines suggested for the assessment step apply here as well. In addition to data collection, it is essential that you solicit feedback from practitioners to gain an understanding of the *perceived* effectiveness of software engineering methods, procedures, and tools. Regular debriefing sessions provide valuable insight and enable technical practitioners to contribute comments, criticisms, and concerns about their changing culture.

After thinking about the implementation life cycle, I've come to the conclusion that it's nothing more than common sense. Would you agree?

Absolutely. The six steps of the software engineering implementation life cycle suggest that you know where you are before you begin; that you understand the technology before you select, that you make choices based on bottom-line issues (quality and productivity improvement), that you install the technology in a stepwise fashion, and that you continually evaluate what you've accomplished. So the next time you hear someone say, "This technology is interesting, but I don't know how to begin," just suggest common sense.

A Manager's Checklist

If your company is only now beginning to move toward software engineering practice, instituting the technology will be the most significant challenge you will face over the next few years. Most companies have relatively little difficulty in understanding the broad spectrum of software engineering technology; most ultimately succeed in selling management on the benefits of this technology; most have sufficient resources to acquire appropriate methods and tools; and most can establish an effective framework for software engineering practice. The primary challenge is making it all happen. This is where many companies struggle and a disproportionate number fail. The actions and questions that follow can help you establish a basis from which technology transition can be implemented. If you begin your transition toward software engineering by addressing each checklist item, you'll have a better chance of implementing the software engineering implementation life-cycle steps described in the chapters that follow.

Actions

- Have a diverse group of managers and technical staff within your organization make two lists. The first should indicate perceived software development strengths and the second perceived software development weaknesses. Once the lists are created, compare them to establish consensus. The results of your work should be compared to a more formal assessment approach, as described in Chapter 5.

- Describe your current software development approach in outline fashion. Be sure to indicate specific task and decision points. Next to each outline entry, indicate the probability (as a percentage) that the task or decision point will be used on a typical project.

- Have a diverse group of managers and technical staff create a list of goals for improved software engineering practice. That is, what does your company want to accomplish by improving the manner in which software is engineered? These goals can serve as a guide for subsequent activities in technology transition.

Questions

- Can you identify an individual who can serve as the "champion" for software engineering technology transition within your company? Does this individual have the political clout to make things happen?

- Has your company implemented other new technologies over the past 5 years? Were the experiences positive or negative? How successful was the implementation? What lessons were learned? Can any of these lessons be applied to software engineering technology transition?

- Does the six-step implementation life cycle described in this chapter seem reasonable in the context of your organization? Can you think of steps that might be deleted or added on the basis of special local circumstances?

- Over what period of time do you intend to make the transition to improve software engineering practice? What are the expectations of senior management? Of technical managers? Of practitioners?

Further Readings

The vast majority of books in the broad category that we call "software engineering" concentrate on one or more elements of the technology. Only a few have defined software engineering technology transition as their primary focus. *Making Software Engineering Happen* (Pressman, Prentice-Hall, 1988) was the first book to consider technology transition issues in software engineering and remains a useful guide for every organization that intends to improve software engineering practices. Humphrey (*Managing the Software Process*, Addison-Wesley, 1989) presents an excellent discussion of software engineering process maturity and the steps required to improve organizational practice. Bouldin (*Agents of Change*, Yourdon Press, 1989) provides useful guidelines for making the transition to better software development practices.

Books by Buckley (*Implementing Software Engineering Practices*, Wiley, 1989) and Utz (*Software Technology Transitions*, Prentice-Hall, 1992) focus primarily on technology issues, but do provide some guidance in the technology transition activities. Articles on technology transition appear regularly in industry newspapers and magazines. Good sources of information include *Computerworld*, *Datamation*, and *Software Magazine*. Industry periodicals and newsletters, such as *American Programmer*, *CASE Outlook*, and *CASE Trends*, also have occasional articles on technology transition.

Few books on the general subject of technology transfer focus on software engineering. However, books by Mogavero and Shane (*What Every Engineer Should Know about Technology Transfer and Innovation*, Dekker, 1982), Rogers (*Diffusion of Innovations*, Free Press, 1982), Glasser et al. (*Putting Knowledge to Use*, Jossey-Bass, 1983), Hall (*Technology Transfer: An Executive Guide*, Random House, 1987), and Reynolds (*Technology Transfer*, Prentice-Hall, 1988) offer useful guidelines that can be adapted to software engineering technology transition.

Reference

[1] Pressman, R.S., and S.R. Herron, *Software Shock*, Dorset House, 1991, p. 115.

Process Assessment— A Look in the Mirror

Managers and technical staff in most companies are all too anxious to make technical decisions—to select new methods and tools and then proceed at a rapid rate toward "modern" software engineering practice. The problem is that many of these same managers and technical people have a weak understanding of procedures, methods, and tools that are currently being applied within their organizations. Because of this, they proceed without a good foundation—without understanding where they are.

The first thing you must do as you proceed toward the integration of software engineering technology is to "look in the mirror." That is, before you worry about technology transfer, take a hard look at your current software development practices.

The phrase *process assessment* refers to both qualitative and quantitative information gathering. You must understand the methods that are currently being applied to develop software (if distinct methods are being used at all!). You should also understand the procedural context into which methods are being applied, the tools that are being used, the modes of communication between customers and software developers, the amount of training that is provided to both technical practitioners and management staff, and many other issues. Finally, you should gather quantitative information—metrics that measure software quality and productivity on past projects.

Process assessment is currently a hot topic in the software engineering community. By determining your current state of practice, you'll lay the foundation for the creation of a transition plan that should lead to improvement in your software engineering procedures, methods, and tools.

You stated that process assessment has both qualitative and quantitative components. Can you describe each in a bit more detail?

The process assessment approach that I will suggest in this chapter requires the collection of both qualitative and quantitative information. Qualitative information provides an indication of an organization's relative maturity[1] in each of eight important areas:

- Organizational policies that guide the use of software engineering practices

- Training that supports the use of procedures, methods, and tools

- The framework (procedural model) that has been established to define a software engineering process

- Quality assurance activities for software

- Project management

- Software engineering methods and techniques

- CASE tools

- Metrics and measurement

By using a detailed questionnaire, a process attribute grade can be developed for each area and an overall process maturity grade can be determined for your organization as a whole.

Quantitative information is obtained by collecting data that describe your organization and its resources. In addition, quantitative software metrics are collected. A detailed discussion of metrics was presented in Chapter 3. The use of metrics for assessment is considered later in this chapter.

It seems like process assessment is a fair amount of work. How do I know if we're ready to begin doing a process assessment and making the technological changes that will occur as a result of it?

In her book on technology transition, Barbara Bouldin [1] suggests a set of 10 initial questions that will help you determine whether you should proceed with technological change:

1. Is your organization newly formed?

2. Are the functions your organization performs new to your organization?

---

[1]Process maturity will be considered in greater detail later in this chapter.

3. Is your organization growing at a reasonably rapid rate?
4. Is your organization responsible for the development of new systems?
5. Is there a general attitude of optimism, and is morale high?
6. Are your [technical staff properly] utilizing tools or methods that improve productivity?
7. Does your management support the concept of productivity in any way?
8. Is staff experiencing motivation problems?
9. Is your staff responsible for mature systems that are primarily in the maintenance mode?
10. Does your organization have a backlog of user [or customer] requests?

Bouldin argues that a positive response to the first five questions followed by a negative response to the last five should convince you to wait—your organization may need to mature a bit before the benefits can be properly recognized. A mixed response ("yes"/"no") to all 10 questions should lead to "soul searching" with the decision to proceed driven by extenuating circumstances. A positive response to the last five questions is a key indicator that change should occur.

How long will a process assessment take?

You should recall that process assessment is the first step in a software engineering implementation life cycle and that the life cycle has a period of 9 to 15 months. The assessment activity is repeated during each period of the implementation life cycle (although the first assessment is the most time-consuming).

In general, a process assessment can be completed in a time period that ranges from 3 weeks to 3 months. The work that occurs during this period includes evaluation of questionnaire responses, group meetings, and limited data collection. In addition, a *Findings and Recommendations Report* (discussed later in this chapter) is generated and a skeleton transition plan is created.

You've mentioned the use of a questionnaire to collect information for process assessment. What kinds of questions are contained in a process assessment questionnaire?

A good software engineering process assessment approach makes use of three types of questions: qualitative, boolean, and quantitative. Answers to questions in the first category demand a narrative response.

Boolean questions elicit a "yes"/"no" response, and quantitative questions result in a numerical response.

Can you provide a few examples of qualitative questions?

Questions in this category focus on elements of software engineering practice that require a narrative explanation. The following questions, adapted from Pressman [2], provide examples of qualitative questions:

- Describe the manner in which project teams are formed. Do you use functional or matrix organization?
- Who is (are) the "customer(s)" for software within your organization?
- Describe the relationship between the customer and the people who develop software. Address the following:
  a. Who initially specifies products with software content?
  b. The degree of understanding of software development practiced by the customer.
  c. Problems associated with communication between customers and software engineering organization.

- Describe the role of your quality assurance, manufacturing, and service organizations with regard to software.
- Describe areas where you believe your management approach to software development is strong. Justify your choices.
- Describe your software development environment: computers (development systems) that are used to develop software; operating system(s); networks.
- Has your organization made a commitment to a specific CASE (computer-aided software engineering) vendor or vendors? Name them.
- Describe individual software development tools—available as OS (operating system) features and as standalone functions—that are used during software development.
  a. Project planning tools
  b. Simulation or prototyping tools
  c. Analysis and design tools
  d. Coding tools (e.g., compilers, editors)
  e. Testing tools
  f. Maintenance and SCM tools

Can you provide a few examples of boolean questions?

Questions in this category elicit a "yes"/"no" response. That is, boolean questions are used to determine whether a specific organizational policy, training approach, procedural model, quality assurance activity, project management approach, method, CASE tool, or metrics and measurement technique is present within the context of current practice. Typical examples (used to assess design, coding, and testing techniques), adapted from R.S. Pressman & Associates, Inc. [4], are presented below:

1. Design
   a. Do you use a specific method for data design?
   b. Do you use a specific method for architectural design?
   c. Do you constrain procedural design to the use of the structured programming constructs?
   d. Do you have a defined method for human–computer interface design?
2. Programming and coding
   a. Is more than 90 percent of your code written in a high-order language?
   b. Are specific conventions for code documentation defined and used?
3. Testing
   a. Do you use specific methods for test case design?
   b. Do you begin test planning before code is written?
   c. Do you create a written test procedure (before coding is completed) that defines all test cases and the logistics required to execute them?
   d. Do you store the results of testing for historical reference?
   e. Is a mechanism used for routinely performing regression testing?
   f. Is a method used to determine the adequacy of regression testing?
   g. Is a mechanism used to ensure that testing covers all software requirements?

Can you provide a few examples of quantitative questions?

Questions in this category enable you to obtain numerical information that can be used in conjunction with software metrics to compute costs and potential payback for new technology. The following questions, adapted from Pressman [2], provide examples of qualitative questions:

- Annual revenue at your component?
- Annual budget for data processing or MIS (management information system)?
- Annual budget for software-related training? Describe the types of training conducted.
- Annual budget for computer hardware?
  a. Mainframes and other production machines?
  b. PC and workstations?
  c. Terminals?

- Annual budget for software tools? Differentiate between hardware and software.
- Number of systems and software practitioners in all application areas?
- Total number of MIS people?
  a. Number of systems and support staff
  b. Number of analysts and system engineers
  c. Number of applications programmers
  d. Number of software specialists (describe)

- Number of software people working on engineered products and systems?
  a. People with the title of "programmer" or "software engineer"
  b. People with the title "engineer" who spend more than 25 percent of their time developing software
  c. Other engineering staff (provide job title) who develop software

- Current number of outside contractors working on software in-house?
- What percentage of software people are working on "maintenance" activities?
- Projected growth or decrease for the above items?

Where can I obtain additional information about process assessment questions, including a list of questions to ask?

There are three good sources that can provide you with a list of appropriate questions. The Software Engineering Institute (SEI), sponsored by the U.S. Department of Defense and located at Carnegie-Mellon University in Pittsburgh, Pennsylvania, has developed an assessment questionnaire [3] that can help a company to assess current software engineering practice. The second source of information on software engineering assessment is contained in the book *Making Software Engineering Happen* [2]. This book contains a questionnaire that stresses qualitative and quantitative questions on many aspects of software development practice. The book also presents a "quasi-expert system" for evaluating the information gathered through the questionnaire.

The third source of questions can be obtained in conjunction with a variety of assessment services offered by software engineering consulting firms. My favorite (not surprisingly!) is *Process Advisor* developed by R.S. Pressman & Associates, Inc. [4] *Process Advisor* includes a videotaped minicourse and automated support that guide a manager through the assessment and a detailed workbook that includes the best elements of the SEI questionnaire with additional qualitative and quantitative questions.[2]

No matter whose questions you use, the bottom line is this: Gather enough information so that you can gain an understanding of your organization, the application of technology within it, and the relative sophistication of the technology that you are applying. Without a detailed look in the mirror, your probability for success in the application of subsequent steps of the software engineering implementation cycle (Chapter 4) will drop dramatically.

Isn't it possible that different groups within our organization would answer process assessment questions differently? How do we handle this phenomenon?

In most cases, quantitative information can be obtained from a single source and will be consistent across an organization. However, qualitative and boolean information is open to broad interpretation. It is not only possible, but likely, that different project groups will provide different answers to qualitative and boolean questions. Interestingly, this is not a cause for concern.

First, all people involved in the assessment should study all questions prior to the start of the assessment. A meeting is then conducted to provide all participants with a chance to ask questions about the assessment questions so that a consistent interpretation is achieved.

Each major project or functional group within your organization completes the questionnaire. Differences and similarities in response

---

[2]If you have further interest in *Process Advisor,* contact R.S. Pressman & Associates, Inc., 620 East Slope Drive, Orange, CT 06477 (USA), phone (203) 795-5044 or fax (203) 799-1023.

provide you with an excellent indication of strengths and weaknesses across your organization and, as importantly, give you an indication of local circumstances that must be addressed individually.

If your organization is large, it may be possible to develop maturity grades for each of the major constituencies. (Be careful here, this can be a political mine field!) Alternatively, the response to boolean questions can be "averaged" to derive a single result for the entire organization.

It is critically important to note that a "single solution" derived from the process assessment may not be best for your organization.

Software engineering practice may have to be customized for local needs. Differences in responses to the questionnaire will provide you with some indication of the amount of customization that is necessary.

O.K., let's assume that I've asked the requisite set of process assessment questions and obtained answers. How do I interpret them?

In an ideal setting, you will be working with an expert in process assessment who has gone through the process many times and has learned to interpret the responses and can provide you with expert guidance. However, limited resources, company policy, or an aversion to outsiders may cause you to "go it alone." Although you should proceed with caution, it is possible to develop meaningful interpretations of the responses you get. To do so you'll need an *expert system* to interpret answers to the qualitative questions, a *grading scheme* to attach meaning to the boolean questions, and an *analysis template* to evaluate the numerical information obtained from qualitative questions.

You mention an "expert system" for interpreting answers to the qualitative questions. Where can I get one?

The phrase expert system conjures an image of a high-tech software-based system that diagnoses the qualitative information that you have gathered as part of process assessment. Although such a system could be developed, I have found that a "low tech" approach works just as well. The first "expert system" for interpreting qualitative questions for process assessment appeared in the book *Making Software Engineering Happen* [3]. Originally represented as an appendix to the book, the expert system contained comments, inferences, and follow-on questions for each qualitative question that was asked as part of the process assessment. This original expert system has been updated and refined and is presented as part of the *Process Advisor* system developed by R.S. Pressman & Associates, Inc. [4].

As an example of the expert system approach described above, I'll use an excerpt from *Process Advisor* [4] that addresses one of the qualitative questions presented earlier in this chapter:

Question: *Describe the relationship between the customer and the people who develop software. Address:*

    a. who initially specifies products with software content?

    b. the degree of understanding of software development practice by customer.

    c. problems associated with communication between customers and software engineering organization.

Comment: Effective communication between customers/users and developers is crucial to successful projects. The intent of these questions is to determine the smoothness of the user–developer interface and to uncover communications bottlenecks, if they exist.

Inferences: The answers to these questions will provide insight into the start-up (often the most important time) of the system development process. How thorough is the system requester in specifying what is needed? Does the user take/desire an active role at the inception of a project? What is the level of software understanding on the part of the customer? What is the level of application understanding on the part of the software engineers?

If   there appears to be little systematicity in the manner in which customers and developers interact, it may be useful to explore the use of *facilitated application specification techniques* [see Chapter 10]. Often, early communication occurs not because information is lacking, but because no mechanism has been developed to impart the information that does exist.

If   you see the comment that "the developers don't understand us" coming from the customer (or the converse coming from the developer), it is likely that each world has been overly insulated from the other. It may be worthwhile to run a nontechnical seminar on software and software engineering for the customer. Determine whether the organization conducts a product technology seminar for analysts and software engineers. Often, software people do not speak in the jargon of their customers. This increases psychological separation.

If   there appears to be friction between customers/users and developers, try to uncover the root cause. It's likely that a team atmosphere has not been created. This leads to unresponsiveness (from either side), personality conflicts, political or organizational issues. Examine the relationship between managers in the customer and developer organizations. Is there friction?

If geographical separation is commonplace for the projects that are undertaken, it is likely that this has something to do with a lack of good communication. It may be useful to emphasize video conferencing, electronic mail, and bulletin boards as a mechanism for improving communication.

Examine the manner in which communication is conducted: the documents, memos that are generated at the inception of a project, etc. Determine whether early meetings are conducted in an effective manner. In almost all cases, poor customer–developer communication is a symptom—you must uncover the cause.

Follow-on Questions:

1. See questions contained in the Inferences section.
2. How does the customer/user select and prioritize system requests?
3. Have there been examples of excellent communication?
4. Who has responsibility for customer/user interface?

Expert system "modules," like the one presented above, have been developed for every qualitative question presented in *Process Advisor* [4]. Using the information provided by respondents from your organization, it is possible to develop a reasonable interpretation for this important category of questions.

You indicated that boolean questions are answered with a "yes"/"no" response. What are the criteria for developing a consistent approach for supplying a positive response?

All boolean questions are answered with a "yes" (**Y**), "no" (**N**), "don't know" (**DK**), or "not applicable" (**NA**) response. A "yes" response should be made only if

- A positive answer applies for a significant majority of the cases or situations (normally 70 percent or more).

- The majority of knowledgeable people in your organization would also respond "yes."

- An independent party could substantiate that the answer is true by using specific project evidence.

If you are wavering between a "yes" and a "no" response, I suggest that the realistic approach is to answer "no." Unless you can answer "yes" without equivocation, you're probably not implementing the software engineering procedure, method, or tool that is implied by the question.

How do we develop a grading scheme for boolean questions?

A grading scheme must be based on a scale that has enough resolution to be meaningful without implying a degree of accuracy that is misleading. In addition, it should provide consistent scaling for global assessment (i.e., a measure of the overall effectiveness of an organization's software engineering practices) as well as a weighting scheme that enables a single boolean response to be weighted. In my opinion, a good assessment grading scheme uses the weighting scheme to develop local and global assessments of software engineering practice.

What do you mean by a "consistent scaling for global assessment"?

The Software Engineering Institute [5a,b] has developed a five-point grading scheme that is appropriate for use with an assessment questionnaire containing boolean questions. The grading scheme provides a measure of the global effectiveness of an organization's software engineering practices and defines five process maturity levels (Figure 5.1) that are defined in the following manner [5a]:

Level 1: *Initial:* The software process is characterized as ad hoc, and occasionally even chaotic. Few processes are defined, and success depends on individual effort.

Level 2: *Repeatable:* Basic project management processes are established to track cost, schedule, and functionality. The neces-

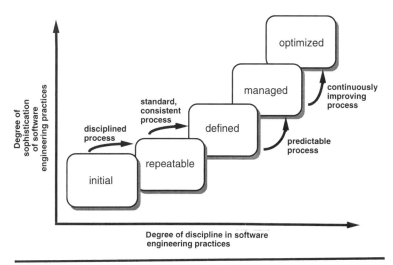

Figure 5.1 Five levels of process maturity [5].

sary process discipline is in place to repeat earlier successes on projects with similar applications.

Level 3: *Defined:* The software process for both management and engineering activities is documented, standardized, and integrated into an organization-wide software process. All projects use a documented and approved version of the organization's process for developing and maintaining software. This level includes all characteristics defined for level 2.

Level 4: *Managed:* Detailed measures of the software process and product quality are collected. Both the software process and products are quantitatively understood and controlled using detailed measures. This level includes all characteristics defined for level 3.

Level 5: *Optimizing:* Continuous process improvement is enabled by quantitative feedback from the process and from testing innovative ideas and technologies. This level includes all characteristics defined for level 4.

The five levels defined by the SEI are derived as a consequence of evaluating responses to the SEI assessment questionnaire and result in a single numerical grade that provides a global indication of an organization's process maturity.

How is a global grade (using the SEI maturity levels) determined?

Figure 5.2 illustrates the manner in which connectivity between the maturity levels and specific boolean questions is established. The SEI has associated *key process areas* (KPAs) with each maturity level. The KPAs describe those software engineering functions (e.g., software project planning, requirements management) that must be present to satisfy good practice at a particular level. Each KPA is described by identifying the following characteristics:

- *Goals:* The overall objectives that the KPA must achieve.

- *Commitments:* Requirements (imposed on the organization) that must be met to achieve the goals.

- *Abilities:* Those things that must be in place (organizationally and technically) that will enable the organization to meet the commitments.

- *Activities:* The specific tasks that are required to achieve the KPA function.

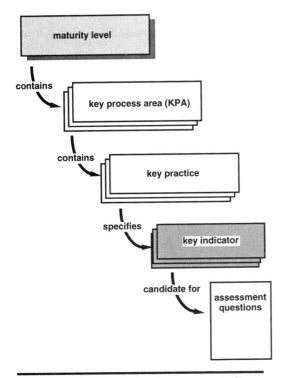

Figure 5.2 The connection between maturity level and assessment questions [5].

- *Methods for monitoring implementation:*   The manner in which the activities are monitored as they are put into place.

- *Methods for verifying implementation:*   The manner in which proper practice for the KPA can be verified.

Eighteen KPAs (each defined using the structure noted above) are defined across the maturity model and are mapped into different levels of process maturity [5a]. For example, the KPAs for level 2, *repeatable* practice, are

- Requirements management
- Software project planning
- Software project tracking and oversight
- Software subcontract management
- Software quality assurance
- Software configuration management

For level 3, *defined* practice (a higher level of practice), all level 2 KPAs must be present and, in addition, the following KPAs are added:

- Organizational process focus
- Organizational process definition
- Training program
- Integrated software management
- Software product engineering
- Intergroup coordination
- Peer reviews

A detailed discussion of each of the maturity model KPAs is beyond the scope of this book. For further information you should obtain a copy of "Key Practices of the Capability Maturity Model" [5b], which may be obtained from the NTIS.[3]

Each of the KPAs is defined by a set of *key practices* that contribute to satisfying its goals. The key practices are policies, procedures, and activities that must occur before a key process area has been fully instituted. *Key indicators* are "those key practices or components of key practices that offer the greatest insight into whether the goals of a key process area have been achieved" [5a]. Assessment questions are designed to probe for the existence (or lack thereof) of a key indicator.

So what you're saying is that the SEI maturity level is based on the collective response to assessment questions?

That's correct. But you should recognize that a single grade (let's say your organization obtains a grade of 2, meaning that your maturity level is repeatable) is not enough. The SEI emphasizes that further evaluation (in the form of face-to-face meetings and other forms of information collection), consulting assistance, and metrics collection are necessary to obtain a complete picture of the state of practice within your company.

I share this point of view. But I also think that the boolean questionnaire can be extended to provide additional insight.

Why not just stick with the SEI approach?

The SEI approach represents a significant achievement in process assessment, but it suffers from a number of minor flaws:

---

[3]NTIS—National Technical Information Service, U.S. Department of Commerce, Springfield, VA 22161.

- Although detailed analysis of the assessment questionnaire can lead to an assessment of the efficacy of KPAs and related key practices, the maturity level alone tells us little about an individual KPA.

- The manner in which the process maturity level is computed[4] currently uses an ordering that causes a low grade if specific questions are answered negatively, even if other questions that represent reasonable sophistication are answered with a "yes."

- Some critics [6] argue that the SEI questionnaire tends to underemphasize the importance of technology and overemphasize the importance of policies and standards.

These flaws disappear if a comprehensive consulting activity occurs in conjunction with the use of the questionnaire. Detailed quantitative and qualitative questions and answers will provide the additional detail and insight that is missing with the SEI questionnaire alone.

Regrettably, it is sometimes "the grade" that is emphasized, and a single grade simply cannot provide any guidance for the manager who must act to improve the state of practice. Additionally, some companies will attempt to use the questionnaire without the consulting that the SEI recommends. (This is a violation of the spirit of the SEI approach.) The resulting maturity level provides little useful information.

What modification to the assessment process do you propose?

As I've already indicated, I believe that the assessment process should have qualitative, boolean, and quantitative elements. The qualitative and quantitative elements are only implied by the SEI maturity model and are not directly addressed by the questionnaire. To be truly effective, an assessment questionnaire should address all three elements.

My suggestions for the qualitative and quantitative elements of the questionnaire have been discussed earlier in this chapter. But what about the boolean questions?

If the boolean questions that have been proposed by the SEI are extended and reorganized, they can be used to produce individual grades for a set of *process attributes* (PAs) that is similar in intent to the KPAs defined by the SEI. The process attributes that we use are listed below.

1. Organizational policies
2. Training

---

[4]It should be noted that at the time of this writing, the SEI is working on a new version of the questionnaire. The SEI should be contacted for further information.

3. Software development framework
4. Quality assurance activities
   a. Documentation
   b. Reviews and analysis of review results
   c. Quality assurance functions
5. Project management
   a. Organizational resources
   b. Oversight
   c. Planning
   d. Monitoring and tracking
   e. Configuration management
   f. Subcontracts
6. Methods and techniques
   a. Customer communication
   b. Analysis and specification
   c. Design
   d. Programming and coding
   e. Testing
   f. Maintenance and support
   g. Component reuse
7. Tools
   a. Categories
   b. Environment
8. Metrics and measurement

Each of the process attributes listed above is assessed through a set of questions. For example, earlier in this chapter the questions that are used for assessing the design, programming and coding, and testing process attributes were presented. A grade is developed for each process attribute.

To be consistent, the grades of the process attributes, when averaged, must result in a process maturity level that is consistent with (but not necessarily identical to) the SEI maturity level.

How is a grade developed for each process attribute?

The response to each boolean question associated with a specific process variable (e.g., design) is weighted on a scale of 1 to 5. The number of "yes" responses adjusted by the weight attached to each question results in a process variable grade that has the following meaning:

1. *Rudimentary practice:* Common in even the most undisciplined organization.
2. *Improved practice:* Representative of those software development

organizations that have begun to improve their software engineering approach.

3. *Advanced practice:* A discipline and related activities that are to be found in the top 5 to 10 percent of all software developers.

4. *Excellent practice:* The best possible approach to a particular software engineering activity, given commercially available technology.

5. *State-of-the-art practice:* Idealized practice that is currently unattainable in industry.

The weight is determined by answering the following question: Which of the practice levels noted above would be able to answer "yes" to this question? Weights for each of the boolean questions in the R.S. Pressman & Associates, Inc. *Process Advisor* system [4] have been developed and are used for computation of process variable grades.

What grades does the "typical" organization obtain when you apply the assessment questionnaire as you've described it?

There really is no such thing as a "typical" software development organization. So many variables—number of people that do software work, characteristics of the customer, types and complexity of applications, size of software projects, and many others—make every software developer unique. I think the question that you want to ask is, "What is common practice throughout the industry?"

R.S. Pressman & Associates, Inc. has conducted many software engineering process assessments over the past decade. We have worked with information systems organizations, engineering software developers, research labs, and other specialized software builders. Based on the grading scheme described above,[5] the Kiviat chart shown in Figure 5.3 represents scaled grades for the process attributes described above. For example, the grade that represents common practice for quality assurance activities is approximately 1.4—between rudimentary and improved practice. Interestingly, if we take the average of all process attributes, the overall grade is 1.95.

Although the grade of 1.95 was developed using the grading scheme that I have proposed, it is reasonably consistent with average data

---

[5]Many of the assessments that we conducted in the early and mid-1980s were completed before the existence of a comprehensive boolean questionnaire. We have reviewed qualitative and quantitative data obtained during these assessments and completed the boolean questionnaire after-the-fact. These results are reflected in Figure 5.3.

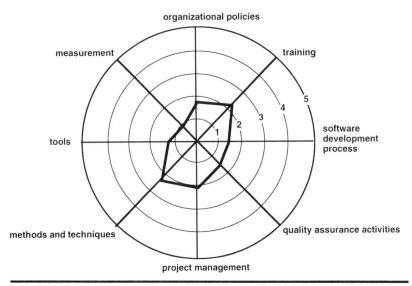

Figure 5.3 Average grades representing common practice for each of eight process attributes.

that have been informally reported for a large number of SEI assessments. Hence, based on our experience, common practice represents a process maturity level that is close to, but not at, the SEI repeatable level.[6]

More important than the single grade, the grading scheme enables you to consider each of the process attributes individually. The Kiviat chart in Figure 5.3 suggests areas of relative strength and relative weakness for common practice. Not surprisingly, organizations in this category are relatively weak in establishing a defined framework for software engineering, SQA activities, tool usage, and measurement. Training, project management, methods use, and organization policy represent relative strengths, although significant improvement is both possible and desirable.

And what about top-of-the-line software developers? Where do they sit in your grading scheme?

Top-of-the-line software developers are those that have achieved best practice in some, if not all, of the process attributes. The Kiviat chart shown in Figure 5.4 represents scaled grades for those software devel-

---

[6]Because assessment questions have been deleted and added, as well as reorganized, we have not done a direct comparison of results for the approach suggested here and the SEI questionnaire.

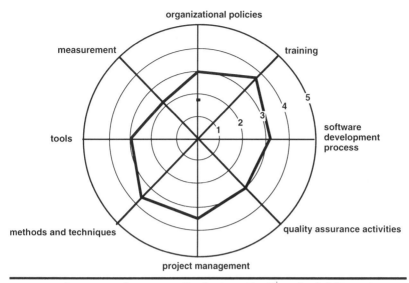

Figure 5.4 Average grades representing best practice for each of eight process attributes.

opers who have achieved best practice. In our experience, this represents the top 5 to 10 percent of all software developers. To illustrate, the best practice organization obtains a grade of 3.1 for quality assurance activities. When compared to the common practice grade of 1.4, the profound difference in approach and sophistication becomes apparent.

Like common practice organizations, best practice software developers have relative strengths and weaknesses, but it's important to note that the distribution of grades across all process attributes is more uniform. Training, project management, and methods utilization represent relative strengths, while measurement remains relatively weak.

Let's assume we acquire the questionnaires and conduct an assessment of our software development practices. Earlier you suggested an "expert system" approach for evaluating quantitative and qualitative questions. How do we interpret the grades derived from boolean questions?

As I mentioned earlier, any set of process assessment questions should be accompanied by detailed guidelines for interpretation. The following excerpt from *Process Advisor* [4] illustrates interpretation guidelines for the process attribute for quality assurance activities:

Questions in the Quality Assurance Activities section of the process assessment questionnaire explore your organization's emphasis on documentation, reviews, and other QA functions. Examine your grade for section 4 and place it in the context of the grade ranges:

Grade range	Identifier
Below 1.65	E
1.65 to 2.25	D
2.26 to 2.75	C
2.76 to 3.25	B
Above 3.26	A

If one or more of the grades for process attribute subtopics are dramatically different than the overall section grade, further investigation into that area is warranted. Here's how to interpret the result for the overall grade for the quality assurance activities section:

E and D: Software quality and the activities that help to ensure it are not a primary focus within your software development organization. Documentation is likely weak, because there are no standard formats to guide developers. You are not conducting effective reviews and you do not use the results of reviews to improve the process. SQA is not a formally defined activity.

Action: You must develop a plan to improve each of the three areas: documentation, reviews, and SQA. The place to begin is with documents and reviews. Pick one or two documents and develop a standard format (recognize that brevity is a virtue) and then develop a set of review guidelines for the documents. Over time, broaden these actions until most important documents are defined, are being produced, and are being reviewed.

C: Your approach to predictable documentation, effective reviews, and basic quality assurance activities is coming together.

Action: You'll need to review responses to each of the subsections to determine which areas are in need of the most improvement. It's likely that quality assurance functions are still in need of improvement, and if this is the case, your focus should be on establishing mechanisms for ensuring compliance with documentation and process standards. You might also look to broaden your review approach, if this can be done in a cost-effective manner. At the same time begin to use CASE tools to create effective documentation in a more productive manner.

B: You are at the state of practice in the QA area. It is likely, however, that you are not using quantitative data to analyze the software engineering process.

Action: Consider a fledgling program in statistical QA for software. Collect data on defects uncovered through other QA activities. Using the data collected, work to improve methods to reduce defects and move to acquire tools that will enable you to build software with high quality more effectively.

O.K., we've used the assessment questions to develop grades and guidelines to interpret their meaning. From a strategic point of view, how can we use the grades that we've computed?

The most important use of the grades that have been derived as part of process assessment is to target relative strengths and weaknesses. Once this is done, you can develop a transition plan that will help your organization improve software engineering practice.

There are, however, other uses for the grades. The questionnaire can be revisited on a yearly cycle. The original set of grades becomes a baseline from which further progress can be measured.

To illustrate, assume that your original grade for the quality assurance process attribute is 1.4. Your organization has work to do in this area. First, you review the *Process Advisor* [4] recommendations for your grade level:

> *Action:* You must develop a plan to improve each of the three areas: documentation, reviews, and SQA. The place to begin is with documents and reviews. Pick one or two documents and develop a standard format (recognize that brevity is a virtue) and then develop a set of review guidelines for the documents. Over time, broaden these actions until most important documents are defined, are being produced, and are being reviewed.

Next, you establish transition plan tasks that will enable you to "improve each of the three areas: documentation, reviews, and SQA." One year later (this time span may vary) you revisit the questionnaire and determine that your grade for the quality assurance process attribute is now 1.9. You have developed one indicator for improvement.

I'm having some trouble with this. After all, the bottom line is that we improve the quality of the software we build, not that we focus all of our attention on improving an arbitrary grade. Am I wrong?

You're absolutely correct! It is critically important not to lose sight of the primary objective when we attempt to improve software engineering practice—and that is: *to improve the quality of the product and the productivity of the people who build it.* Everything else, including assessment grades, is secondary.

With this said, I want to emphasize that the questionnaire can help you achieve the primary objective. Sadly, many managers with budgetary authority find it easier to relate to the Kiviat chart presented earlier in this chapter than they would to a detailed set of metrics delineating software quality. An improvement in a process attribute grade is something they can hang on to when requests for additional expenditures are made. I believe that both "measures"—assessment grades and software metrics—should be used to help convince senior managers that money should be spent to improve the software engineering process.

You indicated that "software metrics" can be used in conjunction with the assessment grades that we have been discussing. What are the metrics that we'll need to collect?

In Chapter 3, I discussed a wide array of software metrics that can be used to assist you in improving the process and the product. If you haven't already done so, I'd suggest that you read Chapter 3 at this point.

In addition to the metrics already discussed, the concept of *work-product analysis* [7] has been proposed as an effective way to collect measures of the product. Work-product analysis focuses on measurement of the tangible outputs (i.e., work products) produced throughout the software engineering process. Work products might include analysis and design model representations (e.g., data flow diagrams, specifications, pseudocode descriptions), source code, test suites, and a variety of other documentation.

To perform work-product analysis, a technical measure of each work product is derived. For example, the Flesch-Kincaid readability index might be computed for all text documents; cyclomatic complexity can be used to assess the algorithmic complexity of a module design. These data can be cross-correlated to defects that have been uncovered throughout the software engineering process.

Can you propose a set of management and technical metrics that will help us to assess product quality?

The U.S. Army Communications Electronics Command (Cecom) [8] has implemented a software metrics program that makes use of both management and technical metrics for assessing software quality. Management metrics focus on process-related issues, while technical metrics focus on the product. The Cecom approach can serve as a worthwhile model for most software organizations. Six management indicators are suggested [8]:

1. A measure of the utilization of computer resources within the organization's development environment. In today's software development

environment this might include tracking of workstation usage, access to file servers and/or repositories, use of I/O devices, and so forth.

2. A measure of applied engineering effort on a per project and per task basis.

3. A measure of requirements stability that provides an indication of the number, timing, and ultimate resolution of customer change requests.

4. A measure of the completeness of each work product as a project progresses to the next phase.

5. A measure of "progress" for each project that indicates how planned and actual costs and schedules deviate from one another.

6. A measure of the availability of software tools.

Each of these measures will provide an indication of the efficacy of the existing process framework and project management approach.

The seven quality indicators proposed by Cecom focus on work-product analysis:

1. *Completeness of specification:* Measured by the number of requirements changes or revisions that occur throughout the software engineering process.

2. *Design structure:* Measures quantifiable characteristics of data, architectural, and procedural design.

3. *Pretest error density:* Measures the number of errors uncovered prior to testing.

4. *Test efficiency:* Measures the number of errors uncovered during testing.

5. *Test coverage:* Measures the completeness of testing based on path coverage and data coverage.

6. *Test sufficiency:* Measures the quality of integration and system tests, based on the number and types of errors uncovered.

7. *Documentation:* Measures the quality of documents produced throughout the process.

By combining management and work-product measures, your organization can develop quantitative indicators for software product quality.

Based on your answers to the last few questions, you're saying that we should record all errors that we find, even before we deliver the software?

That's right. In Chapter 14, I'll present a collection of SQA activities that can be used throughout the software engineering process. One of these activities—the formal technical review—can help you not only find errors but also collect information about them throughout the process. Ultimately, information about errors can be used for statistical software quality assurance. But even if you don't want to go that far, you can use error-rate data to gain insight into your process and ultimately determine whether the real quality of your product is improving.

Are the metrics that you're suggesting collected as part of assessment or is their collection part of the software engineering process itself?

The ideal answer to your question is "Both." Realistically, there are few organizations that have a metrics program that will be ready for use during assessment. Recall that the common practice grade for the process attribute for measurement is 1.0. For this reason, the pragmatic answer to your question is: If you don't currently collect metrics, assessment can act as a catalyst to help you begin. It's unlikely that you'll be able to collect enough useful information to be of help during assessment, but the data that you begin collecting will aid you immeasurably during the second iteration of the software engineering implementation life cycle.

Assuming that we can collect the error data, is there one metric that we could use to get a "bottom-line" indication of improving quality?

Surprisingly, the answer is "Yes." But to compute the metric, you'll have to gather error data throughout the process and then collect defect reports from users as the software enters production. The single metric that I would propose is called *defect-removal efficiency* (DRE) and is computed in the following way:

$$\text{DRE} = \frac{E_p}{E_p + E_u}$$

where E_p is the number of errors uncovered throughout the software engineering process, but before delivery, and E_u is the number of defects uncovered in the field during actual usage.

The beauty of DRE is that it does not penalize an organization that is very aggressive about finding errors prior to delivery. In fact, the higher the value of E_p, the better the overall DRE for a constant number of field defects.

How do we collect the error data that you describe?

I'll assume that you're conducting effective formal technical reviews (see Chapter 14) and that if you aren't, you'll first move to put this activity into place. As reviews, and later tests, are conducted throughout the process, each software engineer records every error encountered. Your data collection should be quite simple:

- Error type (selected from a checklist)
- Process step where found
- Effort (in person days) required to correct

The sum of pretest errors and errors uncovered during testing provides you with a value for E_p.

For the first year or so, you'll do nothing more than collect error data, but after some time has passed (and a sufficient number of data points have been collected), you'll be able to begin computing quality metrics.

But you indicated that "common practice" doesn't include the use of formal technical reviews. Don't we have a chicken-and-egg problem?

You've touched on a real problem. Organizations that obtain an assessment grade (maturity level) in the 1.0 to 2.5 range tend not to have the mechanisms in place to collect quality data effectively. If your organization falls into this category, you'll have to use the following strategy for assessing progress in making the transition to improved software engineering practice:

1. Determine your maturity level.

2. As part of your transition plan, develop a schedule for putting formal technical reviews into place.

3. In the meantime, attempt to collect error-rate data during testing.

4. Compute DRE using errors uncovered during testing as your value for E_p. Later, you'll add additional errors that are uncovered during reviews.

5. While you're working to implement steps 2 and 3, use the value of DRE suggested in step 4 and the assessment grade to assess progress.

Steps 2 and 3 can take time. Depending on your overall transition plan and the priorities you assign to each transition task, steps 2 and

3 can take between 1 and 2 years to accomplish. But in time you will have established a structure that enables you to collect accurate data on product quality.

What value for DRE can we expect?

The answer to your question depends on your process maturity. Although I am unaware of any study that has attempted to correlate process maturity and DRE, it is highly likely that there is a strong positive correlation between these values. As a rough estimate of the DRE you can expect, consider the following table:

Maturity	E_p	E_u	DRE
1.0–1.8	20	8	0.714
1.9–2.3	40	4	0.909
2.4–3.2	55	0.8	0.986
3.3–4.0	65	0.05	0.999
4.0+	Unknown		Unknown

The values represented under the E_p and E_u columns represent average errors per KLOC before and after delivery, respectively; values under the "Maturity" column are the average of assessment grades for the following process attributes: quality assurance activities, process framework, and methods. Values in the "DRE" column represent the DRE to be expected for the upper bound of the maturity range.

It looks like a measurement activity is an integral part of all transition plans. Is that true?

Metrics should be an integral part of your transition plan, but your question asks whether it is a part of all transition plans. Sadly, the answer is "No." For reasons discussed in Chapter 3, many companies shy away from metrics collection. Although managers never completely justify their decision, their strategy to improve software engineering practice does not include metrics collection. I do believe that this is a mistake, but I will not be dogmatic about it.

If your maturity level is low, it is possible to improve the product and the process without measurement. This is not ideal or even advisable, but it is doable. However, as you begin to make progress, it will become essential to measure or any further gains will be quite difficult to attain.

You're saying that if we want to do things correctly, we should measure. What strategy should we use to institute a measurement program?

In a landmark book that outlines a complete strategy for instituting software metrics within a company, Grady and Caswell [9] define 10 "steps to success" that can serve as the basis for any transition strategy for software metrics work:

1. *Define a set of objectives for your measurement program:* Your objectives should provide a realistic indication how you expect software metrics to (1) assist you in technology transition, (2) improve the quality of the software that you produce, and (3) provide a mechanism for process improvement.

2. *Assign responsibility:* In Chapter 4 I indicated that technology transition requires a "champion." The situation is no different for software metrics. You must select those individuals who will make the metrics program a reality.

3. *Do research:* There is an extensive literature on software metrics. Before you begin, you should review important books and articles on the subject.

4. *Select the metrics that you plan to collect during the early stages of your measurement work:* The secret here is "keep it simple." You should focus on both quality and productivity by collecting a subset of the management metrics described in Chapter 3 and in this chapter and a small set of technical metrics that focus on work-product quality.

5. *Sell the metrics program to management and technical people:* Management must provide the resource required to do a good job, and technical people must understand the importance of measurement and make a commitment to collect accurate data.

6. *Obtain tools that enable automatic collection and analysis of metrics data:* Tools can remove much of the drudgery that is associated with measurement and can help ensure that data are collected in a consistent manner.

7. *Establish a metrics education program:* This step is applied in conjunction with step 5. In essence, education must answer the question that every technical person will ask, "What's in this for me?" Before metrics can be collected, practitioners must understand what to collect and why it's collected.

8. *Encourage participation by publicizing success and soliciting*

feedback: If simple data are used to improve management insight or technical control, the benefit of metrics can be demonstrated. If staff feedback is solicited and acted on, problems with metrics will not fester and solutions will become apparent.

9. *Create a metrics database:* Initially, the number of data items should be limited so that collection and analysis remain simple. Over time, the data to be collected should expand somewhat.

10. *Remain flexible:* The guidelines that you establish for metrics collection and analysis will evolve over time. Staff feedback and changing needs for process improvement will have much to do with the way that change occurs.

What happens once the initial assessment has been completed?

Once qualitative, boolean, and quantitative questions have been answered, metrics collection has begun, and follow-up meetings have occurred, a *Findings and Recommendations Report* should be written. Although the format of this report may vary, its intent is always the same—to summarize major findings that have been culled from the assessment and to propose overall recommendations for improvement. The recommendations, often prioritized, will serve as the basis for creation of a *Software Engineering Transition Plan.* The transition plan defines a complete strategy for all remaining steps in the implementation life cycle and is discussed in greater detail in Chapter 6.

What are the objectives for the *Findings and Recommendations Report?*

The *Findings and Recommendations Report* should accomplish the following objectives:

- To define the objectives and limitations of the assessment activity
- To describe the assessment methodology
- To summarize the process attributes grades and the process maturity grade and to discuss their meaning
- To delineate findings and recommendations clearly

The report is a sales document. It must convince management that there is reason for action, and at the same time, provide a clear indication of what action should be taken.

What form do you recommend for the *Findings and Recommendations Report?*

The report should be concise and to the point. After an introductory section that accomplishes the first two objectives noted above, the report should contain a section that summarizes the process maturity grades that have been derived. The final section contains findings and recommendations themselves. The text that follows has been extracted from the *Process Advisor* system [4] and provides a good format for presenting findings and recommendations:

Findings and Recommendations

The findings and recommendations presented in this section have been developed based on results obtained from the questionnaire grades and group discussions. Each finding is presented in **boldface** text and is followed by discussion and recommendations.

Each finding is assigned a priority rating (PR) that ranges from 1 to 3. The priority rating is shown in parentheses after each finding. The priorities can be interpreted as follows:

PR = 1. This finding represents a serious deficiency in software engineering practice. Immediate and continuing action is required to correct it.

PR = 2. This finding represents a moderate deficiency in software engineering practice. It should be corrected as soon as resources are available and schedule commitments permit dedicated effort.

PR = 3. This finding represents an opportunity for improvement. Action is suggested after corrections to more serious deficiencies are made.

FINDING: < The finding is presented as a factual statement.>

EXAMPLE: There is no organized focus on quality. Quality is not perceived as a serious issue even though excessive time is spent "fire fighting" and supporting old work (PR = 1).

DISCUSSION: < The discussion amplifies the finding and, where possible, provides supporting evidence or insight.>

EXAMPLE: There is no formal quality program which transcends the testing function and addresses quality throughout the process. Testing is perceived as the way to achieve quality. Unfortunately, *quality cannot be tested into software.*

While software testing is necessary to uncover certain classes of errors, one of the goals of total quality management is to reduce the need for extensive verification testing and thus the heavy costs associated with this activity.

RECOMMENDATION: < The recommendation should suggest some concrete action that will resolve the problem indicated in the

finding. It need not indicate how the action will be achieved, but rather what the action should be.>

EXAMPLE: <COMPANY NAME> should develop a "quality assurance" function. The role of the function should be (1) to foster SQA activities across all groups, (2) to become the driving force behind the development of a process framework, (3) to establish guidelines and standards for development and maintenance work, deliverables and reviews, (4) to introduce a quality review process that covers the entire software development process from definition through code and test, and (5) to help in the selection of tools to complement other software engineering activities. Quality reviews should be a mandatory "exit condition" for every software release.

Each {FINDING, DISCUSSION, RECOMMENDATION} should be developed in the same manner.

Where do we go from here?

Process assessment is critically important. It provides you with a firm foundation from which to build a strategy for technology transition. The next steps in the implementation life cycle are executed using a strategy that you'll define with a transition plan. We consider the transition plan in the next chapter.

A Manager's Checklist

The activities that surround software engineering technology transition can seem daunting to even the most enthusiastic manager. Yet, the ancient Chinese proverb—a journey of 1000 miles begins with a single step—should draw you to process assessment. Your first step on the long journey to improved software engineering practice is process assessment. But more important than getting you started, process assessment will also provide you with a map for the remainder of your journey.

The following actions and questions will help you prepare to take the first step.

Actions

- Poll project managers and technical staff and ask each to develop a list of your software development strengths and weaknesses. Compare the lists to find those entries that appear most frequently and record them. Save the list for comparison with your findings once a process assessment has been conducted.

- Acquire the *Capability Maturity Model for Software* [5] developed by the Software Engineering Institute. It will provide you with additional insight into process maturity and the key process factors that define different maturity levels.

- Acquire a set of process assessment questionnaires that covers qualitative, boolean, and quantitative issues. I recommend the *Process Advisor* system [4].

- Conduct a process assessment using the guidelines presented in this chapter.

Questions

- How many different major projects are currently under way within your organization's area of responsibility? Do you think that each project manager would have radically different responses to the process assessment questionnaire?

- What do you think your grade would be for each of the process attributes described in this chapter? What do you think your current process maturity is? Save these guesses for comparison with your actual grades.

Further Readings

Because formal software engineering process assessment is a relatively new management technique, the literature on this subject is rather sparse. Pressman (*Making Software Engineering Happen*, Prentice-Hall, 1988) presents a detailed treatment of qualitative and quantitative questions for software engineering process assessment. The Software Engineering Institute and private consulting firms are the source for boolean questions. Process maturity is considered in an excellent book by Humphrey (*Managing the Software Process*, Addison-Wesley, 1989), which also presents the steps required to improve organizational practice.

Weinberg (*Software Quality Management*, volume 1, Dorset House, 1992) presents an intriguing view of process maturity in his discussion of "software subcultures." He uses "patterns" that are analogous to maturity levels to help us understand how technology transition should occur.

Excellent articles on process assessment can be found in *IEEE Software* (July 1991). In a series of articles, the use of process assessment in an industry setting is described by Humphrey and his colleagues (*IEEE Software*, July 1991, pp. 11–23); a critique of the SEI model for process assessment is presented by Bollinger and McGowan [6], and a rebuttal to the critique is presented by Humphrey and Curtis (*IEEE Software*, July 1991, pp. 42–46).

Excellent sources of information on software metrics (a necessary element of process assessment) can be found in books by Putnam and Myers (*Measures for Excellence,* Yourdon Press, 1992), Jones (*Applied Software Measurement,* McGraw-Hill, 1991), Grady and Caswell [9], and Fenton (*Software Metrics,* Chapman & Hall, 1991). Fenton's book contains an extensive bibliography on metrics and describes METKIT, a metrics education tool kit that has been developed by the Espirit project in Europe. Many of the METKIT modules may be useful as you begin to implement a metrics program.

References

[1] Bouldin, B., *Agents of Change,* Yourdon Press, 1989.

[2] Pressman, R.S., *Making Software Engineering Happen,* Prentice-Hall, 1988.

[3] Humphrey, W., and W. Sweet, "A Method for Assessing the Software Engineering Capability of Contractors," Software Engineering Institute, CMU/SEI-87-TR-23, DTIC No. ADA187320, September 1987.

[4] Pressman, R.S., *Process Advisor: A Self-Directed System for Improving Software Engineering Practice,* R.S. Pressman & Associates, Inc., 1992. [phone: (203) 795-5044, fax: (203) 799-1023]. Used with permission.

[5] (a) *Capability Maturity Model for Software,* Software Engineering Institute, Carnegie-Mellon University, Pittsburgh, PA, 1991; (b) Weber, C.V., et al., "Key Practices of the Capability Maturity Model," CMU/SEI-91-TR-25, ESD-TR-91-25, Software Engineering Institute, Carnegie-Mellon University, Pittsburgh, PA, August 1991.

[6] Bollinger, T., and C. McGowan, "A Critical Look at Software Capability Evaluations," *IEEE Software* (July), 25–41 (1991).

[7] Grady, R. B., "Work-Product Analysis: The Philosopher's Stone of Software?" *IEEE Software* (March), 26–34 (1990).

[8] Fenick, S., "Implementing Management Metrics: An Army Program," *IEEE Software* (March), 65–72 (1990).

[9] Grady, R.B., and D.L. Caswell, *Software Metrics: Establishing a Company-Wide Strategy,* Prentice-Hall, 1987.

6

Transition Planning:
A Strategy
for Better Practice

Many organizations attempt to install software engineering technology by forcing a square peg into a round hole. A "methodology" is chosen, but it is too complex, too cumbersome, and too inflexible; staff members dismiss it as a bad idea. Technical methods are recommended, but they are inappropriate for the applications that are under development; practitioners revert to "the old ways." Powerful tools are selected, but they address the wrong aspects of software development or are applied to the wrong problems by the wrong people; frustration and confusion result, and the tools become "shelfware."

I have painted a dark and, sadly, not altogether uncommon picture of problems that occur when some companies attempt to implement software engineering technology. Because they don't have a clear understanding of local strengths and weakness, their strategy is often ill-conceived.

But your company does not have to suffer from these problems. If you've spent the time to conduct a thorough process assessment (Chapter 5) and developed a meaningful set of findings and recommendations, you're ready to develop an effective transition strategy.

You've used the word *transition* many times in this book. What do you really mean when you use it?

Webster's Dictionary defines the word *transition* as "a passing from one condition, form, stage, activity, place, etc., to another." When your company attempts to improve its software engineering practices, it will pass from one condition or stage (relatively low software engineering process maturity) to another (a more mature process). It will change the form of the process that is used to create software and the activities that are applied within the process. It may even change the "place" (the software development environment and the tools within it) where software is created. Transition is about change, and in most companies, change will succeed only if it is planned carefully.

You're saying that the creation of a transition strategy is a planning activity. How should we approach it?

Transition planning treats the implementation of software engineering practices like any technical project. That is, a work-breakdown structure (WBS) of specific tasks for implementation should be defined, responsibilities should be assigned to key individuals, milestones and deliverables should be identified, and a task network and overall project schedule should be developed.

In order to develop a successful strategy, it is necessary to proceed incrementally. Some organizations attempt to improve software engineering practice in one dramatic stroke, but this "big bang" approach introduces too much risk and overly complicates the introduction of new technology.

Who participates in this planning activity?

The transition strategy will be executed by staff members within your organization. For this reason, they should participate in every phase of its development. The transition planning activity can be coordinated by the same people who were involved in the process assessment effort, but more staff should be involved in the creation of the transition plan.

It sounds like you're advocating planning by committee, and that never works. How should we proceed?

You're right, planning by committee is frustrating, time-consuming, and worse, ineffective. Here's what I mean when I say that staff should be involved. The champion (see Chapter 4) and other staff who worked on the assessment should draft a "strawman" transition plan. The strawman document should be distributed to senior staff members, project leaders, and others for comment and criticism. The process proceeds iteratively until and a transition strategy acceptable to your organization's "opinion leaders" has evolved.

What's the first thing we should do?

I'd rather begin by talking about the thing that you shouldn't do first. Don't begin by developing a voluminous set of software engineering standards and procedures. After you've spent some time educating, selecting, and justifying, you may decide to write a "skinny" set of software engineering/CASE guidelines and have these guidelines evolve slowly into more formal standards and procedures. By developing guidelines first, practitioners can contribute to evolution of a standards document and will ultimately have greater ownership in the end result.

You suggest that we spend some time "educating, selecting, and justifying." Aren't these separate steps in the software engineering implementation life cycle that you discussed in Chapter 4?

You're correct. Education, selection, and justification (as well as installation and evaluation) are steps in a common-sense approach to transition planning. Your strategy should be to plan and coordinate these steps while at the same time defining the set of installation activities. You may recall that I mentioned that steps in the implementation life cycle are often concurrent. It is not at all unusual to conduct education, perform selection and justification, and install elements of the technology simultaneously.

You also suggested that transition planning should be treated like project planning for any technical activity. What is the "work-breakdown structure" for transition planning?

To a very great extent, the work-breakdown structure (WBS) for transition planning is derived from the results of the process assessment. Each recommendation (developed as a consequence of the assessment) is decomposed into a series of concrete tasks. In addition, tasks associated with education, selection, and justification are also defined, if these activities have been recommended (they almost always are).

O.K., let's assume that as a consequence of our assessment we find that education in software engineering is weak (e.g., the *training* process attribute earns a grade of 1.8). Can you suggest a WBS for education?

First, we have to study the responses to all process assessment questions (boolean, quantitative, and qualitative). It is true that a process attribute grade of 1.8 (see Chapter 5 for details) indicates that improvement is necessary, but your course of action will be dictated by qualitative and quantitative information as well. For example, the number of managers and technical staff that should be trained must be considered, budgetary constraints must be weighed, and the availability of training courses or media must be noted. In addition, each process attribute grade can be used to provide an indication of courses that may be appropriate.[1]

Finally, education tasks must be coordinated with tasks in other implementation life-cycle steps. For example, the choices that your organization makes for methods and tools will dictate the kinds of education that you perform.

I realize that a canned WBS for education is difficult to specify. How about a generic WBS that leaves room for further refinement once the information that you suggest above is known?

A generic WBS for an education strategy might take the following form:

- Write a training requirements plan.
- Identify training tracks for staff.
- Prepare a requirements specification for each software engineering course.
- Select alternative training media.
- Evaluate commercial course offerings.
- Prepare development plans for unique courses.
- Identify and train instructors.
- Schedule courses, participants, and facilities.
- Define evaluation and feedback process.
- Evaluate and introduce new material and courses.

The details of each transition task are developed on the basis of other assessment information.

How would the education tasks be described in an actual transition plan?

Later in this chapter, I'll suggest an overall format for transition plans. In general, each major transition task (called a "program" in

---

[1]This topic is discussed in more detail in Chapter 7.

the text that follows) is addressed in a separate section (in this case section *n*) of the transition plan. The following format, adapted from an actual transition plan, works reasonably well:

n. Create a Software Engineering Training Program

n.1 Overview   Training is the key to effective use of software engineering methods and tools and effective application of good software project management practices. <company name> software engineering training focuses on three audiences:

- *Those concerned with the management and technical activities of maintaining software products:*   Course content concentrates on the software engineering process and the roles of each participant.
- *Users and their managers:*   Course content focuses on what is to be done. Why is it needed? What is the payoff? What roles are they expected to play?
- *Technical staff and technical management:*   Courses concentrate on specific software engineering topics such as testing, change, and revision control.

Additional software engineering training is to be identified as new technology emerges and courses are deleted as technology becomes obsolete. All courses must be updated periodically to reflect experience and new thinking.

While some of the training courses must be developed because of their unique nature, many can be selected from outside commercially available offerings. A <company name> training plan would act as a template for procurement.

n.2 Applicable Documents   The following documents have a direct bearing on the success of tasks associated with this program and/or are produced as a consequence of tasks performed during the duration of this program:

- *Software Engineering Findings and Recommendations Report <date>:* Guides the direction and philosophy of the training strategy.
- *The <company name> SE Training Requirements Plan:*   A document that describes the software engineering training program (developed by <company name> or a contractor).
- *SE Course Requirements Specification:*   Developed for each SE training course to be offered by <company name>.

n.3 Task Descriptions   The task descriptions (denoted by the symbol §) presented in this section are numbered in the format, *i.j*, where *i* is the program number [in this case, *n*] and *j* is the task number.

§ n.1. **Write a training requirements plan.**   This task defines software engineering training requirements for each of the three constituencies noted in section n.1 and identifies courses needed, the characteristics and size of the audience, the objective for each course, a content outline for each course, and the manner in which success will be measured. An attempt should be made to schedule a development-procurement phase, a prototype or evaluation phase, and a full-availability phase. The SE coordinator (whose role is defined elsewhere in the transition plan) coordinates, administers, and implements the SE training program.

§ n.2. **Identify training tracks for staff.**   Not every member of <company name> should take every SE course offered. The SE coordinator jointly with the advisory group (whose role is defined elsewhere in the transition plan) defines skill objectives for each <company name> staff group and then targets training accordingly. As a minimum, the following groups should be addressed: users/customers, top-level managers, contractors, experienced technical staff, and new hires and junior technical staff.

§ n.3. **Prepare a requirements specification for each SE course.** Using the training requirements plan as a guideline, detailed specifications for each course are developed. The content of the specification includes content outlines, day plans, lab exercises, materials, presentation method, class size, learning objectives, and validation criteria. In many cases, these specifications can be acquired directly from training vendors or adapted from materials obtained from them. For specialized courses, the specifications can be used to assist in internal development of the course. In general, however, courses will be developed or procured from an outside vendor.

§ n.4. **Select alternative training media.** It is often possible to supplement classroom training with other training media such as videotaped courses, computer-based multimedia training, audiotaped presentations, and written materials. Available courseware should be evaluated and selected as an adjunct to classroom training. All alternative courseware should be coordinated with classroom training.

§ n.5. **Evaluate commercial course offerings.** Many SE technical courses are available from vendors off-the-shelf. The course specification can be used to determine the acceptability of various products. In some cases vendors can readily adapt to minor changes. In other cases it may be advisable to accept a course that comes close to meeting the specification, rather than developing a new course.

§ n.6. **Prepare development plans for unique courses.** For those courses that are not off-the-shelf, detailed development plans are prepared and resources assigned. <company name> should not develop a large number of "custom" courses. In most cases, it would be cost-effective to contract the development of unique courses to contractors experienced in SE training and more importantly, curriculum design for large companies.

§ n.7. **Identify and train instructors.** In most cases, courses should be presented by professional trainers who (1) have excellent teaching skills and (2) have an in-depth understanding of the subject matter. In some cases, it would be cost-effective to do the instruction with internal people. It is also a good morale boost for the staff. All instructors need extensive training before teaching a course. The best technologist is not always the best teacher. Look for good communicators and teach them the technology. SE training is one form of sales tool for the SE transition program. It's extremely important that the training accomplish this objective.

Important Note: For the early presentations of new courses, the instructor should always be a training professional. <company name> instructors would observe for the first few sessions before teaching the course themselves.

§ n.8. **Schedule courses, participants, and facilities.** As the courses become available, a registration and logistics function is needed. If <company name> has a training organization, it might be willing to assume this ongoing responsibility. The SE coordinator provides guidance as necessary.

It is important to note that training should be coordinated with project needs so that "just in time" training is offered to managers and technical staff.

§ n.9. **Define the course evaluation and feedback process.** A course and instructor should be evaluated regularly and the responses integrated as appropriate. A one-page evaluation sheet is developed which rates (scale of 1 to 5) course content, relevance, presentation, length, materials, facilities, and overall satisfaction. Space for written comments is also provided.

§ n.10. **Evaluate and introduce new material and courses.** Courses and their content must be evaluated for relevance and applicability. New courses are evaluated and introduced as new technology is integrated into <company name> software development and maintenance processes.

As new employees join <company name>, they should be trained as quickly as possible. Scheduling of courses for new employees is difficult because they enter over a long period of time, rather than all at once. It may be necessary to supplement the kernel SE courses with video versions so that new employees can obtain training on an as-needed basis.

In reviewing the 10 tasks that you recommended above, I noticed that they span a significant time period. Don't you think it would be a good idea to write a transition plan that recommends actions to be performed quickly?

It is natural for both management and staff to be impatient once a decision to improve software engineering practice has been made. However, impatience should not drive the transition planning process. Improving practice takes time.

With this in mind, it is possible to assuage at least some of the impatience that is natural among managers and staff, while at the same time outlining a rational strategy for the long term. To do this, the transition plans that I write always have a section called "6-month quick hits." This section outlines transition tasks that can be conducted within six months of the adoption of the plan. These "6-month quick hits" allow everyone to see progress and help to create small successes that spur everyone forward.

Can you provide an example of these "quick hits"?

To a large extent, quick hits are chosen based on the responses to all process assessment questions (boolean, quantitative, and qualitative). They are rarely, if ever, generic. The example that follows suggests 6-month quick hits for the education program discussed above.

n.4   First 6-Month Quick Hits

- *Develop and teach an SE awareness seminar:*   The SE awareness seminar should be developed and given to all members of the <company name> management, users and their managers, and the technical staff. This should be accomplished early with at least four sessions given in the first three months. The topics covered are the following:

  The SE assessment report results

  The recommendations

  Highlights of the plan and its various programs

  Why it needs to be done

  What results should be expected

  What's expected of "you"

- *Identify and evaluate the following technical courses: information mapping, tool training for any recommended CASE tools, and peer review training:* There are many technical courses available off-the-shelf. These could be offered under the auspices of the SE coordinator and the advisory group (AG) with relatively little effort. In fact, the <company name> training function would probably be glad to be involved and do most of the administrative work.

- *Acquire a video series on software engineering methods and make it available to <company name> staff immediately:*   Staff members will be able to pick and choose those topics of interest and learn about them in a timeframe that is convenient. The video presentation can be used to acclimate the entire organization to software engineering jargon, concepts, and philosophy.

You discussed the format for presenting transition tasks. What is the recommended content and format for the transition plan itself?

As I mentioned earlier, the transition plan is actually a project plan. Therefore, it must present information that is necessary to plan and manage a "software engineering transition project." The plan should contain a work-breakdown structure (WBS) of specific tasks for implementation, responsibilities for each task, milestones and deliverables associated with the tasks, and a task network and overall project schedule.

Ideally, the transition plan exists in two forms: (1) a written document and (2) an electronic form that is maintained by a CASE project management tool. A suggested format for the written document follows:

Introduction

Scope

Objective

The Planning Procedure

The Plan

    Coordination of the Transition Process

      Role of the Software Engineering Coordinator

Role of the Advisory Group

Role of <company> Organizations

Management's Role

User's Role

Organizational Goals—First Year, Second Year, Third Year

Transition Tasks—An Overview

Transition Schedule—An Overview

Program and Task Descriptions

Specific Major Transition Task (referred to as a "program")

n.1   Overview

n.2   Applicable Documents

n.3   Task Descriptions

n.4   First 6-Month Quick Hits

The Transition Schedule

Schedule Overview

Assumptions and Limitations

A Review of the Work-Breakdown Structure

Transition Tasks and Resource Requirements for Program n

Transition Plan Task Network

Timeline Schedules

Project Tables

Schedule Summary

Figures

Task Networks

Task Timelines

Project Tables

Appendix I—Software Engineering Bibliography

The outline that you propose for the transition plan generates a number of questions. First, can you provide an example of the introductory sections of the plan?

The text that follows has been extracted from an actual transition plan that we developed for a client. It is representative of the tone and content of the introductory sections of the plan.

Introduction   The transition plan is the culmination of the second phase of the <company name> software engineering assessment. In the first phase, detailed findings and recommendations were presented to <company name> management and staff. Six program recommendations were presented. The intent of these recommendations was to provide <company name> with guidance in its attempt to bring software engineering practice to a state that is equal to the best practice in the industry. The transition plan addresses an implementation strategy for achieving this goal.

It should be noted that the transition plan is an evolving document. As time passes, it must be updated and modified to reflect the current situation at <company name>.

Scope   The transition plan presents the first level of a work-breakdown structure (WBS) for software engineering implementation. Implementation issues associated with each task are presented in a discussion that accompanies the task statement.

The tasks contained in the WBS are presented in sufficient detail for <company name> to modify, enhance, and expand them to produce the final working plan. From this final plan, work can be allocated to organizations, task forces, or individuals.

This transition plan does not address topics such as organizational issues, funding sources, or specific staff assignments.

Objective   The transition plan provides a WBS and related information that are needed for defining, analyzing, implementing, and incorporating software engineering technology recommended by each of the program recommendations contained in the *Software Engineering Findings and Recommendations Report*. The plan describes both short-term (first 6 months) and long-term tasks and emphasizes frequent evaluation of results. The requirement for ongoing technology introduction and support is also considered.

The Planning Procedure   The transition plan consists of six major tasks that correspond to the program recommendations presented in the *Software Engineering Findings and Recommendations Report*. Each major task is refined into a series of subtasks which comprises the WBS. The intent of each subtask is described, related implementation issues are discussed, resources required are estimated (when possible), and a sequence for execution of the tasks is suggested in the context of an overall schedule. Since many of the programs are interrelated, the interdependencies of WBS tasks are considered in the schedule.

A single master schedule covering a three-year period is provided. The schedule includes the tasks from all programs. The tasks are uniquely labeled so that the program flow is readily identifiable.

It appears that the transition schedule is discussed in some detail in the plan. What form does this discussion take?

The transition plan schedule is developed using the work-breakdown structure implied by tasks described in the plan. Estimated effort and project duration are defined for each task; interdependencies among the tasks are established, and a simple, automated project scheduling tool (e.g., MacProject II for the Apple Macintosh) is used to develop a task network, timeline (Gantt Chart) schedule, and project table for the project as a whole and each program recommendation.

To help simplify review of the schedule, discussion in this section of the transition plan should focus on the following:

- Scheduling assumptions and limitations
- Projections of the effort and duration for each WBS task
- Indication of responsible organization

This is followed by

- The task network
- Task timelines organized globally and by program
- A project table indicating start and finish dates, effort, duration, and number of people by task in tabular format

What are typical assumptions that you make when the transition plan schedule is created?

To complete the transition plan in a timely fashion and keep the scheduling activity relatively simple, it is necessary to make assumptions that may, in fact, be proved incorrect as the transition process begins. Some of the most common assumptions are listed.

1. People will be available in required numbers to address each task when its start date occurs.

2. Effort will be distributed evenly throughout the duration of each task.

3. Budgeting for the WBS occurs instantly—budgeting tasks have zero duration.

4. Acquisition of desired tools and methods occurs "instantly" once the decision to acquire the tool or method has been made.

5. Each milestone represents a management decision point. If a milestone has not been achieved, work on a particular program (or set of programs) may be modified or suspended.

6. No time lag occurs between a milestone and the start of the next task.

In reality, the transition project manager (the person I called the "champion" earlier in this book) must account for these assumptions by adding tasks, effort, and duration to reflect the "real world" operating environment at your company.

What are some of the limitations that affect the transition plan schedule?

The transition schedule is limited by factors that affect all project schedules: resource availability, task interdependence, changing organizational and business needs, and management whim.

How is the schedule presented?

First, the transition tasks associated with a specific program recommendation are summarized using a table similar to the one shown below:

WBS task	Estimated effort, pm	Estimated duration, months	Participating organization
Task 1.1	0.5	0.5	SRC
Task 1.2	0.5	0.5	SRC
Task 1.3	2	0.75	SRC/AG
Task 1.4	3	1.0	SRC/AG/ORG
Task 1.5	1	Continuous	SRC/AG/ORG
Task 1.6	5	Continuous	SRC/DIV
Task 1.7	5	Continuous	SRC
Task 1.8	2	1.0	SRC/AG
Task 1.9	2	1.0	SRC/AG
Task 1.10	2	Continuous	SRC
Task 1.11	18	Continuous	SRC/AG/DIV
Task 1.12	6	Continuous	SRC/AG/TF
Task 1.13	6	Continuous	SRC

The table lists each transition task, the estimated effort in person-months (pm) that will be required to accomplish the task, the chronological duration in calendar months for the task, and the responsible organization (represented by its initials).

How is this information used to create the kind of schedule chart that we use on technical projects?

The classic timeline schedule chart, often called a Gantt Chart, is created using a project scheduling tool. The input to the tool is called a task network—a diagram that depicts each WBS task and its interdependence with other tasks.[2]

To illustrate, consider the top-level task network for a transition

---

[2]It should be noted that some scheduling tools do not use the task network. Instead, a list or a hierarchy of work tasks is entered directly and then organized with a timeline chart.

plan shown in Figure 6.1. Each WBS task is represented as a simple rectangle. Subprojects—tasks associated with program recommendations (in this case five subtasks are shown)—are denoted by rectangles with rounded shading at each corner. A task number and an abbreviated text description are contained in each task rectangle. The projected start date for the task (or subproject) is noted to the upper left above the rectangle; the projected duration for the task is noted to the upper right above the rectangle (the earliest finish date is shown in Figure 6.1; see legend accompanying the figure). Milestones are depicted as

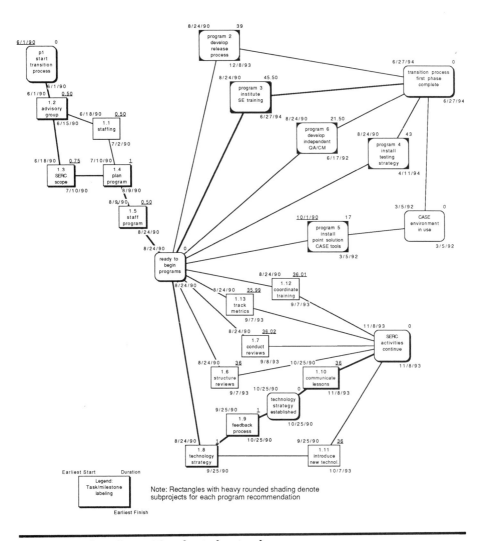

Figure 6.1 Overall transition plan task network.

rectangles with rounded corners. The milestone date appears above the milestone at the upper left. Tasks and milestones are connected with lines that indicate sequential dependence. The critical path [i.e., the schedule path(s) that cannot fall behind schedule without negative impact on major milestones and end dates] is denoted with a bolder linewidth.

Is it correct to assume that each of the major subtasks shown in the figure is itself expanded into a task network?

That's correct. To illustrate, a slightly modified task network for the education task that I discussed earlier is presented in Figure 6.2.

How is a timeline schedule derived from the task network?

Timeline schedules are derived automatically from the task network by the project planning tool. The format of a typical timeline schedule is shown in Figure 6.3. The following characteristics should be noted:

- An annual time scale is used; each vertical column represents one year.

- Milestones are noted as a solid diamond.

- Tasks are noted as a bar that moves horizontally (with time) for the task's duration.

- Subprojects are denoted as bars with shaded, rounded ends.

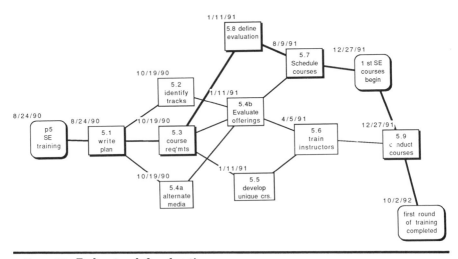

Figure 6.2   Task network for education program.

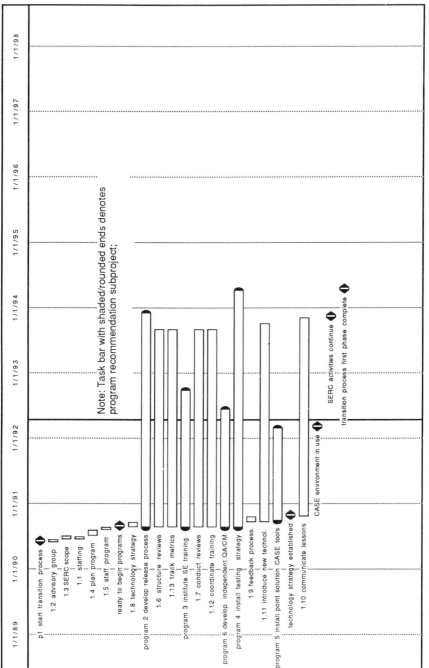

Figure 6.3 Overall transition plan task timeline. (Note: task bar with shaded/rounded ends denotes transition program that contains multiple tasks.)

133

It should be noted that the output format for task networks and schedule timelines varies among project planning tools. The tool that your organization uses may use a different format.

Are other forms of output produced by the project planning tool useful in transition planning?

Another useful output is the *project table*. A project table (Table 6.1) presents the earliest start and finish and latest start and finish for each task, the number of work-months allocated, a suggested number of people (denoted as "number"), and the duration of the task (denoted as "months"). Tasks and milestones that sit on the critical path are denoted with boldface text.

Can you suggest any generic guidelines that will help make the transition strategy successful?

The most important generic guidelines for software engineering transition planning are these:

1. Be certain that a "champion" (Chapter 4) has been chosen to manage the transition strategy.

2. Make sure that the introduction of new technology (procedures, methods, and tools) is supported by "systants" (Chapter 4) who will be available to help staff members overcome the initial frustration that occurs whenever something new must be learned.

3. Define transition tasks that are well focused and have modest, measurable goals.

TABLE 6.1   Project Table for Education Program

Name	Earliest start	Earliest finish	Latest start	Latest finish	Work-weeks	Duration
p5 SE training	8/24/90	8/24/90	5/18/92	5/18/92	0	0
5.1 Write plan	8/24/90	10/19/90	5/18/92	7/13/92	4	8
5.4a Alternate media	10/19/90	11/16/90	1/11/93	2/8/93	4	4
5.2 Identify tracks	10/19/90	11/16/90	1/11/93	2/8/93	1	4
5.3 Course requirements	10/19/90	1/11/91	7/13/92	10/5/92	8	11.94
5.8 Define evaluation	1/11/91	8/9/91	10/5/92	5/3/93	3	29.99
5.4b Evaluate offerings	1/11/91	4/5/91	2/8/93	5/3/93	3	12
5.5 Develop unique courses	1/11/91	4/4/91	3/29/93	6/18/93	2	11.76
5.7 Schedule courses	8/9/91	12/27/91	5/3/93	9/20/93	1	19.99
5.6 Train instructors	4/5/91	7/8/91	6/18/93	9/20/93	4	12.01
1st SE courses begin	12/27/91	12/27/91	9/20/93	9/20/93	0	0
5.9 Conduct courses	12/27/91	10/2/92	9/20/93	6/27/94	8	39.99
1st round of training completed	10/2/92	10/2/92	6/27/94	6/27/94		

4. During early phases, work with staff members who are enthusiastic about the new technology. Don't waste your time trying to cajole those who are hesitant.

5. Be sure that all education does two things: (a) that it informs and (b) that it sells the student on the technology.

In an earlier chapter, you introduced the "systant" as a key role during technology transition. What guidelines can you suggest for implementing this role?

Recalling our earlier discussion, a systant is a member of your technical staff who has received special training and access to detailed information concerning the procedures, methods, and tools that are implemented as part of changes in software engineering practice. Part of the systant's job function is to provide assistance to any staff members who have begun to use any of the components of software engineering practice.

The systant should be selected from knowledgeable and respected staff members who are "people people." That is, each systant should have a tutor's mentality, fielding questions with good grace and providing cheerful guidance to everyone who requests it.

In all cases, the systant should receive training and guidance from technology experts. For example, prior to the installation of a new CASE tool, the systant should be sent to the vendor's site to take training classes, use the tool, and interact with the vendor's instructors to learn how to field questions about the tool. The systant should then bring the tool home and use it for some period of time before it is introduced to a project team or to the organization as a whole.

Every member of the technical staff should be aware of the systant's role and be provided with that person's name, electronic-mail address, and telephone number.

How much time should be allocated for the systant's work?

Time allocation for the systant must be scheduled into that person's daily work schedule. If this does not occur, every request for help will be viewed as an intrusion (by the systant) and the approach will fail. Time allocation varies with the number of months since the technology (e.g., a specific procedure, method, or tool) has been introduced. The following table [1] can be used as a rough guideline:

Months since introduction	% time allocated to systant role
1–3	75
4–9	50
10–18	25
19+	As required

What is the ratio of staff members to systants?

The staff-to-systant ratio is a function of the amount of training received by each staff member, the complexity of the technology that is being introduced, the time since technology transition began, and the skills of the systant. In general, one systant can comfortably service between 10 and 20 staff members.

What if we put together the transition plan and never fully get management support?

If this happens, it's likely that you haven't done your homework. It is essential that managers receive what I call "consciousness raising education" that sells as well as informs. In addition, you must work to collect basic quality and productivity metrics so that you can project the return on investment that will occur when practice improves. When these things are done, management support usually follows.

And what if support is still lacking? You have two options: (1) stop all further transition activity until management can be signed up, or (2) continue transition activities as a grass-roots effort, recognizing that resources will be severely limited.

In the past, our staff has been less than enthusiastic about software engineering. What if this happens again?

Let me begin by saying that you can't expect everyone to be enthusiastic. Human nature doesn't work that way. Sadly, many managers waste valuable time and energy attempting to achieve global consensus before the transition even begins. My experience has been that this approach is doomed to failure.

If you've done a good job of assessment, you'll be able to create a transition plan that many of your staff can endorse. Ideally, many practitioners have worked with you to create the transition plan; therefore, they have a vested interest in making it happen. Work with them and (temporarily) forget about the nay sayers. Later, you'll have to work to bring them around (or find them a more acceptable position elsewhere).

It seems that we always have trouble getting started on something like this. How do we overcome our organizational inertia?

That's where a detailed transition plan and a committed champion (transition plan project manager) come in. The champion must act as a slave driver/cheerleader/preacher/manager at the beginning of transition. If tasks are specific and responsibility is defined; if milestones are measurable and discernible progress can be observed in a relatively short time, you'll overcome organizational inertia.

I'm certain that deadline pressures are going to cause some staff to say that they have "no time" for this. What should we do if that occurs?

There are situations in which "no time" is a reasonable excuse, but each "no time" claim must be considered on it merits. If your resources are stretched to their limits and project deadlines are looming in the near future, it's better to delay certain transition activities. If you decide to proceed, you must recognize that goals may have to be scaled back and that progress will be slow.

A word of caution: In some companies it seems that there is never the time to make improvements that will enable people to have the time to do things well, so time pressure mounts and there is even less time for improvement. This circular chain must be broken, or your organization will be doomed to mediocrity.

What if some of our transition tasks fail?

The installation step occurs iteratively, and it is likely that you will encounter a few small failures along with your successes. However, if you apply the guidelines noted above and treat technology transition as a project, you'll move relatively smoothly as your organization transfers new technology.

A Manager's Checklist

Transition planning occurs as a consequence of process assessment. It translates the findings and recommendations that you developed into a concrete plan of action for technology transition. The transition plan includes a work-breakdown structure for transition and a schedule that defines tasks and their dependencies and the milestones and deliverables that are associated with them.

The following actions and questions will help you to gain additional insight into transition planning.

Actions

- Create a work-breakdown structure for the activities that you'll need to conduct to prepare for process assessment and transition planning.
- Write a description of every activity listed as part of the above action.

Questions

- Make a list of senior managers who you must sell. What are their hot buttons?
- Who among your colleagues would be a good candidate for the champion's role?
- Make a confidential list of those staff members who might be good systants. Would it be possible to free their time for this activity?
- What do you guess would be the five or six major program tasks for the transition strategy for your organization?
- What project scheduling tool does your organization use? Is it capable of creating those elements of the transition schedule discussed in this chapter?

Further Readings

The readings suggested for Chapters 4 and 5 are also applicable to the topic of transition planning. In addition, many of the software project management guidelines proposed in books by King (*Project Management Made Simple*, Yourdon Press, 1992), Whitten (*Managing Software Development Projects*, Wiley, 1989), House (*The Human Side of Project Management*, Addison-Wesley, 1988), Page-Jones (*Practical Project Management*, Dorset House, 1985), and DeMarco (*Controlling Software Projects*, Yourdon Press, 1982) can be adapted to management of the transition strategy.

The *Proceedings of the Workshop on Software Engineering Technology Transfer* (IEEE, 1983) contain somewhat dated, but still useful papers that provide guidance for creating successful transition strategies. Przybylinski and Fowler (*Transferring Software Engineering Tool Technology*, IEEE Computer Society Press, 1988) provide similar guidance that focuses exclusively on the transition to CASE tools.

Reference

[1] Pressman, R.S., *Making Software Engineering Happen*, Prentice-Hall, 1988.

7

Education, Selection, and Justification: Moving toward Software Engineering

The last two chapters emphasized the importance of setting the stage for transition, a common-sense approach that lays a foundation for success. You've learned how to conduct a detailed software engineering process assessment to determine where you are today. You've examined the guidelines required to plan a transition strategy so that you'll have a reasonable chance of moving to where you want to be tomorrow.

In this chapter I'll discuss the steps in the implementation life cycle that will move you forward. *Education* raises the level of software engineering knowledge and at the same time increases the level of enthusiasm among managers and practitioners. *Selection and justification* guide you through choices that may affect your software engineering practices for years to come. It's also during these steps that you must approach management and gain their approval and commitment.

Our job is to institute new technology so that we can build higher-quality systems more productively. We're not a school. Why is it that you emphasize education to such an extent?

I emphasize the importance of education because it is a pivotal activity for technology transition. People tend to resist things that they don't understand. Education will help to improve understanding of software engineering procedures, methods, and tools, thereby reducing staff resistance. People tend to become frustrated when they attempt to use a method or tool that they've never been taught how to use properly. Education helps to reduce frustration. People become pigeon-holed in their jobs and often have no overall feeling for "the big picture." Education helps to put software engineering into a business context. People tend to look for personal benefit when they are asked to use something new. Education helps to answer the question that all practitioners ask, "What's in it for me?"

Resources are limited in our organization. How much education is enough?

Although education needs vary, a good rule of thumb is that software engineering staff should receive at least 1 and as many as 3 weeks of methods training each year. During the early stages of technology transition, the education load may approach the high end of this training allocation. As time passes, your organization will likely achieve a steady-state training level that falls toward the low end of the training allocation suggested above.

How do we know what types of education we need, what subjects should be presented, and in what order training should occur?

Process assessment should help you target areas where education would provide benefit. It will also help you estimate the amount of time that should be dedicated on a per person basis. Using the results of the process assessment as a guide, you should develop an education strategy.

Is it fair to say that the steps involved in developing an education strategy are similar to the steps required to develop an overall transition strategy?

Yes, but developing an effective education strategy is actually somewhat easier. Using the process assessment, organizational needs for education can be determined with relatively little difficulty. However, organizational goals for education may not fit the needs of every practitioner and manager. Each individual has different skills, knowledge, and motivation. Therefore, it's necessary to provide staff members with help in determining their individual educational needs within the context of broader organizational goals.

How do we use the process assessment questionnaire to begin the development of an education strategy?

The boolean questions associated with the process assessment (described in Chapter 5) provide a good starting point. To illustrate how these might be used, I'll use the questions that focus on the *training* process attribute (Chapter 5) contained in the *Process Advisor* system [1] developed by R.S. Pressman & Associates, Inc. Questions related to training are reproduced below.

Training

1. Has your organization developed or acquired a series of software engineering training courses for managers and technical staff?

2. Do you have a training group within your company that has responsibility for education of software developers?

3. Are software engineering courseware and training materials available to all software development staff?

4. Is a course in software project management required for all software managers?

5. Is a course in software analysis and design methods offered on an as-required basis?

6. Is a course in software testing methods and strategies offered on an as-required basis?

7. Is there a required course for formal technical review[1] leaders?

8. Has your organization developed or acquired specialized courses for tools and methods that are used locally?

9. Are a selection of software engineering books, periodicals, conference proceedings, and newsletters readily available to software developers?

10. Are training requirements considered during software project planning?

11. Is a training budget[2] established for each software staff member?

12. Is each software engineering training course evaluated to assess its quality and its conformance to training objectives?

13. Does every staff member receive at least 5 days of software engineering training per year?

---

[1] A *formal technical review* is a review of a software product by peers of the producer(s) of the product for the purpose of identifying defects and improvements. Formal technical reviews are discussed in Chapter 14.

[2] A *training budget* allocates a number of days of training to an individual over a given time period (usually one year).

The "yes"/"no" answers to these questions can be interpreted using guidelines adapted from *Process Advisor* [1]:

Question	Interpretation and action
1	**Yes:** If you have acquired a set of software engineering courses and training materials or if such courses are offered in-house by training vendors, make a list and compare the courses offered in your shop to the list of courses presented later in this chapter. **No:** Candidate courses and/or training materials should be acquired and are discussed later.
2	**Yes:** For political and organizational harmony, be sure that you include this group in the creation of the final plan. You can, however, present a "draft" plan to the training group. **No:** Develop your own training plan.
3	**Yes:** What types are available? Videos? Workbooks? Textbooks? Make a list of available courseware and categorize it by topic and type. Use courseware to complement your education strategy. **No:** Select the types of courseware using guidelines discussed later in this chapter.
4–8	**Yes:** Make a list of all relevant courses. **No:** Determine which of these courses is required? You can determine the answer to this question using an education planning matrix such as the one presented later in this chapter.
9	**Yes:** Compare available titles and periodicals to those contained in the software engineering bibliography presented in Appendix I. **No:** Plan to acquire titles and periodicals contained in the software engineering bibliography, Appendix I.
10	**Yes:** Good. Continue this practice. **No:** Add a training requirements task to the work breakdown structure for project planning.
11	**Yes:** The budget should be tuned to the needs of each individual manager or practitioner. You should work to establish some mechanism for isolating these needs. **No:** Create a budget that has a minimum of 5 training days per year per person.

In addition to the direct interpretation discussed above, it is possible to use an *educational planning matrix* [1] that will target specific software engineering courses.

What courses are typically specified as part of an educational strategy?

The following courses are candidates for inclusion in a software engineering education plan. It is important to note, however, that a decision on the courses to be offered can only be made after (1) interpretation of assessment responses, (2) completion of the education planning matrix [1], and (3) an evaluation of a *Software Engineering Self-Test* described a bit later in this chapter.

General courses

Introduction to software engineering (ISE)

Software engineering methods (SEM)

Introduction to the local process framework (ILPF)

The role of users/customers in the software engineering process (RUC)

Management courses

Software project management (SPM)

Software quality assurance (SQA)

Software configuration management (SCM)

Facilitated application specification (FAS)

Software metrics (SM)

Technical courses

Structured analysis (SA)

Object-oriented analysis and design (OO)

Software design (SD)

Software testing (ST)

Software reviews (SR)

Operational courses

CASE tools (offered by tool vendor)

When you say "courses," I think of a classroom setting. Aren't there other forms of education that are useful?

It is important to understand that education can take many forms. The most common is classroom instruction, conducted on site or through public course offerings. However, other modes of education are also valuable. For example, video-based education in software engineering can prove especially useful when tight project schedules do not allow staff members to spend long periods of time away from the office or when new staff are being hired over a rather long period of time. Although video-based education does not contain the interactive element that is particularly beneficial in classroom work, it still provides a useful mode of information transfer.[3] As the 1990s progress, it is likely that conventional video courses will evolve into multimedia, computer-based training systems.

In addition to formal modes of education delivery, a software engineering library should be established within the software development organization. For an expenditure of 5 to 10 thousand dollars an organization can establish a reasonably comprehensive collection of textbooks and periodicals. The library serves to supplement formal education and to keep staff members up to date on a rapidly changing technology. The software engineering bibliography contained in Appendix I can serve as an excellent "shopping list" for your librarian.

Earlier you mentioned an "education planning matrix" as one technique for developing an education strategy. Can you provide a few more details?

An education planning matrix (Table 7.1) can be used to help you select the appropriate software engineering courses for your organization. The matrix is driven by responses to the boolean questionnaire used as part of the assessment activity. The question numbers in the education planning matrix correspond to the question numbers in the boolean questionnaire. An entry in the matrix is made for each boolean question that receives a "no" response.

Each column of the matrix corresponds to one of the recommended software engineering courses discussed earlier. The entire matrix is summed columnwise. Those courses (columns) with the most entries represent prime candidates for inclusion in an educational strategy. Table 7.1 is an excerpt [1] illustrating the structure of the education planning matrix.

You also mentioned a _Software Engineering Self-Test._ What is this?

The _Software Engineering Self-Test_ (presented in Appendix II) is designed to provide you with an indication of your understanding of important software engineering concepts. Questions span both management and technical topics. The self-test is intended not as a comprehensive examination, but rather as a survey of software engineering knowledge.

The self-test is composed of multiple-choice questions that have been categorized by subject area. In some cases the differences between responses will be subtle. In fact, it is possible to provide more

---

[3]For further information on video-based curricula for software engineering training, contact R.S. Pressman & Associates, Inc. and other software engineering training companies.

TABLE 7.1   Excerpt of a Software Engineering Education Planning Matrix [1]*

4. Quality assurance activities
4.1 Documentation

Question No.	ISE	SEM	ILPF	RUC	SPM	SQA	SCM	FAS	SM	SA	OO	SD	ST	SR
4.1.1a ___		□		□										
4.1.1b ___							□		□					
4.1.1c ___												□		
4.1.1e ___													□	
4.1.1f ___					□	□	□							
4.1.1g ___					□		□							
4.1.2 ___			□											
4.1.3 ___						□								
Subtotal	ISE	SEM	ILPF	RUC	SPM	SQA	SCM	FAS	SM	SA	OO	SD	ST	SR

*Column entries (represented by a box) should be checked in any matrix row that corresponds to a boolean question answered with a "no" response. Subtotals for each section should be computed. For example, if question 4.1.1g has a "no" response, check the box under the SPM and SCM columns.

than one partially correct response. However, the "correct" response provided at the end of Appendix II is felt to be the most appropriate. It is important to note that there is no passing or failing "grade" for the self-test. It is intended solely for your own use in determined areas of strength and weakness. A suggested scheme for interpreting your results is contained in Appendix II.

All of this seems reasonably systematic and potentially beneficial, but it also seems quite expensive in time and dollars. Do we really have to do this?

All education mechanisms send a set of important signals to practitioners. First, education tells them that software engineering is deemed important by management and that management is willing to commit resources to improve their capabilities. Second, it provides all staff members with a consistent source of information that can be translated into practical use. Third, it provides a foundation from which procedures, methods, and CASE can be selected and effectively applied.

O.K., let's assume that we've gotten smarter. The next thing we have to do is begin choosing procedures, methods, and tools that are appropriate for our situation. How do we proceed?

The *selection step* commences as soon as you begin to make choices about the technology. Selection demands three things: (1) an understanding of available methods, procedures, and tools for software engineering practice; (2) the establishment of selection goals and criteria for methods, procedures, and tools; and (3) a rational mechanism for choosing, justifying, and acquiring procedures, methods, and tools.

Selection can be confusing. In some cases, the problem is too many choices, not too few. However, once process assessment is complete and education has begun, you will be better able to target the specific criteria required to make appropriate choices.

Should we begin by defining a set of technical criteria for selection, or are there other criteria that should be considered first?

Technical criteria for selection of software engineering and CASE are important, but overall management goals are even more important. These goals are always the same: *quality* and *productivity*. Each technical criterion that is developed for the selection of a procedure, method, or tool should be traceable to one or both of these goals. If it is not, it should be rejected.

How do we know what needs to be selected?

The transition plan defines the technology areas in which selection must be made. It is likely that choices will be required for procedures, methods, and tools.

What is the sequence of events that occurs during the selection step?

The following steps occur during selection:

1. Develop selection criteria (requirements) for methods, procedures, and CASE tools that are required as part of the transition plan.

2. Review the selection criteria against primary goals and get feedback from staff.

3. Do research and select candidates that appear to meet a substantial subset of the selection criteria.

4. Build a matrix for candidates versus selection criteria.

5. Consider each candidate in the context of selection criteria.

6. Eliminate candidates.

The final choice is based on compliance to criteria, vendor direction and support (if the candidate is to be acquired), discussions with others who have made a similar choice, and a little intuition.

Can you provide an example of how we would identify criteria for the selection of procedures?

Let's assume that the process assessment results in findings and recommendations and a set of transition tasks whose goal is to "develop and institute a common process framework for software engineering." The transition plan description for this major program task follows:

> The common process framework encompasses a common set of tasks, milestones, and deliverables that establish the criteria for task completion at each step in the software engineering process. Organizational responsibility is defined for each deliverable. Reviews are conducted to confirm completion. The framework also incorporates the activities and responsibilities of quality assurance and configuration management.
>
> A common process framework should be easily adapted to different technical methods (e.g., analysis, design, or testing methods) that are used for information system development. It establishes milestones (checkpoints) and deliverables for all projects and should be used for both new work and maintenance.
>
> While a minimum set of document deliverables are necessary at each framework checkpoint, the formats can be tailored to meet organizational and project needs as long as the intent of the common deliverable is met.
>
> A combination of a common framework, a conforming (to the intent of the common framework) set of technical methods, and a set of conforming deliverables define the software engineering process.

In order to develop an appropriate common process framework, it is important to establish a set of criteria for the framework that your organization can live with. The following criteria should get you started:

1. The framework should define tasks, milestones, and deliverables in a way that will serve as a guide for the project manager's work.

2. The framework should be adaptable. That is, it should provide a framework for both large and small projects.

3. The framework should be applicable to both new development and maintenance work.

4. The framework should demand appropriate documentation, but should not bury developers and/or maintainers under an avalanche of documents.

5. The framework should serve as a first step toward the development of software engineering standards.

Appendix III contains a prototype process framework. Review it and make modifications that you think would make it adaptable to your organization.

Can you provide an example of how we would identify criteria for the selection of methods that fit into a common process framework?

As you correctly point out, your goal is to select a set of methods that will complement the software engineering tasks chosen as part of a common process framework. To do this, you can begin with the following criteria that I have listed for each of the major method areas.[4] You should supplement these with criteria of your own.

Analysis

- Does the analysis method support facilitated application specification with customers?

- Does the analysis modeling approach support a graphical notation that is widely used and understood?

- Are data, functional, and behavioral modeling supported?

- Is partitioning of all models supported?

- Does the method lead directly to (1) a specification or (2) a prototype?

- Is the model that is created capable of being mapped into a design?

- Is the method supported by a number of different CASE tools supplied by different vendors on different platforms?

Design

- Does the design method support data design, architectural design, and procedural design?

- Does the design modeling approach support a graphical notation that is widely used and understood?

- Are design fundamentals such as support for abstraction, refinement, functional independence, and modularity directly implemented using the method?

- Are design quality criteria explicitly stated?

- Does the design method result in the derivation of reusable components?

- Is the method supported by a number of different CASE tools supplied by different vendors on different platforms?

---

[4]A technical discussion of software engineering methods is presented in Chapter 17.

Programming languages and 4GLs

- Are the programming languages that have been chosen best for your application domain?
- Are the programming languages that have been chosen best for your design approach?
- Are tools available for automatically generating source code?
- Does the language enable you to maintain coding style standards?
- Are the languages supported by a number of different CASE tools supplied by different vendors on different platforms?

Testing

- Do the testing methods chosen support both black- and white-box testing philosophies?
- Are the testing methods supported by CASE tools?
- Are the testing methods amenable to automated management by CASE tools?
- Do the testing methods provide path and condition coverage?
- Are the testing methods consistent with the testing strategy specified in the common process framework?

Reengineering and maintenance

- Do the analysis, design, and testing methods chosen have the ability to be used during maintenance activities? How must they be modified, if at all?
- Are specialized tools available to support reengineering methods?

Software quality assurance (SQA)[5]

- Do the SQA methods enable quality checking after each major software engineering step?
- Do the SQA methods support the collection of quantitative data?
- Are the methods to be applied by an independent group? Are they easily learned?
- Is the formal technical review (FTR) approach that has been chosen well suited to the culture and personalities of the organization's staff?
- Does the FTR method demand record keeping?

---

[5]SQA is discussed in detail in Chapter 14.

Software configuration management (SCM)[6]

- Do the methods for SCM provide the procedural controls implied by the process framework?
- Does SCM make use of a CASE repository?
- Are the SCM methods supported by a number of different CASE tools supplied by different vendors on different platforms?

Project management[7]

- Are cost estimation methods predicated on the collection of historical data?
- Are cost estimates derived using two different and independent methods?
- Is there a way of assessing the risks inherent in a software project?
- Do scheduling methods make use of the tasks implied in the common process framework?
- Are the project management methods supported by a number of different CASE tools supplied by different vendors on different platforms?

It seems that a recurring criterion for each of the method areas is the availability of CASE tools. Can you provide guidance for selecting the tools themselves?

The selection of CASE tools is actually a process that winnows hundreds of tools down to a reasonably small number of viable candidates for selection. Topper [3] suggests that CASE tools selection is actually a three-phase process: initial survey, detailed analysis, and follow-up observation.

During the *initial survey,* you'll use CASE tools directories (see Appendix I for references) to isolate potential candidates for the methods that you've chosen. In some cases (e.g., structured analysis and design), you'll have dozens of potential candidates; in others (e.g., quality assurance) your choices will be more limited. The criteria that you apply during this phase are the following:

- Is the tool supported in the development environment (hardware platform and operating system) that you use?
- Does the tool support the version or extension of the method that

---

[6]SCM is discussed in detail in Chapter 15.
[7]Project management is discussed in detail throughout Part 3 of this book.

you'd like to use? Note that methods such as SA/SD have real-time, object-oriented, and other versions or extensions?

- Does the tool conform to industry standards for data exchange, repositories, and interfaces?
- Can the tool be directly linked to existing CASE tools or to others that will likely be chosen?
- Is the CASE vendor viable?

These criteria will filter out many tools, leaving a list of candidates that are worth examining further.

During the *detailed analysis* phase, you'll apply a more complete set of technical criteria, evaluate tools during live demonstrations, get staff feedback, conduct benchmarks (where appropriate), talk with other users of the tool, and assess the tool in the context of your overall development environment. During this phase, you may decide to make use of a detailed technical checklist.

In reality, the *follow-up observation* phase is not a selection activity at all. Rather, it is the equivalent of the evaluation step of the software engineering implementation life cycle, applied exclusively to CASE tools. I'll discuss evaluation in greater detail in Chapter 8.

You mentioned that a "detailed technical checklist" for CASE tools can be used during the detailed analysis phase of selection. Can you describe a checklist of this type?

I'll use a technical checklist for CASE tools that has been adapted from a CASE attributes checklist first published in *Making Software Engineering Happen* [2]. The technical checklist for CASE tools, presented in Table 7.2, should be used as a guide in evaluating vendor offerings. For further explanation of the CASE tools categories, refer to Chapter 18. You should look beyond simple "yes"/"no" responses to the sophistication and depth of a given attribute.

As we begin making choices, we're going to have to get management's commitment to spend money. How do we do this?

Your question leads us to the next step in the implementation life cycle—*justification*. There are two different ways to justify: using bottom-line cost justification (e.g., return on investment) and/or using intangibles (e.g., improved staff morale). In most cases, bottom-line justification provides you with the ammunition to get qualified commitment and intangibles provide the icing on the cake. If your management has a reasonable expectation of achieving an attractive re-

TABLE 7.2 Technical Checklist for CASE Tools

CASE tool characteristics

Project planning tools
Support cost estimation using decomposition and empirical modeling
Can be customized for your common process framework
Allow creation of WBS, task networks, timeline charts, project tables
Allow allocation of resources to tasks
Generate progress reports based on planned schedule

Project management tools
Can be customized for your common process framework
Track task assignments
Collect basic project metrics
Enable tracking of customer requirements
Support general project tracking mechanism
Display work standards for practitioners

Documentation tools
Support conventional word processing
Support integrated text and graphics with desk-top publishing
Support import and export of documents and graphics from other CASE tools
Provide general graphics manipulation capability
Maintain a hierarchical document file structure, file nesting
Provide E-mail (electronic-mail) capability or compatibility
Create document templates that fit standard formats
Conform to documentation standards [e.g., DOD Std 2167a]

Analysis and specification tools
Support one or more FAST techniques
Support analysis method and notation (e.g., structured analysis)
Support extensions for specialized applications (e.g., real-time)
Provide data modeling capabilities (e.g., entity-relationship models)
Provide for data content representation (e.g., data dictionary)
Enable definition of data objects
Interface with host-based dictionaries
Isolate data objects and processes
Support specification reuse
Provide query support to data dictionary and/or CASE repository
Support prototyping
    For screen representations
    For reports and graphical representations
    For algorithm design
Allow for behavioral modeling that leads to simulation
Enable the creation of a control specification

Design tools
Support direct integration with analysis and specification tools
Support design method and design notation
Provide mechanism for data design
Provide mechanism for architectural/procedural design
Contain a GUI (graphical user interface) design kit
Support PDL (program design language) representations and manipulation
Enable a module definition/catalog capability
Provide support for design reuse
Provide a design classification and browsing capability
Support direct links to documentation tools
Support direct links to code generation tools

TABLE 7.2   Technical Checklist for CASE Tools (Continued)

Coding tools
    Provide editing and compilation capability for HOLs (high-order languages) chosen
    Provide support for HOL source code
        Code to graphical representations
        Language conversion capability
        Auditing for conformance to ANSI standards
        Feature extraction
        Links to SCM (software configuration management) system
    Provide interface with host-based coding tools
    Support all activities at workstation level
    Automatic code generation/4GL support
        Links to database environment
        Links to analysis and design tools

Program construction and reusability tools
    Integrated with CASE repository
    Provide mechanism for component classification
    Provide mechanism for component retrieval

Testing tools
    Support static and dynamic analysis
    Provide white-box testing support
        Path testing
        Loop testing
        Condition testing
        Data flow testing
    Provide black-box testing support
    Allow automatic test case generation
    Integrate with design and coding tools
    Support for test case management
    Support for regression test management
    Provide test record-keeping mechanism

Reengineering tools
    Support for inventory analysis
    Provide code restructuring capability in chosen HOLs
    Allow data stabilization capability
    Support reverse engineering from HOL source code
    Support limited reengineering
    Produce reports on source code quality

Software configuration management tools
    Provide complete SCI (software configuration item) identification scheme
    Support all configuration objects including code, text, and graphics
    Integrate directly with CASE repository
    Support the change control procedure for all SCIs
    Support version/release control
    Provide configuration auditing and reporting features
    Support an automatic construction function
    Track status of all changes

Quality assurance tools
    Provide support for formal technical reviews
        Record keeping
        Scheduling and control
    Support code auditing
    Support document standards auditing
    Provide error report record keeping
    Provide support for statistical SQA
    Support administrative management of SQA

TABLE 7.2   Technical Checklist for CASE Tools (*Continued*)

Metrics tools
  Provide template for metrics collection
  Support automated computation of function points
  Analyze basic project and product data
  Provide mechanism for on-line data collection
  Integrate with SQA, testing, and other CASE tools
  Integrate with the CASE repository
  Provide metrics reporting function

Tools integration

Each CASE tool candidate is evaluated to determine
  Degree of integration among tools
  Extensibility of the tool to accommodate the schema of the CASE repository
  Consistency of human interface

Method dependence
  Adaptability
    Table-driven notation and symbology
    Rule-based analysis and design tools
  Methods directly supported
    Structured analysis and design
    Object-oriented analysis and design
    Jackson methodology
    Warnier-Orr (DSSD)
    SADT
    Other(s)
  Fourth-generation technique support
  Languages
  Application generators
  Formal methods
  Others

Workstation operating environment
  Hardware configurations supported
    PC families supported
    Support for client-server architectures
    High-performance workstation support
    Resolution of graphics display
    Support for multimedia applications
    Local disk storage capacity
    Local printer/plotters supported
    Local area network protocol
    Mainframe terminal emulation (vendors)
  Software support
    Operating systems supported
    Degree of machine independence
    Database system supported (if any)
    Special utility software provided or required

Vendor profile
  Overall reputation
  Independent reviews of tool by third parties
  Number of different companies using system
  Total number of copies installed
  Number of software developers on vendor staff
  New tools or versions introduced over past 18 months
  Training and support activities
  Cooperative relationships with other companies

turn on their investment and at the same time can see other business and technical benefits, the decision to proceed with technology transition becomes much easier.

How can we demonstrate a quantitative return on investment when we ask management to acquire new software engineering technology?

The following steps represent a reasonable sequence of activities that can result in quantitative justification.

1. *Collect metrics from past projects:*   The key to any quantitative justification model is metrics. If you are unwilling or unable to collect software metrics for past projects, you will have trouble demonstrating return on investment.

2. *Project future demand for software development and maintenance:* On the basis of business issues, customer communication, and internal needs, the total number of lines of code or function points to be newly developed are estimated. The amount of maintenance work can be estimated in a similar manner.

3. *Using the current cost of software development and maintenance, compute the cost of future demand:*   The current cost is determined from the metrics collected in step 1. Future cost is computed by multiplying the estimate determined in step 2 by the cost from step 1.

4. *Suggest future quality and productivity improvement:*   A conservative projection of 10 to 25 percent per year can be realized.

5. *Recompute the cost of future demand:*   Using cost data (step 1) that has been improved by the percentages noted in step 4, the cost of future demand (step 2) is recomputed.

6. *Compute the projected cost savings:*   The difference between the results of step 3 and step 5 is the cost saving.

Can you provide us with a template for metrics collection?

The collection of baseline metrics requires a bit of research and a fair amount of effort. Ideally, information about all new development and maintenance projects conducted over the past 2 or 3 years should be obtained. Practically, this may not be possible. As a minimum, data collected from 5 to 10 major new development projects and 5 to 10 major maintenance efforts conducted over the past 24 months should be obtained.

A *Metrics Collection Worksheet* was suggested in Chapter 3 (Figure

3.6). It can be used as a guideline for the type of information that is used to create the baseline. It is likely that you will not be able to collect all of the data requested. As a minimum, those entries noted below should be collected. Guidelines for the computation of function point metrics are discussed in Chapter 3.

Cost Data—Input	
Description	Units
Labor cost	$/person-month
Labor year	hours/year

Data for Metrics Computation	
Description	Units
Project name or identifier	Alphanumeric
Release type	(development-maintenance)
Number of project staff	People
Effort	Person-hours
Effort, computed	Person-months (pm)
Elapsed time to completion	Months
Newly developed output	KLOC or FP
Modified (existing code)	KLOC or FP
Output delivered (total)	KLOC or FP
Number of defects (1st year after release)	Defects

How are the data collected with the template used in the justification sequence that you described above? Can you suggest a "cookbook" approach?

Using data collected with the *Metrics Collection Worksheet* (or a simplified version of it), the following average values should be computed for all projects that have been evaluated:

- KLOC/pm or FP/pm
- $/KLOC or $/FP
- KLOC/calendar-month or FP/calendar-month
- Defects/KLOC or defects/FP
- Effort/defect
- $/defect
- Total maintenance effort/KLOC or total maintenance effort/FP

With these values calculated, the justification model that follows can be used as a "first cut" quantitative cost justification for software engineering procedures, methods, and tools.

The model is predicated on the collection of baseline metrics, the computation of average values, and projections of future software work. Recalling the justification steps discussed earlier, do the following:

1. Use the average metrics values (see above) as a baseline. These will indicate the current cost of software development and maintenance.

   KLOC/pm or FP/pm =

   $/KLOC or $/FP =

   KLOC/calendar-month or FP/calendar-month =

   Defects/KLOC or defects/FP =

   Effort/defect =

   $/defect =

   Total maintenance effort/KLOC or total maintenance effort/FP =

2. If possible, collect industry data that will allow you to compare your results to "industry results." Although relatively little data have been published, good first sources are Jones [4, 5], Grady and Caswell [6], and Dreger [7].

3. Establish conservative projections of the quality and productivity improvement to be expected when software engineering practice is applied. In general, improvements of between 10 and 25 percent per year can be obtained through the use of better methods and CASE tools.

   PI, projected improvement =

4. Project demand for software over the next 12 to 24 months by estimating the total lines of code or function points to be produced.

$$NL, \text{ new KLOC } =$$

or

$$NFP, \text{ new FP to be developed } =$$
$$ML, \text{ KLOC to be maintained } =$$

or

MFP, FP to be maintained =

PD, projected defects based on new KLOC or FP to be developed =

5. Compute the cost of new lines of code or function points using the baseline average costs described in step 1 above. Also compute the cost of maintenance and defects using the same approach. (Note: Using duration averages, it is also possible to develop an indication of improved responsiveness.)

The following computations are shown only for lines of code. Identical computations can be performed for function points, where each reference to an LOC value (e.g., NL) is replaced by the analogous FP value (e.g., NFP).

$$NL \times \$/KLOC = CNL.old$$

$$NL \times defects/KLOC = PD.old$$

$$PD.old \times \$/defect = CD.old$$

$$ML \times total\ maint.effort/KLOC = Effort.ML.old$$

6. Recompute the cost of new lines of code, maintenance, and defects using the baseline averages reduced by the percent improvement projected in step 3.

$$(1 - PI) \times NL \times \$/KLOC = CNL.new$$

$$(1 - PI) \times NL \times defects/KLOC = PD.new$$

$$PD.new \times \$/defect = CD.new$$

$$(1 - PI) \times ML \times total\ maint.effort/KLOC = Effort.ML.new$$

7. Compute the cost savings. Cost savings are determined by computing the difference between cost of new development, maintenance, and defects using past practice as an indicator (step 5) and the cost of new development determined in step 6.

$$Savings\ of\ new\ development = CNL.old - CNL.new$$

$$Savings\ defects = CD.old - CD.new$$

$$Savings\ maintenance = Effort.ML.old - Effort.ML.new$$

In any justification that we'll have to make, it will be necessary to estimate the cost of acquiring procedures, methods, and CASE. Can you provide some help with this?

The cost of any new technology can be divided into *investment cost* (often spread over 3 to 5 years) and *continuing cost* that recurs annually. A simple model for the cost of CASE has been suggested by Grochow [8]. I have augmented this (see next page) with the additional costs associated with

Organizational profile	
Number of professional staff (total)	100
Number of project managers	10
Investment cost	
Workstation hardware (50 @ $5000)	$250,000
Procedures development and selection	
Evaluation of canned methodologies	
20 person-days @ $1000 per day	20,000
Acquisition of canned methodology	150,000
or	
Development of common process framework	
60 person days @ $1000 per day	$60,000
Methods selection	
Analysis (40 person-days @ $1000 per day)	$40,000
Design (20 person-days @ $1000 per day)	$20,000
Test (20 person-days @ $1000 per day)	$20,000
Systant training	
15 people for 20 days each at $500 per day	$150,000
Miscellaneous (books, publications)	$15,000
CASE software	
Project management tools (10 @ $1500)	$15,000
Analysis and design tools (40 @ $4200)	$168,000
Configuration management tools	$50,000
Prototyping tools (5 @ $5000)	$25,000
Programming tools (workstations)	
50 @ $5000	$250,000
Integration framework	
Database software	$60,000
System software	$40,000
Outside consulting	
30 consulting days at $2000	$60,000
Initial staff training	
5 days per staff member @ $160	$80,000
Total investment cost	**$1,473,000**
Continuing cost	
Software engineering resource group	
2 people @ $80,000 per year (burdened)	$160,000
Hardware maintenance	$25,000
Software tools upgrades and maintenance	
13% of investment expenditure	$80,000
Continuing training	
4 days per staff member @ $160	$64,000
Miscellaneous (media, books, courseware)	$15,000
Total continuing cost per year	**$344,000**
Five-year cost	
Total investment cost	**$1,473,000**
Total continuing cost (5 years × $344,000)	**1,720,000**
Total:	**$3,193,000**

software engineering procedures and methods. You can scale the model to properly reflect your organization's size and needs.

The cost model presented on the previous page assumes a software development organization of 100 professional staff and the requirement to upgrade hardware as well as software. It is important to note that the figures shown in the cost model represent rough estimates only. You must investigate current costs that are relevant to your situation.

Is there a way we can use the above cost estimates to develop a macroscopic justification for software engineering technology?

Using the preceding example for a 100-person organization and keeping the analysis simple, assume a 5-year expenditure of $3.2 million for software engineering. To break even, your organization must save $3.2 million in that time period. One way to justify is to assume increased productivity that results in the above saving. The following analysis can be applied:

Total staff	100
Burdened labor rate	$80,000
Total staff expenditure over 5 years	$40,000,000
Desired savings over 5 years	$3,200,000
Productivity improvement to achieve savings	8%

Even if lower productivity improvement is assumed during the first 2 years, it is difficult to believe that dedicated effort cannot achieve an 8 percent savings over 5 years. To ensure this result, a solid transition plan should be established and the proper procedures, methods, and tools should be selected.

It is important to note that inflationary effects, changing business environment, and many other factors have not been taken into account in this simple example. Also, this discussion does not take the indirect benefits of quality improvement into account. Finally, the example does not define what we mean by "savings." In most cases, staff count will not be reduced by 8 percent at the end of 5 years, so savings will be measured by (1) greater ability to meet customer demands with stable staff levels, (2) a reduction in application backlog, or (3) a reduction in the number of contract employees that may also be used by the organization.

Earlier you mentioned that quantitative justification should be supplemented with a discussion of "intangibles." What are some of these?

An *intangible* is a benefit that accrues to individuals or the entire organization as a result of using software engineering technology. In general, an intangible is difficult (but not impossible) to measure, yet it becomes an argument for adopting a particular element of the technology.

When software engineering procedures are implemented (usually in the context of a common process framework), the following intangibles are likely:

- Better management oversight and control
- Improved ability to predict and measure progress
- Higher likelihood that all projects will be conducted in a more uniform fashion
- Easier for technical staff to move across projects
- Improved ability to use automated tools to help manage projects
- Better morale among technical managers resulting from improved management oversight and control
- More predictable deliverables and documentation
- Ease in enforcing quality assurance activities

When your organization has chosen a specific software engineering method (for analysis, design, or testing) and has implemented it successfully), the following intangibles are likely:

- Uniform approach to modeling that results in better communication of technical information
- A more predictable technical format that makes review easier
- Improved technical quality resulting from consistent application of proven principles
- More thorough coverage of technical detail
- Easier technical communication because all practitioners "speak the same language" and use the same notation
- Improved documentation quality

CASE tools have an impact on the management of software projects and on the ease with which technology is applied. Among the intangibles for CASE are the following:

- Easier application of technical methods
- Improved consistency in documentation, notation, and modeling
- Better enforcement of standards for documentation, notation, and modeling
- Easier to achieve traceability between software models (e.g., analysis and design models)
- Facilitated creation of a central repository for information produced during the process
- Easier flow of information between technical steps
- Easier to assess the impact of change
- Better management control

Not every intangible noted above will accrue to your organization. It is likely, however, that improved software engineering practice will result in a reasonable subset of these intangibles.

Our management is quite skeptical about new technologies. What are typical management objections to all of this, and how can we deal with them?

If you've done your homework—conducted an assessment, educated management and staff, been systematic about selection and careful about justification—it's likely that management objections will be relatively easy to handle. Here are some of the most common:

"We don't have the money this year. We're going to have to put this off." Your cost justification should indicate that any expenditure should pay itself back in a relatively short time period. But if money is really tight, you should develop a transition plan that relies more on people than on external expenditures.

"We can't free up the people to do this; they're all tied up with on-going critical projects." This may be a reasonable statement, but it can also become a chronic excuse for doing nothing. Find out why all projects are critical and how some percentage of time can be freed. It may be that software development problems (that would be eliminated by better practice) have caused projects to go "critical."

"But we already have standards for software work." Explain that standards by themselves offer little benefit. The goal is to improve practice, thereby improving product quality, on-time delivery, and customer satisfaction. Practice is improved by implementing new technology (methods, tools) in the context of a disciplined approach.

"This will put us on a learning curve that will really slow things down. We can't afford the time lag for ongoing projects." There is no doubt that staff will require time to learn new procedures, methods, and tools, but the time spent in learning can be accelerated through good education, the use of systants (Chapter 4), and a transition plan that introduces technology slowly.

"Our people are happy with things as they are. It is likely that they'll resist this stuff." As I noted earlier, people tend to resist things they don't understand and that can be overcome with education. In addition, there will be a substantial number of practitioners and technical managers who will embrace the new technology. These people serve as the core for technical change.

"Show me scientific data that proves that software engineering and CASE will give us the benefits you suggest." Sadly, most data published on this subject are anecdotal—few scientific experiments have been conducted. However, the preponderance of anecdotal evidence suggests that the technology does work.

Is there anything else that we should worry about as the education and selection process proceed?

One of the biggest problems that I have encountered is loss of momentum. In many cases management begins the journey toward improved software engineering practice with reasonable enthusiasm. But as time passes, attention drifts to other things. One of the problems is that technology transition rarely provides instant gratification. Even with good transition planning, it takes time to achieve the benefits and the improvement discussed in this chapter. During the early steps of the software engineering implementation life cycle, time is your enemy. Not because you don't have enough of it, but because people become defocused as it passes.

How can we avoid a loss of momentum?

One way is to develop a transition plan (Chapter 6) that has closely spaced milestones. This will enable you to achieve small successes quickly. It is also important to move toward installation without delay. Until software engineering technology is in use on real projects, you're at risk of losing momentum.

A Manager's Checklist

Education, selection, and justification are the software engineering implementation activities that set the stage for success. Without them, your ability to execute the transition plan and successfully install new software engineering technology will be at risk.

Actions

- Poll your technical staff and make a list of all courses, conferences, seminars, and "educational visits" that have been taken by your staff in the past 18 months. Which of these were dedicated to software engineering topics?

- Using the list of software engineering courses presented in this chapter (and augmented with any specialized needs that you may have), poll your technical staff to determine the three courses that have highest priority. Be sure that you provide a space for "other."

- A universal complaint among technical staff and project managers is that senior managers don't understand the difficulties associated with and importance of software engineering. Schedule a 4-hour seminar (presented by *real* professionals) that will raise senior management consciousness.

- Begin collecting the metrics required to do technology justification. Use the model presented in this chapter to develop draft computations for cost savings and return on investment.

- Review the "intangibles" presented in this chapter and select the top three in each category. Attempt to develop a rough method for quantifying these.

Questions

- What is the first software engineering course that you would like to take?

- What is the first software engineering course that you feel your technical staff should take?

- On the basis of past experience in your organization, what are the "buttons" that must be pressed to gain management commitment to spend money? (If these "buttons" are not pressed by the justification model I've presented, modify it accordingly.)

Further Readings

The best sources of information on available software engineering courses may very well enter your office every day in the form of junk mail. Brochures from software training companies such as Digital Consulting, Inc., The Technology Transfer Institute, The Technology Exchange Co., USPDI, and many, many others provide information on hundreds of public course offerings in software engineering and related topics. It is important to understand that public courses, such as those offered by the companies I've just named, are not an optimal education mechanism. However, they do enable you to sample the merchandise before bringing training in house. Another option is to request brochures from companies (such as R.S. Pressman & Associates, Inc.) that specialize in in-house custom curriculum development, courseware design, and training.

Guidelines for selection of CASE tools can be obtained from many of the books suggested in the Further Readings section of Chapter 18. In addition, the CASE newsletters noted in Appendix I present regular features that provide criteria for comparison of methods and tools.

Brief discussions of technology cost justification can be found in books by Bouldin (*Agents of Change*, Prentice-Hall, 1989) and Pressman (*Making Software Engineering Happen*, Prentice-Hall, 1988).

References

[1] Pressman, R.S., *Process Advisor: A Self-Directed System for Improving Software Engineering Practice*, R.S. Pressman & Associates, Inc., 1992. Used with permission.

[2] Pressman, R.S., *Making Software Engineering Happen*, Prentice-Hall, 1988.

[3] Topper, A., "Evaluating CASE Tools, Guidelines for Comparison," *Am. Programmer* 4 (7), 12–20 (1991).

[4] Jones, C., *Programming Productivity*, IEEE Computer Society Press, 1981.

[5] Jones, C., *Applied Software Measurement*, McGraw-Hill, 1991.

[6] Grady, R.B., and Caswell, D.L., *Software Metrics: Establishing a Company-Wide Program*, Prentice-Hall, 1987.

[7] Dreger, J.B., *Function Point Analysis*, Prentice-Hall, 1989.

[8] Grochow, J.M., "Justifying the Cost of CASE," *Computerworld*, February 8, 1988, p. 19.

8

Installation
and Evaluation:
Making It Happen[1]

The installation of software engineering technology is the bottom line of the implementation life cycle. Assessment, education, selection, and justification have laid the groundwork. Now, it's time to make things happen! It is during installation that your organization will really begin to feel the effects of change. Procedures may be modified, new methods will be put into place, and new CASE tools will be adopted. Each of these activities represents cultural change, with all of the attendant challenges that have already been described in Chapter 4.

In this chapter, we'll discuss the installation of software engineering procedures, methods, and tools. We'll also consider techniques for evaluating what you've done.

We've gone through a reasonable amount of preparation to get to this step, and yet, I have a feeling that there can still be problems. What general guidelines will govern our actions during installation?

The installation step of the software engineering implementation life cycle can be problematic. To help you to short circuit problems before they occur, the following guidelines are appropriate:

1. *Be sure a transition plan exists and that the plan contains a distinct step-by-step strategy for installation:* There is a tendency to con-

---

[1]This chapter has been adapted from *Making Software Engineering Happen* (Prentice-Hall, 1988) by Roger S. Pressman. Reproduced with permission.

duct installation in a disjointed fashion. That is, a software development organization adopts a method here and tool there, but lacks a top-level view of how they all fit together. This guarantees confusion and raises the level of frustration among all involved.

2. *Hit singles, not home runs:*   Successful installation of software engineering technology occurs when a series of small, measurable successes are achieved. Small successes create a momentum that permeates an entire organization. Unfortunately, many companies attempt to perform the installation process in one big step. Massive standards and procedures documents are prepared, large-scale acquisitions of tools and methods occur, and major changes are instituted. Chaos is often the result. The level of management required to successfully achieve a "home run" is exponentially greater than that required to "hit a single."

3. *Before worrying about new technologies, be sure that a process framework is in place:*   Too many organizations attempt to install technology without a proper process framework. This is the equivalent of erecting a skyscraper without its steel skeleton. No matter how sophisticated the facade, the building would be inherently unstable and unsafe. A software engineering process framework provides support for new methods and tools. It enables an organization to apply SQA activities, and to manage software projects more effectively. It must be installed first.

4. *After a framework exists, install methods and CASE tools simultaneously:*   Software engineering methods almost always require the use of new notation, and in many instances, the generation of new documentation. New heuristics must be learned and new modes of representation must be coordinated. These activities put an additional burden on each software developer and no matter how well justified, may be viewed as additional work by technical staff. If CASE tools are available to reduce the amount of "dog work" associated with the representation of a new method, it is far more likely that the method will be adopted without complaint. For this reason, methods and tools should be adopted in conjunction with one another rather than in sequence. It is important to note that more learning will be required, but the overall benefits of a CASE approach outweigh the potential disadvantages of information overload.

5. *Written guidelines are important, but encyclopedic standards and procedures are often the kiss of death, if introduced too early:*   There is a tendency among many companies to develop software engineering standards and procedures as the first step in software engineering installation. Earlier in this book, I indicated that this is often a mistake.

If your organization currently has no standards and procedures for software development and maintenance, a set of "skinny" guidelines should be the first thing that is introduced.

6. *Train one or more individuals to play the role of the "systant."* The importance of the systant has been emphasized in earlier chapters. To review: Software engineering installation sometimes fails simply because no one is around to answer questions. That is, technical staff must have a local source of expertise to whom they can go with technical and procedural questions.

7. *Be certain that the other steps of the software engineering implementation life cycle are under way:* Assessment, education, selection, and justification (Chapters 4 to 7) are all precursors to successful installation. If you've chosen to skip these steps, you're heading for trouble.

What kind of trouble are you talking about?

The guidelines noted above will help to circumvent technology transition problems. You should recognize, however, that things rarely proceed as smoothly as one might hope. I have found that the problems typically encountered during the installation step occur because of (1) incompetent, improper, or incomplete training; (2) inappropriate tools and methods; or (3) an ill-advised process framework or no framework at all. In addition, trouble occurs when the installation strategy attempts to insert technology into a project that is not equipped to assimilate it.

You mentioned that education problems can have a negative impact on installation. Can you describe some of these problems and how we might avoid them?

A software development organization often contracts an outside education vendor to provide appropriate training support for new methods and tools as they are installed. To avoid problems, early training classes must be carefully monitored to ensure that specific and practical guidance (rather than generalities) are provided to technical staff and managers. In addition, it is crucially important to contract for specific instructors—*by name*—who will be doing the training. In many cases, the instructor is more important than the courseware. An organization will assess training presented by a master instructor only to find that day-to-day training is conducted by junior (and often less competent) instructors. To uncover and correct training problems, it is essential that students complete detailed critique sheets that will help to isolate problems when they are encountered.

In addition to problems associated with quality, there are often problems that occur because of the timing of education. To be most effective, training should be timed to coincide with the installation of procedures, methods, and tools on specific projects. Rather than attempting to train an entire organization, education should be targeted at those groups that "have a need to learn" and will make immediate use of what they have learned. If you won't apply what you're going to learn for another 18 months, wait and learn it when you need it.

I think we may be able to circumvent these problems and save some money by doing our own training. What do you think about this?

In most cases, I'd advise against it. You should recognize two realities: (1) doing your own training rarely saves money because courseware development costs are high and (2) the quality of "home-grown" training is often abysmal because inexperienced courseware developers and instructors are involved. In most cases, software engineering training should be left to training professionals. However, if you insist on doing your own training, be sure that the following conditions are met:

- Your organization has an existing training group that is experienced in conducting software engineering training.

- Courseware development costs can be leveraged across many staff members.

- In-house instructors are experienced in software engineering methods and tools.

Unless you have the facilities, budget, and personnel, get professional assistance in this area.

You also mentioned that problems with CASE tools can have a negative impact on installation. Can you describe some of these problems and how we might avoid them?

Problems associated with the installation of CASE tools actually begin during the selection step. No matter how systematically the CASE tools selection process is conducted, it will be impossible to make everyone happy. That is, certain staff members will likely "fall in love" with a particular CASE tool and will emotionally reject all others. The love affair can be predicated on a flashy user interface, a particular function that has strong parochial appeal, a personal relationship with a particular vendor's salesperson, or dozens of other reasons. Although some of these reasons may have merit (when viewed from an individual's perspective), the tool in question may not be appropriate for the organization as a whole.

Once the tools selection decision is made, all staff members who view themselves as "jilted lovers" will likely exhibit lukewarm (at best) enthusiasm for installation of the "other" CASE tool. This could result in poor utilization or misapplication of the tools.

The solution to the "jilted lover" problem lies in eliminating the cause rather than treating the symptom. That is, during the selection step of the software engineering implementation life cycle, staff members should be involved in the definition of criteria for the evaluation and selection of CASE tools. Once staff members have become familiar with a number of candidate tools, it is more likely that they will be willing to "play the field," selecting the best solution from the pack. In essence, staff members should *own* any decisions that are made in the tools area. Once *all* criteria have been stated in black and white, parochial love affairs are less likely to occur.

Another important tools problem occurs immediately after installation. No matter how thoroughly a CASE tool has been assessed, it is difficult to exercise every function in every situation. For this reason, bugs[2] in tools are sometimes encountered only after the tool is put into place. You and the CASE tool vendor must develop a procedure for the isolation and correction of bugs in an expeditious manner. This procedure should be established in advance—before tools are installed. The effects of this problem are far broader than defects in software. An otherwise effective tool may be rejected by technical staff because of a relatively trivial, but bothersome, defect. If confidence in the tool is lost, installing it becomes doubly difficult. For this reason, it is essential that the vendor be responsive in the correction of any bugs that are encountered.

A more subtle tools problem occurs when local applications require customization of a CASE tool. If customization is to be performed by the vendor, it should be done before installation, not in line with current usage. If you perform customization (a process that is generally not recommended), the same guidelines hold.

What about installation problems that are related to methods? What are they, and how can we avoid them?

Because software engineering methods are inseparable from the creative process of building software, the types of problems that are en-

---

[2]In this case, the term *bugs* is used to indicate any failing in the tool. This includes functionality that was expected but not delivered in a fashion that helps your software development activity.

countered during the installation of new methods range from broad philosophical arguments about development approach to nit-picking conflicts over notation or terminology. If a "software as an art form" mentality still exists among your software development staff, any method that is perceived to restrict "artistic freedom" is potentially problematic.

Because the installation of software engineering methods always requires a change in the manner in which developers perform their work, problems associated with cultural change are likely. The following are among the most common problems:

- Project schedules that may be protracted while developers learn to apply new methods

- Requirement for extra work (and time) associated with a new method that provides no apparent benefit to the developer

- Misapplication of a method resulting in poor software quality

- Outright refusal to use a particular method because "it just doesn't work for the types of applications that we develop"

Each of these problems can be traced to one or more of three causes: (1) insufficient technical education, leading to a misunderstanding of the nature and application of the method; (2) lack of systants, resulting in early frustration with the application of the method; or (3) lack of good CASE tools that support the method and remove the drudgery associated with the method.

It is extremely important to review early work to ensure that the method is being applied properly. If problem symptoms are uncovered, actions designed to eliminate the causes noted above should be taken.

We need a more disciplined procedure for doing software engineering work. Therefore, we'll likely install a common process framework. What problems occur when procedures are installed?

Software engineering procedures are usually installed at both macroscopic or microscopic levels. At the macroscopic level, the paradigm for software engineering is chosen and an overall procedural approach is defined. In essence, technical managers and developers are provided with a broad framework from which they can build specific procedural requirements for their organization. Once the organization agrees on a macroscopic approach, microscopic refinement must occur. A detailed *work-breakdown structure* (WBS) for software development practice is defined in the context of a common process framework (see Appendix III). Work steps for each major software engineering activity are identified. Checkpoints and documentation are established for each step. Sign-offs, reviews, and control mechanisms are enforced. Managers and technical staff are provided with definitive rules for software engineering practice.

If an organization already has an established software engineering culture that was originally introduced using macroscopic procedures, it is possible to make a transition to microscopic procedures with relatively little cultural upheaval. This is possible because microscopic procedures will have been derived from your current modus operandi. If, however, you attempt to install microscopic procedures from scratch, the degree of cultural upheaval may be high.

The best strategy is to agree on a macroscopic approach and then define an adaptable microscopic template that can be used by each project team. The key word in the preceding sentence is "adaptable." It is extremely important to allow each project team to adapt the microscopic details of the common process framework to best meet its needs. As long as the detailed approach stays within the broad philosophical boundaries established by the macroscopic procedure, improved software engineering practice will result.

As we begin installation, it seems as if we can take two different paths: (1) move rapidly toward the installation of high-powered methods and tools, or (2) move toward more formalized procedures. Which installation strategy is best?

The best installation strategy for software engineering navigates the fine line between bureaucracy on one hand and chaos on the other! Referring to Figure 8.1, an installation approach that moves rapidly toward the installation of high-powered methods and tools is a high-risk

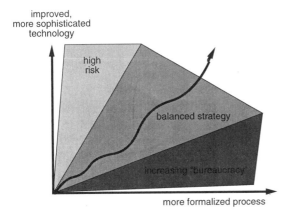

Figure 8.1 The installation strategy.

strategy. Radical changes in the technology that is to be applied by your organization can lead to chaos at the project level. If you choose this approach, it must be managed very, very carefully. But an installation strategy that focuses solely on procedural issues also has risks. Procedures should be installed to control the application of tools and methods and to provide management with a mechanism for tracking progress as a project proceeds. However, too much procedural control too soon will always be viewed as "bureaucratic red tape" and will undoubtedly create resentment among technical staff. Procedures should only be instituted once their rationale has been "sold" to both managers and technical staff.

I advocate a balanced installation strategy (Figure 8.1) in which methods and tools are installed in conjunction with procedures that will control (but not stifle) their use. To achieve balance, it is necessary to consider the timing of installation as well as the content of what is being installed.

What is a good installation strategy?

There is no single, clear-cut strategy for instituting software engineering technology. The results of your process assessment and the transition plan that has been derived from it, along with the choices that you have made during the selection and justification steps, will define your strategy for installation. For example, if your technical approach is strong, but your overall management controls are weak, an installation strategy that stresses early implementation of a consistent process framework for project management is probably appropriate. On the other hand, if you're struggling with software quality, you may opt to focus on methods and tools that can be applied as "point solutions" to relieve quality problems.

Each software organization must choose an installation strategy based on its own culture and experience. The transition plan defines the overall strategy, but activities during the installation step must be adapted to meet ever-changing needs.

O.K., I can accept the fact that each installation strategy is different, but aren't there generic guidelines that apply to them all?

Because the transition plan establishes the basic installation strategy, the guidelines that apply to the creation of a transition plan (Chapter 6) also apply to the installation strategy. As you begin to install procedures, methods, and tools, you'll go through a repeating sequence:

1. Use the results of the process assessment to prioritize your needs by identifying which technology components (i.e., procedures, methods, tools) are most important, when you'd like to have them in place, and what the interdependencies are between components.

2. Select specific technology components.

3. Target the components by deciding their *breadth of installation*.

4. Refine the transition plan by developing an *installation task breakdown*.

5. Be certain to determine the best time for installation (e.g., it makes little sense to install analysis and design tools for a project team that is currently beginning the testing phase).

6. Coordinate component acquisition or development and training to ensure that staff will have the requisite knowledge to use the component.

7. Solicit feedback immediately and work to correct problems before they become fatal.

What do you mean by "breadth of installation"?

In some cases, a specific procedure, method, or tool should be installed across your entire organization. You'll need to develop a plan for educating and selling all staff members, installing the component in a nondisruptive fashion, and ensuring that all constituencies are using it properly and without problems. Alternatively, you may decide to install the component across only a subset of all technical staff, across a single project team, or even for just one individual. Again, it will be necessary to develop a plan for education, installation, and evaluation. *Breadth of installation* refers to the approach that you choose.

Can you provide an example of an "installation task breakdown"?

The transition plan (Chapter 6) identifies the major tasks that are required for technology transition and, at the same time, establishes the foundation of an installation strategy. An *installation task breakdown* (ITB) is nothing more than a detailed refinement of one or more transition tasks that can be used to guide the installation step.

As an example, assume that your organization has decided to install a common process framework across all project teams. The "program task" identified in the transition plan is to *select and install a common process framework for software engineering across the entire department.*

The installation task breakdown refines the WBS contained in the transition plan by providing a detailed set of tasks that will guide installation. For the program task noted above, the ITB is as follows:

Select and Install a Common Process Framework

Create plan to develop the process framework
Set up plan
Obtain approval for plan
Define objectives for common process framework
Review objectives with all staff members
Research and document existing software engineering paradigms
Select a paradigm most appropriate to this department
Create a metamodel that describes the paradigm
Solicit staff feedback
Review final version of metamodel
Research and document submodels for major framework tasks
Solicit staff feedback
Define software engineering tasks, milestones, and deliverables
Define variations dependent on project size and type
Define minimum documentation guidelines
Identify tools usage within framework
Define SQA points
Conduct review of all work done to date
Review recommended framework with management
Evaluate feedback from reviews
Revise draft process framework
Establish training mechanism for the framework
Select pilot project on which framework is to be applied
Schedule all project staff for training
Distribute framework documentation
Conduct training
Acquire tools for framework support
Implement framework on a pilot project
Collect feedback from pilot
Make revisions based on feedback
Establish a rolling installation schedule as new projects begin
Implement the framework on new projects

Because the ITB is actually a set of tasks that can be scheduled, a task network can be created for the ITB and an installation schedule can be derived.

We have to improve our product quality. Therefore, one of the first things that we intend to install is an approach for formal technical reviews. Do you have any guidance for us?

The installation of review procedures should not be taken lightly. If your organization has not previously conducted reviews, new procedures for review can represent a substantial change in culture and can lead to dramatically improved software quality (and, if mismanaged, severe staff problems). It is extremely important to provide training and to establish review guidelines in advance. A detailed discussion of all the issues associated with installing formal technical reviews is beyond the scope of this book. An excellent source of information is presented by Freedman and Weinberg [1]. As a first step, the following guidelines are suggested:

1. Basic review training should be presented to a small cadre of practitioners who will be responsible for defining the review approach.

2. After training, two or three staff members develop a set of local review guidelines.

3. A review team (Chapter 14) is formed, and the review guidelines document is reviewed using the logistics defined in the document. In essence, the first review is used to critique the review approach.

4. On the basis of feedback from the "review of the review approach," modifications are made to the review guidelines.

5. An education strategy for reviews is developed. In general, reviews are introduced on a project-by-project basis. Therefore, it is essential that an entire project team receive review training at the same time.

When we install new procedures and methods, we'll also create a requirement for new forms of documentation. What guidelines should we follow to ensure that improved documentation accompanies better procedures and methods?

Documentation is a natural consequence of good software engineering practice, and yet, many software developers view it as the "D" word. Part of the problem is the notion that more is better, resulting in ill-conceived software engineering standards that bury technical staff in an avalanche of paper.

It is likely that improved documents will be required as your organization matures. But improved documents need not necessarily result in an onerous burden on technical staff, if the following guidelines are followed:

1. *Generic descriptions for all documents, reports, and forms should be prepared in advance.* It is not enough to define a document outline in a standards and procedures manual. An important installation task is the preparation of sample documents that clearly illustrate the content, form, and style that is desired for each software engineering de-

liverable. Without these examples, it is difficult to understand just what is required in certain forms of documentation. In some cases, example documents are created as part of a pilot project in which new technology components are prototyped for the entire organization.

2. *Be certain they produce only those documents that add information value.* Voluminous documentation is counterproductive to the installation of good software engineering practice because it dissuades developers from following recommended standards and practices. It should be noted, however, that customer requirements in certain application areas (e.g., defense, aerospace) often have mandated practices that do result in voluminous documentation.

3. *All documents should be organized hierarchically—that is, the document should be nested so that each level reveals additional detail.* Software should be designed in a hierarchical fashion—its documentation should exhibit the same characteristic. A hierarchical representation enables a reader to delve into an appropriate level of detail. Effective partitioning eases documentation changes that are inevitable.

4. *Diagrams and graphics should be used whenever possible if they improve understanding of complicated text.* The use of graphics is facilitated when desk-top publishing systems are available. However, regardless of your document processing environment, a good picture is often worth a thousand words and can eliminate unnecessary hours spent on the learning curve.

5. *A detailed table of contents is essential. An index and/or glossary is highly recommended.* If one were to add all of the human effort expended on *finding* information in software documents, the number would account for many person-months of effort per year for even a small software development organization. In addition, searching for information can be frustrating, leading a developer to *assume* rather than *find*.

6. *Documents that are delivered to users should be edited for style and reviewed by a third party to assure clarity and correctness.* Although the overall quality of vendor documentation is improving, documentation developed by in-house staff often leaves much to be desired. Documentation clarity has much to do with the perceived quality of software. It should be taken seriously.

7. *Acronyms, symbology, and diagrammatic forms should be consistent and restricted.* One of the most difficult tasks when writing large documents is to remain consistent in the use of terminology, symbology, and even diagrammatic forms. Ideally, a software development organization would have a "copy editor" to help enforce consistency. Realistically, consistency should be a primary review criterion.

8. Documents should be developed with document production tools that support word processing and computer graphics (i.e., a desk-top publishing environment). Low-cost desk-top publishing systems should be a mandatory tool for all serious software development organizations. When text and graphics can be manipulated easily, document content and style will improve dramatically.

In many software organizations, developers often spend as much time creating and editing documents than they spend "programming." Software work creates information that must be documented. As you work to install better procedures and methods, you'll be installing a requirement for better documentation at the same time.

You've emphasized the importance of documentation. What about the installation of the tools that will enable us to produce it?

Software engineers can spend between 20 and 40 percent of their time producing documents. Given this level of effort, it is surprising that many still use document production tools that have changed little since the early 1980s. Today, modern desk-top publishing tools should be *de rigueur* for most software engineers.

To illustrate the sorry state of document production practice, I'll provide a few true-life examples:

- A software engineer at a large manufacturing company complained because he and his colleagues were forced to develop flowcharts for all software designs. The problem wasn't the flowcharts. It was the fact that they had to be drawn using the alphanumeric keyboard available for the local text editor (i.e., boxes created with I's for sides and underscores for top and bottom)! A single flowchart took hours to create.

- A software development manager found a system engineering group spending 30 percent of its time developing transparencies for customer presentations. For important presentations, an outside contractor developed slides for $75.00 each. The group acquired an Apple Macintosh and reduced the cost of presentation visuals by an order of magnitude!

- A word-processing system, originally developed in the early 1970s and designed for line-oriented input, remains in use in some engineering environments. Not only is what you see not even close to what you get, but a series of arcane command strings is required to produce indentation, centering, or boldface text. Of course, it can't manipulate graphics in any form.

Sadly, the tales presented above are not all that uncommon. In almost every software engineering assessment that our company has conducted, document production facilities were found seriously lacking. Because most modern CASE tools are available on workstations, desk-top publishing capability can be installed at relatively low cost. In fact, desk-top publishing should be one of the first automated tools to be installed. It is rarely controversial; almost always received enthusiastically by software development staff; has a high likelihood of improving both productivity and quality; and produces results that will be obvious to everyone reading software documents. Once staff are familiar with these tools, other CASE tools can be integrated to add software development capability to document production capability.

Although few definitive studies have been conducted, it is not unreasonable to state that a 3 to 5 percent improvement in software development productivity can be achieved simply by installing state-of-the-art document production capability. The decision to install tools in this category should be a management "no brainer."

There is little doubt that we'll be installing new CASE tools in the years ahead. Is there a painless way to begin this process?

It's not a bad idea to establish a "tools mind-set" among technical staff and managers. To do this, the installation of CASE tools (acquired from outside vendors) might be accompanied by an internal program for transforming hidden *personal tools* into *community tools*.

In many software development organizations, technical staff members have developed tools for their personal use. These tools are often quite good and might have much broader application and benefit. Unfortunately, there is no formal mechanism for informing others of the existence of these personal tools. Essentially, the software development organization has a collection of hidden software tools assets, which, if uncovered, could have an important impact on day-to-day software engineering tasks.

How do we make these assets available?

One of the most effective (albeit somewhat radical) methods for encouraging people to develop tools and fostering widespread distribution is to create a "software tools awards program" that is similar in concept to the "manufacturing suggestion boxes" used in many industrial settings. First, publish a memo that takes the form illustrated in Figure 8.2.

The program described in the memo is effective because it plays to

To: All software development personnel

From: Department manager

Re: Software tools

As part of our program to improve software quality and productivity, we'd like to recognize the many members of our technical staff who have developed software tools that improve some aspect of software engineering. In the past many of you have developed specialized tools that help you do a better job. To be frank, your efforts have often gone unrewarded. In many cases, we've had no mechanism for making these tools available to a wider audience.

I strongly believe that software engineering is important and that each of you can contribute to its successful implementation. For this reason, I have decided to establish an on-going software tools awards program. Here's how it will work:

1. If you have developed a software tool that you believe could benefit others, document it along with an example of its use, describe how it can be used in broader application and what its benefits are, and submit it to the Software Tools Awards Committee (STAC). Contact {person's name and mail stop} for details.

2. The STAC is a five member committee comprised of three technical staff members and two technical managers. They will meet on a monthly basis to judge each submission for general applicability and quality.

3. If the STAC judges a tool to have widespread benefit, you will receive a special cash award tied to the potential productivity and/or quality impact of the tool. The minimum cash award will be $500. Your tool will be "productized" for general use and then distributed to the software development community.

4. At the end of each year the STAC will determine the "Software Tool of the Year"—the internally developed tool that provides maximum productivity and quality benefit for our software engineering work. Three bonus awards of $5,000, $2,500 and $1,250 will be given to those members of the technical staff that have developed the best software tools.

Please note that only those software tools developed "in your spare time" qualify for this program. That is, if you are assigned to develop a specific software tool, it may not be submitted for consideration by the STAC.

Further details about this program and complete rules for submission will be forthcoming. I welcome your comments and suggestions and look forward to your submissions.

Figure 8.2   A sample memo outlining a tools awards program.

three key motivators for software people: peer recognition, financial reward, and technical competition. For a relatively small cash outlay, a software development organization can acquire dozens of excellent tools over a 1- or 2-year period. "We can't do those kinds of things," you say. You'd be surprised what you can do if you convince management that your efforts can improve the bottom line.

However, other more mundane approaches are also available. A monthly *Software Engineering Newsletter* can be published within your organization. A column on new tools can be a regular feature. Staff can be assigned to uncover and document existing tools that may have wider applicability. If you have electronic mail capability, one or more bulletin boards can be established for software tools information. A centralized library can be created for all software tools.

What are our options as we begin to install vendor-supplied CASE tools?

In Chapter 7, guidelines for CASE tools selection were discussed. Once a specific CASE tool has been selected, you have one of three options for installation:

1. A few copies of CASE tools can be installed on workstations and made available to staff at some centralized location.

2. CASE tools can be provided for all staff members working on a software project.

3. CASE tools can be provided for all software engineers.

Option 1

In order to evaluate the efficacy of CASE, some software development organizations take an "experimental approach." That is, a few CASE tools are acquired and installed either in a centralized location for use by any interested staff member or in the offices of specific individuals. The use of these tools is monitored with the intent of acquiring larger numbers of CASE workstations if initial experience is good.

Unfortunately, the approach described for option 1 is often problematic. Although there is no question that your organization will learn from early experimentation and will gain insight into the benefits of CASE, it will be difficult to draw conclusions about wider application. If you decide to centralize CASE tools for use by all interested parties, you are likely to encounter the same problems that occurred in the early days of centralized interactive computer terminals (the infamous "terminal room"): too many staff members waiting in line for too few workstations. This situation often results in *lower* productivity, staff frustration, and general dislike of CASE. If, on the other hand, you decide to provide CASE tools for a few, selected staff members, the problems associated with a centralized approach disappear. However, many staff members will be precluded from using CASE, possibly leading to resentment and certainly giving you a limited view of broader applications of the technology.

If budgetary constraints demand that only a few (between two and five copies) CASE tools can be acquired, it is probably better to apply them in the context of option 2.

Option 2

A moderately sized software project is selected (see discussion of pilot project selection later in this chapter) and CASE tools (targeted to the needs of the project team) are provided for each member of the technical staff.

The approach described for option 2 can be an effective mechanism for measuring the benefits of new methods and CASE within a realistic project environment. Because use of CASE is constrained to a single project, productivity and quality benefits (or problems) can be more easily monitored. The software engineering implementation team can focus directly on one bounded project, rather than worrying about the "extenuating circumstances" associated with many projects.

If initial experiences using option 2 are positive, justification for additional CASE acquisition will be facilitated and your organization can move toward option 3.

Option 3

The economic justification for providing each technical staff member with a CASE workstation was presented in Chapter 7. However, even when this strategy is economically justified, the logistics for option 3 must be carefully planned in advance. Among the key factors that must be taken into account as CASE installation occurs are the following:

1. Determining which staff members can make best use of CASE tools.
2. Scheduling hands-on education of staff members in a manner that does not disrupt ongoing software project work.
3. Providing special training for and assignment of *systants*—technical staff members who become expert in the CASE environment

and are assigned to answer questions concerning use and application of CASE.

4. Coordination of the installation of software engineering procedures and methods with the installation of CASE.

How do we determine who on the project team gets CASE tools?

To determine who should have their own CASE tools and the types of tools to be assigned, job function must be taken into account. An individual who spends 80 percent of the time testing is not a prime candidate for analysis and design tools. However, testing tools may provide significant benefit.

Some managers expect software engineers to use CASE tools continuously and become upset if no one is sitting at a workstation using the tools. During one software engineering audit, I listened to a senior manager bemoan the fact that "hundreds of thousands of dollars were spent on CASE, and yet I only see the workstations in use 50 percent of the time."

I asked him whether he owned an electric drill. When he said "yes," I asked what percentage of the time he used it, and whether the small percentage negated its payoff when it was needed. The point slowly sank in.

Tool usage is only one part of software engineering. In fact, it is the quality and applicability of CASE tool usage—not quantity of usage—that yield high payoff. Even if a project member will only use a particular tool 20 percent of the time, the tool may provide substantial productivity and quality benefits.

The installation of procedures and methods should result in more consistent forms of information. It's likely that this information will change as time passes. How do we install procedures (and other technology) to control this change?

Installation of better software engineering procedures and methods will almost always be accompanied by a need for software configuration management (SCM). To install SCM procedures and tools (discussed in Chapter 15), a software development organization should (1) establish a systematic identification scheme for all documents, (2) locate a central repository for all documentation, and (3) define set procedures for the control of changes to documentation.

SCM procedures are often viewed as "red tape" by software developers and must be instituted in a manner that reduces the aura of bureaucratic interference in the software engineering process. Like other activities, the best approach to the installation of SCM is to proceed incrementally. For example, rather than establishing a detailed change control approval hierarchy as the first step, acquire a good SCM tool that will eliminate much of the drudgery that is currently required when changes must be made. An SCM tool provides immediate benefit to technical staff, thereby smoothing the way for installation of more formal SCM procedures.

As we install a common process framework for software engineering, we want to stress software quality assurance. Since we don't emphasize SQA currently, how should we begin?

SQA will represent a major cultural change for your organization. Your installation strategy should be to integrate SQA slowly, beginning with basic quality assurance activities. Over a period of 18 to 36 months, a more comprehensive SQA approach can be installed.

The elements of SQA are discussed in Chapter 14. In essence, the role of SQA is to ensure software quality through reviews, measurement, technical methods and tools, and management control. The following guidelines will provide you with a starting point for installation of SQA activities:

1. *Develop a common process framework:* The CPF (Appendix III) establishes the structure into which SQA fits. In addition, the framework will ultimately evolve into formal standards.

2. *Establish quality "checkpoints" throughout the process defined by the framework:* A quality checkpoint normally corresponds to a project milestone—that is, a point in the process when a deliverable has been created and successfully reviewed.

3. *Define the SQA activity that will be applied at the checkpoint:* Formal technical reviews are the most common SQA checkpoint activity, but measurement, testing, standards compliance audits, reporting, and other activities may also be required.

4. *Install formal technical reviews:* Guidelines for installing formal technical reviews were presented earlier in this chapter. If you accomplish nothing else, you will have made an important advance toward SQA if you install formal technical reviews successfully during your first 18 months of effort.

5. *Define a test strategy and install distinct black-box and white-box testing methods:* Testing is a quality assurance activity, and yet, most organizations do not perform it well. Quality improve-

ment is likely if better testing procedures and methods are installed.

6. *Establish a set of simple procedures for change control:* In most software organizations, change occurs haphazardly. Through better change control, "side effects" due to change are reduced and quality is improved.

7. *Integrate the activities implied by the above steps with your company's "total quality management" program:* Almost every major company in the industrialized world has adopted a quality management program. It is likely that your company is no exception. The SQA approach should be integrated with your overall company-wide program.

If the guidelines suggested above are followed, you will begin to see immediate improvement in the quality of software—improvement that can be translated into direct cost savings and improved customer satisfaction.

Should we develop (or acquire) and adopt a set of formal software engineering standards and procedures?

Software engineering standards and procedures (SES&P) lie on a "formality spectrum" that ranges from simple informal guidelines to mandated procedural requirements enforced by government edict. In general, software engineering standards and procedures should be instituted gradually, recognizing that too much formality, introduced too rapidly, can be detrimental to the installation step.

We have already noted that technology transition is a delicate balancing act between the need for cultural change and the desire for organizational and methodological stability. If properly constructed, SES&P can become an agent for change while at the same time improving the stability through which change is instituted. However, if improperly constructed or inappropriately installed, SES&P can create conflict within a software organization and retard the progress of ongoing projects.

In most cases, SES&P will be derived from your common process framework. The tasks, milestones, and deliverables of the CPF will serve as the foundation for a standards document.

A broad array of standards have been developed and are readily available for software engineering practice. For military contractors, the key SES&P document is DOD/Std 2167a along with many other standards that cover different aspects of the development process for computer-based systems. The IEEE publication *Software Engineering Standards* [2] contains standards for many important software engineering activities. These standards, modified for local needs, can serve as a basis for your SES&P.

Regardless of your source of information, a set of guidelines[3] for the development of SES&P is well worth noting:

1. *Begin by developing standards for software engineering activities that are already being conducted and for which everyone already agrees that appropriate procedures and methods are in place.* Standardization, if it has not been instituted in an organization, will often be viewed as an impediment to progress and creativity. Although this point of view is entirely incorrect, it is sometimes understandable when overly aggressive introduction of SES&P occurs. If the first standards introduced in an organization are for activities that everyone already agrees on, little antagonism will be generated and an atmosphere of acceptance can be established.

2. *Call them "guidelines" until SES&P have been proven in practice.* Even the best-intended standards and practices are sometimes inappropriate for a given software organization. The only way to determine the efficacy of SES&P is to apply them in a project environment. It is important to encourage technical staff to provide feedback on the applicability of standards and procedures and to "tune" SES&P as this feedback is acquired. You should not take a dogmatic attitude about standards and procedures. They are meant to improve the process of software engineering—not to become shackles on either management or the development organization.

3. *Build on a foundation that has been created by others.* I have already noted that many existing software standards and procedures have been published by industry groups, government agencies, and many companies in the software and systems community. It is well worthwhile to build on existing work rather than attempting to develop standards and procedures from scratch.

4. *Assess each page of the SES&P by asking the question. "Will this result in a net improvement in software development quality or productivity?"* Discipline for discipline's sake is both unnecessary and wasteful. Standards and procedures should be developed to improve the manner in which projects are managed or the quality with which software is produced. There is no point in developing restrictive SES&P that result in degradation of project schedules or little net benefit beyond current practice.

5. *Be sure to make a clear distinction between actions that are abso-*

---

[3]It should be noted that these guidelines must be modified by defense contractors and others who must apply mandated SES&P for many of their projects.

lutely required and activities that are recommended but not strictly required. The use of precise terminology within an SES&P document is very important. For example, in military standards for software development, the word "shall" is used to indicate an activity or document that must be developed as part of the software engineering process. The word "may" (as in "method x may be used") indicates a suggested activity that is not absolutely required as part of SES&P. Consistency in the use of such words is important. If inconsistent usage occurs, it is difficult for the reader to determine what must be done and what is optional.

6. *Be sure that standards developed for one group within the software organization do not act as an impediment to other groups.* As standards are being developed, you should assess the scope of impact of such standards across the entire software organization. For example, new standards may be developed that dictate detailed requirements specifications prior to the initiation of any software project. The user community may be unfamiliar with such specifications and untrained in the participatory communication necessary to create them. Unless appropriate training is conducted in advance, such standards will be viewed as an impediment to the development of software. One useful mechanism for determining the scope of effect of a particular standard is to create a cross-reference matrix that lists all relevant standards in the left-hand column and all major technical groups (including users and others) across the top row. Check marks can indicate which groups are affected by what standards.

7. *Sell them before implementing them.* The installation of SES&P proceeds much more smoothly if the concepts behind and reasons for each standard are sold to both management and technical staff. The "selling process" occurs in an educational format that includes plenty of feedback. Practitioners must be made to feel that their comments on standards and procedures are being taken to heart and that the final version of such SES&P will incorporate their constructive criticism.

You've provided us with some useful guidelines for installing various software engineering technology components. But I'm still uneasy about getting started. Can you make some suggestions?

Each step of the software engineering implementation life cycle is a precursor to the initiation of a project that actually uses software engineering technology. There are a number of different ways that you can begin to institute software engineering within your organization:

1. *Discrete methods or tools can be implemented across the board for all staff members working in an organization.* For example, all practi-

tioners can be encouraged to use a specific design method, adapt to pre-specified changes in documentation formats, or apply a new CASE tool.

2. *Distinct methods or tools can be applied to one or more pilot projects with the intent of "testing" these methods and tools in a controlled environment.* The use of a *pilot project* creates a "laboratory" environment in which new methods and tools can be tested without major impact across the entire software organization. If things should go awry, the impact will be localized and the opportunity to make corrections without recriminations will be improved.

3. *Implement the complete (or almost complete) spectrum of software engineering practice for one or more pilot projects.* In this case, the scope of implementation broadens dramatically. All elements of software engineering are to be applied to a pilot project that is conducted in a laboratory environment. By applying the full spectrum of software engineering practice, a software organization can assess those elements that work and those elements that are problematic, and make adjustments prior to implementation across the entire organization. The advantage of this approach over the implementation of distinct tools and methods is that all important aspects of software engineering practice are considered and assessed.

4. *Institute comprehensive software engineering practice across an entire software organization.* There is no doubt that this is the most daring (and dangerous) approach to software engineering implementation. If performed in a carefully planned and phased manner, this approach can work. However, if a big-bang approach is taken, cultural change will likely be too rapid and many problems associated with technology transition will occur.

The implementation options described above represent two fundamental schools of thought: (1) implementation through a series of small steps in which "incremental successes" are achieved and built on; (2) implementation using the big-bang philosophy in which the entire methodology is instituted at one time.

What are the advantages and disadvantages associated with the "stepwise" approach to installation?

By implementing software engineering in a piecewise fashion, the amount of upheaval within an organization is reduced dramatically. In addition, both managers and practitioners have less change to worry about and can therefore better focus their attention on the changes that are occurring at the moment. Small successes will serve to build confidence and begin to develop a momentum that will lead to larger successes.

However, the stepwise implementation of software engineering practice also has disadvantages:

- The order in which software engineering practice is implemented (when implemented stepwise) is not typically the order in which it is applied in an actual project. Unless the overall context for software engineering is introduced in advance, the technology may appear to be disjointed and even confusing to practitioners with little software engineering experience.

- It will undoubtedly take longer to implement broad-spectrum software engineering practice. In addition, there will likely be more debate over individual methods and tools. Because practitioners may not be able to assess the application of a procedure, method, or tool in the context of broader software engineering practice, it is possible that the overall benefit of the tool may not be apparent to the user.

- Implementation decisions made early during the installation step may constrain options for later installation.

What are the advantages and disadvantages associated with the "big bang" approach to installation?

The big-bang approach to software engineering installation enables you to apply the technology front to back on one or more pilot projects. Because implementation occurs in the sequence that it will actually be applied in practice, the context of each procedure, method, and tool can be more readily understood. In addition, by applying the entire methodology, it is possible to implement and assess it in a shorter time.

The disadvantages of big-bang implementation are primarily those of upheaval due to cultural change and problems associated with selecting the right pilot project(s) at the right time. While stepwise installation allows a software organization to implement software engineering practice within the context of ongoing projects, big-bang installation requires that a pilot project be available and ready to start at the time that software engineering installation is to commence. In many software organizations, timing is not appropriate, and delays may occur because no pilot project is available.

How do we decide which "school of thought" to adopt?

Each approach to software engineering installation has the advantages and disadvantages that I've outlined above. You must assess the potential availability of pilot projects, the degree of receptiveness that is likely from project managers, and senior management's receptiveness to across-the-board change before you can adopt either of the two schools of thought. As I've already stated, the safest path is an incremental approach to specific software engineering procedures, methods, and tools using a pilot project as a test bed. However, local requirements may dictate a different strategy.

You made a number of references to a "pilot project." Can you provide more details on this?

A pilot project may be selected to act as a "test bed" for software engineering procedures, methods, and tools. It must be significant enough to be realistic, but not so critical that small delays or minor confusion would cause great hardship. Normally, the project team implements a new application or works on a substantial enhancement to an existing application. The pilot project has the following characteristics:

- A duration of 4 to 12 calendar months
- Staff size of 3 to 7 people
- A customer that has worked with your organization before
- An application that is typical (in complexity and difficulty) of the majority of those that your organization encounters
- An experienced project manager who is willing to assess the efficacy of software engineering practice while managing the application effort

Because the pilot project is a test bed, it is important to recognize that time must be budgeted to educate members of the project team and to measure and assess the efficacy of the technology.

What happens when a technology component doesn't work well within the context of the pilot project?

With the proper mix of people and the proper selection of a pilot project, software engineering installation should proceed quite smoothly. There is no question, however, that some tuning of specific technology components will be required. When changes to the software engineering approach are required, two options are available: (1) making on-the-fly modifications as the project is being conducted or (2) noting any complaints or concerns about procedures, methods, and case tools, and making modifications after the project has been completed.

Each approach has advantages and disadvantages. On-the-fly modifications provide staff with instantaneous feedback, but can cause confusion when "the rules change in the middle of the game." After-the-fact modification results in a more controlled atmosphere, but can cause frustration among project staff when reasonable criticisms are not acted on immediately.

It is important for you to maintain a pragmatic, rather than dogmatic, attitude about software engineering. If a serious failing in a procedure, method, or tool is noted, you must act immediately to rectify it. Otherwise, staff will begin to question the efficacy of all software engineering and a negative attitude will develop. It is essential to keep "grumbling" to an absolute minimum. If staff members feel strongly about a particular issue, it is incumbent on you to listen to any criticisms and act on them in an expeditious manner. If staff criticisms find a deaf ear, it is very likely that morale will drop and project success will be jeopardized.

Everyone involved must recognize that they are participating in a "technology laboratory," and some degree of uncertainty is to be expected. However, the project team has a right to expect that ideas that looked good on paper but do not work well in practice will not be forced on them when it is obvious that changes must be made. If a collaborative attitude is fostered, it is likely that the project will proceed at a reasonable pace and that successful completion will be achieved.

How should we evaluate the success of a pilot project?

The success of a pilot project can be evaluated by applying all of the following criteria:

1. Have customer requirements been successfully implemented within the specified development schedule and budget?

2. Have software engineering practices been successfully implemented in a manner that contributed to successful completion of the project?

3. Has the quality of the resultant software improved when compared to other similar application efforts?

4. Have changes in the software configuration (documents, programs, data) resulted in more maintainable programs?

5. Have management and technical staff accepted software engineering practice and adopted it for use on other projects?

6. Have quality and productivity metrics indicated a net improvement over past data?

If each of these questions has been answered in the affirmative, the pilot project can be deemed an unqualified success and broader implementation of software engineering practice can be initiated. However, if one or more of the questions is answered negatively, it is necessary to evaluate the response, assess the reasons, and act to correct those elements of software engineering practice that may have been contributing factors to the negative response.

Let's assume that we've completed the first pilot project successfully. How do we propagate software engineering to other projects?

Once a pilot project has been successfully completed, software engineering procedures, methods, and tools can be propagated across the software organization. The success achieved during the pilot project should increase management confidence in widespread use of software engineering.

The following guidelines are recommended for broader propagation of software engineering:

1. *Be sure that problems encountered during the pilot project have been remedied:* If significant changes have been made as a result of the pilot project, propagation should proceed judiciously. A rule of thumb should be: If you're uncomfortable with the potential for broad-based acceptance and success, choose another procedure, method, or tool that is more likely to succeed.

2. *Use staff participants in the pilot project as "seeds" for other projects:* Technical staff who have successfully applied software engineering often become its best representatives. Participants in the pilot can serve as systants during broader propagation of software engineering.

3. *Follow all guidelines for startup:* With minor adjustments, start-up guidelines apply equally well to broader propagation of software engineering practice.

Our organization has many projects that are at varying stages of completion at any given time. Should we introduce software engineering technologies to ongoing projects or only to projects in the startup phase?

In general, it is best to introduce a software engineering approach at the beginning of a project. This leads most organizations to use a "rolling strategy" for installation. As each new development or maintenance project is scheduled to start, it becomes a candidate for software engineering installation. As the project team forms, the common process framework is presented and all members are provided with sufficient education and tools. The software engineering implementation team, along with the project team, reviews the project scope to determine if any project-specific changes should be made for the installation strategy. All guidelines suggested for the pilot project can be applied to each new installation of software engineering.

Some of our projects span many years, and we want to begin to introduce software engineering practices for them as well. Can we do this without major upheaval?

Absolutely, but the installation strategy must be tuned to the characteristics of the project, and more importantly, to what the project team has already accomplished. If the project is in its early technical stages, it may be possible to implement many components of software engineering (e.g., formal technical reviews, methods for subsequent steps, documentation requirements, CASE tools), but it is still necessary to proceed cautiously. If a weak foundation has been laid (i.e., software engineering practices have not been applied, and the analysis or design work that was done is suspect), it may be best to focus solely on SQA installation and forego the introduction of methods and tools. Overlaid on a weak foundation,[4] methods and tools may cause more harm than good.

Can you suggest an overall installation procedure that answers at least some of these questions?

- What do we do in preparation?

- What methods and tools do we install first?

- How do we install technology components for software projects at various stages of completion?

At the risk of oversimplifying a sometimes difficult technology transition activity, I'll use pseudocode to describe a procedure for installation.[5] If you're unfamiliar with pseudocode or PDL [3], it's re-

---

[4]It can be argued that a weak foundation should be rebuilt, not ignored. Although I agree completely with this sentiment, the realities of business sometimes do not afford us the luxury of reworking the system.

[5]The pseudocode procedure was developed by R.S. Pressman & Associates, Inc. and has been published in *Understanding CASE*, a video educational product distributed by Digital Equipment Corporation.

ally nothing more than a mock programming language in which procedural logic for decisions and loops is represented by boldface operators (e.g., **repeat until** or **if-then-else**), and activities are denoted as English language phrases. Indentation indicates the logical structure of activities.

The procedure that follows focuses primarily on the installation of CASE tools. However, it implies the installation of procedures and methods that are required as a foundation for effective use of the tools. Therefore, whenever you encounter an activity such as

```
install analysis/design CASE tools;
```

be aware that this activity implies that staff must be educated in analysis and design methods, that a procedure that accommodates analysis and design must be in place, and that SQA techniques for analysis and design must be present.

A Procedure for Installation

```
PROCEDURE Software Engineering Component Installation;
   assess status of all ongoing projects and all upcoming projects;
   repeat until a consensus is achieved
      select software engineering paradigm(s) to be used;
      define generic software engineering framework for organization;
      establish review points/milestones;
      document the software engineering approach;
      develop document templates and examples;
      indicate where CASE tools are to be applied;
      review software engineering ''standards'';
   endrep;
   if responsibilities, milestones for installation are unclear
      then begin
         develop a Transition Plan for CASE installation;
         establish measurement criteria and metrics;
         assign project management responsibility for installation;
         define milestones for installation;
         establish evaluation procedure for CASE environment;
      end;
   install workstations for each project team member;
   install desk-top publishing (DTP) tools;
   work with computer vendor to establish network if none exists;
   install communication tools (e.g., E-mail) for all developers;
   develop a phased approach to installation of SCM;
   define manual/automated SCM activities;
   develop preliminary strategy for ensuring software quality;
   consider CASE database and its impact on SCM tools;
   select SCM tools based on degree of integration with environment;
   if version control formalism is desired then install a version
      control tool;
   install a "make" tool;
   repeat in parallel until CASE environment is installed across all
      projects
      consider a project;
      if project has not yet started
         then begin
```

```
install a project management tool for estimation;
install specialized SCM tool(s) for software control;
assign responsibility to oversee application of CASE tools;
educate [staff, project];
if system level analysis is required
  then install a simulation/prototyping tool;
install additional workstations to support analysis/design;
train systants in analysis/design methods/tools;
educate [staff, project];
install analysis/design CASE tools;
check for integration with DTP;
begin use of CASE analysis/design tools;
use DTP tools for specs;
use reviews as an SQA and a debriefing mechanism;
evaluate application of CASE tools using debriefing;
if problems are being encountered
  then problem resolution [problem];
augment existing coding tools with:
  language sensitive editors;
  program construction (e.g., "make") tools;
  compiler and cross compilers;
  code analyzers;
  debugging tools;
if appropriate testing tools can be found
  then acquire and install;
  else consider building tools to meet your specific needs;
endif;
end {tasks that are conducted when project has not yet
started};
else {project is already under way}
  case of project status:
  planning:
    apply all steps associated with a new project;
  analysis/design:
    begin
    if early in analysis step
      then {installation of CASE SA/SD tools is possible}
      apply all steps associated with a new project;
      else {project is in later stages of analysis}
      educate [staff, project];
      use DTP tools to develop specs;
    endif;
  coding:
    begin
    augment existing coding tools with:
    language sensitive editors;
    program construction (e.g., ''make'') tools;
    compiler and cross compilers;
    code analyzers;
    debugging tools;
    if appropriate tools can be found
      then acquire and install testing tools;
      else consider building tools to meet your specific needs;
    endif;
    end;
  endcase;
endif;
if project has been completed
  then
    collect software metrics for project;
    compare metrics with historical baseline noting differences;
    determine benefits and tune CASE application to
    ''optimize'';
```

```
      else
         conduct regular staff debriefing sessions;
         respond quickly to criticisms/problems;
      endif;
end proc {Software Engineering Component Installation}

PROCEDURE educate [staff, project];
   establish a software engineering library;
   use self-test to help staff identify software engineering
   weaknesses;
   identify training needs for the project based on status;
   if training needs are similar to other projects
     then group project staff with staff from other projects for
     training;
     else design specialized training for project team;
   endif;
   if time is critical and project is already ''late''
     then design ''part-time'' training regimen that might include
     introductory seminar;
     readings from library;
     video or audio self-learning;
     else conduct classroom training;
   endif;
end proc {educate}

PROCEDURE problem resolution [problem];
   case of problem:
     staff resistance:
     begin
        determine reasons for resistance;
        demonstrate "what's in it for me";
        educate [resisting staff, project];
        encourage those who are enthusiastic as a model for
        those that are resisting;
     end;
     low productivity:
     begin
        be sure that measures are rational and correct;
        examine where methods and tools are being applied;
        select high-productivity leverage activities and apply CASE;
     end;
     schedule slippage:
     begin
        attempt to determine causes for slippage;
        {it is likely due to factors other than CASE}
        latch all noncritical change requests;
        develop new WBS with shorter duration tasks;
        establish milestones that are more closely spaced;
        micromanage to new WBS;
        continue with application of CASE;
     end;
     poor quality:
     begin
        determine types of quality problems;
        if quality problem is CASE related
          then problem resolution [wrong tool];
          else begin
          evaluate review/testing procedures to determine if changes
          are required;
          update software engineering guidelines to accommodate
          changes;
        endif;
     wrong tool:
```

```
   begin
     attempt to isolate specific tool or tool set;
     if tool is really wrong
       then
         admit that an error in selection has been made;
         use lessons learned from application of existing tool to
         help guide selection of new, better tool;
         return to the Selection Step;
       else determine why tool is perceived to be wrong;
         attempt to determine the real problem;
         educate [staff, project];
         problem resolution [real problem];
     endif;
   endcase;
 end proc {problem resolution}
```

As we move through the installation procedure, it would seem that a formal process of evaluation should take place. Is this correct?

Evaluation should certainly take place, but it isn't always formal. Throughout the installation step of the software engineering implementation life cycle, managers and practitioners should initiate an evaluation process that includes (1) informal discussions about what is working and what isn't, (2) systematic collection of comments and criticism from all people who are working with the installed technology component, (3) collection of data to be used for software metrics, and (4) a reapplication of the process assessment questionnaire to determine whether attribute grades and the maturity level are improving with time.

You suggest systematic collection of comments and criticism from technical staff. How do we go about doing this?

Information gleaned from informal discussions is one approach, but this doesn't always work well. A better approach is to poll all project managers and technical staff on a regular basis. A simple, yet effective polling technique is a questionnaire that asks for a subjective assessment of the efficacy of a particular procedure, method, or tool. Average ratings for various topics will provide you with an indication of what's working and what isn't. Personal follow-up is then required.

Can you provide an example of a questionnaire of this type?

The following questionnaire provides an example of a polling approach for CASE tools. Although the questionnaire is rather general, it could be expanded to target a specific class of tools. Questions could be designed to examine whether tools are meeting specific organizational goals.

Evaluation Questionnaire—CASE Tools Please answer each of the following questions with a percentage. If unsure, make your best guess. If you really don't know, enter "DK."

1. What percentage of your time do you spend using CASE tools?
2. What percentage of your time would you like to be using CASE tools?
3. Estimate the percent change in effort required to accomplish each of the following tasks. If the task takes more time with CASE, note this with a positive percentage; less time should be noted with a negative percentage. If you don't perform the task, enter "NA."
   a. Project status reporting
   b. Analysis modeling
   c. Requirements documentation
   d. Reviews and error detection
   e. Design modeling
   f. Design documentation
   g. Coding
   h. Achieving coding standards
   i. Code documentation
   j. Test case design
   k. Test management
   l. Test documentation
   m. Maintenance work
   n. Maintenance documentation
   o. Change control

For each of the statements that follows, respond with a rating of 1 to 5, where 1 = strongly disagree, 2 = disagree, 3 = neutral, 4 = agree, 5 = strongly agree.

4. The installation and use of CASE tools have resulted in the following:
   a. Higher-quality software
   b. Fewer customer–developer misunderstandings
   c. More rapid development of analysis models
   d. Better analysis models
   e. Easier prototyping
   f. Fewer developers to develop communication problems
   g. More effective reviews of analysis and design
   h. Better adherence to schedules
   i. Fewer errors introduced during analysis and design
   j. Easier coding
   k. Fewer errors in coding
   l. Better consistency across the project team
   m. Improved customer satisfaction
   n. Better staff morale
   o. Reduced maintenance effort
   p. Easier testing
   q. Fewer customer-generated changes
   r. Better insight into system architecture and function

It seems as if we're cycling back to where we started—"looking in the mirror." Is this true?

That's why it's called the software engineering implementation life *cycle*.

A Manager's Checklist

The general strategy for installation of software engineering is to take a stepwise approach, first instituting those elements that are close to current practice and slowly broadening the focus to new and advanced methods and tools. Installation guidelines are available for each step in the software engineering process. In general, the guidelines strive to introduce new technology (and manage the cultural changes that accompany it) with a minimum of upheaval. In addition to specific development steps, umbrella activities such as SQA and SCM must also be installed; standards and procedures should be instituted; and specific people and projects must be selected as subjects for installation.

To gain a better understanding of the installation step and your organization's readiness for installation, the following actions and questions are recommended.

Actions

- Make a list of the installation problems that you're likely to encounter when you begin this step. Try to develop a plan to circumvent each problem and contingency steps if the problem does occur.

- List seven technology components that you would like to install during the first year of the implementation life cycle. Prioritize each item on the list.

- Using the guidelines presented in this chapter, outline an installation strategy that would work for your development organization.

- Research existing software engineering standards and select the one that would be most appropriate for your organization.

- Make a list of upcoming application projects that could serve as the installation pilot project. "Grade" each project against the criteria for pilot projects discussed in this chapter.

Questions

- Which path would you prefer: movement toward a formal framework or movement toward more advanced methods and tools? Which path would your technical staff prefer?

- Is it realistic to assume that you can install a common process framework for your organization? Will it be applicable for all development groups and project teams?

■ What breadth of installation do you think is appropriate for your organization?

■ What is the first CASE tool that you'd like to install and why?

■ For the installation strategy that you outlined as one of the actions above, how many people and how much money will you need to implement it?

■ What new document (something you currently don't produce) would you like to install first?

■ Could your organization implement the software tools awards program suggested in this chapter? If no, why not?

■ Which do you prefer: "stepwise" or "big bang" installation? Why?

Further Readings

Books by Pressman (*Making Software Engineering Happen,* Prentice-Hall, 1988), Humphrey (*Managing the Software Process,* Addison-Wesley, 1989), Bouldin (*Agents of Change,* Yourdon Press, 1989), Buckley (*Implementing Software Engineering Practices,* Wiley, 1989), and Utz (*Software Technology Transitions,* Prentice-Hall, 1992) provide varying degrees of guidance for the manager who wants to create an installation strategy for software engineering.

References

[1] Freedman, D., and G. Weinberg, *Handbook of Walkthroughs, Inspections, and Technical Reviews,* 3d ed., Dorset House, 1990.
[2] *Software Engineering Standards,* 3d ed., IEEE, document no. SH12534, 1989.
[3] Pressman, R.S., *Software Engineering: A Practitioner's Approach,* 3d ed., McGraw-Hill, 1992.

Part 2

Project Management

Project Management: Holding the Reins

Software project management is the first layer of the software engineering process. We call it a *layer,* rather than a step or a task, because it overlays the entire development process from beginning to end. It is an umbrella activity.

In order to conduct a successful software project, managers and technical staff must understand the scope of work to be done, the risks to be incurred, the resources to be required, the tasks to be accomplished, the milestones to be tracked, the effort (cost) to be expended, and the schedule to be followed. Software project management provides that understanding. It begins before technical work starts, continues as the software evolves from concept to reality, and culminates only when the software is retired.

Because software project management is so important to the success of a project, it would seem reasonable to assume that all project leaders understand how to do it, and all practitioners understand how to work within the bounds established by it. Unfortunately, many do not. This chapter is a brief introduction to project management. It is intended to establish the context for Part 3 of this book.

It seems like our software projects often get off to a ragged start. How should we begin a project?

Before a project can be planned, objectives and scope should be established, alternative solutions considered, and technical and management constraints identified. Without this information, it is impossible to define reasonable (and accurate) estimates of the cost, a realistic breakdown of project tasks, or a manageable project schedule that provides a meaningful indication of progress.

The software developer and customer must meet to define project objectives and scope. In many cases, this activity occurs as part of the customer communication process (Chapter 10). Objectives identify the overall goals of the project without considering how these goals will be achieved. Scope identifies the primary functions that software is to accomplish, and more importantly, attempts to *bound* these functions in a quantitative manner.

Once the project objectives and scope are understood, alternative solutions are considered. Although very little detail is discussed, the alternatives enable managers and practitioners to select a "best" approach, given the constraints imposed by delivery deadlines, budgetary restrictions, personnel availability, technical interfaces, and myriad other factors.

Let's assume that customer communication has been successfully completed. Are we ready to begin planning?

Planning is a process of estimation, and to develop reasonable estimates, you'll need to have a good historical baseline. In Chapter 3 we talked about software metrics and their use as the input to an estimation process. So the next thing you have to do is to ensure that data are available to enable you to generate estimates.

My management wants a project plan "yesterday." In many cases we simply use past experience and best guesses. Is there a more systematic approach?

One of the pivotal activities in the software project management process is *planning*. When a software project is planned, estimates of required human effort (usually in person-months), chronological project duration (in calendar time), and cost (in dollars) must be derived. But how is this done?

In many cases estimates are made using past experience as the only guide. If a new project is quite similar in size and function to a previous project, it is likely that the new project will require approximately the same amount of effort, take the same calendar time, and cost the same number of dollars as the older work. But what if the project breaks new ground? Then past experience alone may not be enough.

A number of estimation techniques have been developed for software development. Although each has its own strengths and weaknesses, all have the following attributes in common:

- Project scope must be established in advance.

- Software metrics (past measurements) are used as a basis from which estimates are made.

- The project is broken into small pieces which are estimated individually.

Many managers apply a number of different estimation techniques, using one as a cross-check for another. In Chapter 10, a number of popular software estimation techniques are considered.

What factors affect the accuracy of our estimates?

Whenever a computer program is to be built, there are areas of uncertainty. Are the needs of the customer really understood? Can the functions that must be implemented be accomplished before the project deadline? Will there be difficult technical problems that are currently hidden from view? Will the changes that invariably occur during any project cause the schedule to slip badly?

Risk analysis is crucial to good software project management, and yet many projects are undertaken with no specific consideration of risk. In his book on software engineering management [1], Tom Gilb says, "If you don't actively attack [project and technical] risks, they will actively attack you." Risk analysis is actually a series of risk management steps that enable us to "attack" risk: risk identification, risk assessment, risk prioritization, risk management strategies, risk resolution, and risk monitoring. These steps are applied throughout the software engineering process and are described in Chapter 11.

What should I use as my primary monitoring and control mechanism during a software project?

A schedule is a project manager's most important tool. Every software project has a schedule, but not all schedules are created equal. Did the schedule evolve on its own or was it planned in advance? Was work done "by the seat of our pants" or was a set of well-defined tasks identified? Have managers focused solely on the deadline date or has a critical path been identified and monitored to be sure that the deadline is achieved? Has progress been measured by "Are we done yet?" or has a set of evenly spaced milestones been established?

Software project scheduling is really no different from scheduling for any engineering project. A set of project tasks is identified. Interdependencies among tasks are established. The effort associated with each task is estimated. People and other resources are assigned. A "task network" is created. A timeline schedule is developed. Each of these activities is described in detail in Chapter 12.

Once the development schedule has been established, tracking and control activities commence. Each task noted in the schedule is tracked by the project manager. If the task falls behind schedule, the manager can use an automated project scheduling tool to determine the impact of schedule slippage on intermediate project milestones and the overall delivery date. Resources can be redirected, tasks can be reordered, or (as a last resort) delivery commitments can be modified to accommodate the problem that has been uncovered. In this way, software development can be better controlled.

It's fairly obvious that the most important software development resource is people. What does a project manager have to do to maximize this resource?

The first thing that a project manager must realize is that the people resource includes more than just software development staff. In fact, the most important resources early in a project are the customer and end users of the software-based system that is to be developed or changed. In many cases this resource lies fallow; that is, the software development organization takes a tacit "leave us alone so that we can do our jobs" approach, never getting the customer/user involved. In other situations, the customer/user is asked to help but is "too busy." Both sets of circumstances are recipes for disaster.

The job of the project manager is to ensure that (1) the customer/user resource is involved early in a project; (2) clear, consistent, accurate requirements are derived during this involvement; and (3) other human resources are then integrated into the project to act on the requirements and build a system that accurately reflects them. To accomplish this, the manager must develop a team-oriented approach at all levels, and communicate, educate, organize, motivate, track, control, and monitor all people involved in a software project. Each of these activities is discussed in Chapter 13.

You've already emphasized that quality is a "bottom line" issue in all companies. How does software quality assurance fit into an effective project management approach?

Software quality assurance (SQA) is an umbrella activity that is applied throughout the software engineering process. It begins at the start of a project, when communication with the customer is undertaken, and it ends only after the software is removed from operation. SQA encompasses a set of activities that includes the creation and enforcement of a process framework for software engineering, the conduct of formal technical reviews at all stages of the engineering process, the use of software metrics to improve quality, and the use of testing to filter remaining errors.

SQA is integrated into a project management strategy in three ways:

- All SQA tasks (e.g., formal technical reviews) are scheduled as part of the project plan, and formal or informal audits are conducted to ensure that SQA is ongoing.

- Staff members are educated to understand that quality is everyone's responsibility (a cliché, it's true, but a critically important point of departure).

- Technical people establish a set of qualitative and quantitative criteria that defines quality at each stage of the software engineering process; completion of these quality criteria checklists becomes the "exit condition" for progress to the next stage of the process.

In most cases SQA activities are "low tech." But this makes them no less important than sophisticated methods or tools for software engineering. SQA is discussed in detail in Chapter 14.

I've often heard people say that the only constant in software work is change. Is there a systematic strategy for managing change as part of the project plan?

I was once talking with a seasoned software manager. We were comparing war stories about "unreasonable" customer requests for change and the havoc that they caused in real-life software projects. Suddenly the manager paused, as if pondering some new idea. "You know," he said, "if it wasn't for change, none of us would have jobs."

How true, but that simple fact is cold comfort when a stream of changes (most justified) creates the potential for chaos in a project that you're managing. You'll note my parenthetical comment—most changes are justified. For this reason, we must develop a strategy for accommodating changes throughout a project. The strategy should define methods for requesting changes, evaluating them, controlling the elements of the software that must be modified; performing record keeping; notifying those with a need to know; and reconstructing the system when all changes are in place. This strategy, called *software configuration management,* is presented in Chapter 15.

A Manager's Checklist

In this chapter, I've done nothing more than introduce the project management subjects that will be discussed in greater detail throughout the remainder of Part 3 of this book. However, there are things that you can begin doing before you read Chapters 10 through 15. Here are some suggestions.

Actions

- Spend some time trying to understand how successful projects have been managed. Find one or more projects that have been completed on schedule and within budget. Speak with the project manager informally and attempt to determine how he or she established a project plan and then managed it.

- Understand how project delivery dates are established and how project priorities are set. Is there a systematic approach to this activity or does your company use the "whoever screams loudest" or "whoever carries the biggest stick" approach to project scheduling?

Questions

- Of the last 10 projects completed by your organization, how many were completed within 10 percent of the initially scheduled completion date? Within 20 percent? Within 30 percent?

- Of the last 10 projects completed by your organization, how many were within 10 percent of initial budget? Within 20 percent? Within 30 percent?

- If you were to ask your customers what their biggest complaint (about software developers) is, what would they say? What would be their most consistent compliment?

- If you were to ask your senior management what their biggest complaint (about software developers) is, what would they say? What would be their most consistent compliment?

Further Readings

Dozens of books and hundreds of technical papers have been written about software project management. Fred Brooks' *The Mythical Man-Month* (Addison-Wesley, 1975) remains the classic guidebook for first-time and seasoned software project managers. Books by Gilb [1] and Simpson (*New Techniques in Software Project Management,* Wiley, 1987) and a tutorial by Reifer (*Software Management,* 3d ed., IEEE Computer Society Press, 1986) are worth examining. A book by Boddie (*Crunch Mode,* Prentice-Hall, 1987) contains pragmatic advice for those managers who always seem to be under the gun. A paper by Boehm and Ross (*IEEE Trans. Software Engineering,* July 1989) presents an intriguing "theory" of software project management whose underlying philosophy is to "make everyone [developers, users, customers, maintainers, managers] a winner."

An intriguing book by Abdel-Hamid and Madnick (*Software Project Dynamics,* Prentice-Hall, 1991) introduces an integrated modeling notation that enables project managers to mathematically model the characteristics of a software project (things like personnel loading, changes, turnover, learning curve, etc.) and then simulate changes to determine their impact on cost and schedule. On the lighter side, a book by Ackoff (*Ackoff's Fables,* Wiley, 1991) presents "irreverent reflections on business and bureaucracy" that are invaluable for understanding the information systems milieu.

Reference

[1] Gilb, T., *Principles of Software Engineering Management,* Addison-Wesley, 1988.

10

Estimation: Projecting Future Demand on People and Time

The software project management process begins with a set of activities collectively called *project planning*. The first of these activities is *estimation*. Whenever estimates are made, we look into the future and accept some degree of uncertainty as a matter of course. To quote Frederick Brooks [1]: "our techniques of estimating are poorly developed. More seriously, they reflect an unvoiced assumption that is quite untrue, i.e., that all will go well.... Because we are uncertain of our estimates, software managers often lack the courteous stubbornness to make people wait for a good product."

Although estimating is as much art as it is science, this important activity need not be conducted in a haphazard manner. Useful techniques for time and effort estimation do exist. And because estimation lays a foundation for all other project planning activities, and project planning provides the road map for successful software engineering, you are ill-advised to embark without it.

What is the key issue that affects the correctness of an estimate?

A leading executive was once asked what single characteristic was most important in a project manager. His response: "a person with the ability to know what will go wrong before it actually does." I might add: "and the courage to estimate when the future is cloudy."

Estimation of resources, cost, and schedule for a software project requires experience, access to good historical information, and the courage to commit to quantitative measures when qualitative data are all that exist. Estimation carries inherent risk, and factors that increase risk also increase the likelihood that an estimate will be incorrect.

What general project factors increase estimation risk?

Risk is an issue that most managers consider in an ad hoc fashion. In fact, risk analysis and monitoring[1] is an important management activity that can lead to more accurate estimates. In general, risks can be categorized into three broad categories: risks that increase project complexity, risks associated with project size, and risks that affect the structure of a project.

Project complexity has a strong effect on uncertainty that is inherent in planning. Complexity, however, is a relative measure that is affected by familiarity with past effort. A real-time application might be perceived as "exceedingly complex" to a software group that has previously developed only batch applications. The same real-time application might be perceived as "run of the mill" for a software group that has been heavily involved in high-speed process control. A number of quantitative software complexity measures have been proposed at the design level, but these are of little use to a manager during the planning stage. However, other, more subjective assessments of complexity (e.g., the function-point complexity adjustment factors described in Chapter 3) can be established early in the planning process.

Project size is another important factor that can affect the accuracy and efficacy of estimates. As size increases, the interdependence among various elements of the software grows rapidly. Problem decomposition, an important approach to estimating, becomes more difficult because decomposed elements may still be formidable. To paraphrase Murphy's law: "What can go wrong will go wrong"—and if there are more things that can fail, more things will fail.

The degree of *project structure* also has an effect on estimation risk. In this context, *structure* refers to the ease with which functions can be compartmentalized and the hierarchical nature of information that must be processed. But it can also refer to the structure of development teams, their relationship to the customer and to one another, and the ease with which the human structure can develop the software architecture.

Are there other factors that affect the risk associated with software estimates?

Risk is measured by the degree of uncertainty in the quantitative estimates established for resources, cost, and schedule. If project scope is poorly understood or project requirements are subject to change, uncertainty and risk become dangerously high. The software planner should demand completeness of function, performance, and interface definitions, but realistically, these demands cannot always be met. The

---

[1]Systematic techniques for risk analysis are presented in Chapter 11.

planner and, more importantly, the customer should recognize that variability in software requirements means instability in cost and schedule.

The risks that you mention imply uncertainty, yet our management demands accuracy. How can we reconcile this?

There is no easy answer to your question. Consider the words of Aristotle (330 B.C.): "It is the mark of an instructed mind to rest satisfied with the degree of precision which the nature of a subject admits, and not to seek exactness when only an approximation of the truth is possible."

O.K., I'm ready to begin making estimates. What's the primary objective at this stage?

The software project manager is confronted with a dilemma at the very beginning of a software project. Quantitative estimates are required, but solid information is unavailable. A detailed analysis of software requirements would provide necessary information for estimates, but analysis often takes weeks or months to complete. Estimates are needed "now!"

The objective of software project planning is to provide a framework that enables the manager to make reasonable estimates of resources, cost, and schedule. These estimates are made within a limited timeframe at the beginning of a software project and should be updated regularly as the project progresses.

As noted above, the planning objective is achieved through a process of information discovery that leads to reasonable estimates. Information discovery begins with the customer.

As "information discovery" commences, whom should I talk to and what should I be looking for?

Talk to the customer and look for a bounded description of *software scope*. The *customer* has a problem that may be amenable to a computer-based solution. You (the developer) respond to the customer's request for help. Communication has begun. But the road from communication to understanding is often full of potholes.

How can we initiate the process of information discovery and achieve a bounded description of a project?

The most commonly used technique to bridge the communication gap between the customer and the developer and to get the communication process started is to conduct a preliminary meeting or interview. The first meeting between a software engineer (the analyst) and the customer can be likened to the awkwardness of a first date between two adolescents. Neither person knows what to say or ask; both are worried that what they do say will be misinterpreted; both are thinking about where it might lead (both likely have radically different expectations here); and both want to get the thing over with, but at the same time want it to be a success.

Yet, communication must be initiated. Gause and Weinberg [2] suggest that the analyst start by asking *context-free questions*—that is, a set of questions that will lead to a basic understanding of the problem, the people who want a solution, the nature of the solution that is desired, and the effectiveness of the first encounter itself.

What "context-free" questions should we ask?

The first set of context-free questions focuses on the customer, the overall goals and benefits. For example, you might ask the following:

- Who is behind the request for this work?
- Who will use the solution?
- What will be the economic benefit of a successful solution?
- Is there another source for the solution?

The next set of questions enables you to gain a better understanding of the problem and the customer to voice perceptions about a solution:

- How would you [the customer] characterize "good" output that would be generated by a successful solution?
- What problem(s) will this solution address?
- Can you show me (or describe) the environment in which the solution will be used?
- Are there special performance issues or constraints that will affect the way the solution is approached?

The final set of questions focuses on the effectiveness of the meeting. Gause and Weinberg [2] call these "metaquestions" and propose the following (abbreviated) list:

- Are you the right person to answer these questions? Are your answers "official"?
- Are my questions relevant to the problem that you have?

- Am I asking too many questions?
- Is there anyone else who can provide additional information?
- Is there anything else that I should be asking you?

These questions (and others) will help to "break the ice" and initiate the communication that is essential to establish the scope of the project. But a question and answer meeting format is not an approach that has been overwhelmingly successful. In fact, the Q&A session should be used for the first encounter only and then be replaced by a meeting format that combines elements of problem solving, negotiation, and specification.

The answers to the questions that you've suggested are important, but they tell us little about the scope of the project. How do we get specific information that will enable us to proceed with planning?

Customers and software engineers often have an unconscious "us and them" mind-set. Rather than working as a team to identify and refine requirements, each constituency defines its own "territory" and communicates through a series of memos, formal position papers, documents, and question/answer sessions. History has shown that this approach doesn't work very well. Misunderstandings abound, important information is omitted, and a successful working relationship is never established.

It is with these problems in mind that a number of independent investigators have developed a team-oriented approach to requirements gathering that can be applied to help establish the scope of a project.[2] Called *facilitated application specification techniques* (FAST), this approach encourages the creation of a joint team of customers and developers who work together to identify the problem, propose elements of the solution, negotiate different approaches, and specify a preliminary set of requirements [3].

Is there a single approach to FAST or does every organization customize the technique to its own needs? Why not describe a scenario?

Many different approaches to FAST have been proposed.[3] Each makes

---

[2]It should be noted that these techniques are also applied as a first step in requirements analysis.

[3]Two of the more popular approaches to FAST are *Joint Application Development* (JAD), developed by IBM, and *The METHOD*, developed by Performance Resources, Inc., Falls Church, VA.

use of a slightly different scenario, but all apply some variation of the following approach:

- A meeting is conducted at a neutral site and attended by both developers and customers.
- Rules for preparation and participation are established.
- An agenda is suggested that is formal enough to cover all important points but informal enough to encourage the free flow of ideas.
- A "facilitator" (can be a customer, a developer, or an outsider) controls the meeting.
- A "definition mechanism" (can be worksheets, flip charts, wall stickers, or wallboard) is used.
- The goal is to identify the problem, propose elements of the solution, negotiate different approaches, and specify a preliminary set of solution requirements in an atmosphere that is conducive to the accomplishment of the goal.

How do the participants prepare for the FAST meeting?

An initial meeting between the developer and the customer occurs, and "context-free" questions and answers help to establish the scope of the problem and the overall perception of a solution. Out of this initial meeting, the developer and customer write a one- or two-page "product request." A meeting place, time, and date for FAST are selected, and a *facilitator* is chosen. Attendees from both the development and customer organizations are invited to attend. The product request is distributed to all attendees before the meeting date.

While reviewing the request in the days before the meeting, each FAST attendee is asked to make a list of *objects* (e.g., data files, input devices, graphical displays, reports) that are part of the environment that surrounds the system, other objects that are to be produced by the system, and objects that are used by the system to perform its functions. In addition, each attendee is asked to make another list of *operations* (processes or functions) that manipulate or interact with the objects. Finally, lists of *constraints* (e.g., cost, size, weight) and *performance criteria* (e.g., speed, accuracy) are also developed. The attendees are informed that the lists are not expected to be exhaustive, but are expected to reflect each person's perspective of the system.

What are the logistics of the FAST meeting?

As the meeting begins, the first topic of discussion is the need and justification for the new product—everyone should agree that the product development (or acquisition) is justified. Once agreement has been established, all participants present their lists for critique and discussion. The lists can be pinned to the walls of the room using large sheets of paper, stuck to the walls using adhesive-backed sheets, or written on a wallboard. Ideally, each list entry should be capable of being manipulated separately so that lists can be combined, entries can be deleted, and additions can be made. At this stage, critique and debate are strictly prohibited.

After individual lists are presented in one topic area, a combined list is created by the group. The combined list eliminates redundant entries and adds any new ideas that come up during the presentation, but does not delete anything. After combined lists for all topic areas have been created, discussion—coordinated by the facilitator—ensues. The combined list is shortened, lengthened, or reworded to properly reflect the product or system to be developed. The objective is to develop a consensus list of data objects, process operations, design and interface constraints, and performance requirements. The lists are then set aside for later action.

Once the consensus lists have been completed, the team is divided into smaller subteams; each works to develop a *minispecification* for one or more entries on each of the lists. The minispecification is an elaboration of the word or phrase contained in a list.

Each subteam then presents each of its minispecs to all FAST attendees for discussion. Additions, deletions, and further elaboration are made. In some cases, the development of minispecs will uncover new objects, operations, constraints, or performance requirements that will be added to the original lists. During all discussions, the team may raise issues that cannot be resolved during the meeting. An issues list is maintained so that these ideas can be acted on later.

Am I correct in assuming that the minispecs bound software function and performance and identify constraints? Will these minispecs form the basis from which project estimates are made?

The minispecs provide an excellent foundation for estimation. The information generated as part of the FAST meeting not only bounds the software project but also serves as a first step for software requirements analysis—the first technical activity in the software engineering process.

So the work done during the FAST meeting can be extended into the software engineering process itself?

The original minispecs can be "fleshed out" at the beginning of requirements analysis. They can serve as the basis for an analysis modeling method (Chapter 17). The minispecs are coupled with a list of validation criteria for the product or system and graphical modeling created with a CASE tool. Using this information, a software engineer can create a complete draft specification using inputs from the FAST meeting as an important information source.

O.K., we've bounded the project to the extent necessary to formulate estimates. What's next?

The second task of software planning is estimation of resources required to accomplish the software development effort. Figure 10.1 illustrates development resources as a pyramid. At the foundation, tools—hardware and software—must exist to support the development effort. At a higher level, the primary resource—people—is always required. Each resource is specified with four characteristics: description of the resource, a statement of availability, chronological time that the resource will be required, and duration of time that the resource will be applied. The last two characteristics can be viewed as a *time window*. Availability of the resource for a specified window must be established at the earliest practical time.

What do I specify under "human resources" in a project plan?

The planner begins by evaluating scope and selecting the skills required to complete development. Both organizational position (e.g., manager, senior software engineer) and specialty (e.g., telecommunications, database, graphics) are specified. For relatively small projects (one person-year or less) a single individual may perform all software engineering steps, consulting with specialists as required.

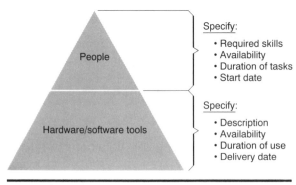

Figure 10.1   Resources.

The number of people required for a software project can be determined only after an estimate of development effort (e.g., person-months or person-years) is made. Techniques for estimating effort are discussed later in this chapter.

In our company each project team works within a different hardware environment. How do we plan for hardware resources when this is the case?

Three hardware categories should be considered during software project planning: the development system, the target machine, and other hardware elements of the new system. The *development system* (also called the *host system*) is a computer and related peripherals that will be used during the software development. For example, a 32-bit computer may serve as the development system for a 16-bit microprocessor—the *target machine*—on which the software will eventually be executed. The development system is used because it can support multiple users,[4] maintain large volumes of information that can be shared by software development team members, and support a rich assortment of software tools. Because most development organizations have multiple constituencies that require development system access, the planner must carefully prescribe the time window required and verify that the resource will be available.

Other hardware elements of the computer-based system may be specified as resources for software development. For example, software for a numerical control (NC) used on a class of machine tools may require a specific machine tool (e.g., an NC lathe) as part of the validation test step; a software project for automated typesetting may need a phototypesetter at some point during development. Each hardware element must be specified by the planner.

I keep hearing about software development environments that include both hardware and software tools. What are the planning issues involved?

Just as we use hardware as a tool to build new hardware, we use software to aid in the development of new software. Today, software engineers use a tool set that is analogous in many ways to the computer-aided design and computer-aided engineering (CAD/CAE) tools used

---

[4]Networked engineering workstations are often used as a development system, even though each workstation supports only a single developer.

by hardware engineers. The tool set, called *computer-aided software engineering* (CASE), is described in detail in Chapter 18.

Is there anything else that we need to consider before developing project estimates? Are there software resources that should be considered in addition to CASE?

Any discussion of the software resource would be incomplete without recognition of *reusability*—that is, the creation and reuse of software building blocks [4, 5]. There is little doubt that the creation and use of reusable software components can have a profound impact on time to delivery and product quality. But to achieve improved productivity and quality, such building blocks must be catalogued for easy reference, standardized for easy application, and validated for easy integration.

Ideally, domain-specific software building blocks[5] would be available to allow construction of large packages with minimum "from scratch" development. Unfortunately, we have not as yet achieved this ideal. Libraries of reusable software do exist for commercial applications, systems and real-time work, and engineering and scientific problems. However, few systematic techniques exist for making additions to a library, standard interfaces for reusable software are difficult to enforce, quality and maintainability issues remain unresolved, and last, the developer is often unaware that appropriate software building blocks even exist!

Let's assume that I want to specify reusable program components as a resource. Is there anything special that needs to be considered?

Two "rules" should be considered by the software planner when reusable software is specified as a resource:

1. If a library of software components meets requirements, acquire it. The cost for acquisition of existing software will almost always be less than the cost to develop equivalent software.

2. If an existing software component library requires "some modification" before it can be properly integrated within the system to be

---

[5]Reusable software components that have been developed for a specific application area. Generic examples include building blocks for graphic user interfaces, device drivers, and mathematical computation. Application-domain-specific examples would include banking applications, medical instrumentation, and factory automation, among many application areas.

built or modified, proceed carefully. The cost to modify existing software can sometimes be greater than the cost to develop equivalent software.

Ironically, software resources are often neglected during planning, only to become a paramount concern during the development phase of the software engineering process. It is far better to specify software resource requirements early. In this way technical evaluation of alternatives can be conducted and timely acquisition can occur.

I realize that it's important to define the types of resources that we'll need to use for a successful project, but aren't you putting the cart before the horse? Shouldn't we first estimate the dollars, person-months, and calendar time that the project will require?

It is true that quantitative estimates of dollars, person-months, and calendar time are absolutely essential at the start of project planning. But in the real world, budgets and deadlines may be driven by outside business concerns and defined with little input from the software engineering organization.[6] In effect, the "estimate" that you make serves as nothing more than a "sanity check" on predefined delivery dates, budgets, and human constraints.

If budgets and schedules are often defined in advance, why should I bother spending time and energy developing systematic estimates?

In a recent discussion, conducted at an industry conference, of why major projects fall behind schedule, a panel of experts developed a list of common causes. Heading the list was *unrealistic project deadlines prescribed by business management.*

Aggressive scheduling is to be expected in the current industry marketplace, but unrealistic (insane?) scheduling serves no one's purposes. It fosters sloppy practices, thereby resulting in low quality, frustrates management and customers whose expectations have been set artificially high, and creates resentment, low morale, and eventual burnout among competent staff members who work too many hours

---

[6]I do *not* endorse this approach and believe that it is the cause of many problems. In theory, software project budgets and schedules should never be established without input from the development organization. But real life doesn't always mirror theory, and it is unrealistic to discuss estimation without stating the situation as it really exists in many companies.

over too long a period of time in a futile attempt to fit more person-days into an ever-shrinking calendar.

For these reasons, you should estimate even when deadlines and budgets have been prescribed in advance so that predefined dates and dollars can be validated against a realistic appraisal of what the project will require. If your sanity check registers insane budgetary and delivery constraints, then immediate action (in the form of project meetings and compromise) must be undertaken. The estimates that you develop will serve as the basis for your arguments at these project meetings.

But my estimates are just that—estimates. I certainly can't guarantee that they are accurate, can I?

Software cost and effort estimation will never be an exact science. Too many variables—human, technical, environmental, economic, political—can affect the ultimate cost of software and effort applied to develop it. However, software project estimation can be transformed from a black art into a series of systematic steps that provides estimates with acceptable risk and a surprisingly high degree of accuracy.

To achieve reliable cost and effort estimates, a number of options arise:

1. Delay estimation until late in the project. (Obviously, we can achieve 100 percent accurate estimates after the project is complete!)

2. Use relatively simple "decomposition techniques" to generate project cost and effort estimates.

3. Develop an empirical model for software cost and effort.

4. Acquire one or more automated estimation tools.

Unfortunately, the first option, however attractive, is not practical. Cost estimates must be provided up front. However, we should recognize that the longer we wait, the more we know, and the more we know, the less likely we are to make serious errors in our estimates.[7]

The remaining three options are viable approaches to software project estimation. Ideally, the techniques noted for each option should be ap-

---

[7]A spiral model (evolutionary) paradigm for software engineering, discussed in Chapter 2 and later in Chapter 16, proposes that project estimates be recomputed regularly (as more information becomes known). This represents an acceptable compromise between the school of thought that demands instant estimates (with little information) and the technical reality that recognizes that the longer we wait to estimate, the more accurate our estimates will be.

plied in tandem, each used as a cross-check for the others. *Decomposition techniques* take a "divide and conquer" approach to software project estimation. By decomposing a project into major functions and related software engineering tasks, cost and effort estimation can be performed in a stepwise fashion. *Empirical estimation models* can be used to complement decomposition techniques and offer a potentially valuable estimation approach in their own right. A model is based on experience (historical data) and takes the form $d = f(v_i)$, where d is one of a number of estimated values (e.g., effort, cost, project duration) and v_i are selected independent parameters (e.g., estimated LOC or FP). *Automated estimation tools* implement one or more decomposition techniques or empirical models. When combined with an interactive human–machine interface, automated tools provide an attractive option for estimating. In such systems, the characteristics of the development organization (e.g., experience, environment) and the software to be developed are described. Cost and effort estimates are derived from these data.

Each software cost estimation option is only as good as the historical data used to seed the estimate. If no historical data exist, estimates rest on a very shaky foundation. This is one of the primary arguments for the collection of software metrics data (Chapter 3).

So how do I begin? What are the first things that need to be done to develop meaningful software project estimates?

Humans have developed a natural approach to problem solving: If the problem to be solved is too complicated, we tend to subdivide it until manageable problems are encountered. We then solve each individually and hope that solutions can be combined to form a whole.

Software project estimation is a form of problem solving, and in most cases, the problem to be solved (i.e., developing a cost and effort estimate for a software project) is too complex to be considered in one piece. For this reason, we decompose the problem, recharacterizing it as a set of smaller (and, hopefully, more manageable) problems.

The statement of software scope provides us with an overview of software requirements, but what is it that we decompose?

In Chapter 3, lines of code (LOC) and function points (FP) were described as normalization data from which productivity metrics can be computed. LOC and FP data are used in two ways during software project estimation: (1) as an *estimation variable* that is used to "size" each element of the software and (2) as *baseline metrics* collected from past projects and used in conjunction with estimation variables to develop cost and effort projections.

LOC and FP estimation are distinct estimation techniques. Yet, both have a number of characteristics in common. The project planner begins with a bounded statement of software scope and from this statement attempts to decompose software into small subfunctions that can each be estimated individually. LOC or FP (the estimation variable) is then estimated for each subfunction. Baseline productivity metrics [e.g., LOC/pm (person-month) or FP/pm] are then applied to the appropriate estimation variable and cost or effort for the subfunction is derived. Subfunction estimates are combined to produce an overall estimate for the entire project.

So what you're saying is that we decompose the software scope functionally and then estimate LOC or FP for each decomposed subfunction?

Yes, but the LOC and FP estimation techniques differ in the level of detail required for decomposition. When LOC is used as the estimation variable, functional decomposition is absolutely essential and is often taken to considerable levels of detail. Because the data required to estimate function points are more macroscopic, the level of decomposition used when FP is the estimation variable is considerably less detailed. It should also be noted that LOC is estimated directly, while FP is determined indirectly by estimating the number of inputs, outputs, data files, inquiries, and external interfaces, as well as the 14 *complexity adjustment values* described in Chapter 3.

Is it realistic to expect a planner to come up with a single number estimate of, say, LOC for a system subfunction? Wouldn't many people feel uncomfortable because of the uncertainty?

Regardless of the estimation variable that is used, the project planner typically provides a range of values for each decomposed function, rather than a single value. Using historical data or (when all else fails) intuition, the planner estimates an optimistic, most likely, and pessimistic LOC or FP value for each function. An implicit indication of the degree of uncertainty is provided when a range of values is specified.

The *expected value* for LOC or FP is then computed. The expected value for the estimation variable E can be computed as a weighted average of the optimistic a, most likely m, and pessimistic b LOC or FP estimates. For example,

$$E = \frac{a + 4m + b}{6}$$

gives heaviest credence to the "most likely" estimate. We assume that there is a very small probability that the actual LOC or FP result will fall outside the optimistic or pessimistic estimates.

Once a value for LOC or FP is estimated, what do we do with it?

Once the expected value for the estimation variable has been determined, historical LOC or FP productivity data are applied. At this stage, the planner can use one of two different approaches.

1. The total estimation variable value for all subfunctions can be multiplied by the average productivity metric corresponding to that estimation variable. For example, if we assume that 310 FP are estimated in total and that average FP productivity based on past projects is 5.5 FP/pm, then the overall effort for the project is estimated to be

$$\text{Effort (pm)} = \frac{310}{5.5} = 56 \text{ pm}$$

2. The estimation variable value for each subfunction can be multiplied by an *adjusted productivity value* that is based on the perceived level of complexity of the subfunction. For functions of average complexity, the average productivity metric is used. However, the average productivity metric is adjusted up or down (somewhat subjectively) according to whether the complexity is higher or lower than average for a particular subfunction. For example, if average productivity is 490 LOC/pm, subfunctions that are considerably more complex than average might reflect an estimated productivity of only 300 LOC/pm and simple functions, 650 LOC/pm.

It is important to note that average productivity metrics should be corrected to reflect inflationary effects, increased project complexity, new people, or other development characteristics.

I've derived an estimate using the decomposition approach and historical LOC or FP data. Is it correct?

The only reasonable answer to your question is: "We can't be sure." Any estimation technique, no matter how sophisticated, must be cross-checked with another approach. Even then, common sense and experience must prevail.

Before we consider another estimation approach, can you provide a detailed example of estimation using the decomposition approach we've just discussed?

Let's consider a software package to be developed for a computer-aided design (CAD) application. The results of FAST meetings indicate that the software is to execute on an engineering workstation and must interface with various computer graphics peripherals including a mouse, a digitizer, high-resolution color display, and a laser printer.

For the purposes of this example, LOC will be used as the estimation variable. It should be noted, however, that FP could also be used and would require estimates of the information domain values discussed in Chapter 3.

A preliminary statement of software scope can be developed:

> The CAD software will accept two- and three-dimensional geometric data from an engineer. The engineer will interact and control the CAD system through a user interface that will exhibit characteristics of good human–machine interface design. All geometric data and other supporting information will be maintained in a CAD database. Design analysis modules will be developed to produce required output which will be displayed on a variety of graphics devices. The software will be designed to control and interact with peripheral devices that include a mouse, a digitizer, a laser printer, and a plotter.

This statement of scope is preliminary—it is *not* bounded. Every sentence would have to be expanded to provide concrete detail and quantitative bounding. For example, before estimation can begin, the planner must determine what "characteristics of good human–machine interface design" means or what the size and sophistication of the "CAD database" is to be.

For our purposes, we assume that further refinement has occurred and that the following major software functions are identified:

- User interface and control facility (UICF)
- Two-dimensional geometric analysis (2DGA)
- Three-dimensional geometric analysis (3DGA)
- Database management (DBM)
- Computer graphics display facility (CGDF)
- Peripheral control (PC)
- Design analysis modules (DAMs)

Following the decomposition technique, an estimation table, shown in Table 10.1, is developed. A range of LOC estimates is developed. Viewing the first three columns of the table, it can be seen that the planner is fairly certain of LOC required for the peripheral control function (only 450 lines of code separate optimistic and pessimistic estimates). On the other hand, the 3DGA function is a relative unknown as indicated by the 4000-LOC difference between optimistic and pessimistic values.

Calculations for expected value are performed for each function and placed in the fourth column of the table (Table 10.2). By summing vertically in the expected value column, an estimate of 33,360 lines of code is established for the CAD system.[8]

The remainder of the estimation table required for the decomposition technique is shown in Table 10.3. Productivity metrics (derived from a historical baseline) are acquired for $/LOC and LOC/person-month. In this case the planner uses different values of productivity metrics for each function according to the degree of complexity. Values contained in the cost and months columns of the table are determined by taking the product of expected LOC and $/LOC and LOC/person-month, respectively.

From the estimation table, the total estimated project cost is $657,000 and the estimated effort is 145 person-months. Later, we will see how the estimated effort can be used with an empirical model to derive an estimate for project duration (in chronological months).

You mentioned that it is important to cross-check an estimate using another approach. What estimation approach should I use in addition to LOC or FP decomposition?

Effort estimation is an excellent complement to LOC or FP decomposition and is widely used in the project management community. Like the estimation approach discussed earlier, effort estimation is also a decomposition approach, but the estimation variable focuses on the process rather than the product. That is, you will estimate the amount of human effort required to accomplish process tasks, rather than the number of LOC or FP associated with the product (software).

Like the LOC or FP technique, effort estimation begins with a delineation of software functions obtained from the project scope. A series of software engineering tasks—requirements analysis, design, code, and test—must be performed for each function. Functions and

---

[8]It should be noted that the estimation precision implied by the three low-order significant digits (i.e., 360) is not attainable. Rounding off to the nearest 1000 LOC would be far more realistic. Low-order digits are maintained for calculation accuracy only.

TABLE 10.1 Estimation Table—Initial Estimate

Function	Optimistic	Most likely	Pessimistic	Expected	$/line	Lines/ month	Cost	Months
User interface control	1800	2400	2650					
2D geometric analysis	4100	5200	7400					
3D geometric analysis	4600	6900	8600					
Data structure management	2950	3400	3600					
Computer graphics display	4050	4900	6200					
Peripheral control	2000	2100	2450					
Design analysis	6600	8500	9800					

TABLE 10.2 Estimation Table—Computed Result

Function	Optimistic	Most likely	Pessimistic	Expected	$/line	Lines/ month	Cost	Months
User interface control	1800	2400	2650	2340				
2D geometric analysis	4100	5200	7400	5380				
3D geometric analysis	4600	6900	8600	6800				
Data structure management	2950	3400	3600	3350				
Computer graphics display	4050	4900	6200	4950				
Peripheral control	2000	2100	2450	2140				
Design analysis	6600	8500	9800	8400				
Total				33,360				

TABLE 10.3 Completed Estimation Table.

Function	Optimistic	Most likely	Pessimistic	Expected	$/line	Lines/month	Cost	Months
User interface control	1800	2400	2650	2340	14	315	32,760	7.4
2D geometric analysis	4100	5200	7400	5380	20	220	107,600	24.4
3D geometric analysis	4600	6900	8600	6800	20	220	136,000	30.9
Data structure management	2950	3400	3600	3350	18	240	60,300	13.9
Computer graphics display	4050	4900	6200	4950	22	200	108,900	24.7
Peripheral control	2000	2100	2450	2140	28	140	59,920	15.2
Design analysis	6600	8500	9800	8400	18	300	151,200	28.0
				33,360			$656,680	144.5

Estimated LOC — Estimated project cost, $ — Estimated effort required, pm

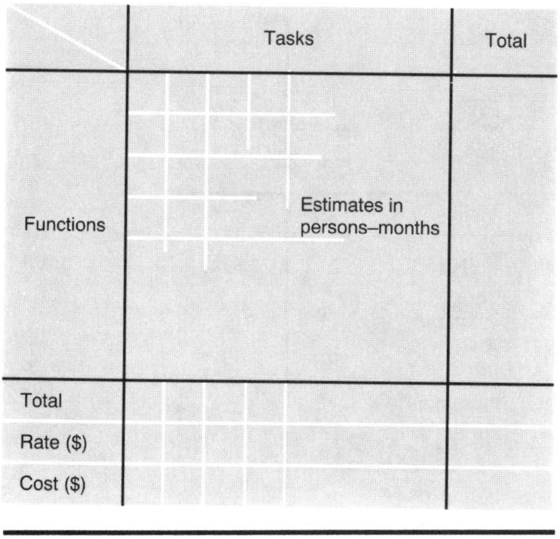

Figure 10.2   Developing an effort matrix.

related software engineering tasks may be represented as part of a table illustrated in Figure 10.2.

The planner estimates the effort (e.g., person-months) that will be required to accomplish each software engineering task for each software function. These data constitute the central matrix of the table in Figure 10.2. Labor rates (i.e., cost/unit effort) are applied to each of the software engineering tasks. It is very likely that the labor rate will vary for each task. Senior staff are heavily involved in requirements analysis and early design tasks; junior staff (who are inherently less costly) are involved in later design tasks, code, and early testing.

Costs and effort for each function and software engineering task are computed as the last step. If effort estimation is performed independently of LOC or FP estimation, we now have two estimates for cost and effort that may be compared and reconciled. If both sets of estimates show reasonable agreement, there is good reason to believe that the estimates are reliable. If, on the other hand, the results of these decomposition techniques show little agreement, further investigation and analysis must be conducted.

Can you provide an example of effort estimation and show how it complements the LOC or FP approach?

To illustrate the use of effort estimation, we again consider the CAD software introduced earlier. The system configuration and all software functions remain unchanged and are indicated by project scope.

Tasks / Functions	Requirements analysis	Design	Code	Test	Total
UICF	1.0	2.0	0.5	3.5	7
2DGA	2.0	10.0	4.5	9.5	26
3DGA	2.5	12.0	6.0	11.0	31.5
DSM	2.0	6.0	3.0	4.0	15
CGDF	1.5	11.0	4.0	10.5	27
PCF	1.5	6	3.5	5	16
DAM	4	14	5	7	30
Total*	14.5	61	26.5	50.5	152.5
Rate ($)	5200	4800	4250	4500	
Cost ($)	75,400	292,800	112,625	227,250	708,075

Estimated effort for all tasks

Estimated cost for all tasks

*All estimates are in person–months except where otherwise noted.

Figure 10.3   Effort estimation table.

Referring to the completed effort estimation table shown in Figure 10.3, estimates of effort (in person-months) for each software engineering task are provided for each CAD software function (abbreviated for brevity). Horizontal and vertical totals provide an indication of effort required. It should be noted that 75 person-months are expended on "front end" development tasks (requirements analysis and design) indicating the relative importance of this work.

Labor rates are associated with each software engineering task and entered in the "Rate($)" row of the table. These data reflect "burdened" labor costs, that is, labor costs that include company overhead. In this example it is assumed that labor costs for requirements analysis ($5200/person-month) will be 22 percent greater than costs for code and unit test. Unlike software productivity data, average labor rates can be accurately predicted in a software development organization.

Total estimated cost and effort for the CAD software are $708,000 and 153 person-months, respectively. Comparing these values to data derived using the LOC technique, a cost variance of 7 percent and effort variance of 5 percent are found. We have achieved extremely close agreement.

What happens when agreement between estimates is poor?

The answer to this question requires a reevaluation of information used to make the estimates. Widely divergent estimates can often be traced to one of two causes:

1. The scope of the project is not adequately understood or has been misinterpreted by the planner.

2. Productivity data (e.g., LOC/pm or FP/pm) is inappropriate for the application, is obsolete (in that it no longer accurately reflects the software development organization), or has been misapplied.

The planner must determine the cause of divergence and reconcile the estimates.

But how close should estimates be before they can be considered "reconciled"?

In general, estimation accuracy of plus or minus 20 percent is a reasonable expectation during early stages of project planning if software scope is defined in an unambiguous manner and historical data are representative of the application and the people who are doing the work. If different estimation techniques fall within 20 percent of one another, they may be considered "reconciled."

It would seem that historical data could be analyzed and that a mathematical model for software estimation could be derived. Has anyone done this?

Estimation models for computer software do exist and use empirically derived formulae to generate effort and time estimates. The empirical data that support most models are derived from a limited sample of projects. For this reason, no estimation model is appropriate for all classes of software and in all development environments. Therefore, the results obtained from such models must be used judiciously.

Can you describe a practical estimation model that we could evaluate for use in our organization?

In his book on software engineering economics, Barry Boehm [6] introduces a hierarchy of software estimation models bearing the name

COCOMO, for *COnstructive COst MOdel.* Boehm's hierarchy of models takes the following form:

Model 1: The basic COCOMO model is a static, single-valued model that computes software development effort (and cost) as a function of program size expressed in estimated lines of code (LOC).

Model 2: The intermediate COCOMO model computes software development effort as a function of program size and a set of "cost drivers" that include subjective assessments of product, hardware, personnel, and project attributes.

Model 3: The advanced COCOMO model incorporates all characteristics of the intermediate version with an assessment of the cost driver's impact on each step (analysis, design, etc.) of the software engineering process.

To illustrate the COCOMO model, we present an overview of the basic and intermediate versions. For a more detailed discussion, you should study reference [6].

The COCOMO models are defined for three classes of software projects. Using Boehm's terminology, these are (1) *organic mode*—relatively small, simple software projects in which small teams with good application experience work to a set of less-than-rigid requirements (e.g., a thermal analysis program developed for a heat-transfer group); (2) *semidetached mode*—an intermediate (in size and complexity) software project in which teams with mixed experience levels must meet a mix of rigid and less-than-rigid requirements (e.g., a transaction processing system with fixed requirements for terminal hardware and database software); (3) *embedded mode*—a software project that must be developed within a set of tight hardware, software, and operational constraints (e.g., flight-control software for aircraft).

The basic COCOMO equations take the form

$$E = a_b(\text{KLOC})^{b_b}$$

$$D = c_b E^{d_b}$$

where E is the effort applied in person-months, D is the development time in chronological months, and KLOC is the estimated number of delivered lines of code for the project (expressed in thousands). The coefficients a_b and c_b and the exponents b_b and d_b are given in Table 10.4.

The basic model is extended to consider a set of "cost driver attributes" [6] that can be grouped into four major categories:

1. Product attributes
   a. Required software reliability

TABLE 10.4   Basic COCOMO

Software project	a_b	b_b	c_b	d_b
Organic	2.4	1.05	2.5	0.38
Semidetached	3.0	1.12	2.5	0.35
Embedded	3.6	1.20	2.5	0.32

    b. Size of application database
    c. Complexity of the product
2. Hardware attributes
    a. Run-time performance constraints
    b. Memory constraints
    c. Volatility of the virtual machine environment
    d. Required turnaround time
3. Personnel attributes
    a. Analyst capability
    b. Software engineer capability
    c. Applications experience
    d. Virtual machine experience
    e. Programming language experience
4. Project attributes
    a. Use of software tools
    b. Application of software engineering methods
    c. Required development schedule

Each of the 15 attributes is rated on a six-point scale that ranges from "very low" to "extra high" (in importance or value). On the basis of the rating, an effort multiplier is determined from tables published by Boehm [6], and the product of all effort multipliers results in an *effort adjustment factor* (EAF). Typical values for EAF range from 0.9 to 1.4. The intermediate COCOMO model takes the form

$$E = a_i(\text{KLOC})^{b_i} \times \text{EAF}$$

where E is the effort applied in person-months and KLOC is the estimated number of delivered lines of code (expressed in thousands) for the project. The coefficient a_i and the exponent b_i are defined in Boehm [6].

COCOMO represents a comprehensive empirical model for software estimation. However, Boehm's own comments [6] about COCOMO (and by extension all models) should be heeded:

> Today, a software cost estimation model is doing well if it can estimate software development costs within 20% of actual costs, 70% of the time, and on its own turf (that is, within the class of projects to which it has

been calibrated...). This is not as precise as we might like, but it is accurate enough to provide a good deal of help in software engineering economic analysis and decision making.

How is the COCOMO model applied in practice?

To illustrate the use of the COCOMO model, we apply the basic model to the CAD software example described earlier in this chapter. Using the LOC estimate developed in Table 10.3 and the coefficients noted in Table 10.4, we use the semidetached model to get

$$E = 3.0(\text{KLOC})^{1.12}$$

$$= 3.0(33.3)^{1.12}$$

$$= 152 \text{ person-months}$$

This value compares quite favorably to the estimates derived earlier in this chapter. To compute project duration, we use the effort estimate described above:

$$D = 2.5E^{0.35}$$

$$= 2.5(152)^{0.35}$$

$$= 14.5 \text{ months}$$

The value for project duration enables the planner to determine a recommended number of people N for the project:

$$N = \frac{E}{D}$$

$$= \frac{152}{14.5}$$

$$\sim 11 \text{ people}$$

In reality, the planner may decide to use only four people and extend the project duration accordingly.

What CASE tools are available to assist the project manager during the estimation process?

The decomposition techniques and empirical estimation models described earlier form the basis for a collection of CASE tools that have been designed to assist in the estimation process. These automated estimation tools allow the planner to estimate cost and effort and to perform "what if" analyses for important project variables such as delivery date or staffing. Although many automated estimation tools exist, all exhibit the same general characteristics and all require one or more of the following data categories:

1. A quantitative estimate of project size (e.g., LOC) or functionality (function-point data).
2. Qualitative project characteristics such as complexity, required reliability, or business criticality.
3. Some description of the development staff and/or development environment.

From these data, the model implemented by the automated estimation tool provides estimates of effort required to complete the project, costs, staff loading, and in some cases, development schedule and associated risk.

BYL (Before You Leap) developed by the Gordon Group and *DECPlan* developed by Digital Equipment Corporation are automated estimation tools that are based on the COCOMO model. Each of these tools requires the user to provide preliminary LOC estimates. These estimates are categorized by programming language and type (i.e., adapted code, reused code, new code). The user also specifies values for the cost driver attributes described earlier.

ESTIMACS [7] is a "macroestimation model" that uses a function-point estimation method enhanced to accommodate a variety of project and personnel factors. The ESTIMACS tool contains a set of models that enables the planner to estimate (1) system development effort, (2) staff and cost, (3) hardware configuration, (4) risk, and (5) the effects of "development portfolio."

SPQR/20, developed by Software Productivity Research, Inc. and based on work by Jones [8, 9], has the user complete a simple set of multiple-choice questions that addresses: project type (e.g., new program, maintenance), project scope (e.g., prototype, reusable module), goals (e.g., minimum duration, highest quality), project class (e.g., personal program, product), application type (e.g., batch, expert system), novelty (e.g., repeat of a previous application), office facilities (e.g., open office environment, crowded bullpen), program requirements (e.g., clear, hazy), design requirements (e.g., informal design with no automation), user documentation (e.g., informal, formal), response time, staff experience, percent source code reuse, programming language, logical complexity of algorithms, and code and data complexity. Project-related cost data (e.g., length of work week, average salary) are also input.

Each of the automated estimation tools conducts a dialog with the planner, obtaining appropriate project and supporting information and producing both tabular and (in some cases) graphical output. All of the tools described above have been implemented on personal computers or engineering workstations.

An interesting comparison of some of the tools described above has been done by Martin [10]. Each tool was applied to the same project. Not surprisingly, a relatively large variation in estimated results was encountered. More importantly, the predicted values sometimes were significantly different from the actual project results. This reinforces the notion that the output of estimation tools should be used as one "data point" from which estimates are derived—not as the only source for an estimate.

You've provided some useful techniques for estimating the cost of developing new software, but what about situations where we have the option to buy or contract software?

In many software application areas, it is often more cost-effective to acquire, rather than develop, computer software. Software engineering managers are faced with a *make–buy decision* that can be further complicated by a number of acquisition options: (1) software may be purchased (or licensed) *off-the-shelf*, (2) off-the-shelf software may be purchased and then modified to meet specific needs, or (3) software may be custom-built by an outside contractor to meet the purchaser's specifications.

The steps involved in the acquisition of software are defined by the criticality of the software to be purchased and the end cost. In some cases (e.g., low-cost PC software), it is less expensive to purchase and experiment than to conduct a lengthy evaluation. For more expensive software packages, the following guidelines can be applied:

1. Develop a specification for function and performance of the desired software. Define measurable characteristics whenever possible.

2. Estimate the internal cost to develop and the delivery date.

3. Select three or four candidate software packages that best meet your specification.

4. Develop a comparison matrix that presents a head-to-head comparison of key functions. Alternatively, conduct benchmark tests to compare candidate software.

5. Evaluate each software package based on past product quality, vendor support, product direction, reputation, and so on.

6. Contact other users of the software and ask for opinions.

In the final analysis, the make–buy decision is based on the following conditions:

1. Will the delivery date of the software product be sooner than that for internally developed software?

2. Will the cost of acquisition plus the cost of customization be less than the cost of developing the software internally?

3. Will the cost of outside support (e.g., a maintenance contract) be less than the cost of internal support?

These conditions apply for each of the acquisition options noted above.

Is there a more systematic way in which we can analyze the make–buy decision?

The steps described above can be augmented using statistical techniques such as *decision tree analysis* [11]. For example, Figure 10.4 depicts a decision tree for a software-based system X. In this case, the software engineering organization can (1) build system X from scratch, (2) reuse an existing system by making modifications to it, (3) buy an available software product and modify it to meet local needs, or (4) contract the software development to an outside vendor.

If the system is to be built from scratch, there is a 70 percent probability that the job will be difficult. Using the estimation techniques discussed earlier in this chapter, the project planner projects that a difficult development effort will cost $450,000. A "simple" development effort is estimated to cost $380,000. The expected value for cost, computed along any branch of the decision tree, is

$$\text{Expected cost} = \sum_i [(\text{path probability})_i \times (\text{estimated path cost})_i]$$

where i is the decision tree path. For the "build" path

$$\text{Expected cost}_{\text{build}} = 0.30(\$380\text{K}) + 0.70(\$450\text{K}) = \$429\text{K}$$

Following other paths of the decision tree, the projected costs for reuse, purchase, and contract, under a variety of circumstances, are also shown. The expected costs for these paths are

$$\text{Expected cost}_{\text{reuse}} = 0.40(\$275\text{K}) + 0.60[0.20(\$310\text{K}) + 0.80(\$490\text{K})]$$

$$= \$382K$$

$$\text{Expected cost}_{\text{buy}} = 0.70(\$210\text{K}) + 0.30(\$400\text{K}) = \$267\text{K}$$

$$\text{Expected cost}_{\text{contract}} = 0.60(\$350\text{K}) + 0.40(\$500\text{K}) = \$410\text{K}$$

According to the probability and projected costs that have been noted in Figure 10.4, the lowest expected cost is the "buy" option.

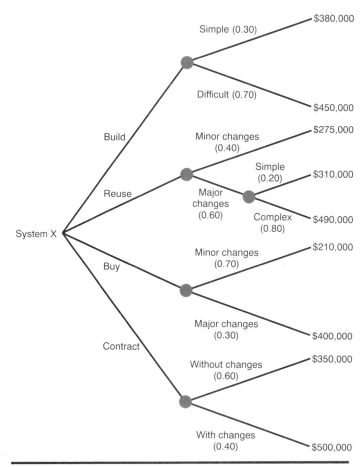

Figure 10.4   A decision tree to support the make–buy decision.

It is important to note, however, that many criteria—not just cost—must be considered during the decision-making process. Delivery and availability, experience of the developer, vendor, and/or contractor, conformance to requirements, local "politics," and the likelihood of change are but a few of the criteria that may affect the ultimate decision to build, reuse, buy, or contract.

A Manager's Checklist

As a software project planner you must estimate three things before a project begins: how long it will take, how much effort will be required, and how many people will be involved. In addition, you must predict the resources (hardware and software) that will be required and the risk involved.

To help you gain some momentum in the use of systematic estimation techniques, here are a few things you can do.

Actions

- Select a software project that was completed by some other group within your organization—one that you are unfamiliar with. Obtain a written statement of scope (if one exists) or a general description of what was built. Using the estimation techniques discussed in this chapter, generate estimates for project effort and duration. Compare these with the actual numbers. Discuss your results with the project manager for the actual project and try to understand what caused the differences.

- Create one or more spreadsheet models that implement the estimation techniques discussed in this chapter. Even if you don't have a budget to acquire estimation tools, the spreadsheet implementation will help you estimate more systematically.

Questions

- How are project budgets developed in your organization? How much input to the process does the software project manager have?

- Select five projects that have been completed recently and for which original estimates have been saved. Compare estimated to actual effort and duration. What is the average percent difference?

- Why do you believe that the differences occurred? Make a list of the primary causes.

Further Readings

Boehm's book on software engineering economics [6] presents detailed project data and provides excellent quantitative insight into the process of estimation. An excellent book by DeMarco (*Controlling Software Projects,* Yourdon Press, 1982) provides valuable insight into the management, measurement, and estimation of software projects. Londiex (*Cost Estimation for Software Development,* Addison-Wesley, 1987) is dedicated to the subject and provides a number of useful examples. Sneed (*Software Engineering Management,* Wiley, 1989) and Macro (*Software Engineering: Concepts and Management,* Prentice-Hall, 1990) consider software project estimation in considerable detail. Putnam and Myers (*Measures for Excellence,* Yourdon Press, 1992) present a detailed discussion of the software equation, another useful model for software project estimation.

Lines-of-code cost estimation is the most commonly used approach in the industry. However, the impact of the object-oriented paradigm (see Chapter 17) may invalidate some estimation models. Laranjeira ("Software Size Estimation of Object-Oriented Systems," *IEEE Trans. Software Engineering,* May 1990) explores this issue in considerable detail.

Each of the techniques described in this chapter can help us derive project duration. In theory, these techniques apply to projects of any size. Ware Myers ("Allow Plenty of Time for Large Scale Software," *IEEE Software,* July 1989) discusses the impact and accuracy of estimation techniques when they are applied to megaprojects (multi-million LOC efforts).

References

[1] Brooks, F., *The Mythical Man-Month,* Addison-Wesley, 1975.
[2] Gause, D.C., and G.M. Weinberg, *Exploring Requirements: Quality Before Design,* Dorset House, 1989.
[3] Zahniser, R.A., "Building Software in Groups," *Am. Programmer* **3** (7/8), (1990).
[4] Freeman, P., *Tutorial: Software Reusability,* IEEE Computer Society Press, 1987.
[5] Tracz, W., *Software Reuse: Emerging Technology,* IEEE Computer Society Press, 1988.
[6] Boehm, B., *Software Engineering Economics,* Prentice-Hall, 1981.
[7] Rubin, H.A., "Macro-estimation of Software Development Parameters: The Estimacs System," *Softfair Proceedings,* IEEE, July 1983, pp. 109–118.
[8] Jones, C., *Programming Productivity,* McGraw-Hill, 1986.
[9] Jones, C., *Applied Software Measurement,* McGraw-Hill, 1991.
[10] Martin, R., "Evaluation of Current Software Costing Tools," *ACM Sigsoft Notes* **13** (3), 49–51 (1988).
[11] Boehm, B., *Risk Management,* IEEE Computer Society Press, 1989.

Risk Analysis: A Project Manager's Due Diligence

In his book on risk analysis and management, Robert Charette [1] presents the following conceptual definition of risk:

> First, risk concerns future happenings. Today and yesterday are beyond active concern, as we are already reaping what was previously sowed by our past actions. The question is, can we, therefore, by changing our actions today, create an opportunity for a different and hopefully better situation for ourselves tomorrow. This means, second, that risk involves change, such as in changes of mind, opinion, actions, or places.... [Third,] risk involves choice, and the uncertainty that choice itself entails. Thus paradoxically, risk, like death and taxes, is one of the few certainties of life.

When risk is considered in the context of software engineering, Charette's three conceptual underpinnings are always in evidence. The future is our concern—what risks might cause the software project to go awry? Change is our concern—how will changes in customer requirements, development technologies, target computers, and all other entities connected to the project affect timeliness and overall success? Finally, we must grapple with choices—what methods and tools should we use, how many people should be involved, how much emphasis on quality is "enough"?

Peter Drucker [2] once said, "While it is futile to try to eliminate risk, and questionable to try to minimize it, it is essential that the risks taken be the right risks." Before we can identify the "right risks" to be taken during a software project, it is important to identify all risks that are obvious to both managers and practitioners.

What types of risks are encountered in a software project? Is there a way that we can categorize them?

It is possible to categorize risks in many different ways. At a macroscopic level, project risks, technical risks, and business risks can be defined.[1] *Project risks* identify potential budgetary, schedule, personnel (staffing and organization), resource, customer, and requirements problems and their impact on the software project. In Chapter 10, project complexity, size, and structure were also defined as risk factors.

Technical risks identify potential design, implementation, interfacing, verification, and maintenance problems. In addition, specification ambiguity, technical uncertainty, technical obsolescence, and "leading edge" technology are also risk factors. Technical risks occur because the problem is harder to solve than we thought it would be.

Business risks are insidious because they can unravel the results of even the best software projects. Candidates for the top five business risks are (1) building an excellent product that no one really wants (market risk), (2) building a product that no longer fits into the overall product strategy for the company, (3) building a product that the sales force doesn't understand how to sell, (4) losing the support of senior management due to a change in focus or a change in people (management risk), and (5) losing budgetary or personnel commitment (budget risks). It is extremely important to note that simple categorization won't always work. Some risks are simply unpredictable in advance.

Another general categorization of risks has been proposed by Charette [1]. *Known risks* are those that can be uncovered after careful evaluation of the project plan, the business and technical environment in which the project is being developed, and other reliable information sources (e.g., unrealistic delivery date, lack of documented requirements or software scope, poor development environment). *Predictable risks* are extrapolated from past project experience (e.g., staff turnover, poor communication with the customer, dilution of staff effort as ongoing maintenance requests are serviced). *Unpredictable risks* are the jokers in the deck. They can and do occur, but they are extremely difficult to identify in advance.

Is there a systematic way in which project risks can be identified?

Risk identification is a systematic attempt to specify threats to the project plan (estimates, schedule, resource loading, etc.). By identify-

---

[1]It should be noted that many of the factors that constitute these risk categories are similar to the "cost driver attributes" defined for the COCOMO model (other empirical models have similar attributes) in Chapter 10. Therefore, some risks can be translated to influence project estimates directly.

ing known and predictable risks, the project manager takes a first step toward avoiding them when possible and controlling them when necessary.

You will encounter two distinct types of risks for each of the categories that have been presented already: generic risks and project-specific risks. Generic risks are a potential threat to every software project. To help you identify some of these, I'll present a few "risk-item checklists" [3] later in this chapter. Project-specific risks can only be identified by those with a clear understanding of the technology, the people, and the environment that are specific to the project at hand. To identify project specific risks, you'll have to examine the project plan and the software statement of scope and ask: "What special characteristics of this project may threaten our project plan?"

We must spend the time to identify risks systematically [4]. If you plan projects under the assumption that all will go well, you'll be far less likely to adapt when problems arise. A word to the wise.

You mentioned a "risk-item checklist" that will help us to identify generic project risks. What topics do the checklists cover?

A risk-item checklist can take a number of different forms (discussed below), but all focus on some subset of known and predictable risks in the following generic subcategories:

- *Product size:*   Risks associated with the overall size of the software to be built or modified.

- *Business impact:*   Risks associated with constraints imposed by management or the marketplace.

- *Customer characteristics:*   Risks associated with the sophistication of the customer and the developer's ability to communicate with the customer in a timely manner.

- *Process definition:*   Risks associated with the degree to which a software engineering process has been defined and is followed by the development organization.

- *Development environment:*   Risks associated with the availability and quality of the tools to be used to build the product.

- *Technology to be built:*   Risks associated with the complexity of the system to be built and the "newness" of the technology that is packaged by the system.

- *Staff size and experience:*   Risks associated with the overall technical and project experience of the software engineers who will do the work.

The risk-item checklist can be organized in different ways. Questions relevant to each of the topics noted above can be answered for each software project. The answers to these questions allow the planner to estimate the impact of risk. A different risk-item checklist format simply lists characteristics that are relevant to each generic subcategory. Finally, a set of "risk components and drivers" [5] is listed along with the probability of occurrence. Drivers for performance, support, cost, and schedule are discussed in answer to later questions.

What are the risks associated with product size?

Few experienced managers would debate the following statement: *Project risk is directly proportional to product size.* The following risk-item checklist should help you to identify generic risks associated with product size:

- Estimated size of the product in LOC or FP?
- Estimated size of product in number of programs, files, and transactions?
- Percentage of deviation in size of product from average for previous products?
- Size of database created or used by the product?
- Number of users of the product?
- Number of projected changes to the requirements for the product?
- Number of changes before delivery? After delivery?
- Amount of reused software?

In each case, the information for the product to be developed must be compared to past experience. If a large percentage deviation occurs or if numbers are similar, but past results were considerably less than satisfactory, risk is high.

What are the risks associated with business impact?

I once visited an engineering manager who had the following framed plaque on his wall: "God grant me brains to be a good project manager and the common sense to run like hell whenever marketing sets project deadlines!" The marketing department was driven by business considerations, and business considerations sometimes come into direct conflict with technical realities. The following risk-item checklist should help you to identify generic risks associated with business impact:

- Effect of this product on company revenue?
- Visibility of this product by senior management?
- Reasonableness of delivery deadline?
- Number of customers who will use this product and the consistency of their needs relative to the product?
- Number of other products or systems with which this product must be interoperable?
- Sophistication of end users?
- Amount and quality of product documentation that must be produced and delivered to the customer?
- Governmental regulatory constraints on the construction of the product?
- Costs associated with late delivery?
- Costs associated with a defective product?

Again, each response for the product to be developed must be compared to past experience. If a large percentage deviation occurs or if numbers are similar, but past results were considerably less than satisfactory, risk is high.

What are the risks associated with customer characteristics?

All customers are not created equal. Pressman and Herron [6] discuss this issue when they state:

- *Customers have different needs:* Some know what they want; others know what they don't want. Some customers are willing to sweat the details, while others are satisfied with vague promises.

- *Customers have different personalities:* Some enjoy being customers— the tension, the negotiation, the psychological rewards of a good product. Others would prefer not to be customers at all. Some will happily accept almost anything that is delivered and make the very best of a poor product. Others will complain bitterly when quality is lacking; some will show their appreciation when quality is good; a few will complain no matter what.

- *Customers also have varied associations with their suppliers:* Some know the product and producer well; others may be faceless, communicating with the producer only by written correspondence and a few hurried telephone calls.

- *Customers are often contradictory:* They want everything yesterday and for free. Often, the producer is caught among the customers' own contradictions.

A "bad" customer can have a profound impact on your ability to complete a project on time and within budget. A bad customer represents a significant threat to the project plan and a substantial risk for the project manager. The following risk item checklist should help you to identify generic risks associated with different customers:

- Have you worked with the customer in the past?
- Does the customer have a solid idea of what is required? Has the customer spent the time to write it down?
- Will the customer agree to spend time in FAST meetings (Chapter 10) to identify project scope?
- Is the customer willing to establish rapid communication links with the developer?
- Is the customer willing to participate in reviews?
- Is the customer technically sophisticated in the product area?
- Is the customer willing to let your people do their job—that is, will the customer resist looking over your shoulder during detailed technical work?
- Does the customer understand the software engineering process?

If the answer to any of these questions is "no," further investigation should be undertaken to assess risk potential.

What are the risks associated with process definition and the environment in which software is developed?

If the software engineering process is ill-defined; if analysis, design, and testing are conducted in an ad hoc fashion; or if quality is a concept that everyone agrees is important, but no one acts to achieve in any tangible way, then you've got a project that is at risk. The following questions are extracted from a workshop on the assessment of software engineering practice[2] developed by R.S. Pressman & Associates, Inc. [7]. The questions themselves have been adapted from the Software Engineering Institute (SEI) questionnaire on process assessment.

- Does your senior management support a written policy statement that defines a process for software development?

---

[2] Only a sampling of questions is presented here. For further information, contact R.S. Pressman & Associates, Inc. at (203) 795-5044.

- Has your organization developed or acquired a series of software engineering training courses for managers and technical staff?
- Are published software engineering standards provided for every software developer and software manager?
- Are specific documentation formats defined for the:

  a. project plan

  b. requirements specification

  c. design document

  d. source code

  e. test plans and procedures

  f. software problem report

  g. software change/enhancement request

- Are formal technical reviews of the requirements specification, design, and code conducted regularly?
- Are formal technical reviews of test procedures and test cases conducted regularly?
- Are the results of each formal technical review documented, including defects found and resources used?
- Is there some mechanism for ensuring that work conducted on a project conforms with software engineering standards?
- Is configuration management used to maintain consistency among system/software requirements, design, code, and test cases?
- Is a mechanism used for controlling changes to customer requirements that impact the software?
- Is there a documented statement of work, software requirements specification, and software development plan for each subcontract?
- Is a procedure followed for tracking and reviewing the performance of subcontractors?
- Are facilitated application specification techniques used to aid in communication between the customer and developer?
- Are specific methods used for software analysis?
- Do you use a specific method for data and architectural design?
- Is more than 90 percent of your code written in a high-order language?
- Are specific conventions for code documentation defined and used?
- Do you use specific methods for test case design?
- Are software tools used to support planning and tracking activities?
- Are configuration management tools used to control and track change activity throughout the software process?
- Are CASE tools used to support the software analysis and design process?
- Are CASE tools used to create software prototypes?
- Are CASE tools used to support the testing process?

- Are CASE tools used to support the production and management of documentation?
- Are quality metrics collected for all software projects?
- Are productivity metrics collected for all software projects?

If a majority of these questions[3] are answered "no," your software engineering process is weak and risk is high.

What are the risks associated with technology to be built?

There's a play on words that many technical managers use when they are asked to develop a system that pushes the state of the technology: "I'm not sure we want to be on the bleeding edge."

Pushing the limits of the technology is challenging and exciting. It's the dream of almost every technical person, because it forces practitioners to use their skills to the fullest. But it's also very risky. Murphy's law seems to hold sway in this part of the development universe, making it extremely difficult to foresee risks, much less plan for them. The following risk item checklist should help you to identify generic risks associated with the technology to be built:

- Is the technology to be built new to your organization?
- Do the customer's requirements demand the creation of new algorithms or input or output technology?
- Does the software interface with new or unproven hardware?
- Does the software to be built interface with vendor-supplied software products that are unproven?
- Does the software to be built interface with a database system whose function and performance have not been proved in this application area?
- Is a specialized user interface demanded by product requirements?
- Do requirements for the product demand the creation of program components that are unlike any previously developed by your organization? What percentage of components are new?
- Do requirements demand the use of new analysis, design, or testing methods?
- Do requirements demand the use of unconventional software devel-

---

[3]Additional discussion of these and other questions was presented in Chapter 5.

opment methods, such as formal methods, AI (artificial intelligence)-based approaches, or artificial neural networks?

- Do requirements put excessive performance constraints on the product?
- Is the customer uncertain that the functionality requested is "doable"?

If the answer to any of these questions is "yes," further investigation should be undertaken to assess risk potential.

What are the risks associated with staff size and experience?

Boehm [4] suggests the following questions to assess risks associated with staff size and experience:

- Are the best people available?
- Do the people have the right combination of skills?
- Are enough people available?
- Are staff committed for the entire duration of the project?
- Will some project staff be working only part time on this project?
- Do staff have the right expectations about the job at hand?
- Have staff received the necessary training?
- Will turnover among staff be low enough to allow continuity?

If the answer to any of these questions is "no," further investigation should be undertaken to assess risk potential.

You mentioned something earlier about risk components and drivers and their use in identifying project risks. Can you go into a bit more detail?

The U.S. Air Force [5] has written a pamphlet that contains excellent guidelines for software risk identification and abatement. The Air Force approach requires that the project manager identify the *risk drivers* that affect *software risk components*—performance, cost, support, and schedule. In the context of this discussion, the risk components are defined in the following manner:

- *Performance risk:*   The degree of uncertainty that the product will meet its requirements and be fit for its intended use.
- *Cost risk:*   The degree of uncertainty that the project budget will be maintained.

COMPONENTS / CATEGORY		PERFORMANCE	SUPPORT	COST	SCHEDULE
CATASTROPHIC	1	Failure to meet the requirement would result in mission failure		Failure results in increased costs and schedule delays with expected values in excess of $500k	
	2	Significant degradation to nonachievement of technical performance	Nonresponsive or unsupportable software	Significant financial shortages, budget overrun likely	Unachievable IOC
CRITICAL	1	Failure to meet the requirement would degrade system performance to a point where mission success is questionable		Failure results in operational delays and/or increased costs with expected value of $100K to $500K	
	2	Some reduction in technical performance	Minor delays in software modifications	Some shortage of financial resources, possible overrun	Possible slippage in IOC
MARGINAL	1	Failure to meet the requirement would result in degradation of secondary mission		Costs, impacts, and/or recoverable schedule slips with expected value of $1K to $100K	
	2	Minimal to small reduction in technical performance	Reponsive software support	Sufficient financial resources	Realistic, achievable schedule
NEGLIGIBLE	1	Failure to meet the requirement would create inconvenience or nonoperational impact		Error results in minor cost and/or schedule impact with expected value of less than $1K	
	2	No reduction in technical performance	Easily supportable software	Possible budget underrun	Early achievable IOC

Note: (1) The potential consequence of undetected software errors or faults.
(2) The potential consequence if the desired outcome is not achieved.

Figure 11.1   Impact assessment [1].

- *Support risk:*   The degree of uncertainty that the resultant software will be easy to correct, adapt, and enhance.

- *Schedule risk:*   The degree of uncertainty that the project schedule will be maintained and that the product will be delivered on time.

The impact of each risk driver on the risk component is divided into one of four impact categories—negligible, marginal, critical, and catastrophic—that are defined in Figure 11.1. The probability of occurrence for risk drivers for each risk component is then determined.

Once risks have been identified, how is the probability of their occurrence assessed?

Risk projection, also called *risk estimation,* attempts to rate each risk in two ways—the *likelihood* or probability that the risk is real and the *consequences* of the problems associated with the risk, should it occur. The project planner, along with other managers and technical staff, performs four risk projection activities [1]: (1) establish a scale that reflects the perceived likelihood of a risk, (2) delineate the consequences of the risk, (3) estimate the impact of the risk on the project and the product, and (4) note the overall accuracy of the risk projection so that there will be no misunderstandings.

A scale can be defined in either boolean, qualitative, or quantitative terms. The best approach might be to assess risk drivers on a qualitative *probability scale* that has the following values: impossible, improbable, probable, and frequent. Alternatively, the planner can estimate the mathematical probability that the risk will be realized [e.g., a probability of 0.7 to 1.0 implies a highly probable (frequent) risk].

Tables 11.1 to 11.4 provide one approach [5] for determining the impact of each risk driver on the risk components discussed earlier. The risk drivers are listed in the left-hand column of each table. Criteria for assessing the probability that the risk will occur are noted in the body of the table. For example, if the *complexity* (of requirements) risk driver in Table 11.1 is judged to be "significant or difficult to allocate," the assigned risk probability will fall between 0.7 and 1.0 (frequent). A probability of occurrence value (noted as "Value" in the table) of 3 is assigned and entered in the far-right-hand column. If desired, each of the risk drivers can be weighted to reflect importance based on a specific project and local conditions, and the entry in the far-right-hand column can be the product of the weight and the probability of occurrence value. An average value for each of the four risk components (performance, cost, support, and schedule) can then be computed.

Now that we've assigned a probability of occurrence, how are the overall consequences of the risk determined?

Three factors affect the consequences that are likely if a risk does occur: its nature, its scope, and its timing. The *nature* of the risk indicates the problems that are likely if it occurs. For example, a poorly defined external interface to customer hardware (a technical risk) will preclude early design and testing and will likely lead to system integration problems late in a project. The *scope* of a risk combines the severity (just how serious it is) with its overall distribution (how much of the project will be affected or how many customers are harmed). Finally, the *timing* of a risk considers when and for how long the impact will be felt. In most cases, a project manager might want the "bad

TABLE 11.1   Quantification of Performance Probability [5]

Performance drivers	Impossible to improbable (0.0 < P < 0.4) Value = 0 or 1	Probable (0.4 < P < 0.7) Value = 2	Frequent (0.7 < P < 1.0) Value = 3	Value
		Probability of drivers adversely affecting impact		
		Requirements		
Complexity	Simple or easily allocatable	Moderate, can be allocated	Significant or difficult to allocate	_____
Size	Small or easily broken down into work units	Medium, or can be broken down into work units	Large, cannot be broken down into work units	_____
Stability	Little or no change to established baseline	Some change in baseline expected	Rapidly changing or no baseline	_____
PDSS*	Agreed to support concept	Roles and missions issues unresolved	No support concept or major unresolved issues	_____
R&M†	Allocatable to hardware and software components	Requirements can be defined	Can only be addressed at the total system level	_____
		Constraints		
Computer resources	Mature, growth capacity within design, flexible	Available, some growth capacity	New development, no growth capacity, inflexible	_____
Personnel	Available, in place, experienced, stable	Available, but not in place, some experience	High turnover, little or no experience, not available	_____
Standards	Appropriately tailored for application	Some tailoring, all not reviewed for applicability	No tailoring, none applied to the contract	_____
GFE/GFP	Meets requirements, available	May meet requirements, uncertain availability	Incompatible with system requirements, unavailable	_____
Environment	Little or no impact on design	Some impact on design	Major impact on design	_____
Performance envelopes	Operation well within boundaries	Occasional operation at boundaries	Continuous operation at boundaries	_____
		Technology		
Language	Mature, approved HOL used	Approved or nonapproved HOL	Significant use of assembly language	_____
Hardware	Mature, available	Some development or available	Totally new development	_____
Tools	Documented, validated, in place	Available, validated, some development	Unvalidated, proprietary, major development	_____
Data rights	Fully compatible with support and follow-on	Minor incompatibilities with support and follow-on	Incompatible with support and follow-on	_____
Experience	Greater than 4 years	Less than 4 years	Little or none	_____

TABLE 11.1   Quantification of Performance Probability [5] *(Continued)*

Performance drivers	Probability of drivers adversely affecting impact			
	Impossible to improbable (0.0 < P < 0.4) Value = 0 or 1	Probable (0.4 < P < 0.7) Value = 2	Frequent (0.7 < P < 1.0) Value = 3	Value
		Development Approach		
Prototypes and reuse	Used, documented sufficiently for use	Some use and documentation	No use or no documentation	_____
Documentation	Correct and available	Some deficiencies, available	Nonexistent	_____
Environment	In place, validated, experience with use	Minor modifications, tools available	Major development effort	_____
Management approach	Existing product and process controls	Product and process controls need enhancement	Weak or nonexistent	_____
Integration	Internal and external controls in place	Internal or external controls not in place	Weak or nonexistent	_____

*PDSS—post deployment support environment.
†R&M—repair and maintenance.

news" to occur as soon as possible, but in some cases, the longer the delay, the better.

Referring to Figure 11.2, risk impact and probability have a distinct impact on management concern. A risk factor that has a high-impact weight but a very low probability of occurrence should not absorb a significant amount of management time. However, high-impact risks with moderate to high probability and low-impact risks with high probability should be carried forward into the risk analysis steps that follow.

Returning once more to the risk analysis approach proposed by the U.S. Air Force [5], the following steps are recommended to determine the overall consequences of a risk:

1. Determine the average probability of occurrence value for each risk component using Tables 11.1 through 11.4. This has already been discussed.

2. Using Figure 11.1, determine the impact assessment for each component based on the criteria shown.

3. Using Figure 11.3 (where the probability and impact have been determined in steps 1 and 2), determine the overall risk (high, moderate, low, or none) associated with the risk component.

TABLE 11.2 Quantification of Cost Probability [5]

	Probability of drivers adversely affecting impact			
Cost drivers	Impossible to improbable (0.0 < P < 0.4) Value = 0 or 1	Probable (0.4 < P < 0.7) Value = 2	Frequent (0.7 < P < 1.0) Value = 3	Value
	Requirements			
Size	Small, noncomplex, or easily decomposed	Medium, moderate, complexity, decomposable	Large, highly complex, or not decomposable	_____
Resource constraints	Little or no hardware-imposed constraints	Some hardware-imposed constraints	Significant hardware-imposed constraints	_____
Application	Non real-time, little system interdependency	Embedded, some system interdependency	Real-time embedded, strong interdependency	_____
Technology	Mature, existent, in-house experience	Existent, some in-house experience	New or new application, little experience	_____
Requirements stability	Little or no change to established baseline	Some change in baseline expected	Rapidly changing or no baseline	_____
	Personnel			
Availability	In place, little turnover expected	Available, some turnover expected	High turnover, not available	_____
Mix	Good mix of software disciplines	Some disciplines inappropriately represented	Some disciplines not represented	_____
Experience	High experience ratio	Average experience ratio	Low experience ratio	_____
Management environment	Strong personnel management approach	Good personnel management approach	Weak personnel management approach	_____
	Reusable Software			
Availability	Compatible with need dates	Delivery dates in question	Incompatible with need dates	_____
Modifications	Little or no change	Some change	Extensive changes	_____
Language	Compatible with system and PDSS requirements	Partial compatibility with requirements	Incompatible with system or PDSS requirements	_____
Rights	Compatible with PDSS and competition requirements	Partial compatibility with PDSS, some competition	Incompatible with PDSS concept, noncompetitive	_____
Certification	Verified performance, application compatible	Some application compatible test data available	Unverified, little test data available	_____
	Tools and Environment			
Facilities	Little or no modifications	Some modifications, existent	Major modifications, nonexistent	_____
Availability	In place, meets need dates	Some compatibility with need dates	Nonexistent, does not meet need dates	_____
Rights	Compatible with PDSS and development plans	Partial compatibility with PDSS and development plans	Incompatible with PDSS and development plans	_____
Configuration management	Fully controlled	Some controls	No controls	_____

TABLE 11.3   Quantification of Support Probability [5]

Support drivers	Probability of drivers adversely affecting impact			Value
	Impossible to improbable (0.0 < P < 0.4) Value = 0 or 1	Probable (0.4 < P < 0.7) Value = 2	Frequent (0.7 < P < 1.0) Value = 3	
Design				
Complexity	Structurally maintainable	Certain aspects difficult	Extremely difficult to maintain	_____
Documentation	Adequate	Some deficiencies	Inadequate	_____
Completeness	Extensive PDSS incorporation	Some PDSS incorporation	Little PDSS incorporation	_____
Data rights	Unlimited	Limited	Restricted	_____
Configuration management	Sufficient, in place	Some shortfalls	Insufficient	_____
Stability	Little or no change	Moderate, controlled change	Rapid or uncontrolled change	_____
Responsibilities				
Management: hardware, software	Defined, assigned responsibilities	Some roles and missions issues	Undefined or unassigned	_____
Configuration management	Single point control	Defined control points	Multiple control points	_____
Software identification	Consistent w/support agency control system	Some inconsistencies	Inconsistent	_____
Technical management	Consistent with operational needs	Some inconsistencies	Major inconsistencies	_____
Change implementation	Responsive to user needs	Acceptable delays	Nonresponsive to user needs	_____
Tools and Environment				
Facilities	In place, little change	In place, some modification	Nonexistent or extensive change	_____
Software tools	Delivered, certified, sufficient	Some resolvable concerns	Not delivered, certified, or sufficient	_____
Computer hardware	Compatible with "ops" system	Minor incompatibilities	Major incompatibilities	_____
Production	Sufficient for fielded units	Some capacity questions	Insufficient	_____
Distribution	Controlled, responsive	Minor response concerns	Uncontrolled or nonresponsive	_____
Supportability				
Changes	Within projections	Slight deviations	Major deviations	_____
Operational interfaces	Defined, controlled	Some "hidden" linkages	Extensive linkages	_____
Personnel	In place, sufficient, experienced	Minor discipline mix concerns	Significant discipline mix concerns	_____
Release cycle	Responsive to user requirements	Minor incompatibilities	Nonresponsive to user needs	_____
Procedures	In place, adequate	Some concerns	Nonexistent or inadequate	_____

TABLE 11.4   Quantification of Schedule Probability [5]

Schedule drivers	Impossible to improbable ($0.0 < P < 0.4$) Value = 0 or 1	Probable ($0.4 < P < 0.7$) Value = 2	Frequent ($0.7 < P < 1.0$) Value = 3	Value
Resources				
Personnel	Good discipline mix in place	Some disciplines not available	Questionable mix and/or availability	_____
Facilities	Existent, little or no modification	Existent, some modification	Nonexistent, extensive changes	_____
Financial	Sufficient budget allocated	Some questionable allocations	Budget allocation in doubt	_____
Need Dates				
Threat	Verified projections	Some unstable aspects	Rapidly changing	_____
Economic	Stable commitments	Some uncertain commitments	Unstable, fluctuating commitments	_____
Political	Little projected sensitivity	Some limited sensitivity	Extreme sensitivity	_____
GFE/GFP	Available, certified	Certification or delivery questions	Unavailable and/or uncertified	_____
Tools	In place, available	Some deliveries in question	Uncertain delivery dates	_____
Technology				
Availability	In place	Some aspects still in development	Totally still in development	_____
Maturity	Application verified	Some applications verified	No application evidence	_____
Experience	Extensive application	Some application	Little or none	_____
Requirements				
Definition	Known, baselined	Baselined, some unknowns	Unknown, no baseline	_____
Stability	Little or no change projected	Controllable change projected	Rapid or uncontrolled change	_____
Complexity	Compatible with existing technology	Some dependency on new technology	Incompatible with existing technology	_____

It is important to note that the risk drivers presented in Tables 11.1 through 11.4 can be supplemented with additional entries that are locally relevant and that weighting can be used to emphasize the importance of a particular driver.

You've suggested a reasonably systematic method for identifying and analyzing individual risks and risk components. How do we assess the information that we've derived?

At this point in the risk analysis process, we have established a set of triplets of the form [1] $[r_i, l_i, x_i]$, where r_i is risk, l_i is the likelihood

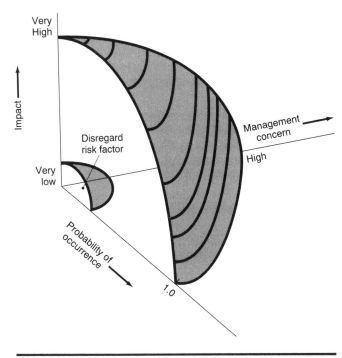

Figure 11.2   Risk and management concern.

Probability Impact	Frequent .7 < P ≤ 1 Value = 3	Probable .4 < P ≤ .7 Value = 2	Improbable 0 < P ≤ .4 Value = 1	Impossible P = 0 Value = 0
Catastrophic	HIGH			
Critical		MODERATE		NONE
Marginal			LOW	
Negligible				

Figure 11.3   Risk assessment [5].

(probability) of the risk, and x_i is the impact of the risk. During *risk assessment,* we further examine the accuracy of the estimates that were made during risk projection, attempt to prioritize the risks that have been uncovered, and begin thinking about ways to control and/or avert risks that are likely to occur.

For assessment to be useful, a *risk referent level* [1] must be defined. For most software projects, the risk components discussed earlier—performance, cost, support, and schedule—also represent risk referent levels. That is, there is a level for performance degradation, cost over-run, support difficulty, or schedule slippage (or any combination of the four) that will cause the project to be terminated. If a combination of risks creates problems that cause one or more of these referent levels to be exceeded, work will stop. In the context of software risk analysis, a risk referent level has a single point, called the *referent point* or *break point,* at which the decisions to proceed with the project or ter-minate it (problems are just too great) are equally acceptable.

Figure 11.4 represents this situation graphically. If a combination of risks leads to problems that cause cost and schedule overruns, there will be a level, represented by the curve in the figure, that (when ex-ceeded) will cause project termination (the shaded region). At a refer-ent point, the decisions to proceed or to terminate are equally weighted.

In reality, the referent level can rarely be represented as a smooth line on a graph. In most cases it is a region in which there are areas of uncertainty; thus, attempting to predict a management decision based on the combination of referent values is often impossible.

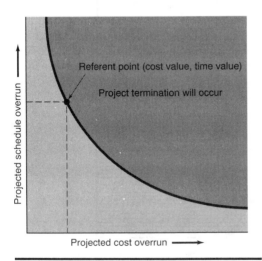

Figure 11.4 Risk referent level.

Therefore, during risk assessment, we perform the following steps:

1. Define the risk referent levels for the project.
2. Attempt to develop a relationship between each (r_i, l_i, x_i) and each of the referent levels.
3. Predict the set of referent points that defines a region of termination, bounded by a curve or areas of uncertainty.
4. Try to predict how compound combinations of risks will affect a referent level.

A detailed discussion is best left to references that are dedicated to risk analysis. For further information, see references [1] and [8].

It would seem that identifying and analyzing risks, however useful, aren't enough. Shouldn't we develop a management strategy for dealing with risk?

A comprehensive risk management strategy includes far more than identification and analysis. It should encompass total quality management and the associated activities that anticipate and eliminate the causes of risk.

Robert Charette [9] has developed a seven-stage hierarchy for managing risk that incorporates this approach. Stage 1 is *crisis management*—the classic fire-fighting activity that begins when it's already too late. The risk has become a real problem and damage has occurred. Stage 2 is *fix-on-failure*—a reactive strategy that is initiated only after a failure has occurred. Damage may be limited through quick action, but the risk was not avoided. Stage 3 is risk *mitigation*—providing the resources to cover a risk (should it occur) but doing nothing to eliminate it in the first place. The first three stages of Charette's hierarchy are reactive, not proactive. Sadly, they are the most common approaches to risk management.

Stage 4 in the hierarchy is *prevention*—an effective plan is created to prevent risks from becoming problems. More important, the plan is executed and managed as part of the software project. As an organization moves to stage 4, it is ready to make the transition to proactive risk management strategies that are integrated with a total quality management (TQM) approach (see Chapter 14).

Stage 5 is *elimination of root causes* of risk. This stage incorporates statistical quality assurance techniques as well as other TQM methods (Chapter 14) to eliminate the underlying causes of risk. Stages 6 and 7—*anticipation* and the *management of change*—represent the highest levels of consciousness in risk management. These stages occur when concrete steps are taken to anticipate change (of all types) and the risks that it will bring. When you are able to manage change to the advantage of your business, the final stage has been reached.

Can you provide an example of risk management?

The risk management and monitoring activity is illustrated schematically in Figure 11.5. The triplet (risk description, likelihood, and impact) associated with each risk is used as the basis from which *risk management* (also called *risk aversion*) *steps* are developed. For example, assume that high staff turnover is noted as a project risk r_1. On the basis of past history and management intuition, the likelihood l_1 of high turnover is estimated to be 0.70 (70 percent, which is rather high), and the impact x_1 is projected to increase project duration by 15 percent and overall cost by 12 percent. Given these data, the following risk management steps are proposed:

- Meet with current staff to determine causes for turnover (e.g., poor working conditions, low pay, competitive job market).

- Act to mitigate those causes that are under your control before the project starts.

- Once the project commences, *assume that turnover will occur* and develop techniques to ensure continuity when people leave.

- Organize project teams so that information about each development activity is widely dispersed.

- Define documentation standards and establish mechanisms to be sure that documents are developed in a timely manner.

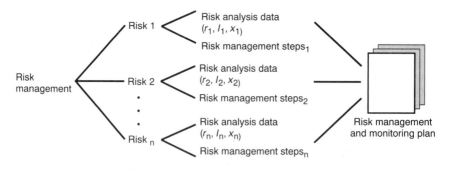

Figure 11.5   Risk management and monitoring.

- Conduct peer reviews of all work (so that more than one person is "up to speed").
- Define a backup staff member for every critical technologist.

It is important to note that these risk management steps incur additional project cost. For example, spending the time to "back up" every critical technologist costs money. Part of risk management, therefore, is to evaluate when the benefits accrued by the risk management steps are outweighed by the costs associated with implementing them. In essence, the project planner performs a classic cost–benefit analysis. If risk aversion steps for high turnover will increase project costs and duration by an estimated 15 percent, and the predominant cost factor is "backup," management may decide not to implement the backup step. On the other hand, if the risk aversion steps are projected to increase costs by 5 percent and duration by only 3 percent, management will likely put all of these steps into place.

For a large project, 30 or 40 risks may be identified. If three to seven risk management steps are identified for each, risk management may become a project in itself! For this reason, we adapt the Pareto 80/20 rule to software risk. Experience indicates that 80 percent of the overall project risk (i.e., 80 percent of the potential for project failure) can be accounted for by only 20 percent of the identified risks. The work performed during earlier risk analysis steps will help the planner determine which of the risks reside in that 20 percent. For this reason, some of the risks identified, assessed, and projected may not make it into the risk management plan—they don't represent the critical 20 percent (the risks with highest project priority).

Are there other areas of risk that are not specifically project related but are still important at this stage?

Risk is not limited to the software project itself. The risks that can occur after the software has been successfully developed and delivered to the customer may be of considerably more management concern than project risks. These safety-related concerns should also be considered.

When you talk about safety in the context of computer software, what do you mean?

Software safety is a software quality assurance activity (Chapter 14) that focuses on the identification and assessment of potential hazards that may impact software negatively and cause an entire system to fail. If hazards can be identified early in the software engineering process, software design features can be specified that will either eliminate or control potential hazards. This topic is discussed in greater detail in Chapter 14.

We've spent a fair amount of effort examining project risks. How does this activity culminate?

Unless you put your strategy into writing, it's likely that the effort that you've spent examining risk will be wasted. A risk management strategy can be included in the software project plan or the risk management steps can be organized into a separate *Risk Management and Monitoring Plan* (RMMP). The RMMP documents all work performed as part of risk analysis and is used by the project manager as part of the overall *Project Plan*. An outline for the RMMP [1] is presented in Table 11.5.

Once the RMMP has been developed and the project has begun, *risk monitoring* commences. Risk monitoring is a project tracking activity with three primary objectives: (1) to assess whether a predicted risk does in fact occur, (2) to ensure that risk aversion steps defined for the risk are being properly applied, and (3) to collect information that can be used for future risk analysis. In many cases, the problems that occur during a project can be traced to many risks. Another job of risk monitoring is to attempt to allocate "blame" [what risk(s) caused which problems] throughout the project.

Risk analysis can absorb a significant amount of project planning effort. Identification, projection, assessment, management, and monitoring all take time. But the effort is worth it. To quote Sun Tzu, a Chinese general who lived 2500 years ago, "If you know the enemy and know yourself, you need not fear the result of a hundred battles." For the software project manager, the enemy is risk.

A Manager's Checklist

Whenever a lot is riding on a software project, common sense dictates risk analysis. And yet, most software project managers do it informally and superficially, if they do it at all. The time spent identifying, analyzing, and managing risk pays itself back in many ways: less upheaval during a project, a greater ability to track and control a project, and the confidence that comes with planning for problems before they occur.

TABLE 11.5   Risk Management and Monitoring Plan Outline [1]

I. Introduction
   A. Scope and purpose of document
   B. Overview
      1. Objectives
      2. Risk aversion priorities
   C. Organization
      1. Management
      2. Responsibilities
      3. Job descriptions
   D. Aversion program description
      1. Schedule
      2. Major milestones and reviews
      3. Budget
II. Risk analysis
   A. Identification
      1. Survey of risks
         a. Sources of risk
      2. Risk taxonomy
   B. Risk estimation
      1. Estimate probability of risk
      2. Estimate consequence of risk
      3. Estimation criteria
      4. Possible sources of estimation error
   C. Evaluation
      1. Evaluation methods to be used
      2. Evaluation method assumptions and limitations
      3. Evaluation risk referents
      4. Evaluation results
III. Risk management
   A. Recommendations
   B. Risk aversion options
   C. Risk aversion recommendations
   D. Risk monitoring procedures
IV. Appendixes
   A. Risk estimate of the situation
   B. Risk abatement plan

Here are a few things you can do right now to give yourself a gentle nudge toward the adoption of risk analysis methods.

Actions

- Evaluate the process framework (the work tasks, deliverables, and milestones) that your organization has adopted for software engineering. Select a point at which the risk analysis activities described in this chapter can be conducted.

- Identify a specific format for risk analysis within your organization. What forms, analysis methods, plans, and so on will you use? You might adopt the approach described in this book, or do some research using one of the references presented at the end of this chapter.

- Decide how risks will be presented and to whom. Will they be part of the project plan, or will they be discussed in a separate document? Will they be presented to software engineering management only, or will you inform your customers/users and their management as well?

- Build a generic risk item checklist that is specific to your organization and the software that it builds. Provide suggested weighting factors for the risk items.

- Create a tutorial for risk analysis that includes a complete analysis of a project that has been conducted within your organization. This will serve as a guide for project managers who want to do risk analysis.

- Begin applying risk analysis methods to real projects. But don't stop there. Track the real problems that occur and compare projected risks with actual project problems. Use this information to adjust your risk-item checklists and to modify your overall approach to risk analysis.

Questions

- If you polled five software project managers and asked them to list their "top 10" project risks, what do you think they would be? Do it in your organization and find out.

- What additional questions or topics would you add to each of the risk-item checklists presented in this chapter? Try to add at least five entries to each checklist.

- Can you develop a weighting scheme for project risk drivers that is more sophisticated than the one implied in Tables 11.1 to 11.4?

- Is software safety an area that should be of concern for your organization?

Further Readings

Boehm [3] suggests excellent questionnaire and checklist formats that can prove invaluable in identifying risk. Charette [1] presents a detailed treatment of the mechanics of risk analysis, calling on probability theory and statistical techniques to analyze risks. In a companion volume, Charette (*Application Strategies for Risk Analysis,* McGraw-Hill, 1990) discusses risk in the context of both system and software engineering and defines pragmatic strategies for risk management. *Air Force Systems Command Pamphlet AFSCP 800-45* [5] describes risk identification and reduction techniques. Gilb [4] presents a set of "principles" (that are often amusing and sometimes profound) that can serve as a worthwhile guide for risk management. Every issue of the *ACM Sigsoft (Software Engineering) Notes* publishes a section entitled "Risks to the Public" (edited by P.G. Neumann). If you want the latest and best software horror stories, this is the place to go.

ITABHI Corporation is a consulting firm (located in Springfield, VA) that specializes in risk analysis. They offer a well-documented "risk engineering" method called CYNIC and conduct specialized training in the subject.

References

[1] Charette, R.N., *Software Engineering Risk Analysis and Management*, McGraw-Hill/Intertext, 1989.
[2] Drucker, P., *Management*, W. Heinemann, Ltd., 1975.
[3] Boehm, B.W., *Software Risk Management*, IEEE Computer Society Press, 1989.
[4] Gilb, T., *Principles of Software Engineering Management*, Addison-Wesley, 1988.
[5] *Software Risk Abatement*, AFCS/AFLC Pamphlet 800-45, U.S. Air Force, September 30, 1988.
[6] Pressman, R.S., and S.R. Herron, *Software Shock*, Dorset House, 1991.
[7] *Making Software Engineering Happen, An Implementation Workshop for Software Engineering and CASE*, R.S. Pressman & Associates, Inc., Orange, CT, 1992.
[8] Rowe, W.D., *An Anatomy of Risk*, Robert E. Krieger Publishing Co., Malabar, FL, 1988.
[9] Charette, R., "CASE and the Management of Risk," ITABHI Corporation, Springfield, VA, 1992.

Chapter

12

Scheduling and Tracking: Where Are We?

I first got involved in computer programming (the operative term for the activity in the late 1960s) as a bright-eyed young engineer. I was chosen to "write" a computer program for an automated manufacturing application because I was the only person in our group who had attended a programming seminar. I knew nothing about software engineering and even less about project scheduling and tracking.

My boss gave me the appropriate manuals and a verbal description of what had to be done. He then informed me that I had 3 months to do it.

I read the manuals, planned my development strategy, and began writing code. After 2 weeks, my boss called me into his office and asked how things were going. "Really great," I said in my youthful innocence, "This was much simpler than I thought. I'm probably close to 75 percent finished."

My boss smiled. "That's really terrific," he said. He then told me that we'd have a status meeting in a week's time.

A week later he called me into his office and asked, "Where are we?" "Everything's going well," I said, I've run into a few small snags, but I've gotten them ironed out and I'm back on track."

"How does the deadline look?" he asked.

"No problem," said I. "I'm close to 90 percent complete." If you've been working in the software world for more than a few years, you can finish my story for me. It will come as no surprise that I stayed 90 percent complete for the entire project duration and finished (with the help of others) one month late.

My introduction to the vagaries of software project scheduling has been repeated tens of thousands of times by hundreds of thousands of software developers during the past 30 years. The big question is *why*.

Why are so many software projects late?

Although there are many reasons why software is delivered late, most can be traced to one or more of the following root causes:

- An unrealistic deadline established by someone outside the software development group and forced on managers and practitioners within the group.
- Changing customer requirements that are not reflected in schedule changes.
- An honest underestimate of the amount of effort and/or the number of resources that will be required to do the job.
- Predictable and/or unpredictable risks that were not considered when the project commenced.
- Technical difficulties that could not have been foreseen in advance.
- Miscommunication among project staff that results in delays.
- A failure by project management to recognize that the project is falling behind schedule and a lack of action to correct the problem.

All of the above causes (with the possible exception of the first) can be controlled and even eliminated. Throughout the remainder of this chapter we'll discuss ways that this can be accomplished.

We often encounter unrealistic deadlines that are demanded by business managers or our customers and end users. What can we do about them?

Aggressive (read "unrealistic") deadlines are a fact of life in the software business. Sometimes such deadlines are demanded for reasons that are legitimate, from the point of view of the person who sets the deadline. But common sense says that legitimacy must also be perceived by the people doing the work.

Napoleon once said: "Any commander-in-chief who undertakes to carry out a plan which he considers defective is at fault; he must put forth his reasons, insist on the plan being changed, and finally tender his resignation rather than be the instrument of his army's downfall." Strong words that many software project managers should ponder.

The estimation and risk analysis activities discussed in Chapters 10 and 11 and the scheduling techniques described in this chapter are often implemented under the constraint of a defined deadline. If best estimates indicate that the deadline is unrealistic, a competent project manager should "protect his or her team from undue [schedule] pressure...[and] reflect the pressure back to its originators" [1].

To illustrate, assume that a software development group has been asked to build a real-time controller for a medical diagnostic instrument that is to be introduced to the market in 9 months. After careful estimation and risk analysis, the software project manager comes to the conclusion that the software, as requested, will require 14 calendar months to create with available staff. How does the project manager proceed?

It is unrealistic to march into the customer's office (in this case the likely customer is marketing/sales) and demand that the delivery date be changed. External market pressures have dictated the date and the product must be released. It is equally foolhardy to refuse to undertake the work (from a career standpoint). So what to do? The following conversation might give you some ideas.

You ask for a meeting with your manager (who has been briefed) and the customer. Prior to the meeting you prepare a detailed estimate and risk management plan, collect historical data from past projects, and study the scope of the software thoroughly (to understand the functions and capability and their interrelationship to one another). After preliminaries, you begin: "I think we may have a problem with the delivery date for the XYZ controller software. I've given each of you an abbreviated breakdown of production rates for past projects and an estimate that we've computed a number of different ways. You'll note that I've assumed a 20 percent improvement in past production rates, but we still get a delivery date that's 14 calendar months rather than 9 months away."

An agitated expression crosses the customer's face, "You software guys are always a bottleneck. Damn, we've got a market window and we cannot wait 14 months to meet it. We absolutely must have the product on the market in 9 months."

Trying not to appear defensive, you respond calmly, "Well, we have a few options, and I'd like you to make a decision based on them. First, we can increase the budget and bring in additional resources so that we'll have a shot at getting this job done in 9 months, but understand that this will increase risk of poor quality due to the tight timeline.[1] Second, we can remove a number of the software functions and capabilities that you're requesting. This will make the preliminary version

---

[1]You might also mention that adding more people will not reduce calendar time proportionally.

of the product somewhat less functional, but we can announce all functionality and then deliver over the 14-month period."

"Third, we can dispense with reality and wish the project complete in 9 months. We'll wind up with nothing that can be delivered to a customer. The third option, I hope you'll agree, is unacceptable. Past history and our best estimates say that it is unrealistic and a recipe for disaster."

There will be a lot of grumbling, but if you've developed solid estimates based on good historical data, it's likely that negotiated versions of either option 1 or option 2 will be chosen. The unrealistic demands on your project team evaporate.

Even when project deadlines are reasonable, many projects still fall behind schedule. How does this happen?

Fred Brooks, the well-known author of *The Mythical Man-Month* [2], was once asked how software projects fall behind schedule. His response was as simple as it was profound: "One day at a time."

The reality of a technical project (whether it involves building a hydroelectric plant or developing an operating system) is that hundreds of small tasks must occur to accomplish a larger goal. Some of these tasks lie outside the mainstream and may be completed without worry about impact on project completion date. Other tasks lie on the "critical path."[2] If these "critical" tasks fall behind schedule, the completion date of the entire project is put into jeopardy.

The objective of the project manager is to define all project tasks, identify the ones that are critical, and then track their progress to ensure that delay is recognized "one day at a time."

How should a project manager view the activity that you call software project scheduling?

Scheduling for software development projects can be viewed from two rather different perspectives. In the first, an end date for release of a computer-based system has already (and irrevocably) been established. The software organization is constrained to distribute effort within the prescribed timeframe. The second view of software scheduling assumes that rough chronological bounds have been discussed but that the end date is set by the software engineering organization. Effort is distributed to make best use of resources and an end date is

---

[2]The critical path will be discussed in greater detail later in this chapter.

defined after careful analysis of the software. Unfortunately, the first situation is encountered far more frequently than the second.

When we approach software project scheduling, a number of questions must be asked. How do we correlate chronological time with human effort? What tasks and parallelism are to be expected? What milestones can be used to show progress? How is effort distributed throughout the software engineering process? Are scheduling methods available? How do we physically represent a schedule and then track progress as the project commences?

Some managers tend to focus on budgets rather than schedules. Are they wrong?

Although a good manager must be concerned with both budget and schedule, the ability to deliver software on time is often more important than the requirement to deliver within a predefined development budget. In a product-oriented environment, added cost can be absorbed by repricing or amortization over large numbers of sales. A missed schedule, however, can reduce market impact, create dissatisfied customers, and raise internal costs by creating additional problems during system integration.

Many of our projects are just 60 or 90 days in duration. Is it really worth the time to develop a detailed schedule for these projects?

Absolutely! Scheduling for a "short" project is at least as important as it is for a longer project. Stated simply, you have less time to react when schedule slippage does occur. Small delays that would be unimportant for a large project can have a significant impact on the delivery date for a small project.

It is, however, important to note that project planning functions (discussed in Chapters 10 through 12) must be accomplished very quickly. You will not have the luxury to plan at a leisurely pace. Project estimates, risk analysis, and scheduling may have to be completed in a day or two—leading to necessary compromises in the thoroughness of these activities.

The process framework for a small project may have to be modified to reflect the limited timeline. For example, analysis and design may be combined into a single project activity, but separate formal technical reviews (Chapter 14) will still be used to assess the efficacy of the analysis and design models. The tasks contained in the work-breakdown structure (WBS) may be scheduled on a day-by-day basis to facilitate timely tracking.

You've already described how estimates of project effort (Chapter 10) can be developed. What is the relationship between people and effort?

In a small software development project a single person can analyze requirements, perform design, generate code, and conduct tests. As the size of a project increases, more people must become involved. (We can rarely afford the luxury of approaching a 10-person-year effort with one person working for 10 years!)

There is a common myth that is still believed by many managers who are responsible for software development effort: "If we fall behind schedule, we can always add more programmers and catch up later in the project." Unfortunately, adding people late in a project often has a disruptive effect on a project, causing schedules to slip even further. I noted the reason for this in Chapter 1. To reiterate: The people who are added must learn the system, and the people who teach them are the same people who were doing the work. While teaching, no work is done and the project falls further behind.

In addition to the time it takes to learn the system, more people increase the number of communication paths and the complexity of communication throughout a project. Although communication is absolutely essential to successful software development, every new communication path requires additional effort and therefore additional time.

As an example, consider four software engineers, each capable of producing 5000 LOC/year when working on an individual project. When these four engineers are placed on a team project, six potential communication paths are possible. Each communication path requires time that could otherwise be spent developing software. We shall assume that team productivity (when measured in LOC) will be reduced by 250 LOC/year for each communication path, because of the overhead associated with communication. Therefore, team productivity is $20{,}000 - (250 \times 6) = 18{,}500$ LOC/year—7.5 percent less than what we might expect.

The one-year project on which the above team is working falls behind schedule and with 2 months remaining, two additional people are added to the team. The number of communication paths escalates to 14. The productivity input of the new staff is the equivalent of $840 \times 2 = 1680$ LOC for the 2 months remaining before delivery.

Team productivity now is 20,000 + 1680 – (250 × 14) = 18,180 LOC/ year.

Although the above example is a gross oversimplification of real-world circumstances, it does serve to illustrate the contention that the relationship between the number of people working on a software project and overall productivity is not linear.

On the basis of the people–work relationship, are teams counterproductive? The answer is an emphatic "no," if communication serves to improve software quality and maintainability. In fact, formal technical reviews (see Chapter 14) conducted by software development teams can lead to better software analysis and design, and more importantly, can reduce the number of errors that go undetected until testing (thereby reducing testing effort). Hence, productivity and quality, when measured by time to project completion and customer satisfaction, can actually improve.

Is there an empirical relationship that can demonstrate how human effort and calendar time are related to one another?

One relationship was introduced with the COCOMO model (discussed in Chapter 10). Another is suggested by the Rayleigh-Norden model [3], an empirical model that predicts a highly nonlinear relationship between chronological time to complete a project and human effort applied to the project. The number of delivered lines of code (source statements) L is related to effort and development time by the equation

$$L = C_k K^{1/3} t_d^{4/3}$$

where C_k is a state of technology constant and reflects "throughput constraints that impede the progress of the programmer." Typical values might be $C_k = 2000$ for a poor software development environment (e.g., no methodology), poor documentation and reviews, a batch execution mode, $C_k = 8000$ for a good software development environment (e.g., methodology in place, adequate documentation, reviews, interactive execution mode), or $C_k = 11,000$ for an excellent environment (e.g., CASE tools and modern techniques). The constant C_k can be derived for local conditions using historical data collected from past development efforts. Rearranging the software equation (above), we can arrive at an expression for development effort K:

$$K = \frac{L^3}{C_k^3 t_d^4}$$

where K is the effort expended (in person-years) over the entire life cycle for software development and maintenance and t_d is the development time in years. The equation for development effort can be related to development cost by the inclusion of a burdened labor rate factor ($/person-year).

This leads to some interesting results. Recalling the CAD software example (originally introduced in Chapter 10), an estimated 33,000-LOC, 12-person-year effort could be accomplished with eight people working for 1.3 years. If, however, we extend the end date to 1.75 years, the Rayleigh-Norden model yields

$$K = \frac{L^3}{C_k^3 t_d^4} \sim 3.8 \text{ person-years}$$

This implies that by extending the end date 6 months, we can reduce the number of people from eight to four! The validity of such results is open to debate, but the implication is clear: benefit can be gained by using fewer people over a somewhat longer time span to accomplish the same objective.

Once effort has been estimated, and the project duration has been defined, the effort must be distributed across the project schedule. Are there any general guidelines for accomplishing this?

Each of the software project estimation techniques discussed in Chapter 10 leads to estimates of person-months (or person-years) required to complete software development. Figure 12.1 illustrates a recommended distribution of effort across the definition and development

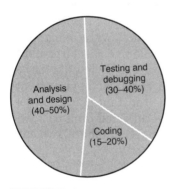

Figure 12.1   Distribution of effort.

phases. This distribution, once called the *40-20-40 rule,*[3] emphasizes front-end analysis and design tasks and back-end testing. You can correctly infer that coding (20 percent of effort) is deemphasized.

The effort distribution shown in Figure 12.1 should be used as a guideline only. The characteristics of each project must dictate the distribution of effort. Effort expended on project planning rarely accounts for more than 2 to 3 percent of effort, unless the plan commits an organization to large expenditures with high risk. Requirements analysis may comprise 10 to 25 percent of project effort. Effort expended on analysis or prototyping should increase in direct proportion with project size and complexity. A range of 20 to 25 percent of effort is normally applied to software design. Time expended for design reviews can absorb as much as 10 percent of design effort.

Because of the effort applied to software design, code should follow with relatively little difficulty. A range of 15 to 20 percent of overall effort can be achieved. Testing and subsequent debugging can account for 30 to 40 percent of software development effort. The criticality of the software often dictates the amount of testing that is required. If software is human-rated (i.e., software failure can result in loss of life), even higher percentages may be considered.

Distributing multiple people over some defined project duration implies parallel tasks. How is the parallel nature of these tasks defined?

When more than one person is involved in a software engineering project, it is likely that development activities will be performed in parallel. Figure 12.2 shows a schematic *task network* for a typical multiperson software engineering project. The network represents all major project tasks and their sequential order and dependencies.

Analysis and specification and the resultant requirements review are the first tasks to be performed and lay the foundation for parallel tasks that follow. Once requirements have been identified and reviewed, design activities (architectural and data design) and test planning commence in parallel. The modular nature of well-designed software lends itself to the parallel development tracks for procedural design, coding, and unit testing, illustrated in Figure 12.2. As components of the software are completed, the integration testing task com-

---

[3]Today, more than 40 percent of all project effort is often recommended for analysis and design tasks for large software development projects. Hence, the name "40-20-40" no longer applies in a strict sense.

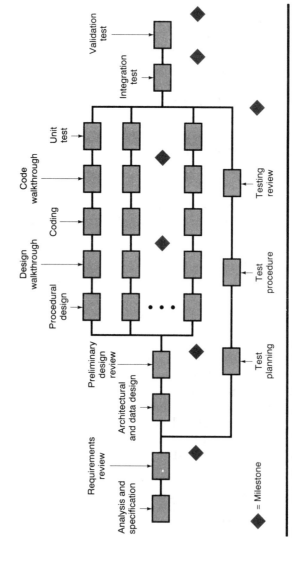

Figure 12.2 Task network and parallelism.

mences. Finally, validation testing readies the software for release to the customer.

Referring to the figure, it is important to note that *milestones* are spaced at regular intervals through the software engineering process, providing a manager with a regular indication of progress. A milestone is reached once a deliverable (e.g., a document, a model, code, test data) produced as part of a software engineering task has been successfully reviewed.

The concurrent nature of software engineering activities leads to a number of important scheduling requirements. Because parallel tasks occur asynchronously, the planner must determine intertask dependencies to ensure continuous progress toward completion. In addition, the project manager should be aware of those tasks that lie on the *critical path*; that is, tasks that must be completed on schedule if the project as a whole is to be completed on schedule. These issues are discussed in more detail later in this chapter.

Are there specific scheduling techniques that can be applied to a software project?

Scheduling of a software project does not differ greatly from scheduling of any multitask development effort. Therefore, generalized project scheduling tools and techniques can be applied to software with little modification.

Program evaluation and review technique (PERT) and *critical path method* (CPM) are two project scheduling methods that can be applied to software development. Both techniques develop a task network description of a project, that is, a pictorial or tabular representation of tasks that must be accomplished from beginning to end of a project (Figure 12.2). The network is defined by developing a list of all tasks, sometimes called the project *work-breakdown structure* (WBS), associated with a specific project and a list of orderings (sometimes called a *restriction list*) that indicates in what order tasks must be accomplished.

Both PERT and CPM provide quantitative tools that allow the software planner to (1) determine the *critical path*—the chain of tasks that determines the duration of the project, (2) establish *most likely* time estimates for individual tasks by applying statistical models, and (3) calculate *boundary times* that define a time "window" for a particular task.

These scheduling techniques have been implemented as automated tools that are available for virtually every personal computer [4] as well as larger machines. Such tools are easy to use and make the scheduling methods described above available to every software project manager.

Can you provide an example of project scheduling using an automated tool?

I'll present a simple project scheduling example using an automated scheduling tool, *MacProject II* (Claris), available for the Apple Macintosh personal computer. The *project task network,* shown in Figure 12.3, is drawn interactively by the project planner. Rectangular boxes represent software engineering tasks and boxes with rounded corners are milestones. The critical path is computed by the tool and is displayed with bold lines. The starting date and duration for each task are specified. In addition, the planner specifies the resources (people) who will be working on each task and the costs of these resources.[4]

Once project data are entered (in the form of the network diagram shown in Figure 12.3), *MacProject II* automatically generates the following information: (1) a timeline chart (Figure 12.4) that describes tasks as a function of chronological date and (2) a resource allocation table (Figure 12.5) that contains task start and finish times, work effort to be applied, and other data that enable a project manager to track progress as the project commences.

How do we establish an appropriate work breakdown structure for a real project?

The work-breakdown structure for software projects should be extracted from the software engineering process framework (e.g., Appendix III) that is established for your software development organization. The process framework is derived once a paradigm for software engineering has been chosen. This topic is discussed in more detail in Chapter 16.

Am I correct in assuming that once we've derived a project schedule, planning stops and the actual management activity begins?

The project schedule provides a roadmap for a software project manager. If it has been properly developed, the project schedule defines the tasks, milestones, and deliverables that must be tracked and con-

---

[4]It should be noted that other scheduling tools use different approaches. Some allow the manager to input project tasks as an outline; others use a Gantt or timeline chart as their primary input representation.

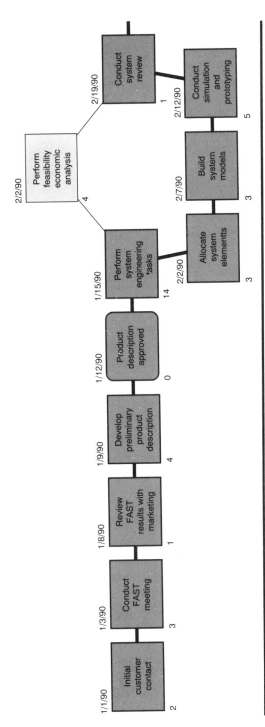

Figure 12.3 A typical task network (bold lines and boxes represent the critical path).

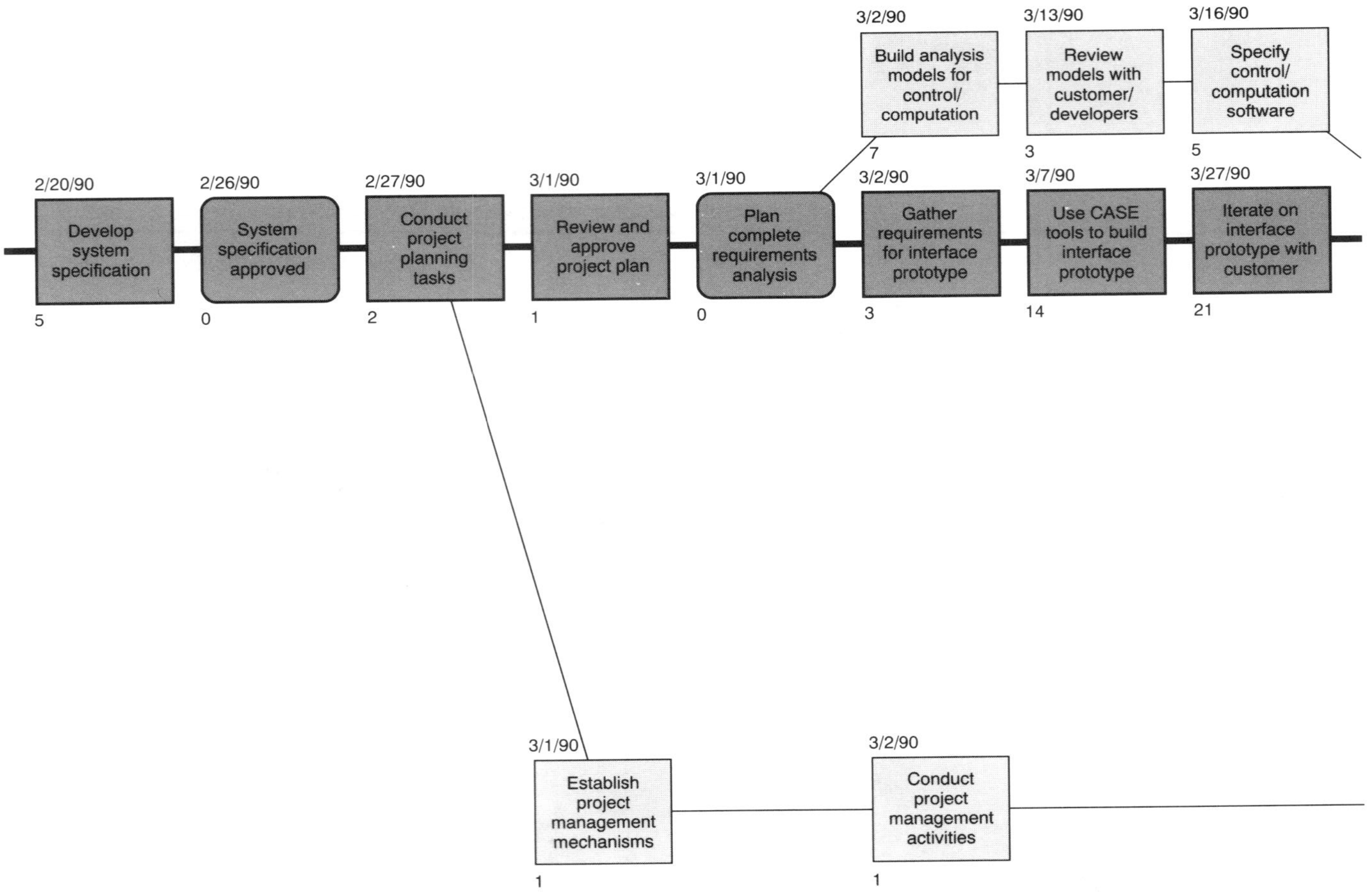

Figure 12.3 A typical task network (*Continued*).

284

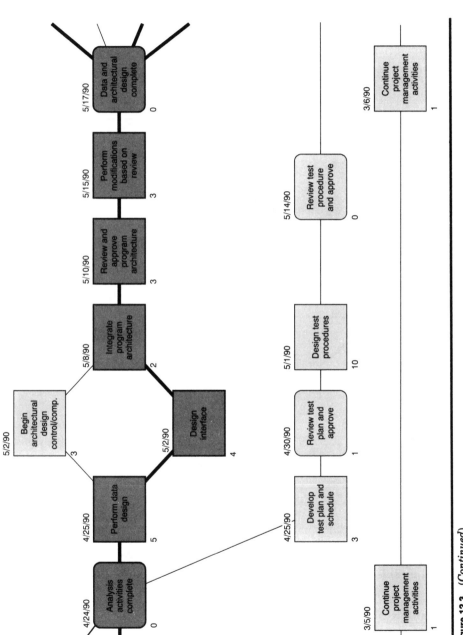

Figure 12.3 (*Continued*)

285

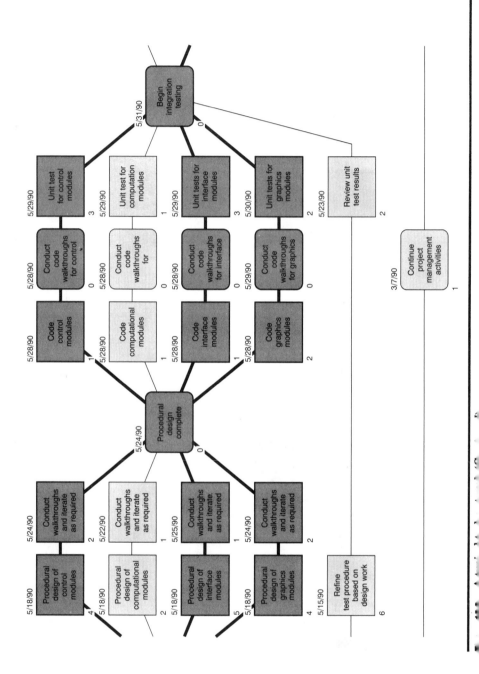

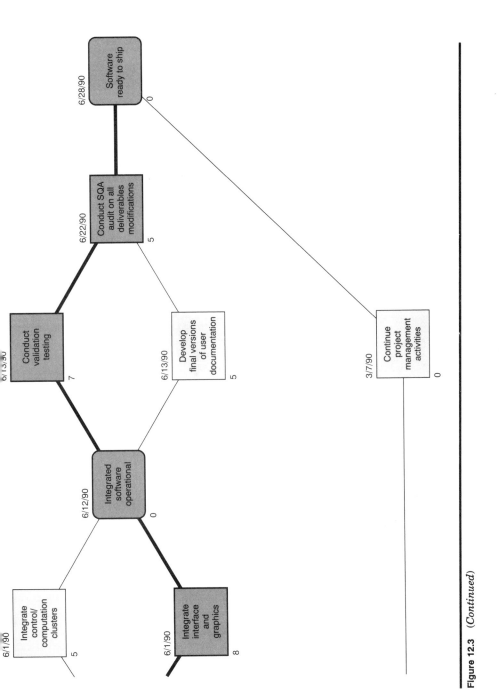

Figure 12.3 (*Continued*)

287

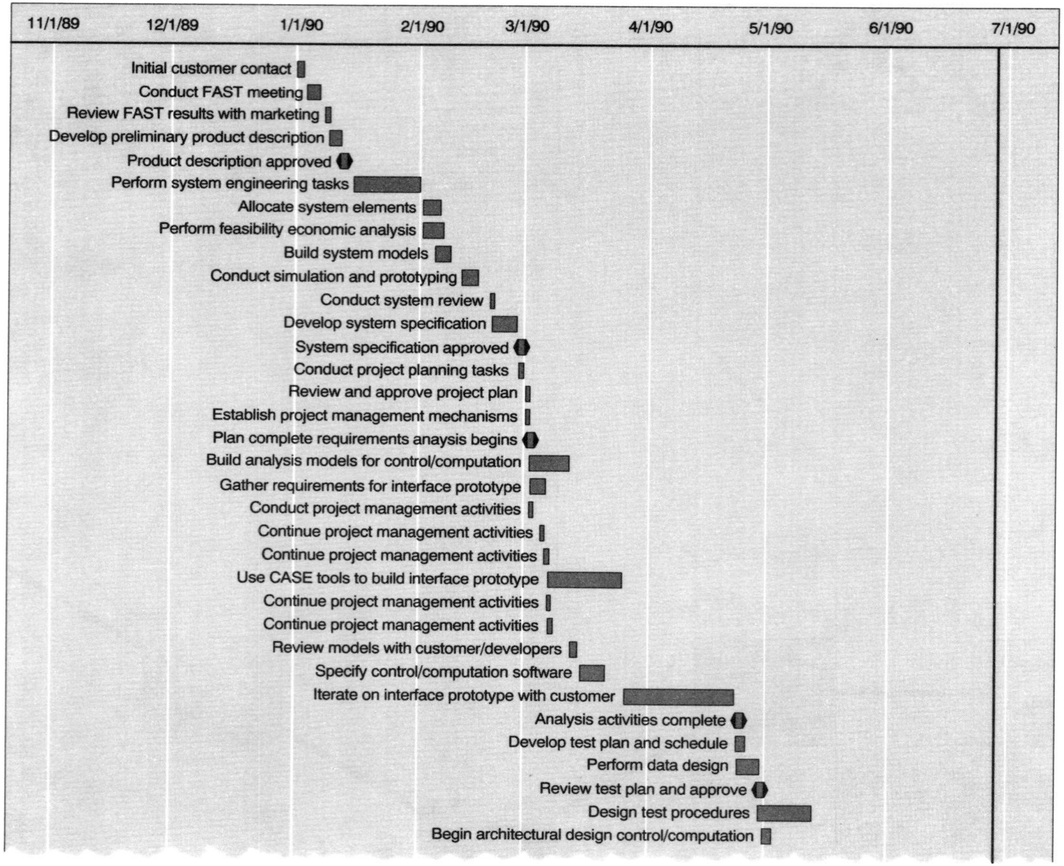

Figure 12.4 Partial task timeline for a typical project (diamonds represent milestones, rect-

trolled as the project gets under way. *Tracking* can be accomplished in a number of different ways:

- Conducting periodic project status meetings in which each team member reports progress and problems
- Evaluating the results of all reviews conducted throughout the software engineering process
- Determining whether formal project milestones (the rectangles with rounded corners shown in Figure 12.3) have been accomplished by the scheduled date
- Comparing actual start date to planned start date for each project task listed in the resource table (Figure 12.5)
- Meeting informally with practitioners to obtain their subjective assessment of progress to date and problems on the horizon

In reality, all of these tracking techniques are used by experienced project managers.

Control is employed by a software project manager to administer project resources, cope with problems, and direct project staff. If things are going well (i.e., the project is on schedule and within budget, reviews indicate that real progress is being made, and milestones are being reached), control is light. But when problems occur or changes are requested, the project manager must exercise control to reconcile them as quickly as possible. After the problem or change has been diagnosed,[5] additional resources may be focused on the problem area; staff may be redeployed or the project schedule can be redefined.

How are estimates, risks, and schedules documented?

Each step in the software engineering process should produce a deliverable that can be reviewed and that can act as a foundation for the steps that follow. The *Software Project Plan* is produced at the culmination of the planning tasks. It provides baseline cost and scheduling information that will be used throughout the software engineering process.

The *Software Project Plan* is a relatively brief document that is addressed to a diverse audience. It must (1) communicate project scope and resources to management, technical staff, and the customer; (2) define risks and suggest risk aversion techniques; (3) define cost and

---

[5]It is important to note that schedule slippage is a symptom of some underlying problem. The role of the project manager is to diagnose what the underlying problem is and then to act to correct it.

Name	Earliest Start	Earliest Finish	Latest Start	Latest Finish
Initial customer contact	1/1/90	1/2/90	1/1/90	1/2/90
Conduct FAST meeting	1/3/90	1/5/90	1/3/90	1/5/90
Review FAST results with marketing	1/8/90	1/8/90	1/8/90	1/8/90
Develop preliminary product description	1/9/90	1/12/90	1/9/90	1/12/90
Product description approved	1/12/90	1/12/90	1/15/90	1/15/90
Perform system engineering tasks	1/15/90	2/1/90	1/15/90	2/1/90
Allocate system elements	2/2/90	2/6/90	2/2/90	2/6/90
Perform feasibility economic analysis	2/2/90	2/7/90	2/13/90	2/16/90
Build system models	2/7/90	2/9/90	2/7/90	2/9/90
Conduct simulation and prototyping	2/12/90	2/16/90	2/12/90	2/16/90
Conduct system review	2/19/90	2/19/90	2/19/90	2/19/90
Develop system specification	2/20/90	2/26/90	2/20/90	2/26/90
System specification approved	2/26/90	2/26/90	2/27/90	2/27/90
Conduct project planning tasks	2/27/90	2/28/90	2/27/90	2/28/90
Review and approve project plan	3/1/90	3/1/90	3/1/90	3/1/90
Establish project management mechanisms	3/1/90	3/1/90	6/22/90	6/22/90
Plan complete requirements analysis begins	3/1/90	3/1/90	3/2/90	3/2/90
Build analysis models for control/computation	3/2/90	3/12/90	4/4/90	4/12/90
Gather requirements for interface prototype	3/2/90	3/6/90	3/2/90	3/6/90
Conduct project management activities	3/2/90	3/2/90	6/25/90	6/25/90
Review models with customer/developers	3/13/90	3/15/90	4/13/90	4/17/90
Use CASE tools to build interface prototype	3/7/90	3/26/90	3/7/90	3/26/90
Specify control/computation software	3/16/90	3/22/90	4/18/90	4/24/90
Iterate on interface prototype with customer	3/27/90	4/24/90	3/27/90	4/24/90
Analysis activities complete	4/24/90	4/24/90	4/25/90	4/25/90
Develop test plan and schedule	4/25/90	4/27/90	5/4/90	5/8/90
Continue project management activities	3/5/90	3/5/90	6/26/90	6/26/90
Perform data design	4/25/90	5/1/90	4/25/90	5/1/90
Review test plan and approve	4/27/90	4/27/90	5/9/90	5/9/90
Begin architectural design control/comp.	5/2/90	5/4/90	5/3/90	5/7/90
Conduct architectural design interface	5/2/90	5/7/90	5/2/90	5/7/90
Design test procedures	4/30/90	5/11/90	5/9/90	5/22/90
Integrate program architecture	5/8/90	5/9/90	5/8/90	5/9/90
Review test procedure and approve	5/11/90	5/11/90	5/23/90	5/23/90
Review and approve program architecture	5/10/90	5/14/90	5/10/90	5/14/90
Perform modifications based on review	5/15/90	5/17/90	5/15/90	5/17/90
Data and architectural design complete	5/17/90	5/17/90	5/18/90	5/18/90
Continue project management activities	3/6/90	3/6/90	6/27/90	6/27/90
Procedural design of control modules	5/18/90	5/23/90	5/18/90	5/23/90
Procedural design of computational modules	5/18/90	5/21/90	5/23/90	5/24/90
Procedural design of interface modules	5/18/90	5/24/90	5/18/90	5/24/90
Procedural design of graphics modules	5/18/90	5/23/90	5/18/90	5/23/90
Refine test procedure based on design work	5/14/90	5/18/90	5/23/90	5/29/90
Conduct walkthroughs and iterate as required	5/24/90	5/25/90	5/24/90	5/25/90
Conduct walkthroughs and iterate as required	5/22/90	5/22/90	5/25/90	5/25/90
Conduct walkthroughs and iterate as required	5/25/90	5/25/90	5/25/90	5/25/90

Figure 12.5   Partial project table.

schedule for management review; and (4) provide an overall approach to software development for all people associated with the project. An outline of the plan is presented in Table 12.1.

A presentation of cost and schedule will vary with the audience to whom it is addressed. If the plan is used only as an internal document,

Type	Elapsed Time	Resource	Work-Days	Resource	Work-Days	Resource	Work-Days
Starting Task	2	Jennifer	1.50				
Task	3	Jennifer	1	Matt	1	Mike	1
Task	1	Jennifer	0.50				
Task	4	Jennifer	2	Matt	2		
Milestone	0						
Task	18	Matt	6	Carolyn	3	Brian	3
Task	5	Matt	1	Carolyn	1	Jennifer	1
Task	6	Mike	3				
Task	3	Matt	3				
Task	5	Matt	3	Carolyn	2		
Task	1	Staff	1				
Task	7	Matt	4	Jennifer	1		
Milestone	0						
Task	2	Norm	1.50	Jennifer	1		
Task	1	Staff	1				
Task	1	Norm	1				
Milestone	0						
Task	11	Matt	5	Carolyn	5	Mike	5
Task	5	Brian	3				
Task	1	Staff	1				
Task	3	Staff	2				
Task	20	Brian	10	Mike	2		
Task	7	Matt	3	Carolyn	3		
Task	29	Brian	10				
Milestone	0						
Task	3	Andy	2				
Task	1	Staff	1				
Task	7	Matt	4	Carolyn	4		
Milestone	0	Andy	0.50	Matt	0.50	Brian	0.50
Task	3	Matt	1	Carolyn	1	Jennifer	1
Task	6	Brian	4	Carolyn	2		
Task	12	Andy	7	Matt	1	Jennifer	1
Task	2	Matt	1	Brian	1		
Milestone	0						
Task	5	Staff	2				
Task	3	Matt	1	Brian	1		
Milestone	0						
Task	1	Staff	1				
Task	6	Matt	4				
Task	4	Carolyn	2				
Task	7	Brian	4				
Task	6	Jennifer	3				
Task	5	Andy	3				
Task	2	Staff	1				
Task	1	Staff	1				
Task	1	Staff	1				

Figure 12.5 (*Continued*)

the results of each costing technique can be presented. When the plan is disseminated outside the organization, a reconciled cost breakdown (combining the results of all costing techniques) is provided. Similarly, the degree of detail contained within the schedule section may vary with the audience and formality of the plan.

TABLE 12.1   Software Project Plan

I. Introduction
   A. Scope and purpose of document
   B. Project objectives
      1. Objectives
      2. Major functions
      3. Performance issues
      4. Management and technical constraints
II. Project estimates
   A. Historical data used for estimates
   B. Estimation techniques
   C. Estimates
III. Project risks (RMMP may be included by reference)
   A. Risk analysis
      1. Identification
      2. Risk estimation
      3. Evaluation
   B. Risk management
      1. Risk aversion options
      2. Risk monitoring procedures
IV. Schedule
   A. Project work-breakdown structure
   B. Task network
   C. Timeline chart (Gantt chart)
   D. Resource table
V. Project resources
   A. People
   B. Hardware and software
   C. Special resources
VI. Staff organization
   A. Team structure (if applicable)
   B. Management reporting
VII. Tracking and control mechanisms
VIII. Appendixes

The *Software Project Plan* need not be a lengthy, complex document. Its purpose is to help establish the viability of the software development effort. The plan concentrates on a general statement of *what* and a specific statement of *how much* and *how long*.

A Manager's Checklist

Scheduling is the culmination of a planning activity that is a primary component of software project management. When combined with estimation methods and risk analysis, scheduling establishes a roadmap for the project manager.

Scheduling begins with the creation of a network that represents each development task and its dependence on other tasks and projected duration. The task network is used to compute the critical project path, a timeline chart, and a variety of project information. Using the schedule as a guide, the project manager can track and control each step in the software engineering process.

Every software development organization schedules. However, many approach the scheduling process in an ad hoc fashion, have poorly defined tasks and milestones, and attempt to define, track, and control the task network without the aid of automated tools. If your organization exhibits one or more of these faults, here are some actions that you should consider.

Actions

- Be certain that your organization has a defined software engineering process framework (see Chapter 16) that defines a generic work-breakdown structure for software projects. If no framework exists, you'll have to create one! See Part 2 of this book.

- If you don't currently use an automated tool for project scheduling, write for literature on three PC-based tools and bring in one of the tools for evaluation.

Questions

- How do you currently measure progress on software projects?

- If you conduct regularly scheduled project meetings, what is the agenda? What is discussed within the context of the agenda?

- What is the average number of people who work on software projects within your organization? Is there a large deviation from the average?

- What types of schedule models (e.g., task network, timeline, or Gantt chart) do you currently use?

- How do you currently handle a situation in which an unrealistic deadline has been defined by some external source?

- Who is your customer and how much does the customer know about software project management issues?

Further Readings

Project scheduling issues are covered in most books on software project management. Boddie (*Crunch Mode*, Prentice-Hall, 1987) has written a book for all managers who "have 90 days to do a 6-month project." Boehm (*Software Engineering Economics*, Prentice-Hall, 1981) presents a comprehensive treatment of software estimating, project planning, and control. Brooks [2] has written a classic text that depicts many of the problems (and some of the solutions) associated with software project management. DeMarco (*Controlling Software Projects*, Yourdon Press, 1982) presents a thorough and pragmatic treatment of all important aspects of software management. Gilb (*Principles of Software Engineering Management*, Addison-Wesley, 1988) writes a thought-provoking discussion of software engineering and its management.

Page-Jones (*Practical Project Management*, Dorset House Publishing, New York, 1985), Simpson (*New Techniques in Software Project Management*, Wiley, 1987), Whitten (*Managing Software Development Projects*, Wiley, 1989), and Ould (*Strategies for Software Engineering*, Wiley, 1990) have written good introductions to project management, presenting the basic elements of estimation, planning and scheduling, project tracking, team organization, and other management topics. Youl (*Making Software Development Visible*, Wiley, 1990) has written one of the few books that emphasizes project tracking.

References

[1] Page-Jones, M., *Practical Project Management*, Dorset House, 1985, pp. 90–91.
[2] Brooks, M., *The Mythical Man-Month*, Addison-Wesley, 1975.
[3] Putnam, L., "A General Empirical Solution to the Macro Software Sizing and Estimating Problem," *IEEE Trans. Software Engineering* 4 (4), 345–361 (1978).
[4] Wood, L., "The Promise of Project Management," *BYTE* (Nov.), 180–192 (1988).

13

Managing Software People: The Human Element

The three major components of software engineering—procedures, methods, and tools—were introduced in Chapter 2. You could have argued that a fourth component was missing. The absent component resides at the heart of any software project. It must work within the confines of software engineering procedures, it applies software engineering methods, and it uses CASE tools. It is always the reason why software projects succeed and is often the cause when projects fail. The fourth software engineering component is *people*.

In a study published by the IEEE [1] the engineering vice presidents of three major technology companies were asked the most important contributor to a successful software project. They answered in the following way:

VP 1: I guess if you had to pick one thing out that is most important in our environment, I'd say it's not the tools that we use, it's the people.

VP 2: The most important ingredient that was successful on this project was having smart people...very little else matters in my opinion....The most important thing you do for a project is selecting the staff....The success of the software development organization is very, very much associated with the ability to recruit good people.

VP 3: The only rule I have in management is to ensure I have good people—real good people—and that I grow good people—and that I provide an environment in which good people can produce.

Indeed, a compelling testimonial on the importance of people in the software engineering process. And yet, all of us, from senior engineering vice presidents to the lowliest technical staff member, often take people for granted. Managers argue (as the group above had done) that people are primary, but their actions sometimes belie their words. How should project managers ensure that good people populate their projects, grow good people when staff acquisition isn't an option, and "provide an environment in which good people can produce"? These are critically important questions, and we'll consider them through this chapter.

Before we start talking about acquiring and nurturing good people and providing them with an effective environment, it might be a good idea to discuss software people themselves. Is there a catalog of traits that describes a "software person"?

Researchers and managers have grappled with this question for decades. "If we could just develop a foolproof checklist of traits that describe a good software person, we'd be able to select the right people for the job," they say somewhat ingenuously.

In reality, there is no foolproof checklist of personality or work traits that defines a software person. In fact, many of the traits that are desirable in a good software person are contradictory. Pressman and Herron [2] provide a list of the common personality traits. Their discussion is reproduced below:

- They are *creative*. A software engineer often begins with a blank sheet of paper and creates a program that solves some complex problem.

- They are *obsessive*. When a problem is encountered, all of a software engineer's energy should be dedicated to a small area of a program that isn't functioning, working tirelessly until it's fixed.

- They are *intuitive*. There are times when intuition (others might call this association or cognitive skill) will lead a software engineer to the source of a problem when technical skill alone will not.

- They are *communicative*. To create a program, a software engineer must understand precisely what needs to be done—and to understand this, the person who builds software must be capable of acquiring substantial knowledge about the problem from those who need a solution.

- They are *consultive*. In many cases, the people who need a solution do not have a firm understanding of what needs to be solved and have absolutely no idea of how to solve it. Rather, the customer has a general understanding of the objectives that must be met. Software engineers must be capable of guiding their customer toward an understanding of what is required to solve the problem.

- They are *disciplined*. To build effective, industry-quality programs, the software engineer must integrate hundreds, and sometimes thousands, of individual components. Without a disciplined approach to this task, chaos will reign.

- They are *retrospective*. Much of what software engineers do is based on work that has already been done. They must be good historians (maybe "archaeologist" is a better term)—able to look at past work, understand it, and then extend it to accommodate present needs.

- They are *pragmatic*. The idealist rarely lasts in this business. In many cases, the development of industry-quality, computer-based systems demands pragmatic tradeoffs that leave no one completely satisfied. Idealists will iterate endlessly, attempting to satisfy each of their ideals while their projects fall further behind schedule. Customers get no solution at all. The pragmatist will recognize that a compromise solution will often provide significant benefit, even if it leaves a few things out.

- They are *skilled*. To develop complex computer software that satisfies customers' needs, a software engineer must have a firm grasp of software development technologies. The days of the coding pad and a seat-of-the-pants approach to programming are behind us. Today, software engineers draw on a broad selection of software development methods and a vast array of programming tools.

- They are *organized*. Even with the best skills, attitudes, and technology, a software developer will get into trouble unless the approach to building large-scale, industry-quality systems has been organized so that everyone's work on the project can be integrated smoothly with the work of others.

- They are *adaptable*. There are few technologies that are changing as rapidly as software development. In little more than 40 years, we have gone from programmers who entered programs by manipulating toggle switches on the front of a computer to software engineers who use specialized methods and tools to create systems that would be the equivalent of billions of toggle switch settings. As the technology changes, the software developer must change with it.

- They are *optimistic*. Without a certain degree of optimism, no one could or would work in the business of software development. Deep down, a software engineer secretly expects that the program will work the first time, that the customer will be so satisfied that few changes will ever be requested, and that the outrageously short development schedule will somehow be accomplished. Unrealistic? Maybe. But it is this trait that allows software developers to achieve real success.

- They have a *sense of humor*. There are many things about the business that are laughable—even if the laughter does not come from all quarters at the same time.

You've noted a number of positive personality characteristics; what are the negative ones?

Again, Pressman and Herron [2] provide a useful discussion:

- They often write poorly and hate to spend time documenting. It is ironic that much of software developers' time is spent trying to figure out what their predecessors have done. Part of the reason why this is difficult is because little information (in the form of documents) about the program exists. Yet the same developers who curse a lack of information about an old program will often resist creating similar information about a current program, and lamentably, will be cursed by their successors.

- They are often opinionated and sometimes obstinate. When disc _.·· ing new technical ideas, many software developers take very str(·.·ᴄ positions on the basis of past experience. A commendable trait, but only if it does not obstruct progress.

- They are loners. Modern software projects demand a team approach. Systems are too large and timelines are too short for one person to do it all. Yet, some software developers have never learned to work together with others.

- They are cynics. The school of hard knocks has taught many software developers to become unwavering disciples of Murphy's law. Although this is often a reasonable defense against the vagaries of project work, some staffers become so cynical that they make Murphy's predictions a self-fulfilling prophecy.

Even if I could use these traits as a checklist, how can I determine whether a person exhibits them?

You shouldn't use them as a checklist. They have been provided simply to help provide insight into the "software person." Most software project managers see traces of each trait in themselves and their people. Later in this chapter we'll discuss how you might be able to discover a bit more about a software person whom you are considering for a new project.

What variation can we expect in the performance of software people?

Like the definition of personality traits, the question of "programmer performance" has been studied for decades. Individual performance differences between best and worst software people can vary by as much as 25 to 1, although a 10-to-1 ratio is more common. In general, the best performers will be about three times as productive as the average staff member! Boehm [3] has found that the performance ratio that separates the 90th percentile software development team from the 15th percentile team is 4 to 1. Still very significant and very troubling to the project manager who must populate a new project.

Although the above ratios can be debated endlessly, one thing is clear: The "one-person project" is at the mercy of the individual. Even with the best software engineering practices in place, a mediocre performer will likely produce results that are substantially less attractive than those of a better performer. The moral? Keep mediocre staff members on team projects rather than assigning them to important individual efforts, but be sure to populate the team with excellent performers as well. The less talented staff members may learn from the best (and are often motivated by them) and the overall performance of the team will remain at an acceptable level.

Have any of the human performance studies that you've alluded to tried to correlate performance with experience, education, or other variables?

The answer is "yes," but the results are generally inconclusive. There appears to be little correlation of software engineering performance with years of experience. Sadly, many people with 15 years of experience actually have a single year of experience repeated 15 times. In general, *breadth* of experience (e.g., the number of different application areas in which an individual has worked, the number of different programming languages that are known by an individual, the methods and tools that are understood and used by a software person) has more to do with performance than the *depth* (measured in chronological years) of experience.

If performance and "breadth of experience" are correlated, is there a way to define gradations for this type of experience?

Attempts to establish an experience scale or spectrum are interesting from an intellectual point of view and may provide some benefit if the experience scale is used to populate project teams. Page-Jones [4] defines a seven-stage scale:

1. *Innocent:*   The software person has no knowledge of software engineering methods and tools and does not see how they can be used.
2. *Aware:*   The software person has been exposed to software engi-

neering and sees the relevance of the technology, but has not applied any of it.

3. *Apprentice:*   The software person has had some formal training in software engineering methods and/or tools and can use a small subset when guided by someone who has had more experience.

4. *Practitioner:*   The software person has used software engineering methods and/or tools a number of times and feels generally comfortable with them.

5. *Journeyman:*   The software person uses software engineering methods and/or tools regularly and becomes the teacher for levels 2 through 4.

6. *Master:*   The software person not only uses software engineering methods and/or tools but adapts them to perform more efficiently or to be applicable to new areas.

7. *Researcher:*   The software person extends the state of the art for software engineering methods and/or tools by publishing papers, writing books, and teaching others outside his or her company.

How can I use an experience scale?

The terminology for an experience scale such as the one posed above is not nearly as important as the distribution of your staff on such a scale. If you are responsible for a software engineering organization, you should make some attempt to determine the number of staff members that fit into one of the levels proposed by Page-Jones. Experience levels 1 through 3 should never work on a critical project without the guidance and interaction of staff members at levels 4 through 6. Technical team leaders should be chosen from those people at levels 5 and 6. Interestingly, people at level 7 rarely work directly on day-to-day development projects. They are often assigned advanced technology applications and spend much of their time laying the foundations that will be used by other levels in the years to come.

How do I go about acquiring the best software people for a new project?

There are two pools from which software people are chosen. In most cases, software project teams (discussed in more detail later) are formed using staff that are already employed by the organization doing the work. The problem is one of selecting the right mix of available people, most of whom are known to the project manager. When an organization is growing, the project manager may have to hire additional staff from the outside.

In either of the above situations, you must determine the experience level of the person to be acquired. From this you can estimate that person's level of performance and use this information to create a balanced software project team.

How do I determine the experience level of a person whom I do not know?

If the person is already employed by your organization, the job is relatively easy. The person will be known to other project managers and staff members. An informal survey of the colleagues and managers who know the person under consideration should provide sufficient information. In addition, an interview, much like the one that I'll describe in a moment, can also be used.

If you're hiring from the outside, references provide only marginal value (particularly when the candidate can collect legal damages if a past employer provides a poor reference). You'll have to learn how to conduct an effective interview.

What are the characteristics of an effective interview?

Before I discuss an effective interview format, a few words on ineffective interviews are appropriate. Many managers don't know how to interview. They monopolize every conversation with the candidate by talking about (1) the great things that they've done, (2) the great things that their group has done, and (3) the reasons why the person should jump at the chance to work for the XYZ company. When the candidate does get a chance to ask questions, they are not answered in a straightforward manner. And when the candidate describes his or her experience, comments are taken at face value.

I've always believed that an effective interview of a software person should be more like an audition and less like a sales meeting. Prior to the day of the interview, the candidate should be asked to bring a "portfolio" of her or his best work. The portfolio should include descriptions of the application, samples of actual deliverables, and a summary of the end results. The candidate should also be asked to prepare a 15-minute formal presentation on a technical topic related to current work.

After reference checks and brief meetings with staff and managers to answer the candidate's questions about the job, the candidate presents his or her work to managers and staff. Much can be learned about a software person by conducting an "audition," and yet, this is rarely done. Hiring a software person without a brief audition is akin to hiring a quarterback for a pro football team using the following approach:

Coach: Can you throw well?

QB: I can throw the ball 60 yards in the air with pin-point accuracy.

Coach: Can you read defenses?

QB: I handle the blitz and zone coverage with the best of them.

Coach: Can you scramble?

QB: I can run a 4.5 forty.

Coach: That's great, you're hired!

What's wrong with this picture? The coach never watched the quarterback play the game. A software project manager should observe first-hand how a candidate software engineer plays the game, *before* a commitment is made to the candidate.

What if we can't acquire software people from the outside and my only option is nurturing talented people from those already on staff? What should our approach be?

Assuming a reasonable level of innate intelligence, talent evolves in one of three ways: (1) a software person is self-taught on the job, learning most new things by experiencing them in a project situation; (2) the software person is apprenticed to a journeyman or expert, who will tutor the "trainee" in a new technology; or (3) the software person receives formal classroom (or nontraditional) training, learning a new technology from an expert teacher.

If only the first option occurs, growth will be slow and many false steps will be made along the way. The second option, although quite effective, depends on the skills and patience of the more experienced mentor. The third option, when considered by itself, can be somewhat sterile and must be bolstered with actual practice and guidance. In the best of circumstances, all three options are applied in tandem.

Let's assume that we have acquired or nurtured reasonably talented people in our organization. How do we motivate them to achieve high performance?

In a landmark study that describes the factors required to motivate and manage software personnel, Cougar and Zawacki [5] define a set of "core job dimensions" that lead to motivated staff:

Skill variety: The degree to which the work to be performed requires different skills and activities.

Task identity: The degree to which the work enables the staff member to complete a whole, identifiable work unit from beginning to end.

Task significance: The degree to which the work to be performed has an impact on others.

Autonomy: The degree to which the worker is free to make independent judgments, to budget time as he or she sees fit, and to determine the order in which activities are conducted.

Feedback: The degree to which the staff member receives feedback about the effectiveness of her or his performance.

In addition to these basic job dimensions, Cougar and Zawacki cite the need for intellectual and professional growth, social interaction, attractive physical environment, and financial reward as additional motivating factors.

How can we achieve improvements in the factors that motivate software people?

It is possible to improve the factors that correlate with staff motivation by making relatively small changes in the way in which software people work and are managed.

Skill variety: Whenever possible, software engineers should be challenged to address a number of different process tasks (e.g., design and testing) so that their focus changes and their skills are stretched. It may also be beneficial to rotate staff among a number of different jobs or application groups.

Task identity: The work-breakdown structure (WBS) defined for your organization's software engineering process framework should define tasks that have a distinct beginning and end. One way to accomplish this is to be certain that each task has a defined deliverable, so that the software engineer produces a "product" (however small) as the consequence of her or his work.

Task significance: The best way to emphasize task significance is to improve communication among team members, the customer, and management.

Autonomy: If measurable milestones are established as part of the software project schedule, a software engineer should be allowed the freedom to budget his or her time within the tasks that lead to the milestone.

Feedback: The use of formal technical reviews (see Chapter 14) is the best known mechanism for establishing feedback from technical peers. Regular informal appraisals provide a mechanism for management feedback.

It is important to note, however, that every person is unique. For every software engineer who desires significant skill variety, there may be one who is perfectly happy to do the same thing day in and day out. In fact, that person would likely be demotivated if her or his activities underwent change.

What about other motivating factors such as the need for intellectual and professional growth, social interaction, an attractive physical environment, and financial reward?

The degree to which core job dimensions are achieved will have a strong bearing on intellectual and professional growth. By providing skill variety and coupling it with good training and mentoring, growth will be achieved. Social interaction is not always a strong need among software people, but it can be achieved by establishing an effective team approach to software projects (more on this a bit later).

The physical work environment has much more to do with motivation and performance than most managers believe. DeMarco and Lister [6] summarize the effects of the workplace when they state: "The bald fact is that many companies provide developers with a workplace that is so crowded, noisy, and interruptive as to fill their days with frustration. That alone could explain reduced efficiency as well as a tendency for good people to migrate elsewhere."

In a study of workplace environment on software engineering job performance, DeMarco and Lister found that those people who performed in the top quarter of all staff members were (on average) four times more likely to have had a quiet, spacious, private work space than those who were in the bottom quarter. Top quarter performers were found to be about 2.5 times as productive as bottom quarter performers.

What is the ideal work environment?

Although the nature of the "ideal" work environment is highly dependent on the industry and the individual, generally accepted guidelines incorporate the following characteristics: approximately 100 square feet of floor space dedicated to each person with 30 square feet of counter space; six-foot soundproofed partitions; a personal workstation; white board and cork board; file cabinets and convenient access to fax, copier, and printers. In addition, the work space should be linked to others via an effective electronic-mail system and to the outside via voice mail. Finally, the ideal work environment should include another workstation that is placed in the software engineer's home.

In addition to individual work space, the group work area should have one meeting room for every 15 to 20 people, a learning center that contains locally relevant periodicals and books, a media room for video-based instruction, and windows that connect workers to the outside world.

What about financial incentives as motivating factors?

Money is what some have referred to as a "hygiene factor." It creates substantial dissatisfaction if it is inadequate, but it does little to make staff members feel good about their jobs if it is present. From a senior manager's point of view, the above statement really says: you're damned if you don't and you're not blessed if you do. Poor pay, inadequate benefits, and an overall pecuniary view of expenditures will invariably create poor morale and will lead to high turnover if competitive pressure exists. Excellent pay and benefits and an expansive attitude toward expenditures will make people comfortable, but will not necessarily motivate them. The core job dimensions discussed earlier are much more important as motivating characteristics.

How should we proceed as we attempt to motivate our staff to better levels of performance?

Ed Yourdon [7] suggests that management should encourage staff to participate in a "breakthrough project." Such projects represent an extraordinary accomplishment in terms of development productivity or product quality or they achieve a result that was thought to be improbable or impossible (e.g., delivery in a very tight timeframe). To achieve a breakthrough, Yourdon suggests the following approach:

- Management must provide a credible reason why the breakthrough is needed.
- Technical staff must understand the consequences of achieving the breakthrough and the negative consequences (for software engi-

neers, the organization, the business, or the customer) if the breakthrough is not achieved.

- Clear objectives must be defined and the risks associated with achieving them explained to all project staff.
- Clear incentives for participation in the breakthrough project must be annunciated (e.g., bonuses, peer recognition, promotion).

Project staff must be given the option to participate in the breakthrough project, and only those who have "signed up" for the work will proceed.

The breakthrough project is managed in much the same way that all software projects are managed, but to encourage an esprit de corps among breakthrough project team members, special perquisites (e.g., flexible work hours, expanded tools budget, catered dinners for those working overtime) should be provided to them.

Throughout this chapter you've talked about the people, but not about how they're organized. What are the organizational issues for software people?

There are almost as many human organizational structures for software development as there are organizations that develop software. For better or worse, organizational structure cannot be easily modified. Concerns with the practical and political consequences of organizational change are not within the software project planner's scope of responsibilities. However, organization of the people directly involved in a new software project is within the project manager's purview.

The following options are available for applying human resources to a project that will require n people working for k years:

1. n individuals are assigned to m different functional tasks, and relatively little combined work occurs; coordination is the responsibility of a software manager who may have six other projects to be concerned with.
2. n individuals are assigned to m different functional tasks ($m < n$) so that informal "teams" are established; an ad hoc team leader may be appointed; coordination among teams is the responsibility of a software manager.
3. n individuals are organized into t teams; each team is assigned one or more functional tasks; each team has a specific structure that is defined for all teams working on a project; coordination is controlled by both the team and a software project manager.

Although it is possible to voice pro and con arguments for each of the above approaches, there is a growing body of evidence that indicates that a formal team organization (option 3) is most productive.

What is the best structure for a software engineering team?

The "best" team structure depends on the management style of your organization, the number of people who will populate the team and their skill levels, and the overall problem difficulty. Mantei [8] suggests three generic team organizations:

Democratic decentralized (DD): This software engineering team has no permanent leader. Rather, "task coordinators are appointed for short durations and then replaced by others who may coordinate different tasks." Decisions on problems and approach are made by group consensus. Communication among team members is horizontal.

Controlled decentralized (CD): This software engineering team has a defined leader who coordinates specific tasks and secondary leaders that have responsibility for subtasks. Problem solving remains a group activity, but implementation of solutions is partitioned among subgroups by the team leader. Communication among subgroups and individuals is horizontal. Vertical communication along the control hierarchy also occurs.

Controlled centralized (CC): Top-level problem solving and internal team coordination are managed by a team leader. Communication between the leader and the team members is vertical.

Are there guidelines that define when each of these team structures is best suited to a particular project?

Mantei [8] describes seven project factors that should be considered when planning the structure of software engineering teams:

- The difficulty of the problem to be solved
- The size of the resultant program(s) in lines of code or function points
- The time that the team will stay together (team lifetime)
- The degree to which the problem can be modularized
- The required quality and reliability of the system to be built
- The rigidity of the delivery date
- The degree of sociability (communication) required for the project

TABLE 13.1 The Impact of Project Characteristics
on Team Structure [8]

Team type	DD	CD	CC
Difficulty			
High	x		
Low		x	x
Size			
Large		x	x
Small	x		
Team lifetime			
Short		x	x
Long	x		
Modularity			
High		x	x
Low	x		
Reliability			
High	x	x	
Low			x
Delivery date			
Strict			x
Lax	x	x	
Sociability			
High	x		
Low		x	x

Table 13.1 [8] summarizes the impact of project characteristics on team organization. Because a centralized structure completes tasks faster, it is the most adept at handling simple problems. Decentralized teams generate more and better solutions than do individuals. Therefore, such teams have a greater probability of success when working on difficult problems. Since the CD team is centralized for problem solving, either CD or CC team structure can be successfully applied to simple problems. A DD structure is best for difficult problems.

Because the performance of a team is inversely proportional to the amount of communication that must be conducted, very large projects are best addressed by teams with a CC or CD structure when subgrouping can be easily accommodated.

The length of time that the team will "live together" affects team morale. It has been found that DD team structures result in high morale and job satisfaction and are therefore good for long-lifetime teams.

The DD team structure is best applied to problems with relatively low modularity, because of the higher volume of communication that is needed. When high modularity is possible (and people can do their own thing), the CC or CD structure will work well.

CC and CD teams have been found to produce fewer defects than DD teams, but these data have much to do with the specific quality assurance activities that are applied by the team. Decentralized teams generally require more time to complete a project than do teams with a centralized structure and at the same time are best when high sociability is required.

Can you provide an example of a specific team structure?

As an example of a specific team structure, consider a controlled centralized (CD) software engineering team. Originally called the *chief programmer team*, this structure was first proposed by Harlan Mills and described by Baker [9]. The nucleus of the team is composed of a *senior engineer* ("the chief programmer") who plans, coordinates, and reviews all technical activities of the team; *technical staff* (normally two to five people) who conduct analysis and development activities; and a *backup engineer* who supports the senior engineer in his or her activities and can replace the senior engineer with minimum loss in project continuity.

The software development team may be served by one or more specialists (e.g., telecommunications expert, database designer), support staff (e.g., technical writers, clerical personnel), and a *software librarian*. The librarian serves many teams and performs the following functions: maintains and controls all elements of the software configuration, such as documentation, source listings, data, and magnetic media; helps collect and format software productivity data; catalogs and indexes reusable software modules; and assists the teams in research, evaluation, and document preparation. The importance of a librarian cannot be overemphasized. The librarian acts as a controller, coordinator, and potentially, an evaluator of the software configuration.

How does the software project manager interact with software engineering teams?

The software project manager acts as the administrative filter for each of the software engineering teams. That is, by taking responsibility for administrative communications, reports, and meetings, the project manager frees team leaders (the senior engineers) to perform technical management duties. The project manager coordinates communication among software engineering teams and conducts regular staff meetings, attended only by team leaders, to stay appraised of progress and problems.

Is there a single "trait" that often leads to a truly successful software engineering team?

In their book *Peopleware*, DeMarco and Lister [10] discuss this issue:

We tend to use the word *team* fairly loosely in the business world, calling any group of people assigned to work together a "team." But many of these groups just don't seem like teams. They don't have a common definition of success or any identifiable team spirit. What is missing is a phenomenon that we call *jell*.

A jelled team is a group of people so strongly knit that the whole is greater than the sum of the parts.

Once a team begins to jell, the probability of success goes way up. The team can become unstoppable, a juggernaut for success.... They don't need to be managed in the traditional way, and they certainly don't need to be motivated. They've got *momentum*.

DeMarco and Lister contend (and I agree) that members of jelled teams are significantly more productive and more motivated than average. They share a common goal, a common culture, and in many cases, a "sense of eliteness" that makes them unique.

How are "jelled" teams created?

To illustrate[1] how a jelled team might be created, consider a startup software company that is struggling through the product quality blues. Version 1.0 of their product was an immediate success. Orders poured in, venture capital materialized, the company grew, and customer requests led to versions 1.1, 1.2, and 2.0. Unfortunately, the blitzkrieg atmosphere left little time for solid software engineering practices, and the quality of the product began to slip. Release 2.0.1 (intended to fix errors in version 2.0) created more problems than it solved.

"When customers began calling me to complain about bugs, I knew that we had to do something," said the 28-year-old VP of Software Engineering. "So I decided to form a software quality assurance and testing (QAT) team."

Unfortunately, not one of the company's 24 software developers volunteered. "Problem was, nobody wanted to join," the VP said, "and our culture here demands that people 'sign up' for any task."

Undaunted, management hired an experienced QAT manager and then offered a 20 percent sign-up bonus for any technical person who would join the team. More importantly, they characterized the QAT team as a prestigious assignment—one on which only the very best people would be rotated. That did it. The team had more applicants than positions. But the challenge was to make the team jell.

The VP explained the company's approach, "Luckily, the QAT man-

---

[1]This illustration has been adapted from R. S. Pressman and S. R. Herron, *Software Shock*, Dorset House, 1991, pp. 122–124.

ager had gone through this before and worked hard to get everyone signed up to a simple goal—making every product, every release, every update coming down the line—fail! The team adopted a name, *The Bug Busters*, and thrived on breaking programs. Nothing gave them a bigger thrill than uncovering an error."

"We have a common goal on this team and we work collectively to come up with devilish tests that will drive the development group nuts," laughs the QAT manager.

"Have you ever seen the little decals that football players have on their helmets?" he asks. "Coaches give those out for particularly good play. I give out little bug decals when someone finds a really subtle or interesting error. QAT team members put them on the white boards in their offices. Might sound hokey, but it works."

Before long, there was a waiting list of people who wanted to join the team. Faces changed as people rotated back onto development assignments, but the effectiveness of the team continued. More importantly, the quality of the company's software products improved dramatically.

It's been our experience that not all teams work as well as we'd like. What are some of the factors that cause the software engineering team concept to fail?

DeMarco and Lister [10] address this issue in their book and give it a catchy name. They call it "teamicide." They emphasize the need to *grow* teams rather than *build* them. A farmer who grows vegetables tills the soil, provides proper amounts of water and nutrients, pulls the weeds, and hopes that nature will then take its proper course. But there are no guarantees. The project manager, like the farmer, can do only so much to grow teams. The rest is up to the nature of the individuals who are involved.

With that said, here are some things [11] to avoid:

Defensive management: Once teams have been formed, you must give the team members enough leeway to make decisions and carry them out. Avoid a "project manager knows best" attitude (even if you *really* think you do). A team will not grow and mature as an effective working unit unless its members are given autonomy to make decisions and then carry them out. In most cases, the whole point of a software engineering team is to decentralize decision making.

Bureaucracy: If you insist that the team members join the corporate paper chase, that they follow arcane and unnecessary policies established for accountants or mail clerks, that they spend too much of their time reporting their progress to every manager who cares and many who don't, the team itself will accomplish very little.

Physical separation: The whole point of establishing a team structure is to concentrate talent. A team is expected to interact—to make decisions, define common objectives, solve problems. The team members will be at a significant disadvantage if they are dispersed over four different floors of an office tower. The common excuse used to justify this situation is "the logistical and cost problems associated with shuffling people geographically." If you want to grow teams that perform, you'll find a way to overcome logistical and cost problems.

Fragmentation of people's time: A team should have a definite objective and work obsessively to achieve it. If team members are constantly being called off the team to "do a small maintenance job," continuity will be difficult to maintain.

Deemphasis of quality: No one will ever admit that quality is unimportant, but when costs and schedule are squeezed, management sometimes forces a team to short-circuit quality checkpoints in the interest of "meeting the customer's schedule." Of course, what really happens is that the team delivers a shoddy product. And that never meets the customer's needs.

Unrealistic deadlines: I discussed unrealistic deadlines in Chapter 12 and suggested a few ways for the project manager to handle them. If they are allowed to persist, the software engineering team is being set up for failure. It cannot grow or jell in a negative environment.

Clique control: Management sometimes acts like the proverbial third world dictator who believes that any cohesive group of four or more people represents a threat to her or his well-being. Instead of being viewed positively, a jelled team may make management uncomfortable. It is not uncommon that such teams are disbanded, even though they are high performers.

A Manager's Checklist

People are the most important component of the software engineering process. Unless they are properly trained, motivated, and organized, even the best technology and intentions will not save a software project from failure.

Sadly, some software project managers are not "people" people. They grew up as technical professionals, have had virtually no management training, and don't have the natural personality traits that are required to manage people effectively. Even if you fall into this category, it's never too late to change. The following actions and questions will provide you with additional insight into your organization and will help you to grow as a technical leader or manager.

Actions

- Without indicating ratings for specific individuals, indicate the percentage of all technical people working within your organization that falls into each of the seven performance levels discussed earlier in this chapter.

- If your project makes use of team structures, study the teams and determine whether they are CC, CD, or DD.

- Rate each of the core job dimensions discussed in this chapter for your organization. Then have your people rate the same things. What differences do you see?

- Rate your physical work environment using some of the issues discussed in this chapter.

Questions

- How do your hiring practices compare with the audition approach discussed in this chapter?

- What, if anything, is your organization doing to improve core job dimensions?

- What is the turnover rate for software people in your organization? How does it compare with other job classifications in your company? With other companies in your area?

- When you conduct personnel appraisals, what are the ways in which you rate performance? Could your approach be improved?

- How many square feet of space (on average) are allocated to each software person?

Further Readings

Books by DeMarco and Lister [10], Cougar and Zawacki [5], and Weinberg (*Understanding the Professional Programmer,* Dorset House, 1988) provide useful insight into software people and how they should be managed. Another excellent book by Weinberg (*Becoming a Technical Leader,* Dorset House, 1986) is must reading for every project manager and every team leader. It will give you insight and guidance in ways to do your job more effectively. House (*The Human Side of Project Management*, Addison-Wesley, 1988) and Crosby (*Running Things: The Art of Making Things Happen*, McGraw-Hill, 1989) provide practical advice for managers who must deal with human as well as technical problems.

Even though they do not relate specifically to the software world, and sometimes suffer from oversimplification and broad generalization, bestselling books such as *The One Minute Manager* and *In Search of Excellence* will provide you with valuable insights that can help you manage people issues more effectively.

A comprehensive anthology of human factors studies conducted over the past few decades has been edited by Bill Curtis (*Human Factors in Software Development*, 2d ed., IEEE Computer Society Press, 1985). Another excellent anthology edited by Don Reifer (*Software Management*, 3d ed., IEEE Computer Society Press, 1986) presents many useful papers on project staffing, organization, and management.

References

[1] Curtis, B. et al., "A Field Study of the Software Design Process for Large Systems," *IEEE Trans. Software Engineering*, **31** (11), 1268–1287 (1988).

[2] Pressman, R.S., and S.R. Herron, *Software Shock*, Dorset House, 1991, pp. 117–122.

[3] Boehm, B., *Software Engineering Economics*, Prentice-Hall, 1981.

[4] Page-Jones, M., "The Seven Stages in Software Engineering," *American Programmer* (July–Aug.), 1990.

[5] Cougar, J.D., and R.A. Zawacki, *Motivating and Managing Computer Personnel*, Wiley-Interscience, 1980.

[6] DeMarco, T., and T. Lister, *Peopleware*, Dorset House, 1987, p. 48.

[7] Yourdon, E., "Peopleware," paper presented at CASE War Games, Digital Consulting, Inc., San Francisco, October 1992.

[8] Mantei, M., "The Effect of Programming Team Structures on Programming Tasks," *CACM* **24** (3), 106–113 (1981).

[9] Baker, F.T., "Chief Programmer Team Management of Production Programming," *IBM Systems J.* **11** (1), 56–73 (1972).

[10] DeMarco, T., and T. Lister, *Peopleware*, Dorset House, 1987, p. 123.

[11] DeMarco, T., and T. Lister, *Peopleware*, Dorset House, 1987, pp. 132–139.

Software
Quality Assurance:
Striving for Excellence

Quality is a challenging concept. Robert Persig [1] describes it in the following way:

> What I (and everybody else) mean by the word quality cannot be broken down into subjects and predicates....If quality exists in an object, then you must explain why scientific instruments are unable to detect it....On the other hand, if quality is subjective, existing only in [the eye of] the observer, then this Quality is just a fancy name for whatever you'd like....Quality is not objective. It doesn't reside in the material world....Quality is not subjective. It doesn't reside merely in the mind.

An interesting thought, but how will it help you to understand software quality, and more importantly, to achieve it in actual practice?

It is true that we cannot measure quality directly, but it can be measured by examining other characteristics that we have come to associate with excellence in design and construction. For example, although you cannot measure the quality of an automobile directly, you can examine its fit and finish. You can sense its handling and ride and the smoothness of its acceleration. You can record the number of times it requires maintenance. All of these are indirect measures of quality—measures that can be translated into quantitative terms and used to provide an indication of the caliber of the automobile.

Like its counterpart in hardware, software quality also cannot be measured directly, but through the use of indirect measures, the quality of computer software can be ascertained.

What is software quality?

Philip Crosby [2], in his landmark book on quality, discusses the milieu that precipitates your question:

The problem of quality management is not what people don't know about it. The problem is what they think they do know.

In this regard, quality has much in common with sex. Everybody is for it. (Under certain conditions, of course.) Everyone feels they understand it. (Even though they wouldn't want to explain it.) Everyone thinks execution is only a matter of following natural inclinations. (After all, we do get along somehow.) And, of course, most people feel that problems in these areas are caused by other people. (If only *they* would take the time to do things right.)

There have been many definitions of software quality proposed in the literature. For our purposes, software quality is defined as *conformance to explicitly stated functional and performance requirements, explicitly documented development standards, and implicit characteristics that are expected of all professionally developed software.*

There is little question that this definition could be modified or extended. In fact, a definitive definition of software quality could be debated endlessly. For our purposes, the above definition serves to emphasize three important points:

1. Software requirements are the foundation from which *quality* is measured. Lack of conformance to requirements is lack of quality.

2. Specified standards define a set of development criteria that guides the manner in which software is engineered. If the criteria are not followed, lack of quality will almost surely result.

3. There is a set of *implicit requirements* that often goes unmentioned (e.g., the desire for good maintainability). If software conforms to its explicit requirements, but fails to meet implicit requirements, software quality is suspect.

Your definition of quality is reasonable, but are there ways that we can measure quality?

Over two decades ago, McCall and Cavano [3, 4] defined a set of quality factors that was a first step toward the development of metrics for software quality. These factors assessed software from three distinct points of view: (1) product operation (using it), (2) product revision (changing it), and (3) product transition (modifying it to work in a different environment, i.e., "porting" it). In their work, the authors describe the relationship between these quality factors (what they call a "framework") and other aspects of the software engineering process:

> First, the framework provides a mechanism for the project manager to identify what qualities are important. These qualities are attributes of the software in addition to its functional correctness and performance

which have life cycle implications. Such factors as maintainability and portability have been shown in recent years to have significant life cycle cost impact....

Secondly, the framework provides a means for quantitatively assessing how well the development is progressing relative to the quality goals established....

Thirdly, the framework provides for more interaction of QA personnel throughout the development effort....

Lastly,... quality assurance personnel can use indications of poor quality to help identify [better] standards to be enforced in the future.

Can you provide additional information on this "quality framework"?

McCall and his colleagues [3] have proposed a useful categorization of factors that affect software quality. These *software quality factors* focus on three important aspects of a software product: its operational characteristics, its ability to undergo change, and its adaptability to new environments:

Correctness: The extent to which a program satisfies its specification and fulfills the customer's mission objectives.

Reliability: The extent to which a program can be expected to perform its intended function with required precision.

Efficiency: The amount of computing resources and code required by a program to perform its function.

Integrity: Extent to which access to software or data by unauthorized persons can be controlled.

Usability: Effort required to learn, operate, prepare input, and interpret output of a program.

Maintainability: Effort required to locate and fix an error in a program. (Might be better termed "correctability.")

Flexibility: Effort required to modify an operational program.

Testability: Effort required to test a program to ensure that it performs its intended function.

Portability: Effort required to transfer the program from one hardware and/or software system environment to another.

Reusability: Extent to which a program [or parts of a program] can be reused in other applications—related to the packaging and scope of the functions that the program performs.

Interoperability: Effort required to couple one system to another.

Is there a way that we can assess these factors in some quantitative manner?

It is difficult, and in some cases impossible, to develop direct measures of the above quality factors. Therefore, a set of quality metrics can be defined and used to develop expressions for each of the factors according to the relationship

$$F_q = c_1 \times m_1 + c_2 \times m_2 + \cdots + c_n \times m_n$$

where F_q is a software quality factor, c_n are regression coefficients, and m_n are the metrics that affect the quality factor. Unfortunately, many of the metrics defined by McCall can be measured only subjectively. The metrics may be in the form of a checklist that is used to "grade" specific attributes of the software [4]. The grading scheme proposed by McCall is a 0 (low) to 10 (high) scale. The following metrics are used in the grading scheme:

Auditability: The ease with which conformance to standards can be checked.

Accuracy: The precision of computations and control.

Communication commonality: The degree to which standard interfaces, protocols, and bandwidth are used.

Completeness: The degree to which full implementation of a required function has been achieved.

Conciseness: The compactness of the program in terms of lines of code.

Consistency: The use of uniform design and documentation techniques throughout the software development project.

Data commonality: The use of standard data structures and types throughout the program.

Error tolerance: The damage that occurs when the program encounters an error.

Execution efficiency: The run-time performance of a program.

Expandability: The degree to which architectural, data, or procedural design can be extended.

Generality: The breadth of potential application of program components.

Hardware independence: The degree to which the software is decoupled from the hardware on which it operates.

Instrumentation: The degree to which the program monitors its own operation and identifies errors that do occur.

Modularity: The functional independence of program components.

Operability: The ease of operation of a program.

Security: The availability of mechanisms that control or protect programs and data.

Self-documentation: The degree to which the source code provides meaningful documentation.

Simplicity: The degree to which a program can be understood without difficulty.

Software system independence: The degree to which the program is independent of nonstandard programming language features, operating system characteristics, and other environmental constraints.

Traceability: The ability to trace a design representation or actual program component back to requirements.

Training: The degree to which the software assists in enabling new users to apply the system.

The relationship between software quality factors and the metrics listed above is shown in Table 14.1. It should be noted that the weight given to each metric depends on local products and concerns.

Have alternative ways of looking at software quality been proposed?

Hewlett-Packard [5] has developed a set of software quality factors that has been given the acronym *FURPS*—functionality, usability, reliability, performance, and supportability. The FURPS quality factors draw liberally from earlier work, defining the following attributes for each of the five major factors:

- *Functionality* is assessed by evaluating the feature set and capabilities of the program, the generality of the functions that are delivered, and the security of the overall system.

- *Usability* is assessed by considering human factors, overall aesthetics, consistency, and documentation.

- *Reliability* is evaluated by measuring the frequency and severity of failure, the accuracy of output results, the mean time between failure (MTBF), the ability to recover from failure, and the predictability of the program.

- *Performance* is measured by processing speed, response time, resource consumption, throughput, and efficiency.

- *Supportability* combines the ability to extend the program (extensi-

TABLE 14.1 Quality Factors and Metrics*

Quality factor	Software quality metric										
	Correctness	Reliability	Efficiency	Integrity	Maintainability	Flexibility	Testability	Portability	Reusability	Interoperability	Usability
Auditability				×							
Accuracy		×									
Communication commonality										×	
Completeness	×										
Complexity		×			×	×	×				
Concision			×		×	×					
Consistency	×	×			×	×				×	
Data commonality										×	
Error tolerance		×									
Execution efficiency			×								
Expandability						×					
Generality						×		×	×	×	
Hardware independence								×	×		
Instrumentation				×	×		×				
Modularity		×			×	×		×	×	×	
Operability			×								×
Security				×							
Self-documentation					×	×	×	×	×		
Simplicity		×			×	×	×				
System independence								×	×		
Traceability	×										
Training											×

*Adapted from L. A. Arthur, *Measuring Programmer Productivity and Software Quality*, Wiley-Interscience, 1985.

bility), adaptability, and serviceability (these three attributes represent a more common term—*maintainability*) and in addition, testability, compatibility, configurability [the ability to organize and control elements of the software configuration (Chapter 15)], the ease with which a system can be installed, and the ease with which problems can be localized.

Although these quality factors provide a useful way of looking at software quality, they can be assessed only qualitatively or pseudo-quantitatively. Are there real measures that relate directly to quality?

Quality can be measured throughout the software engineering process and after the software has been released to the customer and users. Metrics derived before the software is delivered provide a quantitative basis for making design and testing decisions. Quality metrics in this category include program complexity, effective modularity, and overall program size. Metrics used after delivery focus on the number of defects uncovered in the field and the maintainability of the system. It is important to emphasize that after delivery measures of software quality present managers and technical staff with a "postmortem" indication of the effectiveness of the software engineering process.

Later in this chapter, I'll discuss the use of quality metrics as the key component of *statistical quality assurance*. That is, by adding additional information about the types of defects uncovered and their causes, we can provide a mechanism for planning actions to correct the elements of the software process that "introduce" defects in the first place.

O.K., I'll accept the fact that we can establish qualitative and quantitative approaches that will enable us to define software quality. How do we ensure that quality is being built as a software project progresses?

All of the components of software engineering—procedures, methods, tools, and (as we saw in the last chapter) people—work toward a single goal: *to produce high-quality software. Software quality assurance* (SQA) is an "umbrella activity" that is applied throughout the software engineering process. SQA encompasses a number of important activities: (1) analysis, design, coding and testing methods and tools, (2) formal technical reviews that are applied during each software engineering step, (3) a multitiered testing strategy, (4) control of software documentation and the changes made to it, (5) a procedure to ensure compliance with software development standards (when applicable), (6) measurement, and (7) record-keeping and reporting mechanisms.

Do these quality assurance activities for software have parallels in other engineering and manufacturing disciplines?

Prior to the twentieth century, quality assurance was the sole responsibility of the craftsperson who built a product. The first formal quality assurance and control function was introduced at Bell Labs in 1916 and spread rapidly throughout the manufacturing world. Today, every company has mechanisms to ensure quality in its products. Some are applied during the engineering phase and others are introduced during manufacturing. In fact, explicit statements of a company's concern for quality have become a marketing ploy during the past decade.

The history of quality assurance in software development parallels the history of quality in hardware manufacturing. During the early days of computing (1950s and 1960s), quality was the sole responsibility of the programmer. Standards for quality assurance for software were introduced in military contract software development during the 1970s and have spread rapidly into software development in the commercial world.

Can you describe SQA activities in a bit more detail?

Software quality is designed into a product or system. It is not imposed after the fact. For this reason, SQA actually begins with the set of *technical methods and tools* that helps the analyst to achieve a high-quality specification and the designer to develop a high-quality design. Measures of specification and design quality are available and are discussed briefly in Chapter 17.

Once a specification (or prototype) and design have been created, each must be assessed for quality. The central activity that accomplishes quality assessment is the *formal technical review*. The formal technical review (FTR) is a stylized meeting conducted by technical staff with the sole purpose of uncovering quality problems. In many situations, reviews have been found to be as effective as testing in uncovering errors in software. Reviews are discussed later in this chapter.

Software testing combines a multistep strategy with a series of test case design methods that helps ensure effective error detection. Many software developers use software testing as a quality assurance "safety net." That is, developers assume that thorough testing will uncover most errors, thereby mitigating the need for other SQA activities. Unfortunately, testing, even when performed well, is not as effective as we might like for all classes of errors. Software testing is discussed in Chapter 17.

The degree to which formal *standards and procedures* are applied to the software engineering process varies from company to company. In many cases, standards are dictated by customers or regulatory mandate. In other situations standards are self-imposed. If formal (written) standards do exist, an SQA activity must be established to ensure that they are being followed. An assessment of compliance to standards may be conducted by software developers as part of a formal technical review, or in situations where independent verification of compliance is required, the SQA group may conduct its own *audit*.

A major threat to software quality comes from a seemingly benign source: *changes*. Every change to software has the potential for introducing error or creating side effects that propagate errors. The *change control* process (a task that is part of software configuration management, Chapter 15) contributes directly to software quality by formalizing requests for change, evaluating the nature of change, and controlling the impact of change. Change control is applied during software development and, later, during the software maintenance phase.

Measurement is an activity that is integral to any engineering discipline. An important objective of SQA is to track software quality and assess the impact of methodological and procedural changes on improved software quality. To accomplish this, software metrics (Chapter 3) must be collected.

Record keeping and recording for software quality assurance provide procedures for the collection and dissemination of SQA information. The results of reviews, audits, change control, testing, and other SQA activities must become part of the historical record for a project and should be disseminated to development staff on a need-to-know basis. For example, the results of each formal technical review for a procedural design are recorded and can be placed in a "folder" that contains all technical and SQA information about a module.

You've outlined seven SQA activities. Which do you feel is most important?

All SQA activities are important, because all lead to high-quality software. However, if you'll only allow me to select one, my choice is *formal technical reviews*. If reviews are properly conducted (more on this later), they are the single most effective way to uncover and correct errors while they are still inexpensive to find and fix.

Why are reviews such an important SQA activity?

Software reviews are a "filter" for the software engineering process. That is, reviews are applied at various points during software development and serve to uncover defects that can then be removed. Software reviews serve to "purify" the software engineering activities that we have called analysis, design, and coding. Freedman and Weinberg [6] discuss the need for reviews this way:

> Technical work needs reviewing for the same reason that pencils need erasers: *To err is human.* The second reason we need technical reviews is that although people are good at catching some of their own errors, large classes of errors escape the originator more easily than they escape anyone else. The review process is, therefore, the answer to the prayer of Robert Burns:
>
> O wad some power the giftie give us
> to see ourselves as others see us
>
> A review—any review—is a way of using the diversity of a group of people to:
>
> 1. Point out needed improvements in the product of a single person or team;
> 2. Confirm those parts of a product in which improvement is either not desired or not needed;
> 3. Achieve technical work of more *uniform,* or at least more *predictable,* quality than can be achieved without reviews, in order to make technical work more *manageable.*

There are many different types of reviews that can be conducted as part of software engineering. Each has its place. An informal meeting around the coffee machine is a form of review, if technical problems are discussed. A formal presentation of software design to an audience of customers, management, and technical staff is a form of review. In this book, however, we focus on the *formal technical review* (FTR)—sometimes called an *inspection* or *walkthrough.* A formal technical review is the most effective filter from a quality assurance standpoint. Conducted by software engineers (and others) for software engineers, the FTR is an effective means for improving software quality.

Why can't we wait and find errors during testing? Why is it so important to find errors early?

The obvious benefit of formal technical reviews is the early discovery of software errors so that each may be corrected prior to the next step in the software engineering process. For example, a number of industry studies (TRW, Nippon Electric, Mitre Corp., among others) indicate that design activities introduce between 50 and 65 percent of all errors during the development phase of the software engineering process. However, formal review techniques have been shown to be up to 75 percent effective [7] in uncovering design flaws. By detecting and removing a large percentage of these errors, the review process substantially reduces the cost of subsequent steps in the development and maintenance phases.

To illustrate the cost impact of early error detection, consider a series of relative costs that are based on actual cost data collected for large software projects. Assume that an error uncovered during design will cost 1.0 monetary unit to correct. Relative to this cost, the same error uncovered just before testing commences will cost 6.5 units; during testing 15 units; and after release, between 60 and 100 units. It pays to filter errors out of the process as soon as possible.

Reviews themselves cost money. Is there a way that your argument to "find and fix" early can be justified quantitatively?

A *defect amplification model* [8] can be used to illustrate the generation and detection of errors during preliminary design, detail design, and coding steps of the software engineering process. The model is illustrated schematically in Figure 14.1. A box represents a software development step. During the step, errors may be inadvertently generated. A review may fail to uncover newly generated errors and errors from previous steps, resulting in a number of errors that are passed through. In some cases, errors passed through from previous steps are amplified (amplification factor x) by current work. The box subdivisions represent each of these characteristics and the percent efficiency for detecting errors, a function of the thoroughness of review.

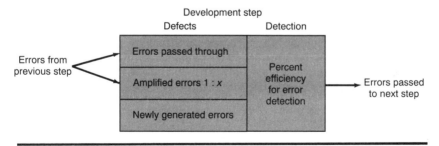

Figure 14.1   Defect amplification model.

Figure 14.2 illustrates a hypothetical example of defect amplification for a software development process in which no reviews are conducted. Referring to the figure, each test step is assumed to uncover

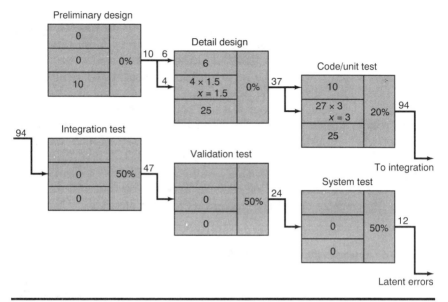

Figure 14.2   Defect amplification—no review.

and correct 50 percent of all incoming errors without introducing any new errors (an optimistic assumption). Ten preliminary design errors are amplified to 94 errors before testing commences. Twelve latent defects are released to the field. Figure 14.3 considers the same conditions except that design and code reviews are conducted as part of each development step. In this case, 10 initial preliminary design errors are amplified to 24 errors before testing commences. Only three latent defects exist. Recalling the relative costs associated with the discovery and correction of errors, overall cost (with and without review for our hypothetical example) can be established.

It seems reasonable to assume that reviews will filter out errors, but doesn't the cost of reviews (in time and money) outweigh their beneficial "filtering" capability?

Referring to Table 14.2, it can be seen that total cost for development and maintenance when reviews are conducted is 783 cost units. When no reviews are conducted, the total cost is 2177 units—nearly three times more costly.

To conduct reviews, a developer must expend time, effort, and money. However, the results of the preceding example leave little doubt that we have encountered a "pay now or pay much more later" syndrome. Formal technical reviews (for design and other technical activities) provide a demonstrable cost–benefit ratio. They should be conducted.

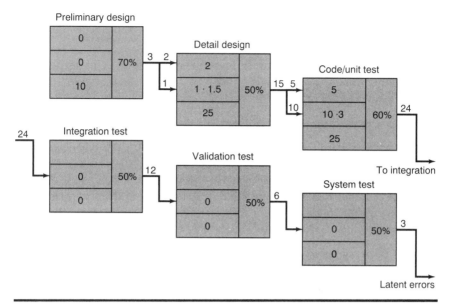

Figure 14.3   Defect amplification—reviews conducted.

TABLE 14.2   Development Cost Comparison

Errors found	Number	Cost unit	Total
Reviews Conducted			
During design	22	1.5	33
Before test	36	6.5	234
During test	15	15	315
After release	3	67	201
			783
No Reviews Conducted			
Before test	22	6.5	143
During test	82	15	1230
After release	12	67	804
			2177

Couldn't the same result be achieved by improving the defect-removal efficiency of our testing approach?

Sadly, the answer is "no." W. Edwards Deming [9], a person that many call the originator of modern statistical quality methods in industry, suggests that to achieve zero-defect products a company must "cease dependence on mass inspection (especially testing)." The reason for Deming's aversion to "mass inspection" (i.e., inspection conducted at the end of the manufacturing or development process) is that it does nothing to remove the causes of defects. Even when mass inspection works, the defects uncovered must be reworked (debugged), and this can involve substantial amounts of time and money. It is far better to eliminate the causes of error or to remove errors as soon as possible after they occur.

What is a formal technical review?

A formal technical review (FTR) is a software quality assurance activity that is performed by software engineering practitioners. The objectives of the FTR are to (1) uncover errors in function, logic, or implementation for any representation of the software; (2) verify that the software under review meets its requirements, (3) ensure that the software has been represented according to predefined standards, (4) achieve software that is developed in a uniform manner, and (5) make projects more manageable. In addition, the FTR serves as a training ground, enabling junior engineers to observe different approaches to software analysis, design, and implementation. The FTR also serves to promote backup and continuity because a number of people become familiar with parts of the software that they may not have otherwise seen.

How should we conduct a formal technical review?

A formal technical review is a meeting with the objectives noted above. Every review meeting should abide by the following constraints:

- Between three and five people (typically) should be involved in the review.
- Advance preparation should occur but should require no more than 2 hours of work for each person.
- The duration of the review meeting should be less than 2 hours.

Given these constraints, it should be obvious that an FTR focuses on a specific (and small) part of the overall software. For example, rather than attempting to review an entire design, walkthroughs are conducted for each module or small group of modules. By narrowing its focus, the FTR has a higher likelihood of uncovering errors.

You argue that the FTR focus should be narrow. But on what do we focus?

The focus of the FTR is on a *product*—a component of the software (e.g., a portion of a requirements specification, a detailed module design, a source code listing for a module). The product is produced as a consequence of a software engineering task.

Who participates in the FTR, and what is the scenario for the review meeting?

The individual who has developed the product—the *producer*—informs the project leader that the product is complete and that a review is required. The project leader contacts a *review leader* who evaluates the product for readiness, generates copies of product materials, and distributes them to two or three *reviewers* for advance preparation. Each reviewer is expected to spend between 1 to 2 hours reviewing the product, making notes, and otherwise becoming familiar with the work. Concurrently, the review leader also reviews the product and establishes an agenda for the review meeting, which is typically scheduled for the next day.

The review meeting is attended by the review leader, all reviewers, and the producer. One of the reviewers takes on the role of the *recorder*, that is, the individual who records (in writing) all important issues raised during the review. The FTR begins with an introduction of the agenda and a brief introduction by the producer. The producer then proceeds to "walk through" the product, explaining the material, while reviewers raise issues based on their advance preparation. When valid problems or errors are discovered, the recorder notes each.

At the end of the review, all attendees of the FTR must decide whether to (1) accept the product without further modification, (2) reject the product due to severe errors (once corrected, another review must be performed), or (3) accept the product provisionally (minor errors have been encountered and must be corrected, but no additional review will be required). The decision made, all FTR attendees complete a *sign-off,* indicating their participation in the review and their concurrence with the review team's findings.

What record-keeping requirements are imposed on the review team?

During the FTR, a reviewer (the recorder) actively records all issues that have been raised. These are summarized at the end of the review meeting and a *review issues list* is produced. In addition, a simple *review* summary report is completed. A review summary report answers three questions:

1. What was reviewed?

2. Who reviewed it?

3. What were the findings and conclusions?

The review summary report takes the form illustrated in Figure 14.4(a). In general, this single page (with possible attachments) form becomes part of the project historical record and may be distributed to the project leader and other interested parties.

The review issues list serves two purposes: (1) to identify problem areas within the product and (2) to serve as an *action-item* checklist

Technical Review Summary Report

Review Identification:

Project: NC Real-Time Controller   Review Number: D-004
Date: 11 July 86   Location: Bldg. 4, Room 3   Time: 10:00 AM

Product Identification:

Material Reviewed: Detailed Design - Modules for motion control

Producer: Alan Frederick

Brief Description: Three modules for x, y, z axis motion control

Material Reviewed: (note each item separately)
1. Detailed design descriptions: modules XMOTION, YMOTION, ZMOTION
2. PDL for modules
Review Team: (indicate leader and recorder)
              Name   Signature:
1. R. S. Pressman (Leader)   _____
2. A. D. Dickerson (Recorder)   Q. Dickerson
3. P. W. Brokerton   Paul W. Brokerton
4. M. Lambert   M. Lambert
5. _____   _____

Product Appraisal:

Accepted: as is ( )   with minor modification (√)
Not Accepted: major revision ( )   minor revision ( )
Review Not Completed: (explanation follows)

Supplementary material attached:

Issues list (√)   Annotated Produce Materials (√)
Other (describe)

(a)

Figure 14.4 (a) Technical review summary report.

Review Number: D-004
Date of Review: 07-11-86
Review leader: R.S. Pressman   Recorder: A.D. Dickerson

Issues List

1. Prologues for module YMOTION, ZMOTION are not consistent with design standards. Purpose of the module should be explicitly stated (reference is not acceptable) and data item declaration must be specified.

2. Loop counter for interpolation in X, Y, Z axes increments one time too many for step motor control. Review team recommends a recheck of stepping motor specifications and correction (as required) of the loop counter STEP.MOTOR.CTR.

3. Typo in reference to current X position, X.POSITION. in modules XMOTION and ZMOTION. See marked PDL for specifics.

4. PDL pseudo code statement must be expanded. The pseudo code statement: "Converge on proper control position as in XMOTION" contained in modules YMOTION and ZMOTION should be expanded to specifics for Y and Z motion control.

5. Review team recommends a modification to the "position comparator" algorithm to improve run time performance. Necessary modifications are noted in annotated PDL. Designer has reservations about the modification and will analyze potential impact before implementing change.

(b)

Figure 14.4   (*b*) Review issues list.

that guides the producer as corrections are made. An issues list that corresponds to the summary report is shown in Figure 14.4(*b*).

It is important to establish a follow-up procedure to ensure that items on the issues list have been properly corrected. Unless this is done, it is possible that issues raised can "fall between the cracks."

Can you provide general guidelines that govern the conduct of a formal technical review?

Guidelines for the conduct of formal technical reviews must be established in advance, distributed to all reviewers, agreed on, and then followed. A review that is uncontrolled can often be worse than no review at all.

The following represents a minimum set of guidelines for formal technical reviews:

1. *Review the product, not the producer:*   An FTR involves people and egos. Conducted properly, the FTR should leave all participants with a warm feeling of accomplishment. Conducted improperly, the FTR can take on the aura of an inquisition. Errors should be pointed out gently; the tone of the meeting should be loose and constructive; the intent should not be to embarrass or belittle. The review leader should conduct the review meeting to ensure that the proper tone and attitude are maintained and should immediately halt a review that has gotten out of control.

2. *Set an agenda and maintain it:*   One of the key maladies of meetings of all types is *drift*. An FTR must be kept on track and on schedule. The review leader is chartered with the responsibility for maintaining the meeting schedule and should not be afraid to nudge people when drift sets in.

3. *Limit debate and rebuttal:*   When an issue is raised by a reviewer, there may not be universal agreement on its impact. Rather than spending time debating the question, the issue should be recorded for further discussion off-line.

4. *Enunciate problem areas, but don't attempt to solve every problem noted:*   A review is not a problem-solving session. The solution of a problem can often be accomplished by the producer alone or with the help of only one other individual. Problem solving should be postponed until after the review meeting.

5. *Take written notes:*   It is sometimes a good idea for the recorder to make notes on a wallboard, so that wording and prioritization can be assessed by other reviewers as information is recorded.

6. *Limit the number of participants and insist on advance preparation:*   Two heads are better than one, but 14 are not necessarily better than 4. Keep the number of people involved to the necessary minimum. However, all review team members must prepare in advance. Written comments should be solicited by the review leader (providing an indication that the reviewer has reviewed the material).

7. *Develop a checklist for each product that is likely to be reviewed:*   A checklist helps the review leader to structure the FTR meeting and helps each reviewer focus on important issues. Checklists should be developed for analysis, design, code, and even test documents.

8. *Allocate resources and time schedule for FTRs:*   For reviews to be effective, they should be scheduled as a task during the software engineering process. In addition, time should be scheduled for the inevitable modifications that will occur as the result of an FTR.

9. *Conduct meaningful training for all reviewers:*   To be effective, all review participants should receive some formal training. The training should stress both process-related issues and the human psychological side of reviews. Freedman and Weinberg [6] estimate a one-month learning curve for every 20 people who are to participate effectively in reviews.

10. *Review your early reviews:*   Debriefing can be beneficial in uncovering problems with the review process itself. The very first product to be reviewed might be the review guidelines themselves.

Are there any management metrics that can be collected to better assess the effectiveness of reviews?

An effective review is one in which the review team has uncovered one or more errors in the product that is undergoing review. Among the many metrics that can be collected for FTRs are the following:

- Review time per page of documentation
- Review time per KLOC or function point
- Errors uncovered per reviewer hour
- Errors uncovered per preparation hour
- Errors uncovered per software engineering task (e.g., design)
- Number of minor errors (e.g., typos)
- Number of major errors (e.g., nonconformance to requirements)
- Defect removal efficiency (Chapter 5)

Once data are collected for dozens of reviews, it will be possible to compute averages that should provide an indication of the amount of review time required on new projects and maintenance activities, and an indication of the effectiveness of the review process itself. You'll be able to ask and answer questions such as these:

- Is the review time per page (per LOC or per FP) too long or too short when compared to past experience?
- Are too many or too few errors uncovered per reviewer hour? Too many errors may indicate a major flaw in the process.
- Are reviews uncovering only minor errors and missing major ones?
- Are too few errors found during preparation?
- Is there an unusual distribution of errors among program modules?
- Is defect removal efficiency improving over time?

The only way to improve the review process is to calibrate it so that weaknesses can be understood and corrected. Effective FTRs are your best hope for achieving high-quality software; ineffective FTRs are a waste of time and resources. Measurement can help you to ensure the effectiveness of your review approach.

Successful reviews find errors in documents, programs, and data. Since the errors are found prior to delivery to the customer, should they be recorded and categorized for future reference?

Although the answer to your question is debatable, many quality assurance experts suggest that *all* errors should be recorded and categorized so that subsequent analysis can be conducted to understand their causes. The database from which information about the types and causes of errors (uncovered during reviews and testing and culled from customer/user reports) forms the basis for statistical quality assurance. It is important to emphasize that the reason for recording errors is *not* to appraise individual or group performance.

What is statistical quality assurance for software?

Statistical quality assurance reflects a growing trend throughout industry to become more quantitative about quality. For software, statistical quality assurance implies the following steps:

1. Information about software errors and defects is collected and categorized.

2. An attempt is made to trace each quality problem to its underlying cause (e.g., nonconformance to specification, design error, violation of standards, poor communication with customer).

3. Using the Pareto principle (80 percent of the quality problems can be traced to 20 percent of all possible causes), isolate the 20 percent (the "vital few").

4. Once the vital few causes have been identified, move to correct the problems that have caused deficiency in quality.

This relatively simple concept represents an important step toward the creation of an adaptive software engineering process in which changes are made to improve those elements of the process that introduce error.

How are statistical data collected and analyzed?

To illustrate the process, assume that a software development organization collects information on errors and defects for a period of one year. Some quality problems are uncovered as software is being developed. Others are encountered after the software has been released to its end user. Although hundreds of different errors are uncovered, all can be traced to one (or more) of the following causes:

- Incomplete or erroneous specification (IES)
- Misinterpretation of customer communication (MCC)
- Intentional deviation from specification (IDS)
- Violation of programming standards (VPS)
- Error in data representation (EDR)
- Inconsistent module interface (IMI)
- Error in design logic (EDL)
- Incomplete or erroneous testing (IET)
- Inaccurate or incomplete documentation (IID)
- Error in programming language translation (PLT) of design
- Ambiguous or inconsistent human–computer interface (HCI)
- Miscellaneous (MIS)

To apply statistical SQA, Table 14.3 is built. In this example, the table indicates that IES, MCC, and EDR are the vital few causes that account for 53 percent of all errors. It should be noted, however, that IES, EDR, PLT, and EDL would be selected as the vital few causes if only serious errors are considered. Once the vital few causes are determined, the software development organization can begin corrective action. For example, to correct MCC, the software developer might im-

TABLE 14.3   Data Collection for Statistical SQA

Error	Total No.	%	Serious No.	%	Moderate No.	%	Minor No.	%
IES	205	22	34	27	68	18	103	24
MCC	156	17	12	9	68	18	76	17
IDS	48	5	1	1	24	6	23	5
VPS	25	3	0	0	15	4	10	2
EDR	130	14	26	20	68	18	36	8
IMI	58	6	9	7	18	5	31	7
EDL	45	5	14	11	12	3	19	4
IET	95	10	12	9	35	9	48	11
IID	36	4	2	2	20	5	14	3
PLT	60	6	15	12	19	5	26	6
HCI	28	3	3	2	17	4	8	2
MIS	56	6	0	0	15	4	41	9
Totals	942	100%	128	100%	379	100%	435	100%

plement facilitated application specification techniques (Chapter 10) to improve the quality of customer communication and specification. To improve EDR, the developer might acquire CASE tools for data modeling and perform more stringent data design reviews.

It is important to note that corrective action focuses primarily on the vital few. As the vital few causes are corrected, new candidates pop to the top of the stack.

In conjunction with the collection of defect information, software developers can calculate an *error index* (EI) for each major step in the software engineering process. After analysis, design, coding, testing, and release, the following data are gathered:

E_i = the total number of errors uncovered during the ith step in the software engineering process
S_i = the number of serious errors
M_i = the number of moderate errors
T_i = the number of minor errors
PS = size of the product (LOC, design statements, pages of documentation, function points) at the ith step
w_j = weighting factor for serious, moderate, and minor errors, where j = 1 to 3

At each step of the software engineering process, a phase index PI_i is computed:

$$PI_i = w_1 \frac{S_i}{E_i} + w_2 \frac{M_i}{E_i} + w_2 \frac{T_i}{E_i}$$

The error index (EI) is computed by calculating the cumulative effect or each PI_i, weighting errors encountered later in the software engineering process more heavily than those encountered earlier.

$$EI = \frac{\sum_i i PI_i}{PS}$$

$$= \frac{PI_1 + 2PI_2 + 3PI_3 + \cdots i PI_i}{PS}$$

The error index can be used in conjunction with information collected in Table 14.3 to develop an overall indication of improvement in software quality.

The application of the statistical SQA and the Pareto principle can be summarized in a single sentence: *Spend your time focusing on things that really matter, but first be sure that you understand what really matters!* Experienced industry practitioners agree that most really difficult defects can be traced to a relatively limited number of root causes. In fact, most practitioners have an intuitive feeling for the "real" causes of software quality problems, but few have spent time collecting data to support their feelings. By performing the basic steps of statistical SQA, the vital few causes for defects can be isolated and appropriate corrections can be made.

Is it possible to achieve zero-defect software using formal technical reviews and statistical SQA?

Formal technical reviews and statistical SQA are pivotal "filters" that must all be applied in any attempt to achieve "zero defect software." In an excellent book on the subject, Schulmeyer [10] argues that "inspections" (formal technical reviews) are the cornerstone of a zero-defect software approach: "The basic concept of a zero-defect software methodology...invokes error prevention and detection techniques at predefined checkpoints where 'errors' are most likely to occur within the software development cycle, such that, as a goal, zero 'defects' are delivered to the customers."

Schulmeyer describes a quality control technique for software that has been adapted from manufacturing quality control methods developed by the Japanese. In Schulmeyer's approach, both manual and automated error detection methods are applied to produce zero-defect software. Manual error detection is achieved through the use of formal technical reviews that are applied throughout the software engineering process. Automated detection is achieved by a variety of CASE tools for testing.

Our company has initiated a total quality management (TQM) program that has its foundation in the Japanese approach you just mentioned. Can you summarize this approach and indicate whether there are parallels for software?

Over the past 30 years, the Japanese have developed a systematic approach that leads to the elimination of root causes of product defects. Although terminology differs across different companies and authors, a basic four-step progression is normally encountered and forms the foundation of any good TQM program.

The first step is called *kaizen* and refers to a system of continuous process improvement. If your organization institutes a statistical software quality assurance approach, you are on your way toward achieving the first step. The goal of *kaizen* is to develop a process (in this case, the software engineering process) that is visible, repeatable, and measurable.

The second step, invoked only after *kaizen* has been achieved, is called *atarimae hinshitsu*. This step examines intangibles that affect the process and works to optimize their impact on the process. For example, your software engineering process may be affected by high staff turnover which itself is caused by constant reorganizations within your company. It may be that a stable organizational structure could do much to improve the quality of your software. *Atarimae hinshitsu* would lead you to suggest changes in your approach to reorganization.

While the first two steps focus on the process, the next step, called *kansei* (translated as "the five senses") concentrates on the user of the product (in this case, software). In essence, by examining the way the user applies the product *kansei* leads to improvement in the product itself, and potentially, to the process that created it.

Finally, a step called *miryokuteki hinshitsu* broadens management concern beyond the immediate product. This is a business-oriented step that looks for opportunity in related areas that can be identified by observing the use of the product in the marketplace. In the software world, *miryokuteki hinshitsu* might be viewed as an attempt to uncover new and profitable products or applications that are an outgrowth from an existing computer-based system.

For most companies *kaizen* should be of immediate concern. Until you have a software engineering process that is visible, repeatable, and measurable (and most companies don't), you need go no further.

How does the reliability of a computer program fit into an overall picture of software quality?

There is no doubt that the reliability of a computer program is an important element of its overall quality. If a program repeatedly and frequently fails to perform, it matters little whether other software quality factors are acceptable.

Software reliability, unlike many other quality factors, can be measured, directed, and estimated using historical and developmental data. Software reliability is defined in statistical terms as "the probability of failure free operation of a computer program in a specified environment for a specified time" [11]. To illustrate, program X is estimated to have a reliability of 0.98 over 8 elapsed processing hours. In other words, if program X were to be executed 100 times and require 8 hours of elapsed processing time (execution time), it is likely to operate correctly (without failure) 98 times out of 100.

Whenever software reliability is discussed, a pivotal question arises: What is meant by the term *failure?* In the context of any discussion of software quality and reliability, failure is nonconformance to software requirements. Yet, even within this definition there are gradations. Failures can be annoying or catastrophic. One failure can be corrected within seconds, whereas another requires weeks or even months to correct. Complicating the issue even further, the correction of one failure may in fact result in the introduction of other errors that ultimately result in other failures.

Are there measures of software reliability?

If we consider a computer-based system, a simple measure of reliability is *mean time between failure* (MTBF), where

$$MTBF = MTTF + MTTR$$

(The acronyms MTTF and MTTR are *mean time to failure* and *mean time to repair*, respectively.)

Many researchers argue that MTBF is a far more useful measure than defects/KLOC. Stated simply, an end user is concerned with failures, not with the total defect count. Because each error contained within a program does not have the same failure rate, the total defect count provides little indication of the reliability of a system. For example, consider a program that has been in operation for 14 months. Defects in this program may remain undetected for decades before they are discovered. The MTBF of such obscure defects might be 50 or even 100 years. Other defects, as yet undiscovered, might have a failure rate of 18 or 24 months. Even if every one of the first category of defects (those with long MTBF) are removed, the impact on software reliability is negligible.

In addition to a reliability measure, we must develop a measure of *availability*. Software availability is the probability that a program is operating according to requirements at a given point in time and is defined as:

$$\text{Availability} = \frac{MTTF}{MTTF + MTTR} \times 100\%$$

The MTBF reliability measure is equally sensitive to MTTF and MTTR. The availability measure is somewhat more sensitive to MTTR, an indirect measure of the maintainability of software.

Our discussion has focused on ways to uncover software defects, but not on the consequences of these defects should they remain undetected. What can we do to evaluate the "safety" of our computer-based systems?

There has been an historical reluctance to use computers (and software) to control safety critical processes such as nuclear reactors, aircraft flight control, weapons systems, and large-scale industrial processes. Although the probability of failure of a well-engineered system is small, an undetected fault in a computer-based control or monitoring system could result in enormous economic damage, or worse, significant human injury or loss of life. But the cost and functional benefits of computer-based control and monitoring often outweigh the risk. Today, computer hardware and software are used regularly to control safety critical systems. Leveson [12] discusses the impact of software in safety critical systems when she writes:

> Before software was used in safety critical systems, they were often controlled by conventional (nonprogrammable) mechanical and electronic devices. System safety techniques are designed to cope with random failures in these [nonprogrammable] systems. Human design errors are not considered since it is assumed that all faults caused by human errors can be avoided completely or removed prior to delivery and operation.

When software is used as part of the control system, complexity can increase by an order of magnitude or more. Subtle design faults induced by human error—something that can be uncovered and eliminated in hardware-based conventional control—become much more difficult to uncover when software is used.

Software safety is a software quality assurance activity that identifies and assesses potential hazards that may impact software negatively and cause an entire system to fail. Initially, hazards are identified and categorized by criticality and risk. For example, some of the hazards associated with a computer-based cruise control for an automobile might be:

- Causes uncontrolled acceleration that cannot be stopped
- Does not respond to depression of brake pedal (by turning off)
- Does not engage when switch is activated
- Slowly loses or gains speed

Once these system-level hazards are identified, analysis techniques are used to assign severity and probability of occurrence.[1] To be effective, software must be analyzed in the context of the entire system. For example, a subtle user input error (people *are* system components) may be magnified by a software fault to produce control data that improperly positions a mechanical device. If a set of external environ-

---

[1]This approach is analogous to the risk analysis approach described in Chapter 11. The primary difference is the emphasis on technology and product issues as opposed to project-related topics.

mental conditions is met (and only if it is met), the improper position of the mechanical device will cause a disastrous failure.

I'm convinced that SQA is an important activity, and yet, it doesn't seem to be widely instituted? Why is that?

Although few managers and practitioners would debate the need for software quality, many shy away from establishing formal SQA functions. Some managers are reluctant to incur the extra up-front cost, even though a cost benefit can be achieved later. Some practitioners feel that they are already doing everything that needs to be done, and that additional SQA activities would be redundant. No one knows where to put such a function organizationally, and everyone wants to avoid the "red tape" that SQA is perceived to introduce into the software engineering process.

In addition to the concerns about cost, technical efficacy, and organization, pragmatic issues often retard the implementation of an effective SQA function:

- *Staffing can be a problem:*   It is difficult to find sufficiently knowledgeable or experienced people.

- *Interaction is a problem:*   SQA staff may have difficulty communicating with technical "gurus."

- *Management is a problem:*   Management is not "signed up" to quality and doesn't support recommendations that the SQA group makes.

- *Standards are a problem:*   Most organizations work without them.

- *Planning is a problem:*   Few software engineering groups develop a quality plan for each project.

Can the problems that retard institution of SQA be solved?

Successful SQA programs have been developed by many companies. The key to the solution of each of the problems noted above is management commitment. Guidelines for creating requisite management commitment and thereby overcoming the problems associated with establishing effective SQA are presented later in this chapter.

What is the organizational role of an SQA group?

First, it is important to note that everyone serves on the SQA team. Software engineers may have a focus different from that of SQA specialists, but everyone—managers, practitioners, specialists, and even users—is responsible for building a high-quality product.

In some software development organizations, quality is the sole responsibility of the individual who may engineer, review, and test the software. The SQA team and the engineering team are one and the same. In other organizations, an SQA group (staffed by specialists) is chartered with the responsibility for (1) preparing and/or adapting a quality management plan, (2) developing policies, procedures, and standards; (3) conducting quality audits, (4) ensuring that SQA enforcement mechanisms are in place, (5) ensuring that verification and validation techniques are complete, (6) encouraging developer education in software engineering, and (7) establishing mechanisms for subcontractor control.

These seven activities are sometimes called *quality certification* functions. In most cases, an independent SQA group is best equipped to perform them effectively.

How do we institute a more formal approach to SQA?

Before formal quality assurance procedures are instituted, a software development organization should adopt software engineering procedures, methods, and tools. This methodology, when combined with an effective framework for software development, can do much to improve the quality of all software produced by the organization.

The first step to be conducted as part of a concerted effort to institute software quality assurance procedures is an *SQA/SCM Audit*. The current "state" of software quality assurance and software configuration management (Chapter 15) is assessed by examining these topics:

Policies: What current policies, procedures, and standards exist for all phases of software development? Are they enforced? Is there a specific (management supported) policy for SQA? Are policies applied to both development and maintenance activities?

Organization: Where does software engineering reside in the current organizational chart? Where does QA reside?

Functional interfaces: What is the current relationship between QA and SQA functions and other constituencies? How does SQA interact with formal technical reviews, with SCM, with testing activities?

Once these questions have been answered, strengths and weaknesses are identified. If the need for a more formal approach to SQA is apparent, a careful assessment of the pros and cons is undertaken.

On the positive side, an independent SQA group offers the following benefits: (1) software will have fewer latent defects, resulting in reduced effort and time spent during testing and maintenance; (2) higher reliability will result in greater customer satisfaction; (3) maintenance costs (a substantial percentage of *all* software costs) can be reduced; and (4) the overall life-cycle cost of software is reduced.

On the negative side, an independent SQA group can be problematic for the following reasons: (1) it is difficult to institute in small organizations, where resources to perform the necessary activities are not available; (2) it represents cultural change—and change is never easy; and (3) it requires the expenditure of dollars that would not otherwise be explicitly budgeted to software engineering or QA.

At a fundamental level, SQA is cost-effective if

$$C_3 > C_1 + C_2$$

where C_3 is the cost of quality problems that occur with no SQA program, C_1 is the cost of the SQA program itself, and C_2 is the cost of defects not found by SQA activities. It is important to note, however, that a more detailed analysis must also consider reduced testing and integration costs, reduced numbers of prerelease changes, reduced maintenance costs, and improved customer satisfaction.

What is the best way to document our plans for establishing an SQA approach?

Once an organization has decided to institute SQA, a plan should be developed and standards should be acquired. The IEEE [13] has developed a standard format for SQA plans that is shown in Table 14.4.

The SQA Plan provides a roadmap for instituting software quality assurance. Table 14.5 presents a list of SQA-related standards that will serve to guide the development of technical procedures for achieving software quality.

Many of the activities you've described sound similar to the activities conducted as part of our company's "total quality management" (TQM) program for manufacturing. Is this coincidental?

Software quality assurance should be part of your company's TQM approach. Formal technical reviews and statistical quality assurance are based on the same principles that guide manufacturing TQM and demand the same level of management commitment and technical dis-

TABLE 14.4   ANSI/IEEE Standards 730-1984 and 983-1986,
***Software Quality Assurance* Plan**

I. Purpose of the plan
II. References
III. Management
    A. Organization
    B. Tasks
    C. Responsibilities
IV. Documentation
    A. Purpose
    B. Required software engineering documents
    C. Other documents
V. Standards, practices, and conventions
    A. Purpose
    B. Conventions
VI. Reviews and audits
    A. Purpose
    B. Review requirements
        1. Software requirements review
        2. Design reviews
        3. Software verification and validation reviews
        4. Functional audit
        5. Physical audit
        6. In-process audits
        7. Management reviews
VII. Software configuration management
VIII. Problem reporting and corrective action
IX. Tools, techniques, and methodologies
X. Code control
XI. Media control
XII. Supplier control
XIII. Records collection, maintenance, and retention

TABLE 14.5   SQA Standards

DOD-STD-2167A	Software engineering
DOD-STD-2168	Software quality evaluation standard
FAA-STD-018	SQA standard for the FAA
IEEE Std. 730-1984	SQA plans
IEEE Std. 983-1986	Software quality assurance planning
IEEE Std. 1028-1988	Software reviews and audits
IEEE Std. 1012-1986	Software verification and validation plans

cipline. The similarity between manufacturing TQM and SQA is not a coincidence.

A Manager's Checklist

Software quality assurance is an "umbrella activity" that is applied at each step in the software engineering process. SQA encompasses procedures for the effective application of methods and tools, formal technical reviews, testing strategies and techniques, procedures for change control, procedures for ensuring compliance to standards, and measurement and reporting mechanisms.

SQA is complicated by the complex nature of software quality—an attribute of computer programs that is defined as "conformance to explicitly defined requirements." But when considered more generally, software quality encompasses many different product and process factors and related metrics.

Software reviews are one of the most important SQA activities. Reviews serve as a filter for the software engineering process, removing errors while they are relatively inexpensive to find and correct. The formal technical review or walkthrough is a stylized review meeting that has been shown to be extremely effective in uncovering errors. To properly conduct software quality assurance, data about the software engineering process should be collected, evaluated, and disseminated.

Actions

- Collect information on defects that have been reported from the field. Categorize defects by type, severity, and cause. If possible, determine the amount of effort required to correct each defect.

- Perform simple statistical analysis to determine the most commonly encountered defects. Work with technical staff to propose changes to your software development process that will remove the cause of the defects.

- Determine the type of reviews that are currently being conducted within your organization.

Questions

- Does your company currently have a total quality management (TQM) program? If so, how can its precepts be applied to software engineering? Has it been applied to software engineering work?

- Does your organization work with an independent SQA group? If not, how is SQA accomplished in your organization?

- Have you developed standards for SQA?

- Do you have guidelines for the conduct of formal technical reviews?

Further Readings

Books by Crosby [2] and Deming [9] are excellent management-level presentations on the benefits of formal quality assurance programs.

Although they do not focus on software, both books are must reading for senior managers with software development responsibility. For more technically minded managers, books by Shingo (*Zero Quality Control: Source Inspection and the Poka-yoke System,* Productivity Press, Cambridge, MA, 1986), Crosby (*Quality without Tears,* McGraw-Hill, 1984), and Juran (*Quality Control Handbook,* 3d ed., McGraw-Hill, 1979) present a more detailed look at techniques for achieving manufacturing quality. An intriguing adaptation of manufacturing quality assurance methods to computer software proposed by Shingo and others is presented by Schulmeyer [10].

Books by Glass (*Building Quality Software,* Prentice-Hall, 1992), Dunn (*Software Quality Assurance,* Prentice-Hall, 1990), Vincent et al. (*Software Quality Assurance,* Prentice-Hall, 1988), Bryan and Seigel (*Software Product Assurance,* Elsevier, 1988), Schulmeyer and McManus (*Handbook of Software Quality Assurance,* Van Nostrand-Reinhold, 1987) and Chow (*Software Quality Assurance: A Practical Approach,* IEEE Computer Society Press, 1985) provide detailed coverage of SQA, quality metrics and the management issues associated with establishing an SQA function. Dunn and Ullman (*Quality Assurance for Computer Software,* McGraw-Hill, 1982) present comprehensive guidelines for planning, establishing, and conducting the SQA function.

Freedman and Weinberg [6] present a comprehensive discussion of every facet of formal technical reviews. In addition, books by Yourdon (*Structured Walkthroughs,* 4th ed., Yourdon Press, 1989) and Hollocker (*Software Reviews and Audits Handbook,* Wiley, 1990) contain useful guidelines for conducting these worthwhile SQA activities.

Schulmeyer (*Zero Defect Software,* McGraw-Hill, 1990) discusses "quality control" for computer software. The book presents a detailed taxonomy of defects and discusses review and inspection techniques, statistical SQA, and software testing.

Books by Shooman (*Software Engineering,* McGraw-Hill, 1983) and Musa et al. [11] contain detailed stochastic models for software reliability. Rook (*Software Reliability Handbook,* Elsevier, 1990) presents a comprehensive anthology that covers basic reliability concepts, models, methods, and measures. Leveson (*Software Safety,* Addison-Wesley, 1990) presents an in-depth discussion of software safety concepts.

References

[1] Persig, R., *Zen and the Art of Motorcycle Maintenance,* Wm. Morrow, 1974, pp. 205–213.
[2] Crosby, P., *Quality is Free,* McGraw-Hill, 1979.
[3] McCall, J., P. Richards, and G. Walters, "Factors in Software Quality," 3 vols., NTIS AD-A049-014, 015, 055, November 1977.
[4] Cavano, J.P., and J.A. McCall, "A Framework for the Measurement of Software

Quality," *Proc. ACM Software Quality Assurance Workshop*, November 1978, pp. 133–139.

[5] Grady, R.B., and D.L. Caswell, *Software Metrics: Establishing a Company-Wide Program*, Prentice-Hall, 1987.

[6] Freedman, D.P., and G.M. Weinberg, *Handbook of Walkthroughs, Inspections and Technical Reviews*, 3d ed., Dorset House, 1990.

[7] Jones, T.C., *Programming Productivity*, McGraw-Hill, 1986.

[8] "Implementing Software Inspections," course notes, IBM Systems Sciences Institute, IBM Corp., 1981.

[9] Deming, W.E., *Out of the Crisis*, MIT Press, 1986.

[10] Schulmeyer, C.G., *Zero Defect Software*, McGraw-Hill, 1990, p. 33.

[11] Musa, J.D., A. Iannino, and K. Okumoto, *Engineering and Managing Software with Reliability Measures*, McGraw-Hill, 1987.

[12] Leveson, N.G., "Software Safety: Why, What, and How," *ACM Computing Surveys*, **18** (2), 125–163 (1986).

[13] *Software Engineering Standards*, 3d ed., IEEE, 1989.

15

Software Configuration Management: Controlling Change

Change is inevitable when computer software is built. And change increases the level of confusion among software engineers who are working on a project. Confusion arises when changes are *not* analyzed before they are made, recorded before they are implemented, reported to those with a need to know, or controlled in a manner that will improve quality and reduce error. Babich [1] discusses this when he states:

> The art of coordinating software development to minimize...confusion is called *configuration management.* Configuration management is the art of identifying, organizing, and controlling modifications to the software being built by a programming team. The goal is to maximize productivity by minimizing mistakes.

Software configuration management (SCM) is an umbrella activity that is applied throughout the software engineering process. Because change can occur at any time, SCM activities are developed to (1) identify change, (2) control change, (3) ensure that change is being properly implemented, and (4) report change to others who may have an interest.

A primary goal of software engineering is to improve the ease with which changes can be accommodated and reduce the amount of effort expended when changes must be made. In this chapter, I'll discuss the specific activities that will enable you to manage change.

What is a "software configuration"?

The output of the software engineering process is information that may be divided into three broad categories: (1) computer programs (both source-level and executable forms), (2) documents that describe the computer programs (targeted at both technical practitioners and users), and

(3) data structures (contained within the program or external to it). The items that constitute all information produced as part of the software engineering process are collectively called a *software configuration*.

As the software engineering process progresses, the number of *software configuration items* (SCIs) grows rapidly. A *System Specification* spawns a *Software Project Plan* and *Software Requirements Specification*. These in turn spawn other documents to create a hierarchy of information.

Why is it that managing the many configuration items isn't a straightforward clerical activity?

If each SCI simply spawned other SCIs, little confusion would result. Unfortunately, another variable enters the process—*change*. Change may occur at any time, for any reason. In fact, the **"First Law of System Engineering"** [2] states: *No matter where you are in the system life cycle, the system will change, and the desire to change it will persist throughout the life cycle.*

Software configuration management (SCM) is a set of activities that has been developed to manage change throughout the software engineering process. SCM can be viewed as a software quality assurance activity that involves considerably more than clerical tasks and that is applied during all phases of the software engineering process.

Every time a software engineer extends a design or writes a line of code, she or he is changing something. Do you mean to say that SCM applies to every action taken by a developer?

Change is a fact of life in software development. Customers want to modify requirements. Developers want to modify technical approach. Management wants to modify project approach. Why all this modification? The answer is really quite simple. As time passes, all constituencies know more (about what they need, which approach would be best, how to get it done and still make money). This additional knowledge is the driving force behind most changes and leads to a statement of fact that is difficult for many software engineering practitioners to accept: Most changes are justified! But not all changes at all times are controlled.

The term "baseline" is often used in discussions of change control. What does it mean?

A *baseline* is a software configuration management concept that helps us control change without seriously impeding justifiable change. One way to describe a baseline is through analogy:

Consider the doors to the kitchen of a large restaurant. To eliminate collisions, one door is marked OUT and the other is marked IN. The doors have stops that allow them to be opened only in the appropriate direction.

If a waiter picks up an order in the kitchen, places it on a tray, and then realizes he has selected the wrong dish, he may change to the correct dish quickly and informally before he leaves the kitchen.

If, however, he leaves the kitchen, gives the customer the dish and then is informed of his error, he must follow a set procedure: (1) look at the check to determine if an error has occurred, (2) apologize profusely, (3) return to the kitchen through the IN door, (4) explain the problem, and so forth.

A baseline is analogous to the kitchen doors in the restaurant. Before a software configuration item becomes a baseline, change may be made quickly and informally. However, once a baseline is established, we figuratively pass through a swinging one-way door. Changes can be made, but a specific, formal procedure must be applied to evaluate and verify each change.

How should I view a baseline in the context of a software project?

In the context of a software engineering project, a baseline can be defined as a milestone in the development of software that is marked by the delivery of one or more software configuration items and the approval of these SCIs that is obtained through a formal technical review (Chapter 14). For example, the elements of a *Design Specification* have been documented and reviewed. Errors are found and corrected. Once all parts of the specification have been reviewed, corrected, and then approved, the *Design Specification* becomes a baseline. Further changes to the program architecture (contained in the *Design Specification*) can be made only after each has been evaluated and approved.

Although baselines can be defined at any level of detail, the most common software baselines are shown in Figure 15.1. Once an SCI becomes a baseline, it is placed in a *project database* (also called a *project library* or *software repository*). When a member of a software engineering team wants to make a modification to a baselined SCI, it is copied from the project database into the engineer's private work space. Referring to Figure 15.2, an SCI labeled B is copied from the project database into a software engineer's private work space. A record of this activity is recorded in an accounting file. The engineer can work on B' (the copy of the SCI) until the required changes are completed. After change control procedures have been completed (discussed later in this chapter), B' can be used to update B. In some cases, the baselined SCI will be locked so that no one else can work on it until the change has been implemented, reviewed, and approved.

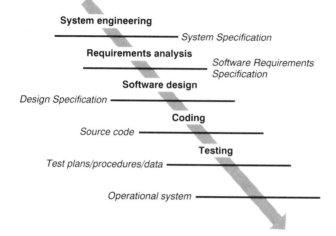

Figure 15.1   Baselines.

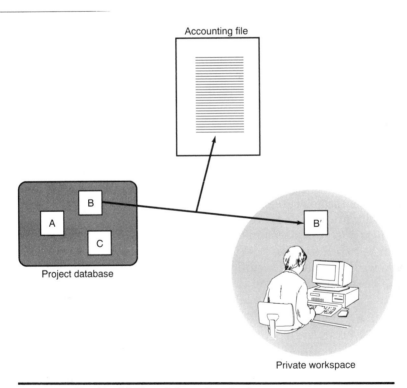

Figure 15.2   Baselined SCIs and the project database.

You named some of the software configuration items that are controlled via SCM. Can you provide a more complete list?

I have already defined a software configuration item as information that is created as part of the software engineering process. In the extreme, an SCI could be considered to be a single section of a large specification or one test case in a large suite of tests. More realistically, an SCI is a document, an entire suite of test cases, or a named program component (e.g., a Pascal procedure or an Ada package).

The following SCIs become the target for configuration management techniques and form a set of baselines:

1. *System Specification*
2. *Software Project Plan*
3. *Software Requirements Specification*; executable or "paper" prototype
4. *Preliminary User Manual*
5. *Design Specification*
   a. Data design description
   b. Architectural design description
   c. Module design descriptions
   d. Interface design descriptions
   e. Object descriptions (if object-oriented techniques are used)
6. Source code listing
7. *Test Plan and Procedure*; test cases and recorded results
8. *Operation and Installation Manuals*
9. Executable program
   a. Module-executable code
   b. Linked modules
10. Database description
    a. Schema and file structure
    b. Initial content
11. *As-built User Manual*
12. Maintenance documents
    a. Software problem reports
    b. Maintenance requests
    c. Engineering change orders
13. *Standards and Procedures for Software Engineering*

Is it correct to assume that SCIs represent work products that are created as part of the software engineering process?

Yes, but other SCIs may also exist. In addition to the SCIs noted above, many software engineering organizations also place software tools under configuration control. That is, specific versions of editors, compilers, and other CASE tools are "frozen" as part of the software configuration. Because these tools were used to produce documentation, source code, and data, they must be available when changes to the software configuration are to be made. Although problems are rare, it is possible that a new version of a tool (e.g., a compiler) might produce different results than the original version. For this reason, tools, like the software that they help to produce, can be baselined as part of a comprehensive configuration management process.

There seem to be a number of ways that SCIs can be related to one another. How are they organized?

In reality, SCIs are organized to form *configuration objects* that may be catalogued in a project database with a single name. A configuration object has a name, has attributes, and is "connected" to other objects by relationships. Referring to Figure 15.3, the configuration objects, **Design Specification, data model, module N, source code,** and **Test Specification,** are each defined separately. However, each of the objects is related to the others as shown by the arrows. A curved

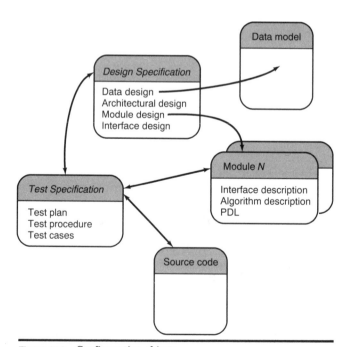

Figure 15.3   Configuration objects.

arrow indicates a compositional relation. That is, **data model** and **module N** are part of the object **Design Specification.** A double-headed straight arrow indicates an interrelationship. If a change were made to the **source code** object, interrelationships enable a software engineer to determine what other objects (and SCIs) might be affected.[1]

What are the key questions that must be answered when an organization decides to manage the SCIs created as part of the software engineering process?

Any discussion of SCM introduces a set of complex questions that must be answered by any organization that wants to control change effectively:

- How does an organization identify and manage the many existing versions of a program (and its documentation) in a manner that will enable change to be accommodated efficiently?

- How does an organization control changes before and after software is released to a customer?

- Who has responsibility for approving and prioritizing changes?

- How can we ensure that changes have been made properly?

- What mechanism is used to notify others of changes that are made?

These questions lead us to the definition of five SCM tasks: *identification, version control, change control, configuration auditing,* and *reporting.*

How should we identify objects in the software configuration?

To control and manage software configuration items, each must be separately named and then organized using an object-oriented approach. Two types of objects can be identified [3]: *basic objects* and *composite objects.* A basic object is a "unit of text" that has been created by a software engineer during analysis, design, code, or test. For example, a basic object might be a section of a requirements specification, a source listing for a module, or a suite of test cases. A composite object is a collection of basic objects and other composite objects. Referring to Figure 15.3, **Design Specification** is a composite object.

---

[1]These relationships are discussed later in this chapter, and the structure of the project database will be discussed in greater detail in Chapter 18.

Conceptually, it can be viewed as a named (identified) list of pointers that specify basic objects such as **data model** and **module N.**

Each object has a set of distinct features that identifies it uniquely: a name, a description, a list of "resources," and a "realization." The object name is a character string that identifies the object unambiguously. The object description is a list of data items that identifies (1) the SCI type (e.g., document, program, data) that is represented by the object, (2) a project identifier, and (3) change and/or version information. Resources are "entities that are provided, processed, referenced or otherwise required by the object" [3]. For example, data types, specific functions, or even variable names may be considered to be object resources. The realization is a pointer to the "unit of text" for a basic object and *null* for a composite object.

Once configuration objects are identified, how are their relationships represented?

Configuration object identification must also consider the relationships that exist between named objects. An object can be identified as <part-of> a composite object. The relationship part-of defines a hierarchy of objects. For example, using the simple notation

```
E-R diagram 1.4 <part-of>  data model;
data model <part-of>  Design Specification;
```

we create a hierarchy of SCIs.

It is unrealistic to assume that the only relationships among objects in an object hierarchy are along direct paths of the hierarchical tree. In many cases, objects are interrelated across branches of the object hierarchy. For example, a data model is interrelated to data flow diagrams (see Chapter 17) and also interrelated to a set of test cases. These cross-structural relationships can be represented in the following manner:

```
data model <interrelated>  data flow model;
data model <interrelated>  test case class m;
```

In the first case, the interrelationship is between a composite object, while the second relationship is between a composite object (**data model**) and a basic object (**test case class m**).

Isn't identification complicated by the changes that occur as an object evolves?

The identification scheme for configuration objects must recognize that objects evolve throughout the software engineering process. Before an object is baselined, it may change many times, and even after a baseline has been established, changes may be quite frequent. It is possible to create an *evolution graph* [4] for any object. The evolution graph describes the change history of the object and is illustrated in Figure 15.4. Configuration object 1.0 undergoes revision and becomes object 1.1. Minor corrections and changes result in versions 1.1.1 and 1.1.2, which are followed by a major update that is object 1.2. The evolution of object 1.0 continues through 1.3 and 1.4, but at the same time, a major modification to the object results in a new evolutionary path, version 2.0. Both versions are currently supported.

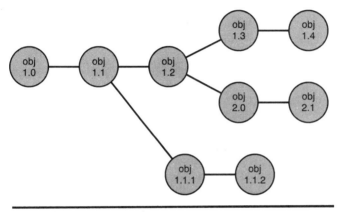

Figure 15.4   Evolution graph.

It is possible that changes may be made to any version, but not necessarily to all versions. How does the developer reference all modules, documents, and test cases for version 1.4? How does the marketing department know what customers currently have version 2.1? How can we be sure that changes to version 2.1 source code are properly reflected in the corresponding design documentation? A key element in the answer to all of the above questions is identification.

It is quite common to manage different versions of the same software package at the same time. How is version control accomplished within the SCM context?

Version control combines procedures and tools to manage different versions of configuration objects that are created during the software engineering process. Clemm [5] describes version control in the context of SCM:

Configuration management allows a user to specify alternative configurations of the software system through the selection of appropriate versions. This is supported by associating attributes with each software version, and then allowing a configuration to be specified [and constructed] by describing the set of desired attributes.

The "attributes" mentioned above can be as simple as a specific version number that is attached to each object or as complex as a string of boolean variables (switches) that indicate specific types of functional changes that have been applied to the system.

One representation of the different versions of a system is the evolution graph presented in Figure 15.4. Each node on the graph is an aggregate object, that is, a complete version of the software. Each version of the software is a collection of SCIs (source code, documents, data), and each version may be composed of different *variants*. To illustrate this concept, consider a version of a simple program that is composed of components 1, 2, 3, 4, and 5 (Figure 15.5).[2] Component 4 is used only when the software is implemented using color displays. Component 5 is implemented when monochrome displays are available. Therefore, two variants of the version can be defined: (1) components 1, 2, 3, and 4; (2) components 1, 2, 3, and 5.

To construct the appropriate variant of a given version of a program, each component can be assigned an "attribute-tuple"—a list of features that will define whether the component should be used when a particular variant of a software version is to be constructed. One or more attributes is assigned for each variant. For example, a *color* attribute could be used to define which component should be included when color displays are to be supported.

Are version control and change control the same thing?

The answer is "no." Version control focuses on the management of specific configuration objects. These objects are created as a consequence of changes that result in the development of different versions of the software. Change control couples procedural activities, technical tasks, and automated tools to manage a change from the time it is requested to the time it is made and integrated into an existing version of the software. In essence, version control can be viewed as an SCM function that occurs as a consequence of change control.

---

[2] In this context, the term "component" refers to all composite objects and basic objects for a baselined SCI. For example, an "input" component might be constructed with six different software modules, each responsible for an input subfunction.

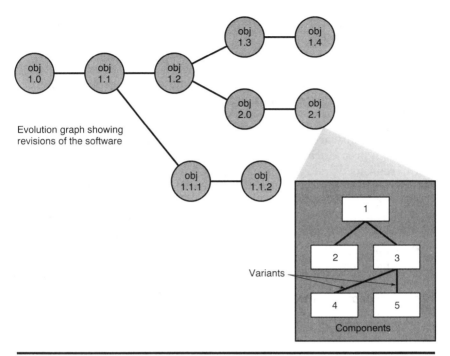

Evolution graph showing
revisions of the software

Variants

Components

Figure 15.5   Versions and variants.

Can you provide an overview of the change control process?

Change control combines human procedures and automated tools to provide a mechanism for the control of change. A *change request*[3] is submitted and evaluated to assess technical merit, potential side effects, overall impact on other configuration objects and system functions, and the projected cost of the change. The results of the evaluation are presented as a *change report* that is used by a *change control authority* (CCA)—a person or group that makes a final decision on the status and priority of the change. An *engineering change order* (ECO) is generated for each approved change. The ECO describes the change to be made, the constraints that must be respected, and the criteria for review and audit. The object to be changed is "checked out" of the project database, the change is made, and appropriate SQA activities are applied. The object is then "checked in" to the database and ap-

---

[3]Although many change requests are submitted during the software maintenance phase, we take a broader view in this discussion. A request for change can occur at any time during the software engineering process.

propriate version control mechanisms are used to create the next version of the software.

Given the procedural nature of the change control process, there must be a step-by-step template for it? Can you provide us with one?

Like many software engineering activities, change control can be reduced to a procedural template, but this can be dangerous for a number of reasons. First, you should not be lured into believing that mere execution of a change control "cookbook" will automatically result in better software quality. Other SQA activities must also be applied. Second, the creation of a cookbook for change control and its acceptance and enthusiastic application within your organization may not necessarily be coincident. It is necessary to plan for the cultural changes that will follow the imposition of a more formal approach to change control.

With these words of warning, the following steps (represented in a process design language) can be defined for change control:

```
procedure: change control
Need for change is recognized;
  case of:
  customer: change in externally observable requirements;
  developer: change in design or implementation;
  manager: change is project context (e.g., cost, delivery date);
  end case
Change request is completed and submitted;
Developer evaluates change request:
  technical impact of requested change is documented;
  cost and schedule impact are noted;
  overall project risk is estimated;
Change Report is generated;
Change control authority (CCA) evaluates Change Report:
  if overall impact is unacceptable and risk is high
  then change is not made:
    change request is denied;
    requester of change is notified;
  else {overall impact is acceptable and risk is low}
    request is queued for subsequent action;
    engineering change order (ECO) is generated:
      change requirements are specified;
      technical specifications for change are noted;
      constraints are identified;
      validation requirements are defined;
    individuals are assigned to configuration objects;
    configuration objects are "checked out;"
    change is made:
      software engineering methods are applied;
      formal technical reviews are conducted;
      all documentation is updated;
      regression testing is conducted;
      SQA activities are performed;
    change is audited by SQA
    modified SCIs are "checked in;"
```

```
appropriate version of software is rebuilt;
baseline for validation testing is established;
final validation tests are performed;
final review of documentation is conducted;
final SQA checks are made;
new software version is distributed;
   endif
end procedure
```

What is meant by check-out and check-in of configuration objects?

The "check-in" and "check-out" process implements two important elements of change control—access control and synchronization control. *Access control* governs which software engineers have the authority to access and modify a particular configuration object. *Synchronization control* helps to ensure that parallel changes, performed by two different people, don't overwrite one another.

Access and synchronization control flow is illustrated schematically in Figure 15.6. Based on an approved change request and ECO, a software engineer checks out a configuration object. An access control function ensures that the software engineer has authority to check out the object, and synchronization control locks the object in the project database so that no updates can be made to it until the currently checked-out version has been replaced. Note that other copies can be checked out, but other updates cannot be made. A copy of the baselined object, called the *extracted version,* is modified by the software

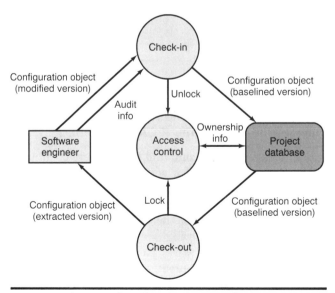

Figure 15.6 Access and synchronization control.

engineer. After appropriate SQA and testing, the modified version of the object is checked in and the new baseline object is unlocked.

It seems like there are many steps involved in making a change. Isn't this approach awfully bureaucratic?

Your question is not uncommon. Without proper safeguards, change control can retard progress and create unnecessary red tape. Most software developers who have change control mechanisms (unfortunately, many have none) have created a number of layers of control to help avoid the problems implied by your question.

Prior to an SCI becoming a baseline, only *informal change control* need be applied. The developer of the configuration object (SCI) in question may make whatever changes are justified by project and technical requirements (as long as changes do not impact broader system requirements that lie outside the developer's scope of work). Once the object has undergone formal technical review and has been approved, a baseline is created.

Once an SCI becomes a baseline, *project-level change control* is implemented. Now, to make a change, the developer must gain approval from the project manager (if the change is "local") or from the CCA if the change impacts other SCIs. In some cases, formal generation of change requests, change reports, and ECOs is dispensed with. However, assessment of each change is conducted and all changes are tracked and reviewed.

When the software product is released to customers, *formal change control* is instituted. The formal change control procedure was described earlier using a process design language.

Given that different layers of change control can be instituted, where does the change control authority (CCA) play a role?

The CCA plays an active role in the second and third layers of control. Depending on the size and character of a software project, the CCA may be composed of one person—the project manager—or a number of people (e.g., representatives from software, hardware, database engineering, support, marketing). The role of the CCA is to take a global view; that is, to assess the impact of change beyond the SCI in question. How will the change impact hardware? How will the change impact performance? How will the change modify the customer's perception of the product? How will the change affect product quality and reliability? These and many other questions are addressed by the CCA.

How can we ensure that the configuration management activities discussed to this point will be conducted within our organization?

Identification, version control, and change control help the software developer maintain order in what would otherwise be a chaotic and fluid situation. However, even the most successful control mechanisms track a change only until an ECO is generated. How can you ensure that the change has been properly implemented? The answer is twofold: (1) *formal technical reviews* and (2) the *software configuration audit*.

The formal technical review (discussed in Chapter 14) focuses on the technical correctness of the configuration object that has been modified. The reviewers assess the SCI to determine consistency with other SCIs, omissions, or potential side effects. A formal technical review should be conducted for all but the most trivial changes.

A software configuration audit complements the formal technical review by assessing a configuration object for characteristics that are seldom considered during review. The audit asks and answers the following questions:

1. Has the change specified in the ECO been made? Have any additional modifications been incorporated?

2. Has a formal technical review been conducted to assess technical correctness?

3. Have software engineering standards been properly followed?

4. Has the change been "highlighted" in the SCI? Have the change date and change author been specified? Do the attributes of the configuration object reflect the change?

5. Have SCM procedures for noting, recording, and reporting the change been followed?

6. Have all related SCIs been properly updated?

In some cases, the audit questions are asked as part of a formal technical review. However, when SCM is a formal activity, the SCM audit is conducted separately by the quality assurance group.

One of our most persistent problems is that people who should know about a specific change aren't informed in a timely manner. Is there an SCM task that will help alleviate this problem?

Configuration status reporting (sometimes called *status accounting*) is an SCM task that answers the following questions:

1. What happened?

2. Who did it?

3. When did it happen?

4. What else will be affected?

Each time an SCI is assigned new or updated identification, a configuration status report (CSR) entry is made. Each time a change is approved by the CCA (i.e., an ECO is issued), a CSR entry is made. Each time a configuration audit is conducted, the results are reported as part of the CSR task. Output from CSR may be placed in an on-line database so that software developers or maintainers can access change information by keyword category. In addition, a CSR report is generated on a regular basis and is intended to keep management and practitioners appraised of important changes.

Configuration status reporting plays a vital role in the success of a large software development project. When many people are involved, it is likely that "the left hand not knowing what the right hand is doing" syndrome will occur. Two developers may attempt to modify the same SCI with different and conflicting intent. A software engineering team may spend months of effort building software to an obsolete hardware specification. The person who would recognize serious side effects for a proposed change is not aware that the change is being made. CSR helps to eliminate these problems by improving communication among all people involved.

Are there published standards for SCM?

Over the past two decades a number of software configuration management standards have been proposed. Many early SCM standards, such as MIL-STD-483, DOD-STD-480A, and MIL-STD-1521A, focused on software developed for military applications. However, more recent ANSI/IEEE standards, such as ANSI/IEEE Std. No. 828-1983, Std. No. 1042-1987, and Std. No. 1028-1988 [6], are applicable for nonmilitary software and are recommended for both large and small software engineering organizations.

Many of the SCM tasks you've described are amenable to automation. Are there CASE tools that support the SCM process?

There are a wide variety of CASE tools that support one or more SCM tasks. Most tools enable a software engineering organization to identify and manage configuration objects, define the relationships between objects, construct new versions of software, and control and report changes that have occurred. When an SCM tool is to be evaluated, the following characteristics should be considered [7]:

- *Component types supported:*   Text, executable code, graphic representations, and data.

- *Versioning strategy:*   Method used to maintain version history.

- *SCM model:*   Based solely on source file changes or focused on versions, baselines, and software engineering paradigms.

- *Data management:*   The way in which configuration objects (COs) are stored.

- *Reporting:*   Types of reports generated by the system.

- *User interface and query capability:*   The ease and robustness of interaction.

- *Traceability:*   The ease with which it is possible to associate one CO with another CO.

- *Automated build method:*   The technique used to automatically construct new versions when changes have been made.

- *Security:*   Controls on the accessibility of COs.

- *Test management:*   The ability to manage test suites and results and relate them to COs.

- *Customization:*   The ability to change the SCM environment and tools to meet local needs.

- *Integration:*   The ease with which other CASE tools can be connected to the SCM environment.

- *Paradigm flexibility:*   The ease with which the tool can be used under different software engineering paradigms.

The CASE repository—the mechanism through which project databases will be created in the future—will be discussed in Chapter 18. Tools for SCM should be designed to manage data contained in the repository.

A Manager's Checklist

Software configuration management is an umbrella activity that is applied throughout the software engineering process. SCM identifies, controls, audits, and reports modifications that invariably occur while software is being developed and after it has been released to a customer. All information produced as part of the software engineering process becomes part of a software configuration. The configuration is organized in a manner that enables orderly control of change.

To help you to understand your current approach to change management, the following actions and questions are recommended.

Actions

- Identify the set of SCIs that your organization currently produces as part of the software engineering process.

- List the configuration objects that comprise each SCI.

- Describe the process through which a change is requested and then made in your organization today.

Questions

- Is the set of SCIs that you currently produce complete? Standardized? Controlled?

- How are requests for change evaluated?

- How do you prioritize requests for change?

- Are records of all software changes made within your organization maintained in a consistent manner?

- How do you currently ensure that a change has been made correctly?

- How do you currently inform those with a need to know?

- Do you currently make use of an on-line "project database" that contains all SCIs produced as part of the software engineering process?

Further Readings

The literature on software configuration management has expanded significantly over the past few years. A book by Berlack (*Software Configuration Management*, Wiley, 1992) is the most comprehensive treatment of the subject published to date. Books by Bersoff et al. [2] and Babich (*Software Configuration Management*, Addison-Wesley, 1986) are good introductions to the procedural elements of SCM. For more detailed discussion of configuration management tools and control mechanisms, the interested reader must resort to conference proceedings and technical papers.

ANSI/IEEE Std. No. 1042-1988 [6] is an excellent tutorial on SCM, providing basic definitions, guidelines for implementing an effective process, and thorough treatment of a wide variety of management and technical issues.

References

[1] Babich, W., *Software Configuration Management*, Addison-Wesley, 1987.

[2] Bersoff, E.H., V.D. Henderson, and S.G. Siegel, *Software Configuration Management*, Prentice-Hall, 1980.

[3] Choi, S.C., and W. Scacchi, "Assuring the Correctness of a Configured Software Description," *Proc. 2d Intl. Workshop on Software Configuration Management*, ACM, Princeton, NJ, October 1989, pp. 66–75.

[4] Gustavsson, A., "Maintaining the Evolution of Software Objects in an Integrated Environment," *Proc. 2d Intl. Workshop on Software Configuration Management*, ACM, Princeton, NJ, October 1989, pp. 114–117.

[5] Clemm, G.M., "Replacing Version Control with Job Control," *Proc. 2d Intl. Workshop on Software Configuration Management*, ACM, Princeton, NJ, October 1989, pp. 162–169.

[6] *Software Engineering Standards*, 3d ed., IEEE Computer Society, 1989.

[7] Forte, G., "Configuration Management Survey," *CASE Outlook* (CASE Consulting Group, Lake Oswego, OR) **90** (2), 24–51 (1990).

The Underlying Technology

Software Engineering Paradigms: A Technology Framework

Every engineering discipline relies on systematic technical methods that have evolved over many years of practice. Whether the objective is to build a new road, fabricate a microchip, construct an office building, develop a control system, or erect a new chemical processing plant, the engineer must apply proven methods that (1) enable the problem requirements to be modeled in a complete and unambiguous manner; (2) specify the design of the entity to be built; (3) implement the design to achieve the function, behavior, and performance that are required by the customer; and (4) test the result to uncover errors and at the same time ensure that all requirements have been met.

Engineering methods are not applied haphazardly. It would make little sense to attempt to construct an office building before a design was created, or to test a microchip before it was fabricated. Therefore, technical methods are applied within some predefined framework that may vary slightly with the people doing the work, the product that is to be built, and the engineering methods that are to be applied. Nonetheless, a framework should always be present.

Like every other engineering discipline, software engineering encompasses a set of proven technical methods that is applied within the context of a process framework. The process framework, often referred to as a software engineering *paradigm,* is chosen based on the nature of the project and application, the methods and tools to be used, and the controls and deliverables that are required. Because software engineering is still maturing, many different paradigms have been proposed (and debated). In this chapter, the most important of these are discussed.

Why is it important for me to understand all of the different paradigms. You're not suggesting that we apply more than one, are you?

A software engineering paradigm provides you with a framework through which you can more effectively manage a software project. A paradigm defines the specific technical steps that should be conducted and, by implication, the milestones to be achieved and the deliverables to be produced. In essence, a paradigm provides a basis for the creation of a work-breakdown structure (WBS) for software engineering.

Over the past two decades, most organizations (that have used a disciplined approach for software development) selected a single paradigm and used it exclusively as a framework for software engineering work. However, the trend today is to be a bit more eclectic. It is possible and often desirable to mix the best features of two or more paradigms or to shift paradigms depending on the situation and development environment. It is for this reason that you should be familiar with each of the major paradigms for software engineering work.

Of the many paradigms that have been suggested for software engineering, which is the one that is most widely used?

The oldest paradigm for software engineering remains the most widely used. Called the *classic life-cycle model*, this paradigm takes a linear sequential view of the software engineering process. Figure 16.1 illustrates a process flow that demands a systematic, sequential approach to software development. The process begins at the system level and progresses through analysis, design, coding, testing, and maintenance. Modeled after a conventional engineering cycle, the life-cycle paradigm encompasses the following activities:

System engineering and analysis: Because software is always part of a larger system, work begins by establishing requirements for all system elements and then allocating some subset of these requirements to software. This system view is essential when software must interface with other elements such as hardware, people, and databases. System engineering and analysis encompasses requirements gathering at the system level with a small amount of top-level design and analysis.

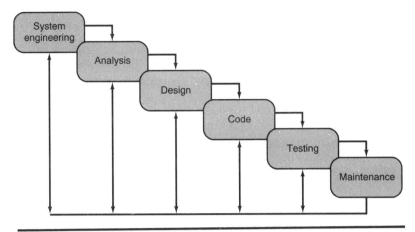

Figure 16.1   The classic life cycle.

Software requirements analysis: The requirements gathering process is intensified and focused specifically on software. To understand the nature of the program(s) to be built, the software engineer ("analyst") must understand the information domain for the software, as well as required function, behavior, performance, and interfacing. Requirements for both the system and the software are documented and reviewed with the customer.

Design: Software design is actually a multistep process that focuses on three distinct attributes of the program: data structure, software architecture, and procedural detail. The design process translates requirements into a representation of the software that can be assessed for quality before coding begins. Like requirements, the design is documented and becomes part of the software configuration.

Coding: The design must be translated into a machine-readable form. The coding step performs this task. If design is performed in a detailed manner, coding can be accomplished mechanistically.

Testing: Once code has been generated, program testing begins. The testing process focuses on the logical internals of the software, ensuring that all statements have been tested, and on the functional externals; that is, conducting tests to uncover errors and ensure that defined input will produce actual results that agree with required results.

Maintenance: Software will undoubtedly undergo change after it is delivered to the customer (a possible exception is embedded software). Change will occur because errors have been encountered, because the software must be adapted to accommodate changes in its external environment (e.g., a change required because of a new operating system or peripheral device), or because the customer requires functional or performance enhancements. Software maintenance reapplies each of the preceding life-cycle steps to an existing program rather than a new one.

A linear, sequential process framework sounds reasonable, but are there any problems with the classic life cycle?

Over the past decade, criticism of the paradigm has caused even active supporters to question its applicability in all situations. Among the problems that are sometimes encountered when the classic life-cycle paradigm is applied are:

1. Real projects rarely follow the sequential flow that the model proposes. Iteration always occurs and creates problems in the application of the paradigm.

2. It is often difficult for the customer to state all requirements explicitly. The classic life cycle requires this and has difficulty accommodating the natural uncertainty that exists at the beginning of many projects.

3. The customer must have patience. A working version of the program(s) will not be available until late in the project time span. A major blunder, if undetected until the working program is reviewed, can be disastrous.

Each of these problems is real. However, the classic life-cycle paradigm has a definite and important place in software engineering work. It provides a template into which methods for analysis, design, coding, testing, and maintenance can be placed. The classic life cycle remains the most widely used procedural model for software engineering. While it does have weaknesses, it is significantly better than a haphazard approach to software development.

You mentioned that the life cycle demands that the customer understand exactly what is required and then wait patiently for it to be constructed. Is there a paradigm that accommodates impatient customers who don't know exactly what they need?

You mean, "Is there a paradigm that accommodates the majority of all software customers?" Surprisingly, the answer is "yes." Most customers have defined a set of general objectives for software, but have not identified detailed input, processing, or output requirements. In other cases, the software developer may be unsure of the efficiency of an algorithm, the adaptability of an operating system, or the form that human–machine interaction should take. In these, and many other situations, a prototyping approach to software engineering may offer the best approach.

The prototyping approach is common in the hardware engineering world. Do you mean to say that we build a mock-up of a software-based system?

Prototyping is a process that enables the developer to create a model or "mock-up" of the software that must be built. The model can take one of three forms: (1) a paper prototype or PC-based model that depicts human–machine interaction in a form that enables the user to understand how such interaction will occur, (2) a working prototype that implements some subset of the function required of the desired software, or (3) an existing program that performs part or all of the function desired but has other features that will be improved on in the new development effort.

The sequence of events for the prototyping paradigm is illustrated in Figure 16.2. Like all approaches to software development, prototyping begins with requirements gathering. Developer and customer meet and define the overall objectives for the software, identify whatever requirements are known, and outline areas where further definition is mandatory. A "quick design" then occurs. The quick design focuses on a representation of those aspects of the software that will be visible to the user (e.g., input approaches and output formats). The quick design leads to the construction of a prototype. The prototype is evaluated by the customer/user and is used to refine requirements for the software to be developed. A process of iteration occurs as the prototype is "tuned" to satisfy the needs of the customer, while at the same time enabling the developer to better understand what needs to be done.

So you're saying that the prototype serves as a mechanism for helping the customer to understand what is required?

Ideally, the prototype serves as a mechanism for identifying software requirements. If a working prototype is built, the developer attempts to make use of existing program fragments or applies tools (e.g., re-

Start

Stop

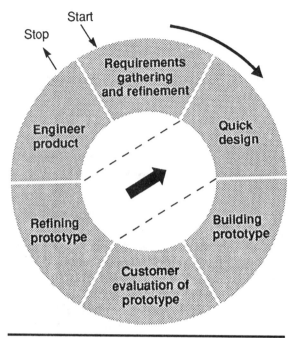

Figure 16.2   Prototyping.

port generators, window managers) that enable working programs to
be generated quickly.

What do we do with the prototype when it has served its purpose?

Brooks [1] provides an answer:

> In most projects, the first system built is barely usable. It may be too
> slow, too big, awkward in use or all three. There is no alternative but to
> start again, smarting but smarter, and build a redesigned version in
> which these problems are solved....When a new system concept or new
> technology is used, one has to build a system to throw away, for even the
> best planning is not so omniscient as to get it right the first time. The
> management question, therefore, is not whether to build a pilot system
> and throw it away. You will do that. The only question is whether to plan
> in advance to build a throwaway, or to promise to deliver the throwaway
> to customers.

The prototype can serve as "the first system." The one that Brooks recommends we throw away. But this may be an idealized view. In many
situations the prototype evolves into the production system. If this evolution occurs in a controlled manner, the paradigm can work effec-

tively, but if the prototype is rushed into use, problems will invariably occur.

The prototyping approach seems quite natural. Why do you imply that it may be problematic?

The customer sees what appears to be a working version of the software, unaware that the prototype is held together "with chewing gum and baling wire," unaware that in the rush to get it working we haven't considered overall software quality or long-term maintainability. When informed that the product must be rebuilt, the customer becomes impatient, crying foul and demanding that "a few fixes" be applied to make the prototype a working product. Too often, software development management relents.

But the problems that can occur while using the prototyping paradigm are not solely the customer's. The developer often makes implementation compromises in order to get a prototype working quickly. An inappropriate operating system or programming language may be used simply because it is available and known; an inefficient algorithm may be implemented simply to demonstrate capability. After a time, the developer may become familiar with these choices and forget all the reasons why they were inappropriate. The less-than-ideal design decision has now become an integral part of the system.

The key for overcoming these problems is to define the rules of the game at the beginning; that is, the customer and the developer must both agree that the prototype is built to serve as a mechanism for defining requirements. It is then discarded (at least in part) and the actual software is engineered with an eye toward quality and maintainability.

During prototyping, software "evolves" toward a working product. Are there other evolutionary paradigms?

The *spiral model* for software engineering [2] has been developed to encompass the best features of both the classic life cycle and prototyping, while at the same time adding a new element—risk analysis—that is missing in these paradigms. The model, represented by the spiral in Figure 16.3, defines four major activities represented by the four quadrants of the figure:

1. *Planning:* Determination of objectives, alternatives, and constraints.
2. *Risk analysis:* Analysis of alternatives and identification and/or resolution of risks.

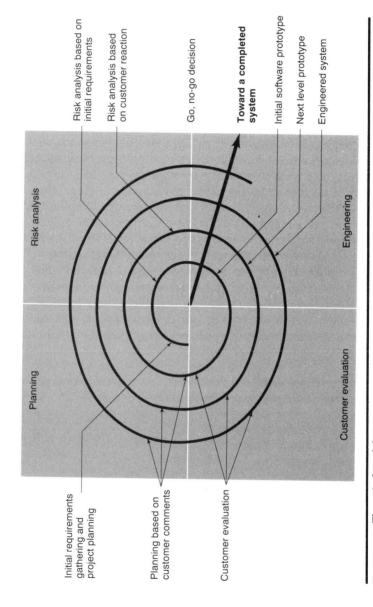

Risk analysis based on initial requirements

Risk analysis based on customer reaction

Go, no-go decision

Toward a completed system

Initial software prototype

Next level prototype

Engineered system

Risk analysis

Planning

Engineering

Customer evaluation

Initial requirements gathering and project planning

Planning based on customer comments

Customer evaluation

Figure 16.3   The spiral model.

3. *Engineering:*   Development of the "next level" product.

4. *Customer evaluation:*   Assessment of the results of engineering.

An intriguing aspect of the spiral model becomes apparent when we consider the radial dimension depicted in Figure 16.3. With each iteration around the spiral (beginning at the center and working outward), progressively more complete versions of the software are built. During the first circuit around the spiral, objectives, alternatives, and constraints are defined and risks are identified and analyzed. If risk analysis (see Chapter 11 for details) indicates that there is uncertainty in requirements, prototyping may be used in the engineering quadrant to assist both the developer and the customer. Simulations and other models may be used to further define the problem and refine requirements.

The customer evaluates the engineering work (the customer evaluation quadrant) and makes suggestions for modifications. On the basis of customer input, the next phase of planning and risk analysis occurs. At each loop around the spiral, the culmination of risk analysis results in a "go/no-go" decision. If risks are too great, the project can be terminated.

In most cases, however, flow around a spiral path continues, with each path moving the developers outward toward a more complete model of the system, and ultimately, to the operational system itself. Every circuit around the spiral requires engineering (lower right quadrant) that can be accomplished using either the classic life-cycle or prototyping approach. It should be noted that the number of development activities occurring in the lower right quadrant increases as activities move further from the center of the spiral.

The spiral model paradigm for software engineering is currently the most realistic approach to the development for large-scale systems and software. It uses an "evolutionary" approach to software engineering, enabling the developer and the customer to understand and react to risks at each evolutionary level. It uses prototyping as a risk reduction mechanism, but more importantly, enables the developer to apply the prototyping approach at any stage in the evolution of the product. It maintains the systematic stepwise approach suggested by the classic life cycle, but incorporates it into an iterative framework that more realistically reflects the real word. The spiral model demands a direct consideration of technical risks at all stages of the project, and if properly applied, should reduce risks before they become problematic.

What problems would be encountered if an evolutionary paradigm were chosen?

Like other paradigms, the spiral model is not a panacea. It may be difficult to convince large customers (particularly in contract situations) that the evolutionary approach is controllable. Each loop around the spiral implies that project cost and schedule are reviewed and may be modified based on customer evaluation. This will create problems in situations in which fixed-price development is undertaken.

The spiral model also demands considerable risk assessment expertise, and relies on this expertise for success. If a major risk is not discovered, problems will undoubtedly occur. Finally, the model itself is relatively new and has not been used as widely as the life-cycle or prototyping approach. It will take a number of years before efficacy of this important new paradigm can be determined with absolute certainty.

Over the last few years, I've heard a lot of discussion about "object-oriented" software development. Is there a paradigm that accommodates this approach?

Object-oriented software development[1] has captured the imagination of much of the software engineering community. Although the object-oriented approach can be used within the context of any of the three paradigms that we have already discussed, a paradigm that explicitly addresses the method, and incorporates the notion of software component reuse, has been developed.

Like other process models, the object-oriented paradigm begins with requirements gathering. Developer and customer meet and define the overall objectives for the software; identify the functional, behavioral, and data requirements that are known; and outline areas where further elaboration is required. The object-oriented paradigm begins with object-oriented analysis (OOA), an activity in which classes and objects (see Chapter 17) are extracted from the initial statement of requirements. Object-oriented design (OOD) creates a model of each program component (object) and the mechanisms for communication between objects. OOA and OOD occur iteratively until a reasonable design model for the system has been derived.

You mentioned the "notion of software component reuse." How does it fit into the object-oriented paradigm?

Once an object-oriented design model has been created, the software engineer browses through a library (repository) that contains existing program components to determine whether any of these components can be reused in the design at hand. "Browsing" is conducted using

---

[1]Object-oriented software development is discussed in Chapter 17.

automated tools and a classification scheme that enables the engineer to categorize required component features. If reusable components are found, they are used as building blocks to construct a prototype of the software. If reusable components are unavailable (or if some modification is required to a reusable component), the design and implementation steps noted in Figure 16.4 are conducted.

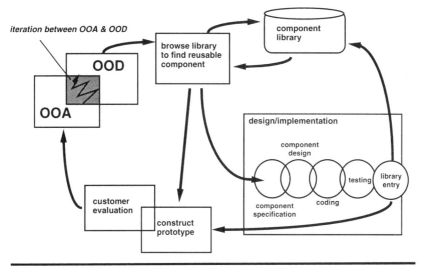

Figure 16.4   An object-oriented paradigm that accommodates reuse.

It is important to note that object-oriented methods result in the creation of program components that are inherently reusable. Therefore, the design and implementation steps result in the creation of another reusable component that is added to the library. Over time, the size of the component library grows and the need to enter the design and implementation step is reduced.

The object-oriented paradigm, like the spiral model, is an evolutionary process model for software engineering. The cycle illustrated in Figure 16.4 continues until the prototype evolves into a production system.

The paradigms that you discussed so far seem to focus on a model for how software is built, without explicit reference to how quality is maintained. Is that true?

It is true that the process models that I have presented emphasize the steps required to create computer software. But it is important to note that each paradigm also assumes that an emphasis on quality will occur throughout the process. As we discussed in Chapter 14, software quality assurance is an umbrella activity that is the responsibility of everyone (managers, engineers, customers, users, and SQA specialists) who is involved in the software engineering process. Therefore, each paradigm makes implicit reference to SQA activities because each assumes that they will be conducted through the process.

Are there paradigms that emphasize "quality" in some formal and explicit way?

Formal program specification and verification (correctness proofs) and statistical SQA have been combined into a paradigm that improves the quality of product software. Called the *cleanroom process* [3] or *cleanroom software engineering,* it is described by Mills et al. [4]:

> With the cleanroom process, you can engineer software under statistical quality control. As with cleanroom hardware development, the process's first priority is defect prevention rather than defect removal (of course, any defects not prevented should be removed). This first priority is achieved by using human mathematical verification [proofs of correctness] in place of program debugging to prepare software for system test.
>
> Its next priority is to provide valid, statistical certification of the software's quality.... The measure of quality is the mean time to failure.

Developers of the cleanroom process argue that mathematical program verification "need take no more time than debugging" and that the resultant number of defects per KLOC can be reduced substantially. For software projects (between 1000 and 50,000 LOC) developed using the cleanroom approach, 90 percent of all defects were found before the first executable tests were conducted.

Is there a pragmatic realization of the cleanroom paradigm?

The high quality of software that has been produced using the cleanroom paradigm is achieved by (1) defining a set of software *increments* that combine to form the required system; (2) using rigorous methods for specification, development, and certification of each increment; (3) applying strict statistical quality control during the testing process;

and (4) enforcing a strict separation of the specification and design tasks from testing activities.

What are the "rigorous methods" that are used as part of the cleanroom engineering paradigm?

The rigorous methods that I have alluded to are actually a collection of formal mathematical methods for software specification and verification. In his introductory discussion of formal methods, Anthony Hall [5] states:

> Formal methods are controversial. Their advocates claim that they can revolutionize [software] development. Their detractors think they are impossibly difficult. Meanwhile, for most people, formal methods are so unfamiliar that it is difficult to judge the competing claims.

Formal methods enable a software engineer to specify, develop, and verify a computer-based system by applying a rigorous, mathematical notation. Using a *formal specification language,* a formal method provides a means for specifying a system so that consistency, completeness, and correctness can be assessed in a systematic fashion.

When formal methods are used during development, they provide a mechanism for eliminating many of the problems that are encountered when software is developed using other paradigms. Ambiguity, incompleteness, and inconsistency can be discovered and corrected more easily—not through ad hoc review, but through the application of mathematical analysis. When formal methods are used during design, they serve as a basis for program verification and therefore enable the software engineer to discover and correct errors that might otherwise go undetected.

Part of the reason why formal methods show promise as a new approach to software engineering is that they make the developer consider a software problem in a manner that is analogous to an algebraic derivation or a proof in analytic geometry. The rigor of a mathematical description forces the engineer to think more carefully about the problem at hand.

You indicate that the cleanroom paradigm demands the "separation" of various engineering activities. How is this accomplished?

To accomplish separation, software engineers are organized into three separate engineering activities that occur within the context of the cleanroom paradigm [6]:

1. A specification team creates a formal specification for each software *increment*. An "increment" is a software component or group of components. The specification provides information necessary for design and establishes a basis from which testing will be conducted.

2. A development team designs and codes each software increment. It is important to note that the team's approach to design and coding is different from that used in less formal paradigms. The team used a *box-structured* [7] strategy in which the design model is represented from three different points of view: external component detail, component behavior, and internal procedural detail. After code has been generated, the development team uses "proof of correctness" methods [8] to demonstrate that the code conforms to the design.

3. A certification team performs all testing and uses statistical quality control techniques (Chapter 14) to track and analyze errors and their causes.

What is the sequence of activities that occurs as the cleanroom engineering team begins the development of a software-based system?

Figure 16.5 illustrates the sequence of events that occurs during the application of the cleanroom paradigm. The specification team devel-

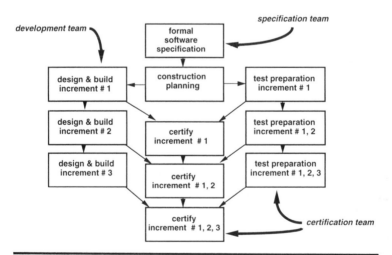

Figure 16.5   The cleanroom engineering paradigm. (Adapted from H. Mills, "Cleanroom Engineering," *CASEWorld Conference Proceedings*, Digital Consulting, Inc., Boston, MA, August 1991.)

ops a formal specification of the software. On the basis of information contained within the specification, the three engineering teams plan the construction process by determining the order in which increments are to be implemented, tested, and certified. The development and certification teams work in parallel on each software increment. The development team uses formal design and implementation methods to build each increment, while the certification team conducts test planning for the increment.

Once the increment is built, the certification team conducts tests and collects statistical data. According to Mills: "It is characteristic that each increment goes through a maturation during testing, becoming more reliable from corrections [made by the development team] required for failures found, serving thereby as a stable base as later increments are delivered and added to the developing system" [6].

The process of development and testing (and the feedback that occurs when errors are discovered) occurs until the software increment is certified. New increments are then added to the certified increment(s) as the system evolves toward the finished product.

My organization makes use of "fourth-generation techniques." Is there a paradigm that has been developed exclusively for them?

The term *fourth-generation techniques* (4GT) encompasses a broad array of software tools that have one thing in common: Each enables the software developer to specify some characteristic of software at a high level of abstraction. The tool then automatically generates source code based on the developer's specification. There is little debate that the higher the level at which software can be specified to a machine, the faster a program can be built.

Fourth-generation techniques can be used with any of the paradigms that have already been discussed in this chapter. However, a paradigm specifically derived for 4GT focuses on the ability to specify software at a level that is close to natural language or using a notation that imparts significant function.

The 4GT paradigm for software engineering is depicted in Figure 16.6. Like other paradigms, 4GT begins with a requirements gathering step. Ideally, the customer would describe requirements and these would be directly translated into an operational prototype. But this is unworkable. The customer may be unsure of what is required, ambiguous in specifying facts that are known, or unable or unwilling to specify information in a manner that a 4GT tool can consume. In addition, current 4GT tools are not sophisticated enough to accommo-

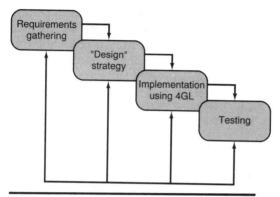

Figure 16.6   Fourth-generation techniques.

date truly "natural language" and won't be for some time. At this time, the customer–developer dialog described for other paradigms remains an essential part of the 4GT approach.

For small applications, it may be possible to move directly from the requirements gathering step to implementation using a nonprocedural fourth-generation language (4GL). However, for larger efforts, it is necessary to develop a design strategy for the system, even if a 4GL is to be used. The use of 4GT without design (for large projects) will cause the same difficulties (poor quality, poor maintainability, poor customer acceptance) that have been encountered when developing software using conventional approaches.

Implementation using a 4GL enables the software developer to represent desired results in a manner that results in automatic generation of code to generate those results. Obviously, a data structure with relevant information must exist and be readily accessible by the 4GL.

To transform a 4GT implementation into a product, the developer must conduct thorough testing, develop meaningful documentation, and perform all other "transition" activities that are also required in other software engineering paradigms. In addition, the software developed using 4GT must be built in a manner that enables maintenance to be performed expeditiously.

Is it fair to say that the 4GT paradigm must be used in conjunction with a set of tools that supports the paradigm?

Currently, a software development environment that supports the 4GT paradigm includes some or all of the following tools: nonprocedural languages for database query, report generation, data manipulation, screen interaction and definition, code generation, high-level graphics capability, and spreadsheet capability. Each of these tools does exist, but only for very specific application domains. There is no 4GT environment available today that may be applied with equal facility across all software application categories.

What are the pros and cons of using fourth-generation techniques and the 4GT paradigm?

There has been much hyperbole and considerable debate surrounding the use of the 4GT paradigm. Proponents claim dramatic reduction in software development time and greatly improved productivity for people who build software. Opponents claim that current 4GT tools are not all that much easier to use than programming languages, that the resultant source code produced by such tools is "inefficient," and that the maintainability of large software systems developed using 4GT is open to question.

There is some merit in the claims of both sides. Although it is somewhat difficult to separate fact from fantasy (few controlled studies have been done to date), it is possible to summarize the current state of 4GT approaches:

1. With very few exceptions, the current application domain for 4GT is limited to business information systems applications; specifically, information analysis and reporting that are keyed to large databases. However, new CASE tools now support the use of 4GT for the automatic generation of "skeleton code" for engineering and real-time applications.

2. Preliminary data collected from companies who are using 4GT seems to indicate that time required to produce software is greatly reduced for small and intermediate applications and that the amount of design and analysis for small applications is also reduced.

3. However, the use of 4GT for large software development efforts demands thorough analysis, design, and testing (software engineering activities) to achieve substantial time savings that are implied by the elimination of coding.

To summarize, fourth-generation techniques have already become an important part of software development in the information systems application area and will likely become widely used in engineering and real-time applications during the middle to late 1990s. The demand for software will continue to escalate throughout the remainder of this century, but software produced using conventional methods and languages is likely to contribute less and less to all software developed. Fourth-generation techniques will fill the gap.

You've already implied that it is possible to combine two or more of the paradigms. Can you provide a bit more detail?

The software engineering paradigms discussed in the preceding sections are often described as alternative approaches to software engineering, rather than complementary approaches. In many cases, however, the paradigms can and should be combined so that the strengths of each can be achieved on a single project. The spiral model paradigm accomplishes this directly, combining prototyping and elements of the classic life cycle in an evolutionary approach to software engineering. But any one of the paradigms can serve as a foundation into which others are integrated.

Figure 16.7 illustrates how some of the software engineering paradigms that we discussed can be combined during a single software development effort. In all cases, work begins with a determination of objectives, alternatives, and constraints—a step that is sometimes called preliminary requirements gathering. From this point, any one of the paths indicated in the figure can be taken. For example, the classic life-cycle steps (far-left-hand path) can be followed, if the system can be fully specified at the beginning. If requirements are uncertain, a prototype can be used to define requirements more fully. Using the prototype as a guide, the developer can then return to the steps of the classic life cycle (design, code, and test). Alternatively, the prototype can evolve toward the production system, with a return to the life-cycle paradigm for testing. Fourth-generation techniques can be used to implement the prototype or to implement the production system during the coding step of the life cycle. 4GT can also be used in conjunction with the spiral model for prototyping or coding steps.

There is no need to be dogmatic about the choice of paradigms for software engineering. The nature of the application should dictate the approach to be taken. By combining paradigms, the whole can be greater than the sum of the parts.

Is there a set of general principles or characteristics that would enable us to assess the efficacy of the paradigms that you've discussed?

Yeh and his colleagues [9] present a set of "common sense principles for tackling complex [software] problems." These principles may also be used to judge the efficacy of a particular software engineering par-

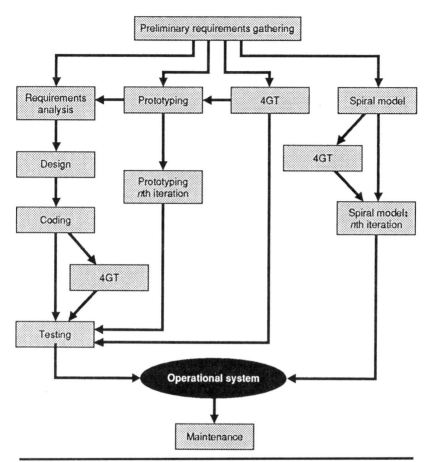

Figure 16.7   Combining paradigms.

adigm. The principles and the questions that they imply are noted below:

Separation of concerns: Large software problems are complex. By subdividing them, they are easier to manage and easier to solve. Does the paradigm make this subdivision relatively easy? Does it reduce overall project complexity? Also, does the paradigm support the means through which the individual subproblems are to be reassembled into a whole?

Coevolution: Many software engineering activities can be conducted concurrently. Does a paradigm support concurrent tasks directly, or does it take a linear, sequential view of development?

Protoiteration: There are many instances during the software engineering process when requirements (at some level of detail) are hazy. Does the paradigm support a prototyping cycle, one in which iterative prototyping can be conducted at a number of points during the process?

Reification: Software projects demand the exchange of information and the need to represent that information in some tangible fashion (e.g., documents, graphical models). Does the paradigm support easy exchange of information across the software engineering process?

Inclusion: Systems are often specified by a diverse group of customers and built by more than one person or group. Does the paradigm accommodate diversity—in terms of both the requirements that are generated by different customers and the development approaches applied by different developers?

Continual improvement: Any process should build a high-quality system, and in so doing, generate data that can be used to improve the process so that the next time it will build an even higher-quality system. Does the paradigm have an explicit focus on continuous quality improvement?

There is no paradigm that satisfies each of these characteristics equally well. However, as a group these principles can provide excellent guidance when an organization establishes its own process framework.

Any one of the paradigms could serve as a framework for managing the software engineering process. Is there a unifying model that would enable us to characterize each of the paradigms?

Yeh and his colleagues [9] extend the principles that were presented above into a "three-dimensional" process model that can be used to characterize any of the paradigms that we have discussed. The Yeh model begins with the assumption that every software engineering process has three different structures: (1) an *activity structure* that defines the tasks to be conducted, and the sequencing, concurrency, and interdependency of these tasks; (2) a *communication structure* that identifies the communication channels that are required to achieve communication among constituencies involved in the software process (reification); and (3) an *infrastructure* that supports overall goals of quality and productivity (the umbrella activities that we have discussed earlier in the book fall within the infrastructure).

Each of the structural dimensions can be characterized on the following qualitative scale:

- *None:* The paradigm places little emphasis on the structural dimension.

- *Slight:* The paradigm places a small amount of emphasis on the structural dimension.

- *Moderate:* The paradigm places a reasonable amount of emphasis on the structural dimension.

- *Heavy:* The paradigm places a heavy emphasis on the structural dimension.

Table 16.1 rates each of the paradigms we have discussed against the structural dimensions proposed by Yeh [9]. Referring to the table, you'll note that most of the paradigms have a moderate level of activity structure, but that emphasis on communication and infrastructure is either *slight* or *none* for the two most commonly used paradigms—the classic life cycle and prototyping. To quote Yeh [9]: "Viewed from a short term perspective, activities are very important, but to achieve long term project objectives, infrastructure and communication structure must have at least an equal emphasis...." If your organization is considering one or more of the paradigms as a model for a software engineering framework, you should keep Yeh's words in mind.

TABLE 16.1 Existing Paradigms and Their Coverage of Activity, Communication, and Infrastructure

Paradigm	Dimensions		
	Activity	Communication	Infrastructure
Classic life cycle	Moderate	None	Slight
Prototyping	Slight	Slight	None
Spiral	Moderate	Moderate	Moderate
Object-oriented/reuse	Moderate	Slight	Moderate
Cleanroom	Moderate	Moderate	Heavy
4GT	Slight	Slight	Slight

A Manager's Checklist

To be used effectively, software engineering technology must be placed within a framework. The framework enables the manager to monitor and track the application of the technology during an actual project. Paradigms provide the conceptual basis for the establishment of a process framework for software engineering. "Older" (but still workable) linear, sequential paradigms are being displaced by more modern evolutionary paradigms that incorporate new management and technical methods such as risk analysis, object-oriented technologies, reuse, statistical SQA, formal methods, and 4GT.

Paradigms can be evaluated using basic characteristics and a process model that considers activity structure, communication structure, and infrastructure.

To better understand the use of paradigms within your organization, the following actions and questions are recommended.

Actions

- List all tasks that are required as part of your organization's software engineering process framework.

- List all milestones and deliverables that are required as part of your organization's software engineering process framework.

- For the two lists developed above, have three or four practitioners and an equal number of project managers grade each task, milestone, and deliverable on an effectiveness scale of 1 to 5, where 1 means ineffective and 5 means very effective.

- For the two lists developed above, have three or four practitioners and an equal number of project managers grade each task, milestone, and deliverable on a usage scale of 1 to 5, where 1 means that the task, milestone, or deliverable is rarely used in real project work and 5 means that it is always used.

- Considering the activity structure, communication structure, and infrastructure introduced in this chapter, categorize each framework task by the dimension (structure) that it addresses.

Questions

- Which of the paradigms presented in this chapter best describes your organization's approach to software engineering?

- Is your approach to software development best characterized as sequential, iterative, or evolutionary?

- To what level of detail is your process framework described? Is it formally documented?

- How much leeway does a project manager have in interpreting your process framework?

Further Readings

Detailed descriptions of software engineering paradigms are presented in software engineering books by Pressman (*Software Engineering: A Practitioner's Approach*, 3d ed., McGraw-Hill, 1992), Sommerville (*Software Engineering*, 4th ed., Addison-Wesley, 1990), Ng and Yeh (*Modern Software Engineering*, Van Nostrand-Reinhold, 1990), and Macro (*Software Engineering*, Prentice-Hall, 1990). Each of these books also discusses the methods and tools that may be used in conjunction with the software process framework. Agresti (*New Paradigms for Software Development*, IEEE Computer Society Press, 1986) discusses a variety of "new" paradigms, including those that are still in the research and exploratory stage.

Thomsett ("Managing Superlarge Projects: A Contingency Approach," *American Programmer*, June 1991) discusses the modifications to any paradigm that are required for very large projects. Yeh and his colleagues [9] introduce a new process model called "Cosmos" that maximizes activity structure, communication structure, and infrastructure.

The Software Engineering Institute has produced a number of excellent publications that enable an organization to assess the current process maturity of its software engineering framework. (These were discussed in Chapter 5.) Books by Utz (*Software Technology Transitions*, Prentice-Hall, 1992), Humphrey (*Managing the Software Process*, Addison-Wesley, 1989) and Pressman (*Making Software Engineering Happen*, Prentice-Hall, 1988) provide additional guidance required to improve the state of practice within a software engineering organization.

References

[1] Brooks, F., *The Mythical Man-Month*, Addison-Wesley, 1975.
[2] Boehm, B., "A Spiral Model for Software Development and Enhancement," *Computer* **21** (5), 61–72 (1988).
[3] Currit, A., M. Dyer, and H.D. Mills, "Certifying the Reliability of Software," *IEEE Trans. Software Engineering* **12** (1), 3–11 (1986).
[4] Mills, H.D., M. Dyer, and R.C. Linger, "Cleanroom Software Engineering," *IEEE Software* (Sept.), 19–25 (1987).
[5] Hall, A., "Seven Myths of Formal Methods," *IEEE Software* (Sept.), 11–20 (1990).
[6] Mills, H.D., "Cleanroom Engineering," *American Programmer* **4** (1), 31–37 (1991).
[7] Parnas, D.L., "A Technique for Software Module Specification with Examples," *CACM* **15** (5), 330–336 (1972).
[8] Baber, R.L., *Error Free Software*, Wiley, 1991.
[9] Yeh, R.T. et al., "A Commonsense Management Model," *IEEE Software* (Nov.), 23–33 (1991).

Software Engineering Methods: Technology Tactics

There was a time—some people call it "the good old days"—when a skilled programmer created a program like an artist creates a painting: she or he just sat down and started. Pressman and Herron [1] draw other parallels when they write:

> At one time or another, almost everyone laments the passing of the good old days. We miss the simplicity, the personal touch, the emphasis on quality that were the trademarks of a craft. Carpenters reminisce about the days when houses were built with mahogany and oak, and beams were set without nails. Engineers still talk about an earlier era when one person did all the design (and did it right) and then went down to the shop floor and built the thing. In those days, people did good work and stood behind it.
>
> How far back do we have to travel to reach the good old days? Both carpentry and engineering have a history that is well over 2,000 years old. The disciplined way in which work is conducted, the standards that guide each task, the step by step approach that is applied, have all evolved through centuries of experience. *Software engineering* has a much shorter history.

During its short history, the creation of computer programs has evolved from an art form, to a craft, to an engineering discipline. As the evolution took place, the free-form style of the artist was replaced by the disciplined methods of an engineer. To be honest, we lose something when a transition like this is made. There's a certain freedom in art that can't be replicated in engineering. But we gain much, much more than we lose.

As the journey from art to engineering occurred, basic principles that guided our approach to software problem analysis, design, and testing slowly evolved. And at the same time, methods were developed that embodied these principles and made software engineering tasks more systematic. Some of these "hot, new" methods flashed to the surface for a few years, only to disappear into oblivion. But others have stood the test of time to become part of the technology of software development.

In this chapter I'll introduce you to the basic principles that support software engineering methods and provide an overview of some of the methods that have already "stood the test of time" and others that are likely to do so.

Now you're going to begin getting technical, aren't you? As a manager, how much do I really need to know?

The only honest answer to your question is: "That depends." If you're a technical manager, it's likely that you'll already be familiar with much of what I'll present in this chapter. (And if you aren't, you should be!) If you're a middle manager, it's still a good idea to have a conversational understanding of the technology that underlies software engineering. After all, you'll be asked to make decisions on the basis of issues that are directly related to the technology.

Frankly, if you intend to *use* the principles and methods that I am going to introduce, this chapter will provide you with an introduction only. You'll have to refer to other books that provide more detailed discussions of this subject. But if you want a broad understanding of what software engineers are doing (or should be doing) when they're working on a new or existing system, this chapter should fit the bill.

When we consider the technical issues associated with software engineering, where should we begin?

To keep this discussion manageable, it's probably a good idea to talk about methods in the order that they are typically applied when new software is to be built. That is, we'll consider analysis methods, design methods, coding, and testing methods. I'll then discuss how these methods apply when existing software is considered.

Analyzing a problem before you start to solve it is common sense. Why is so much made of software requirements analysis?

You're right, it is common sense, and yet many software problems are never analyzed in the proper way. It is true that a complete understanding of software requirements is essential to the success of a software project. No matter how well designed or well coded, a poorly analyzed and specified program will disappoint the user and bring grief to the developer.

The requirements analysis task is a process of discovery, refinement, modeling, and specification. The software scope, initially established by the system engineer and refined during software project planning, is modeled using a "language" that enables the software engineer to specify what needs to be done. Models of the required information and control flow, operational behavior, and data content are created. Alternative solutions are analyzed and allocated to various software elements.

Both the engineer and the customer take an active role in requirements analysis and specification. The customer attempts to reformulate a sometimes nebulous concept of software function and performance into concrete detail. The engineer acts as interrogator, consultant, and problem solver.

Requirements analysis and specification may appear to be a relatively simple task, but appearances are deceiving. Communication content is very high. Chances for misinterpretation or misinformation abound. Ambiguity is probable. The dilemma that confronts a software engineer may best be understood by repeating the statement of an anonymous (infamous?) customer: "I know you believe you understood what you think I said, but I am not sure you realize that what you heard is not what I meant."

What principles guide the analysis task?

The analysis task is guided by four fundamental principles:

1. The information domain of a problem must be represented and understood.
2. Models that depict system data, function, and behavior should be developed.
3. The models (and the problem) must be partitioned in a manner that uncovers detail in a layered (or hierarchical) fashion.
4. The analysis process should move from essential information toward implementation detail.

By applying these principles, the analyst approaches a problem systematically. The information domain is examined so that function may be understood more completely. Models are used so that information can be communicated in a compact fashion. Partitioning is applied to reduce complexity. Essential and implementation views of the software are necessary to accommodate the logical constraints imposed by processing requirements and the physical constraints imposed by other system elements.

What do you mean when you discuss the "information domain"?

Software is built to process data—to transform data from one form to another; that is, to accept input, manipulate it in some way, and produce output. This fundamental statement of objective is true whether we build batch software for a payroll system or real-time embedded software to control fuel flow to an automobile engine.

It is important to note, however, that software also processes *events*. An event represents some aspect of system control and is really nothing more than boolean data—it is either on or off, true or false, there or not there. For example, a pressure sensor detects that pressure exceeds a safe value and sends an alarm signal to monitoring software. The alarm signal is an event that controls the behavior of the system. Therefore, data (numbers, characters, images, sounds, etc.) and control (events) both reside within the *information domain* of a problem.

The information domain contains three different views of the data and control as each is processed by a computer program: (1) information flow, (2) information content, and (3) information structure and relationships. To fully understand the information domain, each of these views should be considered.

What is information flow?

Information flow represents the manner in which data and control change as each moves through a system. Input is transformed into intermediate information, which is further transformed into output. Along this transformation path (or paths), additional information may be introduced from an existing *data store* (e.g., a disk file or a memory buffer). The transformations that are applied to the data are functions or subfunctions that a program must perform. Data and control that move between two transformations (functions) define the interface for each function.

What is information content and structure?

Information content represents the individual data and control items that are combined to form some larger item of information. For example, the data item, **paycheck**, is a composite of a number of important pieces of information: the payee's name, the net amount to be paid, the gross pay, deductions, and so forth. Therefore, the *content* of **paycheck** is defined by the items that are needed to create it. Similarly, the content of a control item called **system status** might be defined by a string of bits. Each bit represents a separate item of information that indicates whether a particular device is on or off line.

Information structure represents the relationships that exist between different pieces of information—pieces that are sometimes called *data items* or *data objects*. Each data object has attributes that describe its contents. Data objects are "connected" to one another by relations that define how the objects fit together to form an information system.

How is modeling used to represent requirements?

We create models to gain a better understanding of the actual entity to be built. When the entity is a physical thing (a building, a plane, a machine), we can build a model that is identical in form and shape, but smaller in scale. However, when the entity to be built is software, our model must take a different form. It must be capable of modeling the information that software transforms, the functions (and subfunctions) that enable the transformation to occur, and the behavior of the system as the transformation is taking place.

During software requirements analysis, we create models of the system to be built. The models focus on *what* the system must do, not on *how* it does it. In many cases, the models that we create make use of a graphical notation that depicts information, processing, system behavior, and other characteristics as distinct and recognizable icons. Other parts of the model may be purely textual. Descriptive information can be provided using a natural language or a specialized descriptive language.

Models created during requirements analysis serve a number of important roles:

- The model aids the analyst in understanding the information, function, and behavior of a system, thereby making the requirements analysis task easier and more systematic.

- The model becomes the focal point for review, and, therefore, the key to a determination of completeness, consistency, and accuracy of the specification.

- The model becomes the foundation for design, providing the designer with an essential representation of software that can be "mapped" into an implementation context.

The modeling method that is used is often a matter of personal (or organizational) preference. Yet, regardless of the modeling approach that is chosen, the modeling activity is fundamental to good analysis work.

Why is "partitioning" so important during the early stages of problem analysis?

Problems are often too large and complex to be understood as a whole. For this reason, we tend to *partition* (divide) such problems into parts that can be easily understood and establish interfaces between the parts so that an overall function can be accomplished. During requirements analysis, the information, functional, and behavioral domains of software can be partitioned.

In essence, partitioning divides a problem into its constituent parts. Conceptually, we establish a hierarchical representation of function or information and then partition the uppermost element by (1) exposing increasing detail by moving vertically in the hierarchy or (2) functionally decomposing the problem by moving horizontally in the hierarchy.

To illustrate horizontal and vertical partitioning, consider the functional characteristics of a word-processing package. Horizontal partitioning of the package is illustrated in Figure 17.1. The functions represented in the figure are major system subfunctions. Each must be present for the package to meet minimal requirements for word processing. Vertical partitioning focuses on one major subfunction, partitioning it to provide increasingly more detail. Figure 17.2 illustrates vertical partitioning for the document production subfunction of the word-processing package.

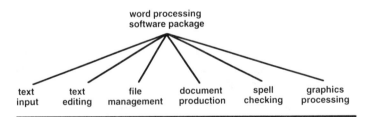

Figure 17.1   Horizontal partitioning.

The partitioning approach that applies to word-processor functions can also be applied to the information domain and behavioral domain as well. In fact, partitioning of information flow and system behavior will provide additional insight into system requirements. As the prob-

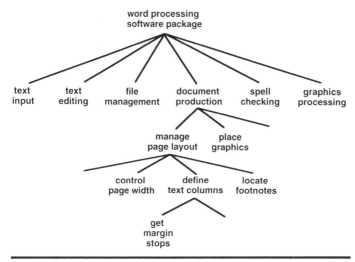

Figure 17.2   Vertical partitioning.

lem is partitioned, interfaces between functions are derived. Data and control items that move across an interface should be restricted to inputs required to perform the stated function and outputs that are required by other functions or system elements.

What is the difference between an essential view and an implementation view[1] of a problem?

An *essential view* of software requirements presents the functions to be accomplished and information to be processed without regard to implementation details. For example, an essential view of the word-processor function **text input** does not concern itself with the physical form of the data or the type of input device that is used. Similarly, an essential *data model* of the data object **document** (implied by the function **document production**) can be represented at this stage without regard to the underlying data structure used to implement the data object. By focusing attention on the essence of the problem at early stages of requirements analysis, we leave our options open to specify implementation details during later stages of requirements specification and software design.

The *implementation view* of software requirements presents the real-world manifestation of processing functions and information structures. In some cases, a physical representation is developed as

---

[1]Many people use the terms *logical* and *physical* views to connote the same concept.

the first step in software design. However, most computer-based systems are specified in a manner that dictates accommodation of certain implementation details. A word-processing package primary input device is a keyboard (not a human voice or a tablet). The general characteristics of the keyboard should be noted as part of a software requirements specification. The analyst must recognize the constraints imposed by predefined system elements (e.g., the keyboard) and consider the implementation view of function and information when such a view is appropriate.

We have already noted that software requirements analysis should focus on *what* the software is to accomplish, rather than on *how* processing will be implemented. However, the implementation view should not necessarily be interpreted as a representation of *how*. Rather, an implementation model represents the current mode of operation, that is, the existing or proposed allocation for all system elements. The essential model (of function or data) is generic in the sense that realization of function is not explicitly indicated.

What is the most widely used analysis method, and what are its basic characteristics?

There is probably no other software engineering method that has generated as much interest, been tried (and often rejected and then tried again) by as many people, provoked as much criticism, and sparked as much controversy as *structured analysis*. But the method has prospered and has gained widespread use throughout the software engineering community.

Structured analysis, like all software requirements analysis methods, is a model building activity. Using a notation that is unique to the structured analysis method, we create models that depict information (data and control) flow and content; we partition the system functionally and behaviorally, and we depict the essence of what must be built. Structured analysis is not a single method applied consistently by all who use it. Rather, it is an amalgam that has evolved over almost 20 years.

The term *structured analysis* was popularized by DeMarco [2]. In his seminal book on the subject, DeMarco introduced and named the key graphical symbols that enable an analyst to create information flow models, suggested heuristics for the use of these symbols, argued that a *data dictionary* and *processing narratives* could be used as a supplement to the information flow models, and presented numerous examples that illustrated the use of this new method. In the years that followed, variations of the structured analysis approach were suggested by Page-Jones [3], Gane and Sarson [4], and many others. In every instance, the method focused on information systems applications and did not provide an adequate notation to address the control and behavioral aspects of real-time engineering problems.

By the mid 1980s, the deficiencies of structured analysis (when attempts were made to apply the method to control-oriented applications) became painfully apparent. Real-time "extensions" were introduced by Ward and Mellor [5] and later by Hatley and Pirbhai [6]. These extensions resulted in a more robust analysis method that could be applied effectively to engineering problems.

What is the basic notation of structured analysis?

Information is transformed as it *flows* through a computer-based system. The system accepts input in a variety of forms; applies hardware, software, and human elements to transform input into output; and produces output in a variety of forms. Input may be a control signal transmitted by a transducer, a series of numbers typed by a human operator, a packet of information transmitted on a network link, or a voluminous data file retrieved from disk storage. The transform(s) may represent a single logical comparison, a complex numerical algorithm, or a rule-inference approach of an expert system. Output may light a single LED (light-emitting diode) or produce a 200-page report. In effect, we can create a *flow model* for any computer-based system, regardless of size and complexity.

Structured analysis is an information flow and content modeling technique. A computer-based system is represented as an information transform as shown in Figure 17.3. Overall function of the system is represented as a single information transform, noted as a "bubble" in the figure. One or more inputs, shown as labeled arrows, originate from external entities, represented as a box. The input drives the transform to produce output information (also represented as labeled arrows) that is

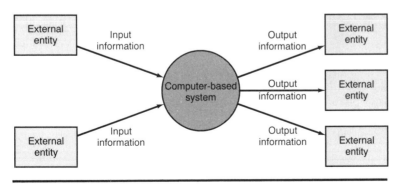

Figure 17.3   Information flow model.

passed to the external entities. It should be noted that the model may be applied to the entire system or to the software element only. The key is to represent the information fed into and produced by the transform.

Does the information flow model represented in the figure have a name?

Information flow is represented with a *data flow diagram* (DFD)—a graphical notation that depicts information flow and the transforms that are applied as data move from input to output. The data flow diagram may be used to represent a system or software at any level of abstraction. In fact, DFDs may be partitioned into levels that represent increasing information flow and functional detail. A level 0 DFD, also called a *fundamental system model* or a *context model*, represents the entire software element as a single bubble with input and output data indicated by incoming and outgoing arrows, respectively. Additional processes (bubbles) and information flow paths are represented as the level 0 DFD is partitioned to reveal more detail. For example, a level 1 DFD might contain five or six bubbles with interconnecting arrows. Each of the processes represented at level 1 are subfunctions of the overall system depicted in the context model.

The basic notation[2] used to create a DFD is illustrated in Figure 17.4. A box is used to represent an *external entity*, that is, a system element

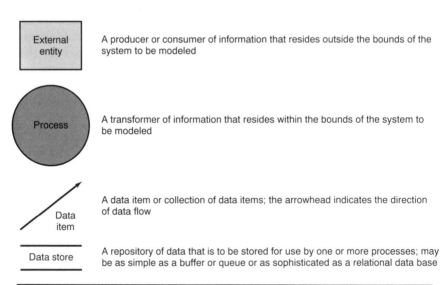

External entity	A producer or consumer of information that resides outside the bounds of the system to be modeled
Process	A transformer of information that resides within the bounds of the system to be modeled
Data item	A data item or collection of data items; the arrowhead indicates the direction of data flow
Data store	A repository of data that is to be stored for use by one or more processes; may be as simple as a buffer or queue or as sophisticated as a relational data base

Figure 17.4 Basic DFD notation.

---

[2]Extensions to the basic notation have been developed for real-time system modeling.

(e.g., hardware, a person, another program) or another system that produces information for transformation by the software or receives information produced by the software. A circle represents a *process* or *transform* that is applied to data (or control) and changes it in some way. An arrow represents one or more data items. All arrows on a DFD should be labeled. The double line represents a *data store*—stored information that is used by the software. The simplicity of DFD notation is one reason why structured analysis techniques are the most widely used.

It is important to note that no explicit indication of the sequence of processing is supplied by the diagram. Procedure or sequence may be implicit in the diagram, but explicit procedural representation is generally delayed until software design.

Earlier, you talked about different "levels" of a DFD. Is this how partitioning is achieved within structured analysis?

Functional and data flow partitioning are achieved by developing a hierarchy of DFDs. Each of the bubbles may be refined or layered to depict more detail. Figure 17.5 illustrates this concept. A fundamental model for system F indicates the primary input is A and ultimate out-

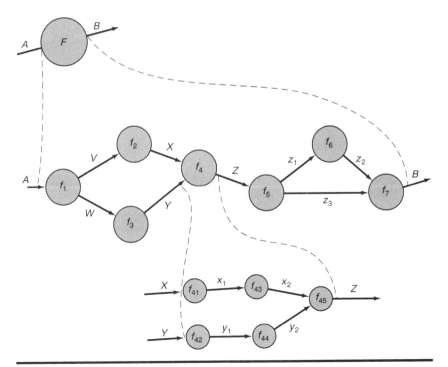

Figure 17.5   Information flow refinement.

put is B. We refine the F model into transforms f_1 to f_7. Note that *information flow continuity* must be maintained, that is, input and output to each refinement must remain the same. This concept, sometimes called *balancing,* is essential for the development of consistent models. Further refinement of f_4 depicts detail in the form of transforms f_{41} to f_{45}. Again, the input X,Y and the output Z remain unchanged.

The data flow diagram is a graphical tool that can be very valuable during software requirements analysis. However, the diagram can cause confusion if its function is confused with the flowchart. A data flow diagram depicts information flow without explicit representation of procedural logic (e.g., conditions or loops). It is not a flowchart with rounded edges!

The basic notation used to develop a DFD is not in itself sufficient to describe requirements for software. For example, an arrow shown in a DFD represents a data item that is input to or output from a process. A data store represents some organized collection of data. But what is the *content* of the data implied by the arrow or depicted by the store? If the arrow (or the store) represents a collection of items, what are they? These questions are answered by applying another component of the basic notation for structured analysis—the *data dictionary.*

What is the purpose and use of the data dictionary?

An analysis of the information domain would be incomplete if only data flow were considered. Each arrow of a data flow diagram represents one or more items of information. Each data store is often a collection of individual data items. Each control item may be defined in terms of other control items. Even the content of an external entity may require expansion before its meaning can be explicitly defined. Therefore, some method for representing the content of each flow model component must be available to the analyst.

The *data dictionary* has been proposed as a quasi-formal grammar for describing the content of objects defined during structured analysis. This important modeling notation has been defined in the following manner [7]: "The data dictionary is an organized listing of all data elements that are pertinent to the system, with precise, rigorous definitions so that both user and system analyst will have a common understanding of inputs, outputs, components of stores and [even] intermediate calculations."

Today, the data dictionary is almost always implemented as part of a CASE structured analysis and design tool. Although the format of dictionaries varies from tool to tool, most contain the following information:

- *Name:* The primary name of the data or control item, the data store, or an external entity.

- *Alias:* Other names used for the first entry.

- *Where used/how used:* A listing of the processes that use the data or control item and how it is used (e.g., input to the process, output from the process, as a store, as an external entity).

- *Content description:* A notation for representing content.

- *Supplementary information:* Other information about data types, preset values (if known), restrictions, or limitations, and so on.

Once a name and its aliases are entered into the data dictionary, consistency in naming can be enforced. That is, if an analysis team member decides to name a newly derived data item *xyz,* but *xyz* is already in the dictionary, the CASE tool supporting the dictionary posts a warning to indicate duplicate names. This improves the consistency of the analysis model and helps to reduce errors and inconsistency.

Why does the data dictionary contain "where used" and "how used" information?

"Where used" and "how used" information is recorded automatically from the flow models. When a dictionary entry is created, the CASE tool scans DFDs to determine which processes use the data or control information and how it is used. Although it may appear unimportant, this is actually one of the most important benefits of the dictionary. During analysis there is an almost continuous stream of changes. For large projects, it is often quite difficult to determine the impact of a change. Many a software engineer has asked, "Where is this data item used? What else will have to change if we modify it? What will the overall impact of the change be?" Because the data dictionary can be treated as a database,[3] the analyst can ask "where used" or "how used" questions and get answers to the queries noted above.

In addition to flow models and the data dictionary, what other information is generated as part of structured analysis?

Three additional types of modeling information are often created as part of structured analysis:

---

[3]In reality the data dictionary can be one element of a larger CASE repository. This is discussed in Chapter 18.

- A processing narrative that provides a description of the transforms represented by the flow model.

- A behavioral model that describes how software reacts to the occurrence of external events.

- A data model that identifies data items and their relationships to one another.

Each of these modeling formats complements the information that is contained in the data flow diagram and the data dictionary.

What does the processing narrative describe?

A *processing narrative*—a paragraph that describes a process bubble—can be used to specify the processing details implied by the bubble within a DFD. The processing narrative describes the input to the bubble, the algorithm that is applied to the input and the output that is produced. In addition, the narrative indicates restrictions and limitations imposed on the process, performance characteristics that are relevant to the process, and design constraints that may influence the way in which the process will be implemented.

How does system "behavior" differ from system "function," and what notation is used to describe it?

The *behavior* of a system describes externally observable reactions that occur as a consequence of a specific data input or event. *Function* describes the processing activities that occur to achieve some specific behavior.

Behavioral modeling is one of the fundamental principles for all requirements analysis methods. Yet, only extended versions of structured analysis [5, 6] provide a notation for this type of modeling. The state transition diagram[4] (STD) represents the behavior of a system by depicting its states and the events that cause the system to change state. In addition, the STD indicates what actions (e.g., process activation) are taken as a consequence of a particular event.

A simplified state transition diagram for photocopier software is shown in Figure 17.6. The rectangles represent system states and the arrows represent *transitions* between states. Each arrow is labeled with a ruled expression. The top value indicates the event(s) that

---

[4]Instead of a diagram, a tabular representation for state transition can also be used. For additional information, see reference [6].

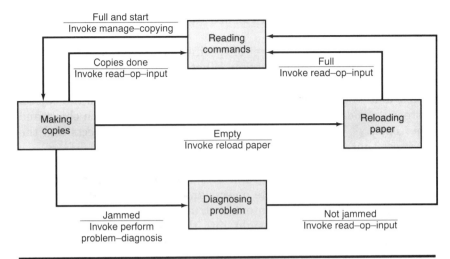

Figure 17.6   Simplified state transition diagram for photocopier software.

causes the transition to occur. The bottom value indicates the action that occurs as a consequence of the event. Therefore, when the paper tray is **full** and the **start** button is pressed, the system moves from the *reading commands* state to the *making copies* state. Note that states do not necessarily correspond to functions on a one-to-one basis. For example, the *making copies* state would encompass both **manage copying** and **produce user displays** functions.

Behavioral modeling enables a software engineer to examine the manner in which the system will react when specific combinations and sequences of events occur. In fact, some CASE tools enable the engineer to create an executable STD so that the operation and behavior of a system can be simulated to gain a better understanding of the future operation of the software.

I was under the impression that the data dictionary enabled us to model data. But isn't there another data modeling notation that is used in structured analysis?

The basic notation for structured analysis—the data flow diagram and the data dictionary—works well when relatively simple information flows through a series of processes. However, in many information systems applications (and a growing number of engineering and scientific applications), there is a need to represent the relationship between complex collections of data. To accomplish this, structured analysis notation has been extended to encompass a *data modeling* component.

Data modeling answers a set of specific questions that are relevant to any data-processing application. What are the primary *data objects* to be processed by the system? What is the composition of each data object, and what attributes describe the object? Where do the objects currently reside? What are the relationships between each object and other objects? What is the relationship between the objects and the processes that transform them?

To answer these questions, data modeling methods make use of the *entity-relationship* (E-R) diagram. The E-R diagram enables a software engineer to identify data objects and their relationships using a graphical notation. In the context of structured analysis, the E-R diagram provides additional insight into the detail of data stores and their relationship to processes within the flow model. In addition, the E-R diagram complements the representation of data content contained in the requirements dictionary.

Is structured analysis the only analysis modeling method in use today?

Absolutely not. There are many analysis modeling techniques that provide equal or greater capability. However, a discussion of them is beyond the scope of this book. For more information, see reference [8].

You've argued that analysis is a modeling activity that helps us describe what must be accomplished by the software. Does modeling stop when analysis is complete?

Modeling continues throughout the software engineering process and leads directly to the next major technical activity—*software design.* Software design sits at the technical kernel of the software engineering process and is applied regardless of the development paradigm that is used. Beginning once software requirements have been analyzed and specified, software design is the first of three technical activities—*design, code,* and *test*—that are required to build and verify the software.

Software requirements, manifested by information, functional, and behavioral models, feed the design step. Using one of a number of design methods, the design step produces a data design, an architectural design, and a procedural design.[5] The *data design* transforms the in-

---

[5]In many instances a fourth design activity is also present—human–computer interface (HCI) design. This design activity occurs when interactive software is built.

formation domain model created during analysis into the data structures that will be required to implement the software. The *architectural design* defines the relationship among major structural components of the program. The *procedural design* transforms structural components into a procedural description of the software. Source code is generated, and testing is conducted to integrate and validate the software.

Design, code, and test absorb 75 percent or more of the cost of software engineering (excluding maintenance). It is here that we make decisions that will ultimately affect the success of software implementation and, as important, the ease with which software will be maintained.

Why is design so important?

The importance of software design can be stated with a single word: *quality*. Design is the place where quality is fostered in software development. Design provides us with representations of software that can be assessed for quality. Design is the only way that we can accurately translate a customer's requirements into a finished software product or system. Software design serves as the foundation for all software engineering and software maintenance steps that follow. Without design, we risk building an unstable system—one that will fail when small changes are made; one that may be difficult to test; one whose quality cannot be assessed until late in the software engineering process, when time is short and many dollars have already been spent.

How do we assess the quality of a design, and what are the criteria that should be applied?

Throughout the design process, the quality of the evolving design is assessed with a series of *formal technical reviews* or *design walkthroughs* that were described in Chapter 14. In order to evaluate the quality of a design representation, we must establish criteria for good design. The following guidelines provide basic criteria for assessing quality:

1. A design should exhibit a hierarchical organization that makes intelligent use of control among components of software.

2. A design should be modular; that is, the software should be logically partitioned into components that perform specific functions and subfunctions.

3. A design should contain distinct and separable representation of data and procedure.

4. A design should lead to modules (e.g., subroutines or procedures) that exhibit independent functional characteristics.

5. A design should lead to interfaces that reduce the complexity of connections between modules and with the external environment.

6. A design should be derived using a repeatable method that is driven by information obtained during software requirements analysis.

These characteristics of a good design are not achieved by chance. The software engineering design process encourages good design through the application of fundamental design principles, systematic methodology, and thorough review.

Is there a set of design fundamentals (like the requirements fundamentals we discussed earlier) that guide all software design methods?

A set of fundamental software design concepts has evolved over the past three decades. Although the degree of interest in each concept has varied over the years, each has stood the test of time. Each provides the software designer with a foundation from which more sophisticated design methods can be applied. Each helps the software engineer to answer the following questions:

- What criteria can be used to partition software into individual components?

- How is function or data structure detail separated from a conceptual representation of the software?

- Are there uniform criteria that define the technical quality of a software design?

M. A. Jackson [9] once said: "The beginning of wisdom for a computer programmer [software engineer] is to recognize the difference between getting a program to work, and getting it *right*." Fundamental software design concepts provide the necessary framework for "getting it right."

Can you provide a description of these design fundamentals and the methods that are derived from them?

A detailed description of design fundamentals and the methods that have been derived from them is beyond the scope of this book. If you have additional interest, books by Pressman [8] and Sommerville [10] consider software design in considerable detail.

I'm hearing a lot about "object-oriented thinking" in discussions of analysis and design (as well as programming). What is object-oriented thinking?

To answer your question, I'll begin by addressing the term *object-oriented*. What is an object-oriented viewpoint? Why is a method considered to be object-oriented? What is an object? There are many different opinions about the correct answers to these questions. In the discussion that follows, I'll attempt to synthesize the most common of these.

To understand the object-oriented point of view, consider an example of a real-world object—the thing you are sitting in right now—a chair. **Chair** is a member (the term *instance* is also used) of a much larger *class* of objects that we call **furniture.** A set of generic *attributes* can be associated with every object in the class **furniture.** For example, all furniture has a **cost, dimensions, weight, location,** and **color,** among many possible attributes. These apply whether we are talking about a table or a chair, a sofa, or an armoire. Because **chair** is a *member* of the class **furniture, chair** *inherits* all attributes defined for the class. This concept is illustrated schematically in Figure 17.7.

Once the class has been defined, the attributes can be reused when new instances of the class are created. For example, assume that we

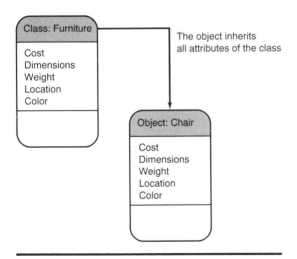

Figure 17.7 Inheritance from class to object.

were to define a new object called **chable** (a cross between a chair and a table) that is a member of the class **furniture. Chable** inherits all of the attributes of **furniture.**

We have attempted an anecdotal definition of a class by describing its attributes, but something is missing. Every object in the class **furniture** can be manipulated in a variety of ways. It can be bought and sold, physically modified (e.g., you can saw off a leg or paint the object purple), or moved from one place to another. Each of these *operations* (other terms are *services* or *methods*) will modify one or more attributes of the object. For example, if the attribute **location** is actually a composite data item defined as

```
location = building + floor + room
```

then an operation named **move** would modify one or more of the data items (**building, floor,** or **room**) that comprise the attribute **location.** To do this, move must have "knowledge" of these data items. The operation **move** could be used for a chair or a table, as long as both are instances of the class **furniture.** All valid operations (e.g., **buy, sell, weigh**) for the class **furniture** are "connected" to the object definition as shown in Figure 17.8 and are inherited by all instances of the class.

The object **chair** (and all objects in general) *encapsulates* data (the attribute values that define the chair), operations (the actions that are applied to change the attributes of **chair**), other objects (*composite ob-*

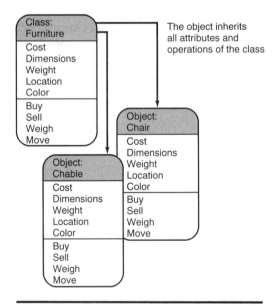

Figure 17.8   Inheritance of operations from class to object.

jects can be defined), constants (set values), and other related information. *Encapsulation* means that all of this information is packaged under one name and can be reused as one specification or program component.

Can we use object-oriented thinking to create analysis models?

Object-oriented analysis (OOA) is making slow but steady progress as a requirements analysis method in its own right and as a complement to other analysis methods. Instead of examining a problem using the classic input-processing–output (information flow) model or a model derived exclusively from hierarchical information structures, OOA introduces a number of new concepts. These new concepts seem unusual to many people, but they are really quite natural. Coad and Yourdon [11] consider this issue when they write:

> OOA—object-oriented analysis—is based upon concepts that we first learned in kindergarten: objects and attributes, classes and members, wholes and parts. Why it has taken us so long to apply these concepts to the analysis and specification of information systems is anyone's guess— perhaps we've been too busy "following the flow" during the heyday of structured analysis to consider the alternatives.

It is important to note that there is no universal agreement on the "concepts" that serve as a foundation for OOA. But one thing is clear, the primary goal of OOA is to identify objects and model them.

How are objects identified using OOA?

If you look around a room, there is a set of physical objects that can be easily identified, classified, and defined (in terms of attributes and operations). But when you "look around" the problem space of a software application, the objects may be more difficult to comprehend.

We can begin to identify objects[6] by examining the problem statement [12]. Objects can be determined by underlining each noun or noun clause and entering it in a simple table. Synonyms should be noted. If the object is required to implement a solution, then it is part of the *solution space*; otherwise, if an object is necessary only to describe a solution, it is part of the *problem space*. Objects manifest themselves in one of the following ways:

---

[6]In reality, OOA actually attempts to define *classes* from which objects are *instantiated*. Therefore, when we isolate potential objects, we also identify potential classes.

- *External entities* (e.g., other systems, devices, people) that produce or consume information to be used by a computer-based system

- *Things* (e.g., reports, displays, letters, signals) that are part of the information domain for the problem

- *Occurrences* or *events*[7] (e.g., a property transfer or the completion of a series of robot movements) that occur within the context of system operation

- *Roles* (e.g., manager, engineer, salesperson) played by people who interact with the system

- *Organizational units* (e.g., division, group, team) that are relevant to an application

- *Places* (e.g., manufacturing floor or loading dock) that establish the context of the problem and the overall function of the system

- *Structures* (e.g., sensors, four-wheeled vehicles, or computers) that define a class of objects or in the extreme, related classes of objects

Is there an object-oriented design approach that models the objects that we've identified during OOA?

It is sometimes difficult to make a clear distinction between object-oriented analysis and object-oriented design. In essence, object-oriented analysis (OOA) is a classification activity. That is, a problem is analyzed in an effort to determine the classes of objects that will be applicable as a solution is developed. Object-oriented design (OOD) enables a software engineer to indicate the objects that are derived from each class and how these objects interrelate. In addition, OOD should provide a notation that depicts the relationships among objects. The terminology, notation, and approach presented for OOA are equally applicable to OOD.

The first attempts to describe an object-oriented design method did not surface until the early 1980s. Early investigators contended that OOD begins with a natural language (e.g., English) description of the solution strategy for the software realization of a real-world problem. From this description, the designer can isolate objects and operations. Later contributions (e.g., Booch [13] and Coad and Yourdon [14]) introduced a more comprehensive notation to support this approach and argued that this activity is more properly characterized as analysis.

At its current stage of evolution, OOD methods combine elements of all three design categories discussed earlier in this chapter: data de-

---

[7]In this context, the term *event* connotes any occurrence. It does not necessarily imply control as it did in our discussion of behavioral modeling.

sign, architectural design, and procedural design. By identifying classes and objects, data abstractions are created. By coupling operations to data, modules are specified and a structure for the software is established. By developing a mechanism for using the objects, interfaces are described. By specifying the algorithmic details of operations, procedural design is accomplished.

What happens after a design model has been created and reviewed?

The coding step translates a design representation of software into a programming language realization. The translation process continues when a compiler accepts *source code* as input and produces machine-dependent *object code* as output. Compiler output is further translated into *machine code*—the actual instructions that drive microcoded logic in the central processing unit.

The initial translation step—from procedural and data design to programming language—is a primary concern in the software engineering context. "Noise" can enter the translation process in many ways. Improper interpretation of a design specification can lead to erroneous source code. Programming language complexity or restrictions can lead to convoluted source code that is difficult to test and maintain. More subtly, characteristics of a programming language can influence the way we think, propagating unnecessarily limited software designs and data structures.

Programming language characteristics have an impact on the quality and efficiency of translation. Programming languages are a vehicle for communication between humans and computers. The coding process—communication via a programming language—is a human activity. As such, the psychological characteristics of a language have an important impact on the quality of communication. The coding process may also be viewed as one step in the software engineering process. The engineering characteristics of a language have an important impact on the success of a software development project. Finally, technical characteristics of a language can influence the quality of design (recall that practicality often dictates that detail design be directed toward a specific programming language). Therefore, technical characteristics can affect both human and software engineering concerns.

I listen to many debates about which programming language is best. Do engineering characteristics provide a way to make this judgment?

The software engineering characteristics of a programming language must be coupled with psychological [15] and technical characteristics in an effort to select the best programming language for a given application. Software engineering characteristics encompass (1) ease of design to code translation, (2) compiler efficiency, (3) source code portability, (4) availability of development tools, and (5) maintainability.

The coding step begins after a design model has been defined, reviewed, and modified, if necessary. In theory, source code generation from a design specification should be straightforward. *Ease of design to code translation* provides an indication of how closely a programming language mirrors a design representation.

Although rapid advances in processor speed and memory density have begun to mitigate the need for "superefficient code," many applications still require fast, "tight" (low memory requirement) programs. An ongoing criticism of high-level language compilers is directed at an inability to produce fast, tight, executable code. Languages with optimizing compilers may be attractive if software performance is a critical requirement.

Source code portability is a programming language characteristic that may be interpreted in three different ways:

1. Source code may be transported from processor to processor and compiler to compiler with little or no modification.

2. Source code remains unchanged even when its environment changes (e.g., a new version of an operating system is installed).

3. Source code may be integrated into different software packages with little or no modification required because of programming language characteristics.

Of the three interpretations of portability, the first is by far the most common. Standardization [by ISO (International Standards Organization) and/or ANSI (American National Standards Institute)] continues to be a major impetus for improvement of programming language portability. Unfortunately, most compiler designers succumb to a compelling urge to provide "better" but nonstandard features for a standardized language. If portability is a critical requirement, source code must be restricted to the ISO or ANSI standard, even if other features exist.

Availability of development tools can shorten the time required to generate source code and can improve the quality of the code. Many programming languages may be acquired with a suite of tools that include debugging compilers, source code formatting aids, built-in editing facilities, tools for source code control, extensive subprogram libraries in a variety of application areas, cross-compilers for microprocessor development, macroprocessor capabilities, reverse engineering tools, and others. In fact, the concept of a good *software development environment* that includes both conventional and automated tools has been recognized as a key contributor to successful software engineering.

Maintainability of source code is critically important for all nontrivial software development efforts. Maintenance cannot be accomplished until software is understood. Earlier elements of the software configuration (i.e., design documentation) provide a foundation for understanding, but ultimately source code must be read and modified according to changes in design. Ease of design to code translation is an important element in source code maintainability. In addition, self-documenting characteristics of a language (e.g., allowable length of identifiers, labeling format, data type/structure definition) have a strong influence on maintainability.

How should we go about choosing a programming language?

The choice of a programming language for a specific project must take into account both engineering and psychological characteristics. However, the problem associated with choice may be moot if only one language is available or dictated by a requester. Mack and Heath [16] suggest a general philosophy when a programming language must be chosen: "the art of choosing a language is to start with the problem, decide what its requirements are, and their relative importance, since it will probably be impossible to satisfy them all equally well (with a single language)...available languages should be measured against a list of requirements."

Among the criteria that are applied during an evaluation of available languages are (1) general application area, (2) algorithmic and computational complexity, (3) environment in which software will execute, (4) performance considerations, (5) data structure complexity, (6) knowledge of software development staff, and (7) availability of a good compiler or cross-compiler. The applications area of a project is a criterion that is applied most often during language selection. As we noted in Chapter 1, a number of major software application areas have evolved and de facto standard languages may be selected for each.

Which languages are the most common for various application areas?

C is often the language of choice for the development of systems software, while languages such as Ada, C, and Modula-2 (along with FORTRAN and assembly language) are encountered in real-time applications. COBOL is the language for business applications, but increasing use of fourth-generation languages has already begun to displace it from its pre-eminent position. In the engineering/scientific area, FORTRAN remains a dominant language, although C is also widely used. Embedded software applications make use of the same languages applied in systems and real-time applications. The predominant language for personal computer users remains BASIC, but the language is rarely used by the developers of personal computer software products—more likely choices are Pascal or C. Artificial intelligence applications make use of languages such as LISP, PROLOG, or OPS5, although other more conventional programming languages are used as well.

The rush toward object-oriented software development across most application domains has spawned many new languages and conventional language dialects. The most widely used object-oriented programming languages are Smalltalk, C++, and Objective-C. But languages such as Eiffel, Object-Pascal, Trellis, and many others are also used by growing numbers of software engineers.

How do we verify that the source code that has been generated conforms to the design and meets all requirements?

We achieve traceability to design and requirements through a series of quality assurance activities (Chapter 14) that begins long before source code ever exists. By the time you reach the point where source code is available, your attention should focus primarily on finding errors in the program, rather than demonstrating that the code conforms to the design and requirements. It is at this time that you will begin testing.

What are the objectives of testing?

Glen Myers [17] states a number of rules that can serve well as testing objectives:

1. Testing is a process of executing a program with the intent of finding an error.
2. A good test case is one that has a high probability of finding an as-yet undiscovered error.
3. A successful test is one that uncovers an as-yet undiscovered error.

The above objectives imply a dramatic change in viewpoint. They move counter to the commonly held view that a successful test is one in which no errors are found. Our objective is to design tests that systematically uncover different classes of errors and to do so with a minimum amount of time and effort.

If testing is conducted successfully (according to the objective stated above), it will uncover errors in the software. As a secondary benefit, testing demonstrates that software functions appear to be working according to specification, that performance requirements appear to have been met. In addition, data collected as testing is conducted provide a good indication of software reliability and some indication of software quality as a whole. But there is one thing that testing cannot do: *Testing cannot show the absence of defects, it can only show that software defects are present.* It is important to keep this (rather gloomy) statement in mind as testing is being conducted.

I often hear the phrase "verification and validation" used in conjunction with testing. What does this phrase mean?

Software testing is one element of a broader topic that is often referred to as *verification and validation* (V&V). *Verification* refers to the set of activities that ensures that software correctly implements a specific function. *Validation* refers to a different set of activities that ensures that the software that has been built is traceable to customer requirements. Boehm [18] states this another way:

Verification: "Are we building the product right?"
Validation: "Are we building the right product?"

The definition of V&V encompasses many of the activities that we have referred to as software quality assurance (SQA): formal technical reviews, quality and configuration audits, performance monitoring, simulation, feasibility study, documentation review, database review, algorithm analysis, development testing, qualification testing, and installation testing. Although testing plays an extremely important role in V&V, many other activities are also necessary.

How do we achieve the testing objectives that you've described?

Testing presents an interesting anomaly for the software engineer. During earlier software engineering tasks, the engineer attempts to build software from an abstract concept to a tangible implementation. Now comes testing. The engineer develops a strategy for conducting tests and tactics for designing test data that results in a series of test cases that is intended to "demolish" the software that has been built. In fact, testing is the one step in the software engineering process that could be viewed (psychologically, at least) as destructive rather than constructive.

Software developers are by their nature constructive people. Testing requires that the developer discard preconceived notions of the "correctness" of software just developed and overcome a conflict of interest that occurs when errors are uncovered.

What strategy should we use when we begin testing?

A strategy for software testing integrates software test case design techniques into a well-planned series of steps that results in the successful construction of software. It defines a *template* for software testing—a set of steps into which we can place specific test case design techniques and testing methods.

A number of software testing strategies have been proposed in the literature. All provide the software developer with a template for testing, and all have the following generic characteristics:

- Testing begins at the module level and works "outward" toward the integration of the entire computer-based system.

- Different testing techniques are appropriate at different points in time.

- Testing is conducted by the developer of the software and (for large projects) an independent test group.

- Testing and debugging are different activities, but debugging must be accommodated in any testing strategy.

A strategy for software testing must accommodate low-level tests that are necessary to verify that a small source code segment has been correctly implemented as well as high-level tests that validate major system functions against customer requirements. A strategy must provide guidance for the practitioner and a set of milestones for the manager. Because the steps of the test strategy occur at a time when deadline pressure begins to rise, progress must be measurable and problems must surface as early as possible.

What are the specific steps in a software testing strategy?

The software engineering process may be viewed as a vortex illustrated in Figure 17.9. Initially, system engineering defines the role of

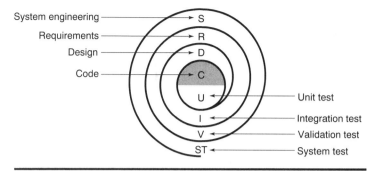

Figure 17.9 Testing strategy.

software and leads to software requirements analysis, where the information domain, function, behavior, performance, constraints, and validation criteria for software are established. Moving inward along the vortex, we come to design and finally to coding. To develop computer software, we spiral in along streamlines that decrease the level of abstraction on each turn.

A strategy for software testing may also be viewed in the context of the vortex (Figure 17.9). *Unit testing* begins at the center of the vortex and concentrates on each unit of the software as implemented in source code. Testing progresses by moving outward along the vortex to *integration testing,* where the focus is on design and the construction of the software architecture. Taking another turn outward on the vortex, we encounter *validation testing,* where requirements established as part of software requirements analysis are validated against the software that has been constructed. Finally, we arrive at *system testing,* where the software and other system elements are tested as a whole. To test computer software, we spiral out along streamlines that broaden the scope of testing with each turn.

Considering the process from a procedural point of view, testing within the context of software engineering is actually a series of four steps that are implemented sequentially. The steps are shown in Figure 17.10. Initially, tests focus on each module individually, ensuring that it functions properly as a unit. Hence, the name *unit testing.* Unit testing makes heavy use of white-box testing techniques, exercising specific paths in a module's control structure to ensure complete coverage and maximum error detection. Next, modules must be assembled or integrated to form the complete software package. *Integration testing* addresses the issues associated with the dual problems of verification and program construction. Black-box test case design techniques that exercise required output are the most prevalent during integration, although a limited amount of white-box testing may be used to

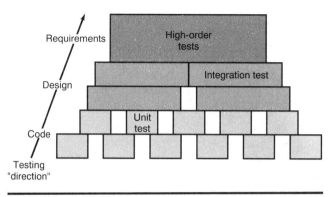

Figure 17.10   Software testing steps.

ensure coverage of major control paths. After the software has been integrated (constructed), a set of *high-order tests* is conducted. Validation criteria (established during requirements analysis) must be tested. *Validation testing* provides final assurance that software meets all functional, behavioral, and performance requirements. Black-box testing techniques are used exclusively during validation.

The last high-order testing step falls outside the boundary of software engineering and into the broader context of computer system engineering. Software, once validated, must be combined with other system elements (e.g., hardware, people, databases). *System testing* verifies that all elements mesh properly and that overall system function and performance are achieved.

What are the "tactics" for test case design?

The design of tests for software and other engineered products can be as challenging as the initial design of the product itself. Yet, for reasons that we have already discussed, software engineers often treat testing as an afterthought, developing test cases that may "feel right" but have little assurance of being complete. Recalling the objectives of testing, we must design tests that have the highest likelihood of finding the most errors with a minimum amount of time and effort.

Over the past decade a rich variety of test case design methods have evolved for software. These methods provide the developer with a systematic approach to testing. More importantly, methods provide a mechanism that can help to ensure the completeness of tests and provide the highest likelihood for uncovering errors in software.

Any engineered product (and most other things) can be tested in one of two ways: (1) if the specified function that a product has been designed to perform is known, tests can be conducted that demonstrate each function is fully operational; (2) if the internal workings of a product are known, tests can be conducted to ensure that "all gears mesh," that is, that internal operation performs according to specification and all internal components have been adequately exercised. The first test approach is called *black-box testing* and the second, *white-box testing*.

When computer software is considered, black-box testing alludes to tests that are conducted at the software interface. Although they are designed to uncover errors, black-box tests are used to demonstrate that software functions are operational; that input is properly accepted, and output is correctly produced; that the integrity of external information (e.g., data files) is maintained. A black-box test examines some aspect of system function with little regard for the internal logical structure of the software.

White-box testing of software is predicated on close examination of procedural detail. Logical paths through the software are tested by providing test cases that exercise specific sets of conditions and/or loops. The "status of the program" may be examined at various points to determine if the expected or asserted status corresponds to the actual status.

If we use a combination of white-box and black-box tests, wouldn't it be possible to exercise every program path and demonstrate that no errors exist?

At first glance it would seem that very thorough black-box and white-box testing would lead to "100 percent correct programs." All we need do is define all logical paths, develop test cases to exercise them, and evaluate results, that is, generate test cases to exercise program logic exhaustively. Unfortunately, exhaustive testing presents certain logistical problems. For even small programs, the number of possible logical paths can be very large. For example, consider the flowchart shown in Figure 17.11. The procedural design illustrated by the flowchart might correspond to a 100-line C program with a single loop that may be executed no more than 20 times. There are approximately 10^{14} possible paths that may be executed!

To put this number in perspective, assume that a *magic* test processor ("magic" because no such processor exists) has been developed for exhaustive testing. The processor can develop a test case, execute it, and evaluate the results in 1 ms. Working 24 hours a day, 365 days a year, the processor would work for 3170 years to test the program represented in Figure 17.11. This would, undeniably, cause havoc in most

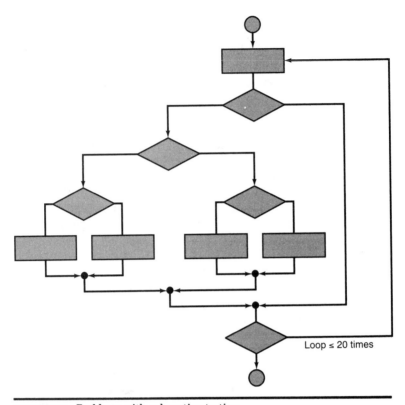

Loop ≤ 20 times

Figure 17.11 Problems with exhaustive testing.

development schedules. Exhaustive testing is impossible for large software systems.

Why spend time and energy worrying about (and testing) logical minutiae when we might better expend effort ensuring that program requirements have been met?

Using white-box testing methods, the software engineer can derive test cases that (1) guarantee that all *independent paths* within a module have been exercised at least once, (2) exercise all logical decisions on their *true* and *false* sides, (3) execute all loops at their boundaries and within their operational bounds, and (4) exercise internal data structures to ensure their validity. We derive test cases with these characteristics because of the nature of software defects:

- *Logic errors and incorrect assumptions are inversely proportional to the probability that a program path will be executed:* Errors tend to creep into our work when we design and implement functions, conditions, or control that are out of the mainstream. Everyday processing tends to be well understood (and well scrutinized), while "special case" processing tends to fall into the cracks.

- *We often believe that a logical path is not likely to be executed when, in fact, it may be executed on a regular basis:* The logical flow of a program is sometimes counterintuitive, meaning that our unconscious assumptions about flow of control and data may lead us to make design errors that are uncovered only once path testing commences.

- *Typographical errors are random:* When a program is translated into programming language source code, it is likely that some typing errors will occur. Many will be uncovered by syntax checking mechanisms, but others will go undetected until testing begins. It is as likely that a typo will exist on an obscure logical path as on a mainstream path.

Each of these reasons provides an argument for conducting white-box tests. Black-box testing, no matter how thorough, may miss the kinds of errors noted above. As Beizer has stated [19]: "Bugs lurk in corners and congregate at boundaries." White-box testing is far more likely to uncover them.

When is black-box testing conducted, and what types of errors are likely to be found using it?

Black-box testing methods focus on the functional requirements of the software. That is, black-box testing enables the software engineer to derive sets of input conditions that will fully exercise all functional requirements for a program. Black-box testing is *not* an alternative to white-box techniques. Rather, it is a complementary approach that is likely to uncover a different class of errors than white-box methods.

Black-box testing attempts to find errors in the following categories: (1) incorrect or missing functions, (2) interface errors, (3) errors in data structures or external database access, (4) performance errors, and (5) initialization and termination errors.

Unlike white-box testing, which is performed early in the testing process, black-box testing tends to be applied during later stages of testing. Because black-box testing purposely disregards control structure, attention is focused on the information domain. Tests are designed to answer the following questions:

- What *classes* of input will make good test cases?

- Is the system particularly sensitive to certain input values?
- How are the boundaries of a data class isolated?
- What data rates and data volume can the system tolerate?
- What effect will specific combinations of data have on system operation?

By applying black-box techniques, we derive a set of test cases that satisfy the following criteria [17]: (1) test cases that reduce, by a count that is greater than one, the number of additional test cases that must be designed to achieve reasonable testing and (2) test cases that tell us something about the presence or absence of classes of errors, rather than an error associated only with the specific test at hand.

Who should do all of the work implied by the testing strategy and tactics that you've described?

For every software project, there is an inherent conflict of interest that occurs as testing begins. The people who have built the software are now asked to test it. This seems harmless in itself; after all, who knows the program better than its developers? Unfortunately, these same developers have a vested interest in demonstrating that the program is error-free, that it works according to customer requirements, and that it will be completed on schedule and within budget. Each of these interests mitigates against thorough testing.

Earlier in this chapter I mentioned that software analysis and design (along with coding) are *constructive* tasks from a psychological point of view. The software engineer creates a computer program, as well as its documentation and related data structures. Like any builder, the software engineer is proud of the edifice that has been built and looks askance at anyone who attempts to tear it down. When testing commences, there is a subtle, yet definite, attempt to "break" the thing that the software engineer has built. From the point of view of the builder, testing can be considered to be (psychologically) *destructive*. So the builder treads lightly, designing and executing tests that will demonstrate that the program works, rather than uncovering errors. Unfortunately, errors will be present. And if the software engineer doesn't find them, the customer will!

There are often a number of misconceptions that can be drawn from the above discussion: (1) that the developer of software should do no testing at all, (2) that the software should be "tossed over the wall" to strangers who will test it mercilessly, or (3) that testers get involved with the project only when the testing steps are about to begin. Each of these statements is incorrect.

The software developer is always responsible for testing the individual units (modules) of the program, ensuring that each performs the function for which it was designed. In many cases, the developer also conducts *integration testing*—a testing step that leads to the construction (and test) of the complete program structure. Only after the software architecture is complete does an independent test group become involved.

The role of an *independent test group* (ITG) is to remove the inherent problems associated with letting the builder test the thing that has been built. Independent test removes the conflict of interest that may otherwise be present. After all, personnel in the independent group team are paid to find errors.

However, the software developer doesn't turn the program over to the ITG and walk away. The developer and the ITG work closely throughout a software project to ensure that thorough tests will be conducted. While testing is conducted, the developer must be available to correct errors that are uncovered.

The ITG is part of the software development project team in the sense that it becomes involved during the specification process and stays involved (planning and specifying test procedures) throughout a large project. However, in many cases the ITG reports to the software quality assurance organization, thereby achieving a degree of independence that might not be possible if it were a part of the software development organization.

Is there a difference between testing and debugging?

Debugging occurs as a consequence of successful testing. That is, when a test case uncovers an error, debugging is the process that results in the removal of the error. Although debugging can and should be an orderly process, it is still very much an art. A software engineer, evaluating the results of a test, is often confronted with a "symptomatic" indication of a software problem. That is, the external manifestation of the error and the internal cause of the error may have no obvious relationship to one another. The poorly understood mental process that connects a symptom to a cause is debugging.

Debugging is *not* testing, but always occurs as a consequence of testing.[8] The debugging process begins with the execution of a test

---

[8]In making this statement, we take the broadest possible view of *testing*. Not only does the developer test software prior to release, but the customer/user tests software every time it is used!

case. Results are assessed and a lack of correspondence between expected and actual is encountered. In many cases, the noncorresponding data are a symptom of an underlying cause as yet hidden. The debugging process attempts to match symptom with cause, thereby leading to error correction.

The debugging process will always have one of two outcomes: (1) the cause will be found, corrected, and removed or (2) the cause will not be found. In the latter case, the person performing debugging may suspect a cause, design a test case to help validate this suspicion, and work toward error correction in an iterative fashion.

Why is debugging so difficult?

In all likelihood, human psychology has more to do with an answer than software technology. However, a few characteristics of bugs provide some clues:

1. The symptom and the cause may be geographically remote. That is, the symptom may appear in one part of a program, while the cause may actually be located at a site that is far removed. Poorly designed programs exacerbate this situation.

2. The symptom may disappear (temporarily) when another error is corrected.

3. The symptom may actually be caused by nonerrors (e.g., round-off inaccuracies).

4. The symptom may be caused by human error that is not easily traced.

5. The symptom may be a result of timing problems, rather than processing problems.

6. It may be difficult to accurately reproduce input conditions (e.g., a real-time application in which input ordering is indeterminate).

7. The symptom may be intermittent. This is particularly common in embedded systems that couple hardware and software inextricably.

8. The symptom may be due to causes that are distributed across a number of tasks running on different processors.

During debugging, we encounter errors that range from mildly annoying (e.g., an incorrect output format) to catastrophic (e.g., the system fails, causing serious economic or physical damage). As the consequences of an error increase, the amount of pressure to find the cause also increases. Often, pressure forces a software developer to fix one error and inadvertently introduce two more.

You haven't spent much time talking about software maintenance methods, yet at the beginning of this book you indicated that maintenance accounts for 70 percent of all software effort. Do the methods you've described in this chapter apply to maintenance work as well?

Software maintenance has been described as "the recursive application of software engineering methods." Each of the methods discussed in this chapter is applicable to maintenance activities, but each must be adjusted to accommodate the constraints imposed by work that is conducted on an existing program. To review a discussion of maintenance that was presented earlier in this book, consider the four activities that are normally associated with software maintenance.

The first maintenance activity occurs because it is unreasonable to assume that software testing will uncover all latent defects in a large software system. During the use of any large program, quality problems will occur and be reported to the developer. The process that includes diagnosis and correction of one or more defects is called *corrective maintenance.*

The second activity that contributes to a definition of maintenance occurs because of the rapid change that is encountered in every aspect of computing. New generations of hardware seem to be announced on a 24-month cycle; new operating systems, or new releases of old ones, appear regularly; and peripheral equipment and other system elements are frequently upgraded or modified. The useful life of application software, on the other hand, can easily surpass 10 years, outliving the system environment for which it was originally developed. Therefore, *adaptive maintenance*—an activity that modifies software to properly interface with a changing environment—is both necessary and commonplace.

The third activity that may be applied to a definition of maintenance occurs when a software package is successful. As the software is used, recommendations for new capabilities, modifications to existing functions, and general enhancement requests are received from users. To satisfy requests in this category, *perfective maintenance* is performed. This activity accounts for the majority of all effort expended on software maintenance.

The fourth maintenance activity occurs when software is changed to improve future maintainability or reliability, or to provide a better basis for future enhancements. Once called *preventive maintenance,* this activity is characterized by a *reengineering* paradigm that is discussed later in this chapter.

Some software professionals are troubled by the inclusion of the second and third activities as part of a definition of maintenance. In actuality, the tasks that occur as part of adaptive and perfective maintenance are the same tasks that are applied during the development phase of the software engineering process. To adapt or perfect, we must determine new requirements, redesign, generate code, and test new and existing program components. Traditionally, such tasks, when they are applied to an existing program, have been called *maintenance.*

How does the application of the software engineering methods described in this chapter affect the manner in which maintenance work is conducted?

The flow of events that can occur as a result of a maintenance request is illustrated in Figure 17.12. If the only available element of a software configuration is source code, maintenance activity begins with a painstaking evaluation of the code, often complicated by poor internal documentation.[9] Subtle characteristics such as program structure, global data structures, system interfaces, performance, and/or design constraints are difficult to ascertain and frequently misinterpreted. The ramifications of changes that are ultimately made to the code are difficult to assess. Regression tests (repeating past tests to ensure that modifications have not introduced faults in previously operational software) are impossible to conduct because no record of testing exists. We are conducting *unstructured maintenance* and paying the price (in wasted effort and human frustration) that accompanies software that has not been developed using a well-defined methodology.

If a complete software configuration exists (i.e., if software engineering methods were applied when the software was built), the maintenance task begins with an evaluation of the design documentation. Important structural, performance, and interface characteristics of the software are determined. The impact of required modifications or corrections is assessed and an approach is planned. The design is modified and reviewed. New source code is developed, regression tests are conducted using information contained in the *Test Specification,* and the software is released again.

This sequence of events constitutes *structured maintenance* and occurs as a result of earlier application of a software engineering frame-

---

[9]A new generation of reverse engineering tools (discussed briefly later in this chapter and in Chapter 18) makes the evaluation of source code easier. However, these tools do not replace the need for good design documentation.

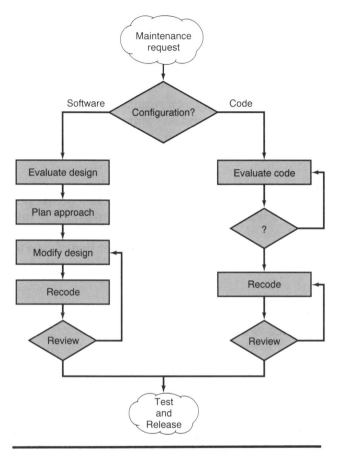

Figure 17.12 Structured versus unstructured maintenance.

work. Although the existence of a software configuration does not guarantee problem-free maintenance, the amount of wasted effort is reduced and the overall quality of a change or correction is enhanced.

Does the activity that you call "unstructured maintenance" result in costs other than the absorption of large amounts of effort?

The dollar cost of maintenance is the most obvious concern. However, other less tangible costs may ultimately be a cause for greater concern. To quote Daniel McCracken [20]: "Backlogs of new applications and major changes that measure in years are getting longer. As an industry, we can't even keep up—let alone catch up—with what our users want us to do." McCracken alludes to the "maintenance-bound" organization. One intangible cost of software maintenance is development opportunity that is postponed or lost because available resources must be channeled to maintenance tasks. Other intangible costs include:

- Customer dissatisfaction when seemingly legitimate requests for repair or modification cannot be addressed in a timely manner.

- Reduction in overall software quality as a result of changes that introduce latent errors in the maintained software.

- Upheaval caused during development efforts when staff must be "pulled" to work on a maintenance task.

The final cost of software maintenance is a dramatic decrease in productivity (measured in LOC per person-month or function points per person-month) that occurs when maintenance of old programs is initiated. In the extreme, productivity reductions of 40 to 1 have been reported. That is, a development effort that cost $25.00 per line of code to develop might cost $1000.00 for every line of code that is maintained.

What are the most common problems that are encountered when unstructured maintenance is conducted?

Most problems that are associated with software maintenance can be traced to deficiencies in the way software was planned and developed. A lack of control and discipline in software engineering development activities nearly always translates into problems during software maintenance.

Among the many classic problems [21] that can be associated with software maintenance are the following:

- It is often difficult or impossible to trace the evolution of the software through many versions or releases. Changes are not adequately documented.

- It is often difficult or impossible to trace the process through which software was created.

- It is often exceptionally difficult to understand "someone else's" program. Difficulty increases as the number of elements in a software configuration decrease. If only undocumented code exists, severe problems should be expected.

- "Someone else" is often not around to explain. Mobility among software personnel is high. We cannot rely on a personal explanation of the software by the developer when maintenance is required.

- Proper documentation doesn't exist or is awful. Recognition that software must be documented is a first step, but documentation must be understandable and consistent with source code to be of any value.

- Most software is not designed for change. Unless a design method accommodates change through concepts such as functional independence or object classes, modifications to software are difficult and error-prone.

- Maintenance has not been viewed as very glamorous work. Much of this perception comes from the high frustration level associated with maintenance work.

All of the problems described above can, in part, be attributed to the large number of programs currently in existence that have been developed with no thought of software engineering. A disciplined methodology should not be viewed as a panacea. However, software engineering does provide at least partial solutions to each problem associated with maintenance.

You mentioned "reengineering" as one element of software maintenance. What do you mean by this term?

Almost all companies that use information systems or build computer-based products will face an "aging software plant" during the 1990s.[10] Many programs that are pivotal to business operations are becoming more and more difficult to maintain. "Patches" are placed on top of patches, resulting in programs that work inefficiently, fail too often, and do not respond to users' needs. In fact, the maintenance of aging programs has become prohibitively expensive for many information systems, manufacturing, and engineering organizations. Yet, many managers think that the cost to reengineer all of these programs is also prohibitively expensive.

At first, it would appear that few acceptable options exist. But this is not the case. A strategy for reengineering existing software can be developed, if company management is willing to pay now, rather than waiting to pay (much more) later. In reality, reengineering may be a "low cost" alternative to ongoing software maintenance. The *IEEE Software Engineering Glossary* defines reengineering as "a complete process that encompasses an analysis of existing applications, restructuring, reverse and forward engineering phases."

A reengineering paradigm that reflects the IEEE definition is illustrated in Figure 17.13. Work begins with an inventory analysis and proceeds through a variety of engineering activities that range from simple code restructuring to comprehensive reengineering of a software architecture.

---

[10]The notion of an aging software plant was discussed in Chapter 1.

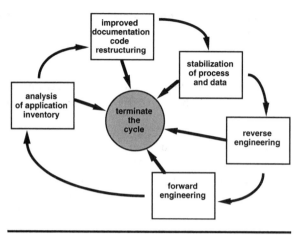

Figure 17.13   A reengineering paradigm.

What is "inventory analysis" when it is discussed in the context of reengineering?

Inventory analysis is a reengineering activity that attempts to isolate those applications that are likely candidates for reengineering. The following steps are applied during inventory analysis:

1. Select those programs that are used heavily at the present time and are likely to be used for the next 5 to 10 years.

2. Estimate the yearly cost of maintaining a program selected in step 1. Maintenance cost should include error correction, environmental adaptation, and functional enhancements.

3. Estimate the number of annual changes that will be requested for each program and the cost of these changes.

4. Prioritize the programs selected in step 1 by importance, number of projected changes and their cost, and the cost to maintain each.

5. Estimate the cost to reengineer (rebuild) the programs selected in step 1. [Note: Because a prototype exists (the old program), reengineering costs may be less than first imagined.] Estimate the annual cost to maintain these reengineered programs.

6. For each program selected, compare the cost to maintain the programs to the cost of reengineering the programs.

7. Compute the time required to show a return on the reengineering investment.

8. Consider intangible issues such as improved responsiveness to change, better system reliability, superior system performance, and improved user interfaces.

These eight steps will provide you with an inventory of candidate applications for reengineering. How many of these programs are actually reengineered is a business decision that each software development organization must make.

Restructuring and stabilization seem to be intermediate levels of reengineering activity. Can you describe these in a bit more detail?

Restructuring and stabilization focus on information that can be extracted from source code and lead to modifications (to source code) that do not change program architecture or data. Restructuring analyzes source code and rearranges the program logic to eliminate "unstructured algorithms" and reduce code complexity. Stabilization analyzes data definitions contained in source code in an attempt to extract data objects for inclusion in a data dictionary or CASE repository.

What does "reverse engineering" mean, when the term is applied to software?

The term *reverse engineering* has its origins in the hardware world. A company disassembles a competitive hardware product in an effort to understand its competitor's design and manufacturing "secrets." These secrets could be easily understood if the competitor's design and manufacturing specifications were obtained. But these documents are proprietary and are not available to the company doing the reverse engineering. In essence, successful reverse engineering derives one or more design and manufacturing specifications for a product by examining actual specimens of the product.

Reverse engineering for software is quite similar. In most cases, however, the program to be reverse-engineered is not a competitor's. Rather, it is the company's own work (often done many years earlier). The "secrets" to be understood are obscure because no specification or design documentation was ever developed. Therefore, reverse engineering for software is the process of analyzing a program in an effort to create a representation of the program at a higher level of abstraction than source code. Reverse engineering is a process of *design recovery*. Reverse engineering tools extract data and architectural and procedural design information from an existing program.

What is "forward engineering," when the term is applied to software?

Forward engineering, also called *renovation* or·*reclamation,* not only recovers design information from existing software but also uses this information to alter or reconstitute the existing system in an effort to improve its overall quality. In most cases, reengineered software reimplements the function of the existing system and also adds new functions and/or improves overall performance.

By what criteria can we judge reengineering methods and tools?

Reengineering conjures an image of the "magic slot." We feed an unstructured, undocumented source listing into the slot, and out the other end comes full documentation for the computer program. Unfortunately, the magic slot doesn't exist. Reverse engineering can extract design information from source code, but the abstraction level, the completeness of the documentation, the degree to which tools and a human analyst work together, and the directionality of the process are highly variable [22].

The *abstraction level* of a reverse engineering process and the tools that are used to effect it refer to the sophistication of the design information that can be extracted from source code. Ideally, the abstraction level should be as high as possible. That is, the reverse engineering process should be capable of deriving procedural design representations (a low-level abstraction), program and data structure information (a somewhat higher level of abstraction), data and control flow models (a relatively high level of abstraction), and entity-relationship models (a high level of abstraction). As the abstraction level increases, the software engineer is provided with information that will allow easier understanding of the program.

The *completeness* of a reverse engineering process refers to the level of detail that is provided at an abstraction level. In most cases, the completeness decreases as the abstraction level increases. For example, given a source code listing, it is relatively easy to develop a complete procedural design representation. Simple data flow representations may also be derived, but it is far more difficult to develop a complete set of data flow diagrams.

Completeness improves in direct proportion to the amount of analysis performed by the person doing reverse engineering. *Interactivity* refers to the degree to which the human is "integrated" with automated tools to create an effective reverse engineering process. In most cases, as the abstraction level increases, interactivity must increase or completeness will suffer.

If the *directionality* of the reverse engineering process is one-way, all information extracted from the source code is provided to the software engineer, who can then use it during any maintenance activity. If directionality is two-way, the information is fed to a forward engineering tool that attempts to restructure or regenerate the old program.

Why hasn't more emphasis been placed on reengineering?

Because every large company (and many small ones) have millions of lines of code that are candidates for reengineering, it would seem that every company should undertake a massive effort to reengineer every program in its library. Unfortunately, this is unrealistic for a number of reasons: (1) some of these programs are used infrequently and are not likely to change; (2) reverse and forward engineering tools are still in their infancy;[11] (3) therefore, these tools are capable of performing reengineering for only a limited class of applications; and (4) the cost (in effort and dollars) would be prohibitive.

It is important to reemphasize, however, that reengineering is often a viable management and technical strategy. Companies that dismiss it out of hand do so at their own risk.

A Manager's Checklist

Software engineering methods encompass a wide variety of modeling and implementation techniques. By providing a set of principles, objectives, modeling techniques, and quality criteria, methods provide the technical foundation for the software engineering process.

An abbreviated discussion of software engineering methods can be dangerous if the reader assumes that "that's all there is." In fact, entire textbooks have been written about each of the technical principles and methods that have been discussed in this chapter. If you need additional information, the Further Readings section of this chapter should provide you with some useful pointers.

If your organization is typical, you're only beginning to apply software engineering methods on a broad scale. To help you gain a better understanding of your organization's methodology, the following actions and questions should be pursued.

Actions

- Collect all documentation produced for a software project that has been completed in the past 6 months. Examine the documentation and determine whether (1) models of requirements or design were created, (2) a consistent notation for the models has been used, and (3) black-box and white-box tests were conducted.

- Have your technical staff make a checklist that contains the criteria by which they would assess an analysis method, a design method,

---

[11]Some CASE tools in limited application domains are relatively sophisticated, but overall, reengineering tools are quite rudimentary.

and a testing method. Does the list reflect the fundamental concepts discussed in this chapter?

Questions

- What training courses are available to teach a specific software engineering method to your staff? What is the method that is taught?
- What tools are available to support the methods that are used for analysis, design, and testing?
- Ask a practitioner to describe the methods that are currently used to perform analysis, design, and testing. How do these conform to the ideas introduced in this chapter?

Further Readings

There are hundreds of books that present the analysis, design, and testing principles and methods that have been discussed in this chapter. Yet, a reasonably small subset can provide you with an excellent understanding of these important software engineering methods. Here are some of the better offerings from the subset:

Analysis

DeMarco's book [2] remains a good introduction to the basic notation. Books by Dickinson (*Developing Structured Systems,* Yourdon Press, 1980), Page-Jones (*The Practical Guide to Structured Systems Design,* 2d ed., Prentice-Hall, 1988), and Mittra (*Structured Techniques of System Analysis, Design and Implementation,* Wiley-Interscience, 1988) are worthwhile references. Yourdon's most recent book on the subject [7] remains the most comprehensive coverage published to date. For the analysis of real-time systems, Ward and Mellor [5] and Hatley and Pirbhai [6] are the books of preference.

Many variations on structured analysis have evolved over the last decade. Cutts (*Structured Systems Analysis and Design Methodology,* Van Nostrand-Reinhold, 1990) and Hares (*SSADM for the Advanced Practitioner,* Wiley, 1990) describe SSADM, a variation on structured analysis that is widely used in the United Kingdom and Europe.

The data dictionary has been the subject of books by Braithwaite (*Analysis, Design, and Implementation of Data Dictionaries,* McGraw-Hill, 1988) and Wertz (*The Data Dictionary: Concepts and Uses,* QED Information Sciences, Inc., 1989). These books present the data dictionary in the context of database applications.

Design

An excellent survey of software design is contained in an anthology edited by Freeman and Wasserman (*Software Design Techniques*, 4th ed., IEEE, 1983). In addition to papers on every important aspect of design, this tutorial reprints many of the "classic" papers that have formed the basis for current trends in software design. Good discussions of software design fundamentals can be found in books by Pressman [9] and Sommerville [10], Blum (*Software Engineering*, Oxford Univ. Press, 1992), and Macro (*Software Engineering: Concepts and Management*, Prentice-Hall, 1990). An excellent survey of different design notations can be found in a book by Martin and McClure (*Diagramming Techniques for Analysts and Programmers*, Prentice-Hall, 1985). Stevens (*Software Design: Concepts and Methods*, Prentice-Hall, 1990) presents a worthwhile treatment of data, architectural, and procedural design.

Coding

Kernihan and Plauger's classic text (*The Elements of Programming Style*, Addison-Wesley, 1978) remains *must* reading for all individuals who intend to generate source code. The authors have provided an extensive, annotated set of rules for coding (and design) that are well worth heeding. In addition, Jon Bentley (*Programming Pearls*, Addison-Wesley, 1986; *More Programming Pearls*, Addison-Wesley, 1988) presents a worthwhile collection of style guidelines and clever language solutions to common programming problems. Books by Weiler (*The Programmers Craft*, Reston, 1983), Liffick (*The Software Development Source Book*, Addison-Wesley, 1985), and Ledgard (*Professional Software: Programming Concepts*, Addison-Wesley, 1987) provide additional information about style.

Testing

A number of excellent books are available for those readers who desire additional information on software testing. Myers [17] remains a classic text, covering black-box techniques in considerable detail. Beizer [19] provides comprehensive coverage of white-box techniques, introducing a level of mathematical rigor that has often been missing in other treatments of testing. Perry (*How to Test Software Packages*, Wiley, 1986) provides practical guidelines and useful checklists for testing purchased software (as well as software developed internally).

A detailed discussion on testing strategies can be found in books by Evans (*Productive Software Test Management*, Wiley-Interscience, 1984), Hetzel (*The Complete Guide to Software Testing*, QED Information Sciences, 1984), and Ould and Unwin (*Testing in Software Development*, Cambridge University Press, 1986). Each delineates the steps of an effective strategy, provides a set of techniques and guidelines, and suggests procedures for controlling and tracking the testing process.

Maintenance and reengineering

Martin and McClure (*Software Maintenance*, Prentice-Hall, 1983) discuss the impact of fourth-generation techniques on the maintenance process. Parikh (*Handbook of Software Maintenance*, Wiley-Interscience, 1986) discusses software maintenance using an effective question and answer format. Glass and Noiseux (*Software Maintenance Guidebook*, Prentice-Hall, 1981) is still another worthwhile treatment of the subject. Data collected by Lientz and Swanson (*Software Maintenance Management*, Addison-Wesley, 1980) remains the most comprehensive study on maintenance published to date.

Parikh's anthology (*Techniques of Program and System Maintenance*, Winthrop Publishers, 1981) and another anthology by Parikh and Zvegintzov (*Software Maintenance*, IEEE Computer Society Press, 1983) contain collections of papers on maintenance.

Reengineering is an extremely hot topic in the software engineering community, but the literature is only beginning to form. A special issue of *IEEE Software* (January 1990) is dedicated to maintenance and reverse engineering and contains a thorough treatment of the subject. An issue of *Software Magazine* (May 1990) contains a listing of popular reverse engineering tools. *CASE Outlook* and other industry newsletters contain a continuing stream of information on reengineering tools.

References

[1] Pressman, R.S., and S.R. Herron, *Software Shock*, Dorset House, 1992.
[2] DeMarco, T., *Structured Analysis and System Specification*, Prentice-Hall, 1979.
[3] Page-Jones, M., *The Practical Guide to Structured Systems Design*, Yourdon Press, 1980.
[4] Gane, T., and C. Sarson, *Structured Systems Analysis*, McDonnell Douglas, 1982.
[5] Ward, P.T., and S.J. Mellor, *Structured Development for Real-Time Systems* (3 vols.), Yourdon Press, 1985.
[6] Hatley, D.J., and I.A. Pirbhai, *Strategies for Real-Time System Specification*, Dorset House, 1987.
[7] Yourdon, E., *Modern Structured Analysis*, Prentice-Hall, 1990.
[8] Pressman, R.S., *Software Engineering: A Practitioner's Approach*, 3d ed., McGraw-Hill, 1992.
[9] Jackson, M., *Principles of Program Design*, Academic Press, 1975.
[10] Sommerville, I., *Software Engineering*, 3d ed., Addison-Wesley, 1990.
[11] Coad, P., and E. Yourdon, *Object-Oriented Analysis*, Prentice-Hall, 1990.

[12] Cashman, M., "Object Oriented Domain Analysis," *ACM Software Engineering Notes* **14** (6), 67 (1989).

[13] Booch, G., *Object-Oriented Design,* Benjamin-Cummings, 1991.

[14] Coad, P., and E. Yourdon, *Object-Oriented Design,* Prentice-Hall, 1991.

[15] Weinberg, G., *The Psychology of Computer Programming,* Van Nostrand, 1971.

[16] Mack, B., and P. Heath (eds.), *Guide to Good Programming,* Halsted Press (Wiley), 1980.

[17] Myers, G., *The Art of Software Testing,* Wiley, 1979.

[18] Boehm, B., *Software Engineering Economics,* Prentice-Hall, 1981, p. 37.

[19] Beizer, B., *Software Testing Techniques,* 2d ed., Van Nostrand-Reinhold, 1990.

[20] McCracken, D., "Software in the 80s—Perils and Promises," *Computerworld* **14** (spec. ed., 38), 5 (Sept. 17, 1980).

[21] Schneidewind, N.F., "The State of Software Maintenance," *IEEE Trans. Software Engineering* **SE-13** (3), 303–310 (1987).

[22] "Case Tools for Reverse Engineering," *CASE Outlook* (CASE Consulting Group, Lake Oswego, OR), **2** (2), 1–15 (1988).

CASE Tools: The Technologist's Workshop

Imagine that you own a house and that next to the house a very large tree has grown. This tree, which is 3 ft in diameter and 100 ft tall, offers shade and beauty year round. A violent storm blows through your region and pulls the tree up by its roots, tilting it ominously toward your house. Regretfully, you decide that the tree must be cut down.

In past years you've used a small hand ax to cut down small trees on your property. Figuring that the task will scale upward, you decide to cut down the large tree. You know nothing about safety procedures for cutting down large trees. You know little about the technical methods that professional tree cutters use when a large tree is to be taken down. You do know, however, that a very powerful tool exists for cutting down large trees.

You rush to the hardware store and buy their most powerful chain saw. Returning home, you pull the cord and the 10-horsepower motor roars to life. You begin to cut.

At this point, one of three things will happen:

1. You cut the tree down successfully; it will fall inside your yard and be removed without incident.

2. You cut the tree down, but it will fall on your house. Now you will sustain the embarrassment of failure and the economic hardship of hiring professionals to remove the tree and correct the damage.

3. You cut the tree down, and it falls on you. This mitigates the need for further concern on your part!

Computer-aided software engineering (CASE) is a lot like the chain saw in my story. It is a powerful tool that can create as many problems as it solves, if the user doesn't understand the software engineering procedures and methods that must be used in conjunction with it. When CASE is properly used in conjunction with effective procedures and methods, it provides enormous leverage for the software engineer. It is a powerful tool.

In this chapter, the technical aspects of computer-aided software engineering are discussed. CASE technologies span a wide range of topics that encompass project management procedures and software engineering methods. In the preceding chapter I attempted to provide you with a reasonable understanding of the underpinnings of the technology. In this chapter, the focus shifts to the tools and environments that will help to automate software engineering.

What is CASE?

Computer-aided software engineering can be as simple as a single tool that supports a specific software engineering activity or as complex as a complete *environment* that encompasses tools, a database, people, hardware, a network, operating systems, standards, and myriad other components.

The building blocks for CASE are illustrated in Figure 18.1. Each building block forms a foundation for the next, with tools sitting at the top of the heap. It is interesting to note that the foundation for effective CASE environments has relatively little to do with software engineering tools themselves. Rather, successful environments for software engineering are built on an *environment architecture* that encompasses appropriate hardware and systems software. In addition,

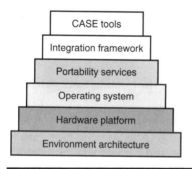

Figure 18.1   CASE building blocks.

the environment architecture must consider the human work patterns that are applied during the software engineering process.

During the 1960s, 1970s, and 1980s, software development was a mainframe activity.[1] Terminals were linked to a central computer, and each software developer shared the resources of that computer. Software tools that were available (and there were relatively few) were designed to operate in a terminal-based timesharing environment.

Today, the trend in software development is away from the mainframe computer and toward the workstation as a software engineering platform. Individual workstations are networked so that software engineers can communicate effectively. The project database (discussed later in this chapter) is available through a network file server that is accessible from all workstations. An operating system that supports the hardware, the network, and the tools ties the environment together.

The environment architecture, composed of the hardware platform and operating system support (including networking and database management software), lays the groundwork for CASE. But the CASE environment itself demands other building blocks. A set of *portability services* provides a bridge between CASE tools and their *integration framework* and the environment architecture. The integration framework is a collection of specialized programs that enables individual CASE tools to communicate with one another, to create a project database, and exhibit the same look and feel to the end user (the software engineer). Portability services allow CASE tools and their integration framework to migrate across different hardware platforms and operating systems without significant adaptive maintenance.

What do you mean when you talk about an "integration framework" for CASE?

The building blocks depicted in Figure 18.1 represent a comprehensive foundation for the integration of CASE tools. However, most CASE tools in use today have not been constructed using all of the building blocks discussed above. In fact, the majority of CASE tools are "point solutions." That is, a tool is used to assist in a particular software engineering activity (e.g., analysis modeling), but does not directly communicate with other tools, is not tied into a project database, and is not part of an *integrated* CASE *environment* (I-CASE). Although this situation is not ideal, a CASE tool can be used quite effectively, even if it is a point solution.

---

[1]Certainly, there were exceptions, but it was not until the late 1980s that workstations and PCs began to be used in significant numbers to build computer-based systems.

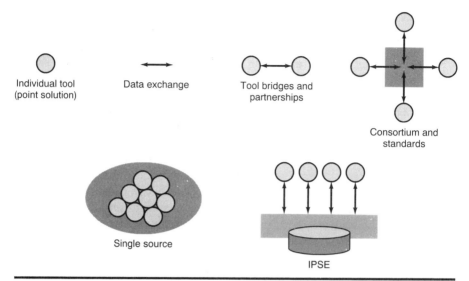

Figure 18.2   Integration options.

The relative levels of CASE integration are shown in Figure 18.2. At the low end of the integration spectrum is the *individual* (point solution) *tool.* When individual tools provide facilities for *data exchange* (most do), the integration level is improved slightly. Such tools produce output in a standard format that should be compatible with other tools that can read the format. In some cases, the builders of complementary CASE tools work together to form a *bridge* between the tools (e.g., an analysis and design tool that is coupled with a code generator). Using this approach, the synergy between the tools can produce end products that would be difficult to create using either tool separately. *Single-source integration* occurs when a single CASE vendor integrates a number of different tools and sells them as a package. Although this approach is quite effective, the closed architecture of most single-source environments precludes easy addition of tools from other vendors.

At the high end of the integration spectrum is the *integrated project support environment* (IPSE). Standards for each of the building blocks described above are created. CASE vendors use these IPSE standards to build tools that will be compatible with the IPSE and therefore compatible to one another.

Is it fair to say that CASE is similar in many ways to automated tools that are applied in other engineering disciplines?

Today, CASE is where CAD, CAE, and CIM (computer-aided design, computer-aided engineering, and computer integrated manufacturing) were in 1980. Individual tools are being used by some companies, usage across the industry is spreading rapidly, and serious effort is under way to integrate the individual tools to form a consistent environment.

There is little doubt that CASE will impact software engineering in substantially the same way that CAE/CAD/CIM have impacted other engineering disciplines. However, there are some important differences. During its early years of evolution CAD/CAE/CIM implemented engineering practices that had been tried and proved over the past hundred years. CASE, on the other hand, provides a set of semi-automated and automated tools that is implementing an engineering culture that is new to many companies. The difference in impact and in acceptance is profound.

CAD/CAE focuses almost exclusively on problem solving and design. It continues to struggle with a bridge to manufacturing through CIM. The primary goal of CASE (over the long haul) is to move toward the automatic generation of programs from a design-level specification. Unlike CAD/CAE, many people believe that analysis and design by themselves are not enough for CASE, but that analysis and design must ultimately lead to the direct generation of the end product—computer software. There is little doubt that this makes the challenge significantly more difficult, but the end result, if it can be effectively accomplished, may be significantly more powerful.

Is there a way that we can categorize CASE tools?

A number of risks are inherent whenever we attempt to categorize CASE tools. There is a subtle implication that to create an effective CASE environment one must implement all categories of tools—this is simply not true. Confusion (or antagonism) can be created by placing a specific tool within one category when others might believe it belongs in another category. Some readers may feel that an entire category has been omitted—thereby eliminating an entire set of tools for inclusion in the overall CASE environment. In addition, simple categorization tends to be flat—that is, we do not show the hierarchical interaction of tools or the relationships among them. But even with these risks, it is necessary to create a taxonomy of CASE tools—to better understand the breadth of CASE and to better appreciate where such tools can be applied in the software engineering process.

CASE tools can be classified by function, by their role as instruments for managers or technical people, by their use in the various steps of the software engineering process, by the environment archi-

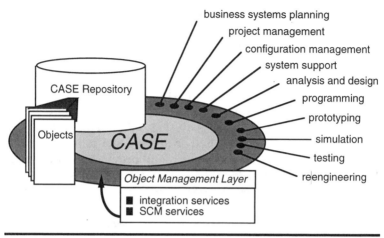

Figure 18.3   A CASE taxonomy.

tecture (hardware and software) that supports them, or even by their origin or cost. The taxonomy created in this book (Figure 18.3) uses function as a primary criterion.

It appears that some CASE tools focus on technical minutiae while others are applied to project-related activities. But are there CASE tools that can be used to analyze business operations and information systems needs?

By modeling the strategic information requirements of an organization, *business systems planning tools* provide a "metamodel" from which specific information systems are derived. Rather than focusing on the requirements of a specific application, business information is modeled as it moves between various organizational entities within a company [1]. The primary objective for tools in this category is to help improve the understanding of how information moves as day-to-day business activities are conducted.

It is important to note that business systems planning tools are not for every organization. They require a major commitment in resources and a major philosophical commitment by management to produce a complete model and then act on the information derived from it. However, such tools do provide substantial insight when information systems strategies are to be constructed and when current systems and methods do not meet the needs of an organization.

What about CASE tools that assist in the day-to-day management of software projects—what are my options in this category?

There is a broad array of CASE project management tools that can have a profound impact on the quality of project management for software development efforts, both large and small. Today, most CASE project management tools focus on one specific element of project management, rather than providing all-encompassing support for the management activity. By using a selected set of CASE tools, the project manager can generate useful estimates of effort, cost, and duration of a software project; define a work-breakdown structure (WBS); plan a workable project schedule; and track projects on a continuing basis. In addition, the manager can use tools to collect metrics that will ultimately provide an indication of software development productivity and product quality. For those managers who have responsibility for contract software development, CASE tools are available to trace requirements from the original customer RFP (request for proposal) to the software development work that implements these requirements in a deliverable system.

Are there tools that support the umbrella activity that helps us to control change—software configuration management?

CASE tools can assist in all five major SCM tasks—identification, version control, change control, auditing, and status accounting. The CASE database provides a mechanism for identifying each configuration item and relating it to other items, the control process discussed in Chapter 15 can be implemented with the aid of specialized tools, easy access to individual configuration items facilitate the auditing process, and CASE communication tools can greatly improve status accounting (reporting information about changes to all who need to know). Software configuration management lies at the kernel of every CASE environment. By controlling changes to the software configuration, SCM tools enforce human cognizance of each change, thereby reducing misunderstanding and improving system quality.

The use of the project database, configuration management tools, and specialized "browsing" tools provide a first step toward the creation of a library for software that will encourage the reuse of software components. Although relatively little reuse has been accomplished to date, CASE offers the first real promise for achieving broader reuse for computer software components.

You've already discussed project management tools, but there are other day-to-day project activities as well. What CASE tools support them?

The *support tools* category encompasses systems and application tools that complement the software engineering process. Tools in this broad category encompass the "umbrella activities" that are applicable across the entire software engineering process. They include documentation tools, systems software and networking tools, quality assurance tools, and database management tools (also members of the framework tools category).

Document production and desk-top publishing tools support nearly every aspect of software engineering and represent a substantial "leverage" opportunity for all software developers. Most software development organizations spend a substantial amount of time developing documents, and in many cases the documentation process itself is quite inefficient. It is not unusual for a software development organization to spend as much as 20 or 30 percent of all software development effort on documentation. For this reason, documentation tools provide an important opportunity to improve productivity.

Documentation tools are often linked to other CASE tools using a data bridge implemented by the vendor of the technical tool. For example, a number of analysis and design tools have links to one or more desk-top publishing systems, so that models and text created during analysis and design can be transmitted to a documentation tool and embedded in the specification created using the documentation tool.

CASE is a workstation technology. Therefore, the CASE environment must accommodate high-quality network system software, electronic mail, bulletin boards, and other communication capabilities. Although the operating system of preference for most engineering workstations (and an increasing number of high-end PCs) is UNIX, the portability services provided by an IPSE may enable CASE tools to migrate to other operating systems without great frustration. Database management software serves as a foundation for the establishment of a CASE database (repository).

In the last chapter, you discussed analysis and design methods at some length and indicated that these methods are supported by CASE tools. Can you provide more details?

Analysis and design tools enable a software engineer to create a model of the system to be built. The model contains a representation of data and control flow, data content (through a definition of a data dictionary), process representations, control specifications, and a variety of other modeling representations. Analysis and design tools assist in the creation of the model and also in an evaluation of the model's quality. By performing consistency and validity checking on the model, analysis and design tools provide a software engineer with some degree of insight into the analysis representation and help to eliminate errors before they propagate into the design, or worse, into implementation itself.

Tools in the analysis and design category often implement the structured analysis and structured design (SA/SD) method discussed in Chapter 17. SA/SD tools enable a software engineer to create progressively more complex models of a system, beginning at the requirements level and finishing with an architectural design.

We already use a wide variety of programming tools. Is this a legitimate category for CASE?

Programming or code generation is the culmination of analysis and design tasks. Tools that support programming are a legitimate entry in the CASE tool set.

The *programming tools* category encompasses compilers, editors, and debuggers that are available to support most conventional programming languages. In addition, object-oriented programming environments, fourth-generation languages, application generators, and database query languages also reside within this category.

There was a time when the only tools available to a software engineer were conventional coding tools—compilers, editors, and debuggers. Pressman and Herron [2] discuss this when they state:

> There's an old saying: "When the only tool that you have is a hammer, every problem looks like a nail." Think about it. You can use a hammer to pound nails, but if it's the only tool that you have, you can also use it to pound screws (sloppy, but workable), bend metal (noisy, but workable), punch a hole in wood or concrete (very sloppy, but possible), dig holes,.... We do the best we can by adapting the tools that we have on hand.

For almost 30 years, the only tools available to programmers were conventional coding tools, and therefore, every software engineering problem looked like a coding problem. Today, conventional tools continue to exist at the front lines of software development, but they are supported by many other CASE tools.

What are "fourth-generation" programming tools?

The thrust toward the representation of software applications at a higher level of abstraction has caused many developers to move headlong toward fourth-generation programming tools. Database query systems, code generators, and fourth-generation languages have changed the nature in which systems are developed. There is little doubt that the end goal of CASE is automatic code generation—that is, the representation of systems at a higher level of abstraction than conventional programming languages and the overlay of tools that not only translate a system description into an operational program but also serve to help verify the correctness of the system specification so that the resulting output will conform to user requirements.

Fourth-generation languages are already used widely in information systems applications. It is not unusual to read claims such as: "Rank Xerox in the U.K....created an application with 350,000 lines of COBOL code...yet it was created with three full-time people and one part-time person in ten weeks" [3]. Although such accomplishments are possible in very limited domains of applicability, they represent a harbinger of things to come in broader application areas. We are already beginning to see the first code generation tools appear in the engineered products and systems market. (Most focus on Ada.) As the 1990s progress, it is likely that less and less source code will be "written" manually.

In many cases we find that the user is unsure of what a human–computer interface should look like. What kinds of prototyping tools are available to assist in interface design and development?

Even with the evolution of user interface standards (e.g., X Windows System, Motif), the design and development of human–computer interfaces remains a challenge for software engineers. Industry studies have found that between 50 to 80 percent of all code generated for interactive applications is generated to manage and implement the human–computer interface [4].

Interface design and development tools are actually a tool kit of program components such as menus, buttons, window structures, icons, scrolling mechanisms, and device drivers. However, this tool kit is being replaced by interface prototyping tools that enable rapid on-screen creation of sophisticated user interfaces that conform to the interfacing standard that has been adopted for the software.

All *prototyping tools* reside somewhere on an implementation spectrum. At the low end of the spectrum, tools exist for the creation of a "paper prototype." A PC- or workstation-based drawing tool can create realistic screen images that can be used to illustrate system function and behavior to the customer. These images cannot be executed. *Screen painters* enable a software engineer to define screen layout rapidly for interactive applications. In some cases, a screen painter will also generate the source code to create the screens. More sophisticated CASE prototyping tools enable the creation of a data design, coupled with both screen and report layouts. Many analysis and design tools have extensions that provide a prototyping option. Simulation tools generate skeleton Ada and C source code for engineering (real-time) applications. Finally, a variety of fourth-generation tools (discussed earlier) have prototyping features.

As prototyping tools evolve, it is likely that some will become *domain-specific*. That is, the tool will be designed to address a relatively narrow application area. Prototyping tools for telecommunications, aerospace applications, factory automation, and many other areas may become commonplace by the mid-1990s. Such tools will use a knowledge base that "understands" the application domain, facilitating the creation of prototype systems.

Are there CASE tools that enable a software engineer to simulate the behavior of a system before it is built?

Simulation tools provide the software engineer with the ability to predict the behavior of a real-time system prior to the time that it is built. In addition, these tools enable the software engineer to develop mockups of the real-time system that allow the customer to gain insight into the function, operation, and response prior to actual implementation. There is little doubt that such capability provides distinct benefits in an area where success has been unpredictable, and software development itself is something of a black art.

Most simulation tools provide the software engineer with a means for creating functional and behavioral models of a system. Tools in this category provide a means for specifying projected performance characteristics of each system element (e.g., execution speed of a hardware or software function), defining input and output data characteristics (e.g., input data arrival rates or interrupt characteristics), and modeling the interfaces and interconnectivity among system elements.

Many simulation tools provide code generation for Ada and other programming languages that will likely become considerably more sophisticated as new generations of these tools evolve. In addition, all tools in this category make use of an underlying formal specification language, opening the door to more comprehensive code generation capability and formal verification of the system specification.

It seems that most discussions of CASE tools focus on analysis and design. Is there a robust tool set for testing?

A wide variety of *testing tools* exist, and they are the most under-utilized category in the CASE tools taxonomy. In its directory of software testing tools, Software Quality Engineering [5] defines the following testing tools categories:

- *Data acquisition:* Tools that acquire data to be used during testing.
- *Static measurement:* Tools that analyze source code without executing test cases.
- *Dynamic measurement:* Tools that analyze source code during execution.
- *Simulation:* Tools that simulate function of hardware or other externals.
- *Test management:* Tools that assist in the planning, development, and control of testing.
- *Cross-functional tools:* Tools that cross the bounds of the above categories.

Many of the most widely used testing tools have features that span two or more of the above categories.

Static testing tools assist the software engineer in deriving test cases. Although a number of different types of static tools exist, the majority accept source code as input and perform a number of analyses that result in the generation of test cases. *Dynamic testing tools* interact with an executing program, checking path coverage, testing assertions about the value of specific variables, and otherwise instrumenting the execution flow of the program. *Test management tools* are used to control and coordinate software testing for each of the major testing steps (Chapter 17). Tools in this category manage and coordinate regression testing, perform comparisons that ascertain differences between actual and expected output, and conduct batch testing of programs with interactive human–computer interfaces.

It would seem that many of the CASE tools described above are applicable to software maintenance as well. Are there specialized tools that focus exclusively on software maintenance activities?

It is true that most CASE tools can be applied to maintenance work as well. However, specialized tools for maintenance do exist and are capturing an increasing share of the CASE market. The *maintenance tools* category can be subdivided into the following areas:

- *Reverse engineering to specification tools:*   Take source code as input and generate graphical structured analysis and design models, where-used lists, and other design information.

- *Forward engineering tools:*   Analyze program syntax, generate a control flow graph, and automatically build a structured program; used to modify on-line database systems (e.g., convert IDMS or DB2 files into entity-relationship format).

The above tools are limited to specific programming languages (although most major languages are addressed) and require some degree of interaction with the software engineer.

Reverse engineering tools perform a postdevelopment analysis on an existing program. Like testing tools, reverse engineering tools can be categorized as *static* or *dynamic*. A static reverse engineering tool (by far the most common) uses program source code as input and analyzes and extracts program architecture, control structure, logical flow, data structure, and data flow. Dynamic reverse engineering tools monitor the software as it executes and use information obtained during monitoring to build a behavioral model of the program. Although such tools are relatively rare, they provide important information for software engineers who must maintain real-time software or embedded systems.

Although forward engineering tools offer significant promise, relatively few industry quality tools are in use today. Existing reengineering tools can be divided into two subcategories—code restructuring tools and data reengineering tools. Code restructuring tools accept unstructured source code as input and then restructure the code to conform to modern structured programming concepts. Although such tools can be useful, they focus solely on the procedural design of a program. Data restructuring tools work at the other end of the design spectrum. Such tools assess data definitions or a database description represented in a programming language (usually COBOL) or database description language. They then translate the data description into graphical notation that can be analyzed by a software engineer.

You mentioned the importance of integration, but you haven't discussed tools that will help us in accomplishing it. Are such tools available?

The industry trend toward I-CASE environments will continue to gain momentum during the 1990s. *Framework tools*—software tools that provide database management, configuration management, and CASE tools integration capabilities—are the first thrust in the IPSE direction.

Tools in this category exhibit functional components that support data, interface, and tools integration. Most implement an object-oriented database, with an internal tool set for establishing smooth interfaces with tools from other CASE vendors. Most framework tools provide some configuration management capability, enabling the user of the tool to control changes to configuration objects created by all CASE tools that are integrated with the framework tool.

What strategy are CASE users and CASE vendors using to achieve integration?

The term *integration* implies both *combination* and *closure*. I-CASE combines a variety of different tools and a variety of different information in a way that enables closure of communication among tools, between people, and across the software engineering process. Tools are integrated so that software engineering information is available to each tool that needs it; usage is integrated so that a common look and feel are provided for all tools; and a development philosophy is integrated, implying a standardized software engineering approach that applies modern practice and proven methods.

To define *integration* in the context of the software engineering process, it is necessary to establish a set of requirements for I-CASE: An integrated CASE environment should serve these functions [6]:

- Provide a mechanism for sharing software engineering information among all tools contained in the environment.

- Enable a change to one item of information to be tracked to other related information items.

- Provide version control and overall configuration management for all software engineering information.

- Allow direct, nonsequential access to any tool contained in the environment.

- Establish automated support for a procedural context for software engineering work that integrates the tools and data into a common process framework (Appendix III).

- Enable the users of each tool to experience a consistent look and feel at the human–computer interface.

- Support communication among software engineers.

- Collect both management and technical metrics that can be used to improve the process and the product.

To achieve these requirements, each of the building blocks of a CASE architecture discussed earlier in this chapter must fit together to create an *integration architecture.*

What is the most commonly discussed integration architecture?

The integration architecture or framework facilitates transfer of information into and out of a pool of software engineering information. To accomplish this, the following architectural components must exist: a database must be created (to store the information), an object management system must be built (to manage changes to the information), a tools control mechanism must be constructed (to coordinate the use of CASE tools), and a user interface that provides a consistent pathway between actions made by the user and the tools must be contained in the environment. Most models of the integration framework represent these components as *layers.* A simple model of the framework depicting only the components noted above is shown in Figure 18.4.

The *user interface layer* incorporates a standardized interface tool kit with a common presentation protocol. The *interface tool kit* contains software for human–computer interface management and a library of display objects. Both provide a consistent mechanism for communication between the interface and individual CASE tools.

The *tools layer* incorporates a set of tools management services with the CASE tools themselves. *Tools management services* (TMS) control the behavior of tools within the environment. If multitasking is used during the execution of one or more tools, TMS performs multitask synchronization and communication, coordinates the flow of information from the repository and object management system to the tools, accomplishes security and auditing functions, and collects metrics on tool usage.

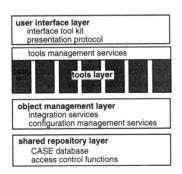

Figure 18.4   Integration framework architecture for CASE.

The *object management layer* (OML) performs the configuration management functions described in Chapter 15. In essence, software in this layer of the framework architecture provides the mechanism for tools integration. Every CASE tool is "plugged into" the object management layer. Working in conjunction with the CASE repository, the OML provides *integration services*—a set of standard modules that couples tools with the repository. In addition, the OML provides configuration management services by enabling the identification of all configuration objects, performing version control, and providing support for change control, audits, and status accounting.

The *shared repository layer* is the CASE database and the access control functions that enable the object management layer to interact with the database.

It seems that the repository sits at the center of the integration issue. What is the role of the repository in CASE?

The repository for an I-CASE environment is the set of mechanisms and data structures that achieves data–tool and data–data integration, that is, the ability to integrate CASE tools with a common shared data store and the ability to establish relationships among the configuration objects that are contained within the data store. The repository provides the obvious functions of a database management system,[2] and, in addition, performs or precipitates the following functions [7]:

- *Data integrity:* Includes functions that validate entries to the repository, ensure consistency among related objects, and automatically perform "cascading" modifications when a change to one object demands changes to objects that are related to it.

- *Information sharing:* Provides a mechanism for sharing information among multiple developers and between multiple tools; manages and controls multiuser access to data; and locks or unlocks objects so that changes are not inadvertently overlaid on one another.

- *Data–tool integration:* Establishes a data model that can be accessed by all tools in the I-CASE environment; controls access to the data; and performs appropriate configuration management functions.

- *Data–data integration:* The database management system (DBMS)

---

[2]Although many investigators feel that an object-oriented database management system is the correct approach, others believe that a relational DBMS can do the job adequately.

enables relations among data objects so that other functions can be achieved.

- *Methodology enforcement:* The E-R (entity-relationship) model of data stored in the repository can imply a specific paradigm for software engineering; as a minimum, the relationships and objects define a set of steps that must be conducted to build the contents of the repository.

- *Document standardization:* The definition of objects in the database leads directly to a standard approach for the creation of software engineering documents.

To achieve these functions, the repository is defined in terms of a *metamodel*. The metamodel determines how information is stored in the repository, how data can be accessed by tools and viewed by software engineers, how well data security and integrity can be maintained, and how easily the existing model can be extended to accommodate new needs.

Are standards for I-CASE and the repository likely to evolve?

A number of different standards efforts are under way for I-CASE environments and the CASE repository. In some cases, a proposed standard goes beyond the definition of a repository to consider many different aspects of an integrated environment. In the United States, a number of proposed standards are competing for dominance. In Europe, a single standard has been adopted. Similarly, Japan and other Far Eastern countries have adopted a single (but different) standard for I-CASE. Each standards effort is described briefly:

Information Resource Dictionary Standard (IRDS), ANSI (X3.I38-1988): The only formally approved ANSI standard presented in this section, IRDS was originally developed as a standard definition for requirements dictionaries. (This standard can also be used for repositories.) It focuses on the management of corporate information resources and is characterized using a multilevel metamodel. This standard helps in the creation of "bridges" between complementary tools such as analysis and design tools and code generators and in CASE tool portability across different platforms.

Atherton/DEC Tool Integration Standard (ATIS): Originally developed by Atherton Technology (a developer of framework tools) and Digital Equipment Corporation, ATIS has been adopted by the CASE Integration Standards Committee of the Software Productivity Consortium. ATIS focuses on the definition of a repository architecture and addresses SCM, tool integration, data security, and portability across platforms.

Common Ada Interface Standard (CAIS):   Focusing primarily on tools for Ada software development, the CAIS standard defines interfaces between tools that will comprise the Ada development environment.

Portable Common Tools Environment (PCTE):   PCTE was developed for use by the European software development community (the Esprit project) and has been adopted by the European Computer Manufacturers' Association (ECMA). PCTE is an interface standard and architectural model for CASE. It addresses portability, concurrency control, network distribution, data architecture, and the user interface in the context of a CASE environment.

Software Industrialized Generator and Maintenance Aids (SIGMA):   SIGMA is similar to PCTE in intent and scope and has been adopted in Japan and other Far Eastern countries.

Electronic Design Interchange Format (EDIF):   This standards effort focuses on data formats for information exchange between CASE tools (and any other programs that want to exchange data). A CASE tool that produces output information in this format can easily transmit the information to other tools that accommodate input in EDIF format.

In addition to the standards introduced above every major computer vendor and other government agencies have proposed "solutions" for I-CASE. A list of some of the more common follows:

- *Cohesion*—Digital Equipment Corporation
- *Softbench*—Hewlett-Packard
- *AD/Cycle*—IBM
- *NSE*—Sun Microsystems

One or more of these integration architectures may evolve to become a de facto standard if widespread industry adoption occurs.

A Manager's Checklist

Computer-aided software engineering tools span every step in the software engineering process and those umbrella activities that are applied throughout the process. CASE combines a set of building blocks that begins at the hardware and operating system software level and ends with individual tools.

In this chapter we have considered a taxonomy of CASE tools and the manner in which these tools may be integrated. Tool categories encompass both management and technical activities and span most software application areas. Integration mechanisms have been developed for data, tools, and human–computer interaction. The CASE repository is a relational or object-oriented database that is the center of accumulation and storage for software engineering information. The repository is implemented using a database management system that provides all standard features expected in a DBMS and special features required to accommodate the software engineering process.

Your organization should be using CASE tools today. To help you investigate the status of CASE within your shop, the following actions and questions are recommended:

Actions

- Make a list of all software development tools that you use. Organize them according to the taxonomy presented in this chapter. Note categories within the taxonomy in which you use no tools.

- Gather product information on at least three tools within each of the following categories: project management tools, configuration management tools, analysis and design tools, testing tools, and reengineering tools. Establish local requirements for tools in each of these categories.

Questions

- Where does your organization spend the majority of its time during software development? During maintenance? Are you currently using tools to assist in these high-intensity areas?

- What percentage of project managers in your organization currently use CASE tools for project management?

- What percentage of your software engineers currently make use of CASE tools other than programming tools? What other tools categories are used by more than 25 percent of staff?

- Do you currently have any plans for creating an I-CASE environment? If not, when do you think your organization will be ready to proceed with integration planning?

Further Readings

A number of books on CASE have been published in an effort to capitalize on the high degree of interest in the industry. Unfortunately, many suffer from one or more of the following failings: (1) the book focuses only on a narrow band of tools (e.g., analysis and design) while claiming to cover a wider categorization, (2) the book spends relatively little time on CASE and more time surveying (often poorly) the underlying methods that the tools deliver, (3) the book spends little time discussing integration issues, or (4) the presentation is outdated because of an emphasis on specific CASE products.

The books that follow have avoided at least some of these failings:

Braithwaite, K.S., *Application Development Using CASE Tools*, Academic Press, 1990.

Gane, C., *Computer-Aided Software Engineering: The Methodologies, The Products and the Future*, Prentice-Hall, 1990.

Fisher, C., *CASE: Using Software Development Tools*, Wiley, 1988.

Lewis, T.G., *Computer-Aided Software Engineering*, Van Nostrand-Reinhold, 1990.

McClure, C., *CASE Is Software Automation*, Prentice-Hall, 1988.

CASE: The Potential and the Pitfalls, QED Information Sciences, Inc., Wellesley, MA, 1989.

Schindler, M., *Computer-Aided Software Design*, Wiley, 1990.

Towner, L.E., *CASE: Concepts and Implementation*, McGraw-Hill, 1989.

An anthology by Chikofsky (*Computer-Aided Software Engineering*, IEEE Computer Society Press, 1988) contains a useful collection of early papers on CASE and software development environments.

The best sources of current information on CASE tools are technical periodicals and industry newsletters. *CASE Outlook* and *CASE User* (CASE Consulting Group, Lake Oswego, OR), *The CASE Report* (Auerbach Publishers, Boston, MA), *CASE Strategies* (Cutter Information Corp., Arlington, MA), *CASE Trends* (Software Productivity Group, Shrewsbury, MA), and *CASEWorld* (Blum Publications, Yorktown Heights, NY) are all industry newsletters that provide in-depth analysis of new products and worthwhile tutorials on software engineering topics that affect CASE.

If you need information concerning specific CASE tools, the following directories provide useful information:

CASEBASE, an on-line database (P-Cube Corp., Brea, CA, 714-990-3169)

CASE Locator, an on-line database (CASE Associates, Oregon City, OR, 503-656-3207)

CASE Product Guide (Software Magazine, Westborough, MA, 800-225-9218)

Tool Finder/Plus (CASE Consulting Group, Lake Oswego, OR, fax: 503-245-6935)

Guide to Software Productivity Aids (Applied Computer Research, Phoenix, AZ, 800-234-2227)

Testing Tools Reference Guide (Software Quality Engineering, Jacksonville, FL, 904-268-8639)

References

[1] Martin, J., *Information Engineering,* 3 vols., Prentice-Hall, 1989.
[2] Pressman, R.S., and S.R. Herron, *Software Shock,* Dorset House, 1991.
[3] *CASE News* **3** (4), 1 (1989).
[4] Lee, E., "User-Interface Development Tools," *IEEE Software* (May), 31–33 (1990).
[5] *Testing Tools Reference Guide,* version 9.0, Software Quality Engineering, Jacksonville, FL, 1991.
[6] Forte, G., "In Search of the Integrated Environment," *CASE Outlook* (March/April), 5–12 (1989).
[7] Forte, G., "Rally Round the Repository," *CASE Outlook* (Dec.), 5–27 (1989).

The Future:
What You Can Expect

The day-to-day grind of the information systems environment causes you to stay focused on today's problems. Your time is absorbed trying to meet competing and sometimes conflicting requests for software work, balancing available resources, acquiring and instituting new technology, mediating personnel problems, and negotiating political conflicts. While all this is going on, you try to get high-quality work out the door. If you're typical, you have very little time to think about the future.

Max Hopper [1] suggests the current state of affairs when he states:

> Because changes in information technology are becoming so rapid and unforgiving, and the consequences of falling behind are so irreversible, companies will either master the technology or die.... Think of it as a technology treadmill. Companies will have to run harder and harder just to stay in place.

Changes in software engineering technology are indeed "rapid and unforgiving," but at the same time real progress is often quite slow. By the time a decision is made to adopt a new method (or a new tool), conduct the training necessary to understand its application, and introduce the technology into the software development culture, something new (and even better) has come along, and the process begins anew.

In this chapter, I'll suggest a few cultural, management, and technical trends that may have an impact on your organization over the decade of the 1990s. No one has a crystal ball. My attempt to prognosticate about the future of software engineering should be viewed for what it is: one person's opinion of the direction of the technology.

Will we see a real change in software development culture over the next few years?

A flip answer might be "not as much as I'd like, but more than many managers and practitioners are comfortable with!" Changes in the way software has been developed have occurred at a relatively slow pace over the past 20 years. Most changes were predicated by hardware technologies that forced software developers to use specialized tools and new approaches.

Today, things are different. New paradigms, CASE, object-oriented thinking, reusability, formal methods, measurement, and reengineering are "hardware independent" developments that will have a profound effect on the culture of software developers over the long term. Yet, integrating these new technologies and coping with the culture changes that occur as a consequence can be unsettling for managers, practitioners, and even end users.

What will be the most likely cultural changes within the "typical" software development organization?

The primary changes in software development culture can be summarized in the following way:

- Managers will be forced to manage quality—an activity that is foreign to most of them.
- Practitioners will use tools to construct programs in an evolutionary manner, rather than write them in a sequential fashion.
- Customers and end users will be asked to take a proactive role in the definition of requirements and will serve as bona fide members of the "team" that builds a computer-based system.

Although each of these predictions seems relatively innocuous, the cultural changes that each portends will be profound.

For the first time, managers will be forced to measure so that total quality management for software can be achieved. They will be asked to use project management tools that enable them to plan more effectively, assess risks more completely, and track progress more comprehensively. They will manage a process framework that will channel the energies of technical staff and change the way in which projects are conducted. They will promote software quality assurance as a way of life rather than an after-the-fact activity.

For the first time, practitioners will move away from writing code, and because of this, will be forced to reassess the way in which they build computer software. They will construct programs from preexisting software building blocks (reusable components) or create programs using nonprocedural languages and code generation tools. They will finally come to the realization that design—not coding—is the creative part of software engineering. Some will begin to use formal methods for software development—an activity that will radically change their approach to "programming." Those that are mired in maintenance groups will gain some relief as reengineering tools reduce the drudgery that is associated with support work. All will be encouraged to build software within a management framework that emphasizes quality.

Customers, and in some cases end users, will be asked to define requirements using the facilitated application specification techniques described in Chapter 10. They will negotiate key system characteristics and evaluate progress as the software evolves. Because they will play a more active role, demands on customer staff time and resources will increase. They will no longer be passive observers.

It is important to note that the changes that I have predicted will not occur uniformly across the software development community. Your organization may see only a few of them in the short term. But over the long haul, most will occur. When taken as a group, they portend significant cultural change.

You mentioned new paradigms as one of the technology developments that would likely have an impact on software development cultures. Earlier in the book, you mentioned a number of paradigms. Which do you think will predominate?

There is little doubt that evolutionary paradigms will predominate throughout the 1990s. The spiral model (Chapter 16) and variations that accommodate formal methods or object-oriented development and reuse will become more common.

Managers and customers who have become used to sequential development models will have to adapt to the iterative nature of evolutionary development. Fixed-price and fixed-time projects will give way to a price/time model that is adjusted according to customer changes as the software evolves. The evolutionary paradigm results in software that adapts to changing needs. It also demands a management structure that adapts to an approach in which software "grows."

It's fair to state that CASE has not yet lived up to its promise. How does CASE need to evolve to better satisfy the real needs of the software engineering community?

First, a comment on your assumption. Many of the problems that have been attributed to CASE are actually problems with the procedural and methodological components of software engineering. If CASE tools are used within a well-defined and well-executed process framework, if they support methods that are appropriate for the applications that are to be built, and if they are applied by trained software engineers who have appropriate support, there is every likelihood that CASE will work successfully today.

With that said, there are a number of areas in which CASE can be improved:

1. *Tools must be integrated with a repository to accomplish the information transfer that is essential for successful software engineering:* Integration, however, is much more than tying the tools together. In an ideal setting, integration provides managers and practitioners with insight.

2. *The CASE environment must be adaptable:*   That is, it must support multiple paradigms and development approaches. For example, an ideal integrated environment would be capable of accommodating an evolutionary macromodel (e.g., the spiral model paradigm) that has been adapted to accommodate component reuse, fourth-generation technology, and conventional third-generation object-oriented development.

3. *The CASE environment must provide active support for project management:*   Tools that do estimating, scheduling, and even risk analysis are not enough. The environment itself must assist in metrics collection, progress assessment (in real time), intrateam communication, and a variety of other support activities.

4. *The CASE environment must contain facilities that support distributed work groups and concurrent engineering:*   Large software projects are often undertaken by many development teams working at different geographic sites. The success of these large projects depends heavily on communication, collaboration, and coordination among teams. The CASE environment must be integrated with a distributed network environment.

5. *Individual tools must become "agents" for the software engineer:* A new generation of rule-based tools should provide domain-specific guidance for the analyst, the designer, and the software tester. Instead of simply doing the engineer's bidding, the tools should offer suggestions, note inconsistencies, and provide limited forms of advice.

6. *Design tools should support the creation, management, and reapplication of reusable design components:*   Such tools will enable a software engineer to reuse earlier design work.

7. *The current generation of reengineering tools must improve substantially to provide real benefits to the majority of software engineers:* To reduce the crushing burden of maintenance, CASE tools must do

more than restructure spaghetti-bowl code or extract basic design information. Next-generation reengineering tools need not rebuild programs automatically. Rather, they must provide facilities that will enable a software engineer to perform rebuilding much more productively.

You alluded to object-oriented (OO) thinking in a number of different chapters. Some people think that OO is just a flash in the pan—that it will fade over the next few years. What do you think about this position?

I think it's incorrect. Although it is true that a lot of hype has been connected with OO, it is also true that the underlying technology offers substantial promise. The reason is reuse. When OO is used properly, the software engineer creates reusable design and program components. Over the long haul, libraries of these components could have significant impact on our ability to build software more productively and with significantly higher quality.

What are the primary challenges that face OO over the next few years?

Many observers argue about the efficacy of specific OO languages or justifiably criticize the immaturity of object-oriented analysis and design techniques. However, the real problem, I believe, resides in our inability to create object-oriented development environments that can make the best use of the reusable software components created as a consequence of OO technology.

An object-oriented software engineering environment (that makes effective use of reuse) must support *specification technologies* that define standards for interchangeable software components, *implementation technologies* to speed production of each new component, *testing technologies* to verify that standards are met, *classification technologies* that enable each component to be described in a generic way, *extraction technologies* that enable a software engineer to describe (classify) and extract a software component from an existing library, and *fabrication technologies* to enable components to be assembled into high-quality software.

It is important to note that the "technologies" that I've just mentioned must be developed in any software engineering approach that intends to achieve reuse, regardless of whether OO is to be used. Although research is under way and some progress has been made, the availability of truly effective classification, extraction, and fabrication technologies is still a number of years away.

Conventional methods (e.g., structured analysis and design), OO methods, and formal methods appear to be competing for the hearts and minds of software engineers. Would you venture a guess on the future penetration of each of these methods?

Figure 19.1 presents my estimate of the market penetration (i.e., the percentage of all software engineers who will be using the method[1]) for each of the methods that you've mentioned over the decade of the 1990s. Today, structured analysis and design (SA/SD) is clearly the leader, but it is likely that OO methods will approach and eventually overtake SA/SD as the method of choice during the mid- to late 1990s. The use of formal methods will evolve more slowly, but will gain substantial market penetration (particularly in safety critical systems) by the late 1990s.

The potential benefits of formal methods make them particularly attractive, and yet they represent a radically different approach to software engineering. Is it realistic to expect that the "average" software engineer will be able to use these mathematically based techniques effectively?

There is considerable debate on this issue. Proponents of formal methods argue that anyone can be trained to use formal methods effec-

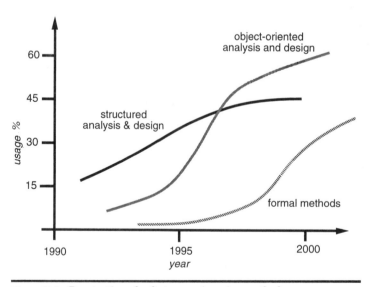

Figure 19.1   Penetration of software engineering methods.

---

[1]Note that the total percentage toward the end of the decade is greater than 100 percent because some software engineers will use different methods in different situations.

tively. Other industry observers argue that they are very difficult for the "average" practitioner to learn and apply.

It is likely that formal methods will gain a nontrivial market penetration only if easy-to-use CASE tools eliminate most of the burden of applying the methods. It is also true, however, that other factors may force the use of formal methods. As concerns about software safety mount, and risks to the public become more severe, regulatory agencies may mandate the use of formal methods for safety critical systems. I suspect that this will happen sometime in the late 1990s and the result will be much wider use of this powerful software engineering approach.

In Chapter 3 you noted that most software developers do not measure. Is this likely to change over the next few years?

Everyone wants to talk about (and debate) software metrics and measurement, but real progress in this area will be slow. The key to progress in software metrics is an emphasis on software quality. When software development organizations decide that product quality is paramount and that to achieve it, the software engineering process must be instrumented, software measurement will begin in earnest.

My best guess is that fewer than 5 percent of all software developers have an active software metrics program.[2] By the end of the decade of the 1990s, I would guess that between 20 and 30 percent will be collecting and analyzing software metrics.

Earlier in this chapter you called software maintenance a "crushing burden." Is this likely to change in the short term?

No. In fact, it's likely that maintenance work will absorb an increasingly high percentage of software budgets. This will result in two important trends: (1) some companies will use outsourcing[3] as a way to reduce the direct burden of maintenance work, but this will do little to reduce the cost of maintenance and may hurt the competitiveness of a company over time; (2) other companies will resist developing anything new, opting to buy packaged software instead. All in-house resources will be applied to maintenance.

---

[2]It is important to recognize that collecting a few productivity numbers on an ad hoc basis is *not* an active metrics program.

[3]Outsourcing occurs when a company subcontracts part or all of its software maintenance and/or development work to a third party.

You mentioned outsourcing as a trend. Do you think that this approach to information systems work is wise?

No, I don't. In fact, if we're not careful, outsourcing may destroy our competitiveness in software technologies in much the same way that outsourcing has destroyed our competitiveness in consumer electronics technologies.

Outsourcing is a manifestation of a deep (and potentially fatal) problem in U.S. industry and commerce: *the short-term view.* Rather than becoming more productive and building our own high-quality products, taking the time to develop technologies that will help us do this, and demanding that quality pervades everything that a company does, senior management looks for the most effective short-term solution. They do save money in the short term (and financial analysts are thrilled), and give up competitiveness in the long term. Over time, entire markets may be lost.

In the first chapter of this book I argued that software differentiates, that it provides a company with strategic advantages. Pressman and Herron [2] capture the essence of software when they state:

> Software is a mechanism for automating business, industry, and government. It is a medium for transferring new technology, a method of capturing knowledge so that it can be used by others, a means for differentiating one company's products from its competitors, and a window into a corporation's decision making processes. It is pivotal to nearly every aspect of business and is a business in and of itself. Software is the fuel that will power us into the next century.

And yet, management opts to outsource these things—to give up control over the "fuel" that can power their companies into the future. Sometimes, all I can do is shake my head.

Throughout this book, you've emphasized a focus on quality as a key to good software engineering. Yet, our company seems to be struggling with its total quality management (TQM) program. Are we missing something or is our situation typical?

In a recent article published in *The Wall Street Journal,* a study of 584 companies in North America, Germany, and Japan indicates that "despite plenty of talk and much action, many American companies are stumbling in their implementation of quality improvement efforts" [3]. Among many problems cited in the study were "amorphous quality management plans" and "diffused effort" that occurs when a company attempts to solve all quality problems at once. In addition, lack of measurement, lack of real employee involvement, and lack of management commitment are typical among many American companies.

The software engineering community in the United States can learn from the experiences of TQM programs that have been applied in a broader context. We must define explicit plans for improving software quality—plans that focus on a limited number of software development issues. We must measure, applying software metrics in both the management and technical arena. We must get all constituencies involved—managers, practitioners, and customers. And finally, as a manager involved in software development, you have to make a commitment to software quality and convince your management to support that commitment with appropriate resources.

Overall, are you optimistic about the future of software engineering?

I'm guardedly optimistic. It is true that the penetration of software engineering has increased dramatically over the past decade and will likely increase even further during this decade. But my experience over the past 20 years is that changes in software development cultures occur at a painfully slow rate.

The key for most companies is to inculcate a "quality culture" for software development. Obviously, software engineering is a key element in doing this. Better paradigms, improved methods, and more powerful CASE tools will help. But the key is people. If your company has a management team that recognizes the strategic importance of software, positive changes will occur. If it employs technical managers who understand how to manage software projects, on-time delivery is possible. If it provides training and resources to technical staff, high-quality systems will result. If people support the software engineering concept, recognize how to manage it, and understand how to apply it, the future is bright.

Further Readings

Books that discuss the road ahead for software and computing span a vast array of technical, scientific, economic, political, and social issues. Naisbitt and Aburdene (*Megatrends 2000*, William Morrow & Co., 1990) provide an intriguing picture of changes in each of these arenas as we move toward the twenty-first century. Rich and Waters (*The Programmer's Apprentice*, Addison-Wesley, 1990) present one view of "what to expect in the future of software development."

Within the more narrow context of computing and software, Allman

(*Apprentices of Wonder,* Bantam Books, 1989) describes the potential impact of artificial neural networks—a book that suggests radical changes in what we will mean when the word "software" is used. Stoll (*The Cuckoo's Egg,* Doubleday, 1989) presents a fascinating look into the world of computer networks, hackers, and computer security—topics that are of significant importance as we become an integrated "electronic community."

Alvin Toffler (*Powershift,* Bantam Publishers, 1990) finishes the trilogy that began with *Future Shock* by discussing the disintegration of well-established power structures that is occurring throughout the world—a shift in power that he attributes directly to software and the information that it produces.

References

[1] Hopper, M.D., "Rattling SABRE, New Ways to Compete on Information," *Harvard Business Review* (May–June), 118–125 (1990).

[2] Pressman, R.S., and S.R. Herron, *Software Shock,* Dorset House, 1991, p. 5.

[3] Fuchsberg, G., "Quality Programs Show Shoddy Results," *The Wall Street Journal,* May 14, 1992, p. B1.

Software Engineering Bibliography

R.S. Pressman & Associates, Inc.[1] has developed an annotated list of books that should be made available in any library that desires a well-rounded collection in software engineering. The annotated list is organized in the following manner:

Software Engineering Management
>   General Interest
>   Metrics and Productivity Issues
>   Project Management
>   People Management
>   Technology Transition
>   Legal Issues

Software Engineering Technology
>   Full-Coverage Textbooks
>   Systems Engineering: Hardware and Software
>   Analysis and Specification
>   Formal Methods
>   Software Design
>>   Conventional Methods
>>   User Interfaces
>>   Object-Oriented Methods

---

[1]This bibliography is reproduced with permission of R.S. Pressman & Associates, Inc.

Fundamental Topics

Real-Time Systems

Software Quality Assurance

Software Testing

Software Maintenance

CASE, Tools, Environments, and Other Topics

Software Engineering: Other Information Sources

To help you get started, especially valuable books have been identified with the symbol Δ before the bibliography entry.

Software engineering is changing constantly. New ideas, techniques, and procedures are introduced on a monthly basis. You should strive to update this bibliography as new literature becomes available.

Software Engineering Management

General interest

Δ   Crosby, P., *Quality Is Free,* McGraw-Hill, 1979.
This book describes how to manage quality so that it becomes a source of profit. Not specifically directed at software, the book nonetheless provides excellent insight into quality issues associated with software. To quote *Business Week:* "The executive who spends half the day digesting this book may find it one of the most valuable investments of time he or she has made."

Felgenbaum, E.A., and P. McCorduck, *The Fifth Generation,* Addison-Wesley, 1983.
A *New York Times* bestseller that describes (in what some have criticized as overly dramatic terms) the impact of artificial intelligence and expert systems and the business implications of knowledge engineering.

Kidder, T., *The Soul of a New Machine,* Little, Brown & Co., 1981.
This Pulitzer-prize-winning, nonfiction bestseller chronicles the development of a state-of-the-art computer system. It provides good insight into the psyche of both hardware and software engineers.

Stoll, C., *The Cuckoo's Egg,* Doubleday, 1989.
A *New York Times* bestseller that describes the world of computer networks and the invasion of hackers. Nonfiction, but written like a high-tech detective novel, this book makes interesting reading for anyone interested in computer security.

Toeffler, A., *Powershift,* Bantam, 1990.
A *New York Times* bestseller, Toeffler completes a trilogy that included *Future Shock* and *The Third Wave.* In this book, he contends that computers and software are creating a shift in the world's power structures. Fascinating reading by a master futurist.

Yourdon, E., *Decline and Fall of the American Programmer,* Yourdon Press, 1992.
This controversial and thought-provoking book sounds a clear warning for managers and technologists alike: we (in the United States) may be in jeopardy of losing our software industry. Yourdon argues his case convincingly, and offers a strategy for recovery.

Metrics and productivity issues

Arthur, L.J., *Measuring Programmer Productivity and Software Quality,* Wiley, 1985.
A somewhat superficial, but still useful, survey of software metrics. Presents mea-

sures of the software development process and technical measures of software. Considers both quantitative and qualitative measures.

Arthur, L.J., *Programmer Productivity*, Wiley, 1983.
An extremely readable treatment of software productivity, this book presents a good qualitative overview of the topic. Presents a concise description of function points and their impact on productivity measurement.

Dreger, J.B., *Function Point Analysis*, Prentice-Hall, 1989.
The first book dedicated to function-point analysis, the metrics approach that is preferred by many software development organizations. Provides a solid tutorial that indicates how to compute function points and how to use them.

Fenton, N.E., *Software Metrics*, Chapman & Hall (Van Nostrand-Reinhold), 1991.
Although some parts of this book seem to stray from the main topic, it contains interesting chapters on fundamentals of measurement, establishing a framework for software measurement and metrics collection and analysis.

Δ   Grady, R.B., and D.L. Caswell, *Software Metrics: Establishing a Company-Wide Program*, Prentice-Hall, 1987.
An excellent book describing Hewlett-Packard's efforts to institute a software metrics program. Must reading for anyone who is contemplating a similar endeavor.

Jones, T.C. (ed.), *Programming Productivity: Issues for the Eighties*, IEEE Computer Society Press, 1981.
This book is an anthology of important papers that address software "productivity" and quality. Methods for measurement of productivity, life-cycle analysis, methodologies, and programming environments are considered. The reader can pick and choose from among many topics.

Jones, T.C., *Programming Productivity*, McGraw-Hill, 1986.
In this significant extension of his original anthology, Jones presents an in-depth discussion of methods for measuring, interpreting, and improving software engineering productivity and quality. A thorough and pragmatic treatment of the subject.

Δ   Jones, T.C., *Applied Software Measurement*, McGraw-Hill, 1991.
This book contains an abundance of information on the function-point metric and includes useful sections on U.S. productivity and quality averages and the mechanics of measurement.

Parikh, G., *Programmer Productivity*, Reston Publishing, 1984.
Still another of a growing number of texts on this subject. The author presents a useful (although somewhat superficial) survey of "productivity methods, tools and procedures."

Project management

Abdel-Hamid, T., and S.E. Madnick, *Software Project Dynamics*, Prentice-Hall, 1991.
This book presents an "integrative model" of software project management that focuses on four areas: human resource management, software production, project control, and project planning. The authors use the notation of system dynamics to model the software process.

Babich, W.A., *Software Configuration Management*, Addison-Wesley, 1986.
An abbreviated, yet effective, treatment of pragmatic issues in software configuration management. More readable and current than Bersoff et al., this book covers all important SCM tasks and surveys existing tools.

Bell, P., and C. Evans, *Mastering Documentation*, Wiley, 1989.
This book contains outlines for all important documents as well as many useful guidelines for writing specifications and user guides.

Δ   Berlack, H.R., *Software Configuration Management*, Wiley, 1992.
An up-to-date survey of SCM concepts, this book covers all SCM activities and is the first to emphasize the importance of the repository and tools in the management of change.

Bersoff, E., V. Henderson, and S. Siegal, *Software Configuration Management*, Prentice-Hall, 1980.
This book is one of the few that focuses on software configuration management. Al-

though the treatment is somewhat general, a number of excellent case studies are presented, good overall guidelines are proposed, and key terminology and concepts are introduced.

Boddie, J., *Crunch Mode*, Prentice-Hall, 1987.
Recommended reading for all managers who "have 90 days to do a 6-month project." This little book focuses on the real-life compromises that occur when time pressure overrides all else.

Δ **Boehm, B., *Software Engineering Economics*, Prentice-Hall, 1981.**
This book presents a comprehensive treatment of software estimating, project planning, and control. Somewhat mathematical and technical in parts, the text introduces Boehm's COCOMO estimation modeling scheme and provides useful data on software development productivity.

Δ **Boehm, B., *Risk Management*, IEEE Computer Society Press, 1989.**
An excellent tutorial on risk analysis and management, this book contains many excellent papers on risk and related topics as well as Boehm's notes on the subject. Presents a number of worthwhile checklists, forms, and guidelines for managing risk.

Δ **Brooks, F., *The Mythical Man-Month*, Addison-Wesley, 1975.**
This classic text, written by a manager of one of IBM's largest software development efforts, depicts many of the problems (and some of the solutions) associated with software. The book is written in an informal, sometimes humorous style. Anecdotes abound.

Case, A.F., *Information Systems Development: Principles of Software Engineering and CASE*, Prentice-Hall, 1986.
This book is one of the first to emphasize the use of computer-aided software engineering (CASE) as an approach to information systems development. Emphasizes management issues and presents an overview of important techniques. Contains useful guidelines for the implementation of software engineering and CASE.

Δ **Charette, R., *Software Engineering Risk Analysis and Management*, McGraw-Hill, 1989.**
One of the first books dedicated to risk assessment and its role in the management of software projects. Topics covered include risk identification, estimation, evaluation, and control.

Δ **Charette, R., *Application Strategies for Risk Analysis*, McGraw-Hill, 1990.**
This book, a companion volume to Charette (1989), is the most comprehensive treatment published to date of the pragmatic aspects of risk analysis in the software engineering context.

DeGrace, P., and L. Hulet-Stahl, *Wicked Problems, Righteous Solutions*, Yourdon Press, 1990.
A worthwhile survey of software engineering paradigms and their strengths and weaknesses.

Δ **DeMarco, T., *Controlling Software Projects*, Yourdon Press, 1982.**
A thorough and pragmatic treatment of all important aspects of software management. Excellent sections on project metrics and a useful discussion of software quality issues.

Frank, W.L., *Critical Issues in Software*, Wiley, 1983.
This book provides a practical guide to software economics, strategy, and profitability. Useful statistics and case studies abound. Contains a comprehensive bibliography.

Freeman, P., *Software Perspectives*, Addison-Wesley, 1987.
This book considers software engineering from a unique system perspective. Freeman discusses the major components of the software engineering process in a style that is particularly well suited to managers.

Δ **Gilb, T., *Principles of Software Engineering Management*, Addison-Wesley, 1988.**
A thought-provoking discussion of software engineering and its management by an industry iconoclast and respected consultant. Gilb discusses everything from scheduling to risk assessment, from walkthroughs to motivation of staff. An interesting read.

Glass, R., *Software Conflict*, Yourdon Press, 1991.
A short collection of essays on software engineering. Procedures, methods, and tools

are each considered in a style that is often humorous, sometimes irreverent, and always thought-provoking.

Gunther, R.C., *Management Methodology for Software Product Engineering,* **Wiley, 1978.**
This book provides excellent guidance for managers who must plan and control products in which software is a critical (but not the only) element. The concept of "software as a product" is introduced and the management disciplines to control product planning, development, services, documentation, support, testing, and maintenance are discussed. A number of interesting case studies, guidelines, and outlines are included.

Hooper, J.W., and R.O. Chester, *Software Reuse: Guidelines and Methods,* **Plenum Press, New York, 1991.**
An anthology of contributed chapters that provides a useful survey of the state of the art in software reuse.

Δ **Leveson, N.,** *Software Safety,* **Prentice-Hall, 1989.**
This book presents essential information required to assess the technology risks associated with computer-based systems. Leveson is the recognized expert on the subject, and her book is one of the few on software safety available to the industry.

Londiex, B., *Cost Estimation for Software Development,* **Addison-Wesley, 1987.**
This book contains a detailed presentation of the Putman estimation model, with consideration of other models for comparison. Its strength lies in many useful examples.

Ould, M.A., *Strategies for Software Engineering,* **Wiley, 1990.**
Discusses management decision making in the context of software projects with an emphasis on risk reduction and product quality.

Page-Jones, M., *Practical Project Management,* **Dorset House, New York, 1985.**
A good introduction to information systems project management. Presents basic elements of estimation, planning and scheduling, project tracking, team organization, and other management topics. Must be supplemented with other texts for detailed study.

Δ **Pressman, R.S.,** *Software Engineering: A Practitioner's Approach,* **3d ed., McGraw-Hill, 1992.**
This bestselling book presents a thorough treatment of software engineering and includes both management and technical topics. Recommended for those who need an understanding of each step in the software engineering process. Contains an extensive bibliography.

Δ **Pressman R.S., and S.R. Herron,** *Software Shock,* **Dorset House, 1991.**
A book on software that is directed toward the nontechnical professional. The people, the process, the tools, the problems, and the opportunities are each covered. Makes excellent reading for senior managers and others who must understand the danger and opportunity offered by software.

Reifer, D.J. (ed.), *Software Management,* **2d ed., IEEE Computer Society Press, 1981.**
This book is an anthology of important papers on software management. Topics include planning, organizing, staffing, directing, and controlling software projects. A number of case studies are presented.

Roetzheim, W.H., *Developing Software to Government Standards,* **Prentice-Hall, 1991.**
One of the few books that is dedicated to a discussion of software development under DOD-STD 2167A. A good overview of important topics prior to wading into the voluminous government standards.

Simpson, W.D., *New Techniques in Software Project Management,* **Wiley, 1987.**
A good overview of software project management, this book provides useful information for the new manager. The author emphasizes team management.

Whitten, N., *Managing Software Development Projects,* **Wiley, 1989.**
An introduction for new managers and those that need to understand the important issues associated with software project management.

Youl, D.P., *Making Software Development Visible,* **Wiley, 1990.**
This small book emphasizes project tracking—a topic that is often given short shrift in other software project management texts.

People management

Cougar, J.D., and R.A. Zawacki, *Motivating and Managing Computer Personnel,* Wiley-Interscience, 1980.
This book is a comprehensive view of "human resource management" for companies involved in the development of computer-based systems. The authors suggest methods, based on findings culled from a large industry study, that help reduce employee turnover, improve work quality, and motivate professional development.

Δ DeMarco, T., and T. Lister, *Peopleware,* Dorset House, 1987.
This book considers the management of the most important software development resource—people. Writing style is light and anecdotal, but the message is an important one. The authors present particularly useful discussions of office layout, "productivity," hiring the right software people, and team building.

House, R.H., *The Human Side of Project Management,* Addison-Wesley, 1988.
Takes a psychological/behavioral view of the management of large technical projects. A pragmatic treatment that focuses on an area of management that is often neglected.

Licker, P.S., *The Art of Managing Software Development People,* Wiley, 1985.
This book presents a somewhat academic but still useful treatment of the subject. The author considers typical management problems and their solutions, human resources management, and training of new managers in the software development world.

Δ Weinberg, G.M., *Becoming a Technical Leader,* Dorset House, 1986.
This book is *must* reading for all technical managers and any technical person who aspires to a management or technical leadership position. Written in an entertaining style filled with anecdotes, self-tests, and challenging ideas, Weinberg's book has become a classic. The author presents important models for leadership style, innovation, and motivation that benefit every reader.

Weinberg, G.M., *Understanding the Professional Programmer,* Dorset House, 1988.
This collection of essays provides an intriguing look into the "head" of software engineers. Filled with amusing anecdotes and useful insight this book will help managers better understand their people.

Technology transition

Bouldin, B.M., *Agents of Change,* Yourdon Press, 1989.
Provides guidance for managing technological change within a software development organization. A good companion text to Pressman, *Making Software Engineering Happen.*

Buckley, F.J., *Implementing Software Engineering Practice,* Wiley, 1989.
Presents a reasonable overview of management topics in software engineering and provides simple guidelines for implementing the technology.

Δ Humphrey, W.S., *Managing the Software Process,* Addison-Wesley, 1989.
Introduces a software process maturity model (developed at the SEI) that is very useful for assessing the status of software engineering practice within an organization. Presents many management topics in the context of the process maturity model.

Δ Pressman, R.S., *Making Software Engineering Happen,* Prentice-Hall, 1988.
The first book to treat the problems associated with the installation of software engineering practice. Defines a "life cycle" for software engineering implementation and provides practical, proven methods for making the transition to software engineering practice.

Utz, W.J., *Software Technology Transitions,* Prentice-Hall, 1992.
This book presents an overview of software engineering and CASE. In addition, it suggests a transition strategy for integrating the technology.

Legal issues

Auer, J., and C.E. Harris, *Computer Contract Negotiations,* Van Nostrand-Reinhold, 1981.
Presents useful guidelines for negotiating hardware and software contracts. Includes checklists and contract formats.

Gemignani, M., *Law and the Computer*, CBI Publishing, Boston, 1981.
This book provides a useful overview of legal issues associated with computer-based systems. Topics include an introduction to legal concepts and terminology, legal protection of software, liability, contracts, and other issues.

Harris, T.D., *The Legal Guide to Computer Software Protection*, Prentice-Hall, 1985.
Focusing solely on software, this guide provides useful, up-to-date information on copyrights, patents, trademarks, software publishing, and trade secrets. Written for the layperson.

Knight, P., and J. Fitzsimons, *The Legal Environment of Computing*, Addison-Wesley, 1990.
With chapters on copyright, patents, privacy, contracts, negligence, antitrust, and other topics, this book provides a useful overview of computing and software legal issues for the nonlawyer.

Software Engineering Technology

Full-coverage textbooks

The following books cover most or all aspects of software engineering. In most cases the topic is presented by considering various steps in the software engineering process.

DeMarco, T., and T. Lister, *Software State-of-the-Art*, Dorset House, 1990.
A comprehensive anthology of important papers published in the field over the past 20 years.

Fairley, R., *Software Engineering Concepts*, McGraw-Hill, 1985.
A life-cycle treatment of the software engineering process. Presents a worthwhile overview of important aspects of the technology. Contains a good bibliography.

Ince, D., *Software Engineering*, Van Nostrand-Reinhold, 1990.
An abbreviated treatment that could serve as an overview to the subject.

Lamb, D.A., *Software Engineering: Planning for Change*, Prentice-Hall, 1988.
A concise treatment of software engineering that touches on each of the important steps in the process. Good example documents are contained in an appendix.

Ledgard, H., *Software Engineering Concepts* (vol. 1) and *Programming Practice* (vol. 2), Addison-Wesley, 1987.
This two-volume set presents a concise treatment of software engineering. Contains useful discussions of team approaches, human factors as a software design criterion, and elements of programming style.

Macro, A., and J. Buxton, *The Craft of Software Engineering*, Addison-Wesley, 1987.
This survey of the software engineering discipline covers the most important aspects of the "craft." Although a bit superficial in places (particularly design), the book contains an interesting case study that illustrates important software engineering principles.

Ng, P., and Yeh, R.T., *Modern Software Engineering*, Van Nostrand-Reinhold, 1990.
A full-coverage textbook with specific emphasis on research topics and directions. Contains worthwhile chapters on analysis and design as well as coverage of specialized topics.

Pressman, R.S., *Software Engineering: A Beginner's Guide*, McGraw-Hill, 1988.
This book is intended to introduce software engineering at an introductory level. Designed for use in introductory college courses, the book contains a step-by-step "cookbook" for software engineering practice.

Δ **Pressman, R.S., *Software Engineering: A Practitioner's Approach*, 3d ed., McGraw-Hill, 1992.**
The most widely used textbook dedicated to software engineering. Covers all steps in the software engineering process, presenting in-depth treatment of important project management, analysis, design, coding, testing methods and CASE as well as "umbrella activities" such as SQA, SCM, and reviews.

Shooman, M., *Software Engineering,* McGraw-Hill, 1983.
An overview of all steps of the life cycle; in-depth discussion of software reliability issues.

Software Engineering Handbook, McGraw-Hill, 1986.
Originally developed by the General Electric Company for internal use, this handbook can serve as a foundation for developing local software engineering guidelines.

Δ Sommerville, I., *Software Engineering,* 3d ed., Addison-Wesley, 1989.
An in-depth treatment of software engineering that treats most important topics thoroughly and clearly. Expanded treatment in this third edition considers object-oriented techniques, the design of user interfaces, and other current topics.

Vick, C.R., and C. Ramamoorthy (eds.), *Handbook of Software Engineering,* Van Nostrand-Reinhold, 1984.
An encyclopedic discussion of wide-ranging topics related to software and computer-based systems development. A good reference source.

Weiner, R., and R. Sincovec, *Software Engineering with Modula-2 and Ada,* Wiley, 1984.
A reasonably complete treatment of software engineering. The primary importance of this book is its use of Modula-2 and Ada, two important programming languages, to illustrate important concepts.

Systems engineering: hardware and software

Athey, T., *Systematic Systems Approach,* Prentice-Hall, 1982.
Presents an integrated method for solving systems problems. Stresses quantitative analysis techniques.

Blanchard, B.S., and W. Fabrycky, *Systems Engineering and Analysis,* Prentice-Hall, 1981.
A detailed treatment of all aspects of systems engineering. Includes analytical engineering techniques.

Thayer, R.H., and M. Dorfman, *System and Software Requirements Engineering,* IEEE Computer Society Press, 1990.
A voluminous tutorial on system and software requirements analysis. Contains reprints of over 30 papers on methods, tools, and management issues.

Analysis and specification

Boar, B.H., *Application Prototyping,* Wiley, 1985.
A discussion of prototyping in a data-processing environment. Contains good arguments for prototyping as an alternative to conventional specification.

Braithwaite, K., *Analysis, Design, and Implementation of Data Dictionaries,* McGraw-Hill, 1988.
One of the few texts that is dedicated to data dictionaries, this book presents an extremely thorough treatment of the subject. Data dictionary concepts, design, and examples in various application areas are presented. However, treatment of CASE implementations is weak.

Davis, A.M., *Software Requirements Analysis and Specification,* Prentice-Hall, 1990.
A full-coverage textbook on analysis and specification methods and tools. Distinguished by a comprehensive bibliography containing well over 100 references to recent work in this area.

Δ DeMarco, T., *Structured Analysis and System Specification,* Prentice-Hall, 1979.
A definitive treatment of data-flow-oriented specification techniques. Stresses the use of data flow diagrams and the data dictionary.

Jackson, M.A., *System Development,* Prentice-Hall, 1983.
Still another approach to data-structure-oriented system design. Jackson offers many intriguing insights into the construction of software-based systems.

Martin, C.F., _User-Centered Requirements Analysis,_ Prentice-Hall, 1988.
An interesting treatment of analysis that suggests methods for drawing the user into the process. Written with a definite IS focus, the book covers both functional and data analysis.

Δ **McMenamin, S., and J. Palmer, _Essential Systems Analysis,_ Yourdon Press, 1984.**
This book introduces an important refinement of the logical and physical modeling approach proposed by most system analysis texts. Called the _essence-implementation model,_ this approach does much to clarify the amount of detail required to describe systems.

Mittra, S.S., _Structured Techniques of System Analysis, Design and Implementation,_ Wiley-Interscience, 1988.
Designed primarily for a data-processing/IS audience, this book emphasizes front-end activities. Contains a good discussion of feasibility analysis. Good case studies.

Orr, K., _Structured Requirements Definition,_ Ken Orr & Associates, Topeka, KS, 1981.
A description of the Warnier-Orr technique of data-structure-oriented specification. Introduces the notation and concepts that form the foundation of data-structured systems development (DSSD).

Page-Jones, M., _The Practical Guide to Structured Systems Design,_ Yourdon Press, 1980.
Another treatment of data-flow-oriented techniques. Jones provides additional insight.

Perkinson, R.C., _Data Analysis: The Key to Data Base Design,_ QED, Wellesley, MA, 1984.
A worthwhile treatment of data analysis and design. Includes discussions of normalization, database design, data requirements analysis, and various database architectures.

Ross, R.G., _Entity Modeling: Techniques and Applications,_ Data Research Group, Inc., Boston, 1988.
One of the few books dedicated to E-R modeling, this short text presents an excellent overview of the subject. E-R techniques are presented with many examples, and the use of CASE tools is considered.

Warnier, J.D., _Logical Construction of Systems,_ Van Nostrand-Reinhold, 1981.
A discussion of data-structure-oriented specification by one of the founding fathers.

Δ **Yourdon, E., _Modern Structured Analysis,_ Prentice-Hall, 1989.**
A comprehensive treatment of structured analysis by one of the "fathers" of the technique. Yourdon revisits, and in many cases, updates earlier concepts. Excellent discussion of both techniques and tools.

Δ **Yourdon, E., and Coad, P., _Object-Oriented Analysis,_ Yourdon Press, 1990.**
The first attempt at coupling structured analysis and design with the underlying concepts of OO. Introduces a new notation and extends existing concepts.

Formal methods

Baber, R.L., _Error-Free Software,_ Wiley, 1991.
A concise book that covers the "know-how and know why" of program correctness, key concepts that are required to understand the thrust toward formal methods.

Dijkstra, E., _The Formal Development of Programs and Proofs,_ Addison-Wesley, 1989.
An advanced treatment of the subject, Dijkstra is one of the true innovators in computer science.

Dromey, R.G., _Program Derivation,_ Prentice-Hall, 1989.
A detailed presentation of the mathematics of formal specification, this book establishes the necessary groundwork and then provides useful examples to illustrate the approach.

Tanik, M.M., _Fundamentals of Computing for Software Engineers,_ Van Nostrand-Reinhold, 1991.
This book presents the mathematics and theory associated with formalism in software engineering. A worthwhile guide for those with little background in the subject.

Woodcock, J., and M. Loomis, *Software Engineering Mathematics*, Addison-Wesley, 1988.
A good introduction to formal systems, propositional and predicate calculus, set theory, and other topics that are relevant to formal specification techniques.

Software design—conventional methods

Δ Cameron, J., *JSP&JSD: The Jackson Approach to Software Development*, IEEE Computer Society Press, 1989.
The most comprehensive treatment of the Jackson methodology published to date. This book combines original writing and reprinted papers to cover both the analysis and design components of the approach. Useful examples are presented.

Hansen, K., *Data Structured Program Design*, Ken Orr & Associates, Topeka, KS, 1984.
A simplified description of Orr's data-structured system development (DSSD) method for software design.

Jones, C., *Software Development: A Rigorous Approach*, Prentice-Hall, 1980.
As its name implies, this book is intended for a more academic audience than most in this bibliography. However, it will be of interest to those with a computer science background.

King, M.J., and J.P. Pardoe, *Program Design Using JSP*, Halsted, 1985.
An excellent summary of the Jackson structured programming (JSP) approach. A worthwhile companion volume to Jackson's excellent book, *System Development*.

Δ Linger, R., H. Mills, and B. Witt, *Structured Programming*, Addison-Wesley, 1979.
The definitive treatment of structured programming as a procedural design tool. Excellent use of PDL and detailed discussion of design correctness proofs.

Marca, D.A., and C.L. McGowan, *SADT*, McGraw-Hill, 1988.
The most thorough treatment of SADT published to date, this book presents excellent coverage of this important analysis and design technique. Detailed discussion of SADT diagramming and examples from many different industry applications make this a worthwhile addition to the software engineering literature.

Martin, J., and C. McClure, *Diagramming Techniques for Analysts and Programmers*, Prentice-Hall, 1985.
Probably the most comprehensive survey of analysis and design notation produced to date. Topics include structure charts, HIPO, Warnier-Orr, N-S diagrams, flowcharts, state transition diagrams, PDL, decision trees/tables, Jackson diagrams, and many others.

Peters, L., *Software Design: Methods and Techniques*, Yourdon Press, 1981.
An overview of major design techniques, representation methods, and procedural approaches. Contains source material on a number of obscure methods.

Warnier, J.D., *Logical Construction of Programs*, Van Nostrand-Reinhold, 1976.
Describes an important data-structure-oriented design approach. Warnier takes a formal view, focusing on the hierarchy of information as the guiding criterion for good design.

Yourdon, E., and L. Constantine, *Structured Design*, Prentice-Hall, 1979.
The seminal textbook describing data-flow-oriented design techniques. Detailed discussion of transform and transaction analysis, functional independence, and other design issues.

Software design—user interfaces

Dumas, J.S., *Designing User Interfaces for Software*, Prentice-Hall, 1988.
A good introduction for user interface design. Provides worthwhile guidelines for data entry, information display, and user–machine interaction.

Monk, A. (ed.), *Fundamentals of Human Computer Interaction*, Academic Press, 1984.
Contains invited chapters on many important aspects of human–machine interface design. Combines human psychological research with technical issues of machine interaction.

Rubin, T., *User Interface Design for Computer Systems*, Wiley, 1988.
Particularly useful for its discussion of "help" techniques, the use of color, and guidelines for evaluating user interface designs, this book is a worthwhile addition to every software engineering library.

Δ **Shneiderman, B., *Designing the User Interface*, Addison-Wesley, 1987.**
A thorough treatment of human–machine interface design by one of the experts in the field. Covers basic concepts and presents many guidelines for user interface design.

Software design—object-oriented methods

Booch, G., *Software Engineering with Ada*, 2d ed., Benjamin-Cummings, 1987.
A useful treatment of object-oriented techniques applied in the context of Ada. Includes a set of worthwhile examples. Also an excellent introductory text on the programming language Ada.

Booch, G., *Software Components with Ada*, Benjamin-Cummings, 1987.
An extension and refinement of his earlier book, Booch refines his approach to object-oriented design using Ada, presenting new and improved examples and substantially broader insight. The author emphasizes software reusability and its accomplishment through the Ada programming environment.

Δ **Booch, G., *Object-Oriented Design*, Benjamin-Cummings, 1990.**
A detailed treatment of object-oriented design that introduces a comprehensive notation for design, guidelines for a design method, and a number of excellent examples that illustrate the process.

Buhr, R.J.A., *System Design with Ada*, Prentice-Hall, 1984.
The design method presented in this book combines data flow and object-oriented approaches and then couples them with an Ada implementation.

Cox, B., *Object-Oriented Programming*, Addison-Wesley, 1986.
A detailed treatment of object-oriented design and programming using the Smalltalk/Objective-C point of view. Introduces important concepts such as inheritance, encapsulation, and messages.

Khoshafian, S., and R. Abnous, *Object-Orientation*, Addison-Wesley, 1990.
A thorough introduction to object-oriented technologies. Covers languages, databases, and user interfaces, emphasizing C++ and Ada.

Δ **Myer, B., *Object-Oriented Software Construction*, 2d ed., Prentice-Hall, 1990.**
The best treatment of object-oriented methods published to date, Myer's book presents basic object-oriented concepts and a detailed discussion of key features of object-oriented systems. The Eiffel programming language is used to illustrate key points.

***Object-Oriented Design Handbook*, EVB Software Engineering, Inc., Rockville, MD, 1985.**
A pragmatic "how to" treatment of object-oriented design. EVB has adopted the object-operation approach proposed by Booch and has established a systematic OOD methodology best suited to the Ada programming language.

Peterson, G.E., *Tutorial: Object-Oriented Computing* (2 vols.), IEEE Computer Society, 1987.
Another excellent IEEE tutorial, these volumes are an anthology of important papers on object-oriented techniques with connecting text and explanation provided by Peterson. Basic concepts are presented in the first volume and followed with specific applications in the second volume.

Rumbaugh, J., et al., *Object-Oriented Modeling and Design*, Prentice-Hall, 1991.
Introduces a comprehensive notation and step-by-step approach for OOD. Contains an interesting and reasonably detailed discussion of how one might relate functional modeling (structured analysis) with object-oriented modeling.

Shlaer, S., and S.J. Mellor, *Object-Oriented Systems Analysis*, Yourdon Press (Prentice-Hall), 1988.
A discussion of object-oriented approaches to analysis as opposed to design. Although the treatment focuses primarily on data design and entity-relationship modeling, the book is a worthwhile addition for those who want all views of OO techniques.

Winblad, A.L., et al., *Object-Oriented Software,* Addison-Wesley, 1990.
A useful introduction to object-oriented technologies for the uninitiated. Covers languages, databases, and user interfaces as well as an overview of methods for analysis and design.

Software design—fundamental topics

The following books (annotated comments have been omitted) may be used to review fundamental topics that are associated with software design and coding.

Data structures (data design)

Barker, R., *Entity-Relationship Modeling,* Addison-Wesley, 1990.
Bracket, M.H., *Practical Data Design,* Prentice-Hall, 1990.
Braithwaite, K.S., *Analysis, Design, and Implementation of Data Dictionaries,* McGraw-Hill, 1988.
Date, C.J., *An Introduction to Data Base Systems,* 4th ed., Addison-Wesley, 1986.
Dutka, A.F., and H.H. Hanson, *Fundamentals of Data Normalization,* Addison-Wesley, 1989.
Gupta, R., and E. Horowitz (eds.), *Object-Oriented Databases with Applications to CASE, Networks, and VLSI CAD,* Prentice-Hall, 1991.
Horowitz, E., and S. Sahni, *Fundamentals of Computer Algorithms,* Computer Science Press, 1978.
Kruse, R.L., *Data Structures and Program Design,* Prentice-Hall, 1984.
Lewis, T.G., and M.Z. Smith, *Applying Data Structures,* Houghton-Mifflin, 1976.
Tenenbaum, A.M., and M.J. Augenstein, *Data Structures Using Pascal,* Prentice-Hall, 1981.
Weiderhold, G., *Database Design,* 2d ed., McGraw-Hill, 1983.

Programming languages

Ledgard, H., and M. Marcotty, *The Programming Language Landscape,* SRA, 1981.
Martin, J., *Fourth Generation Languages: Principles, Representative Languages* (2 vols.), Prentice-Hall, 1985, 1986.
Pratt, T.W., *Programming Languages,* 2d ed., Prentice-Hall, 1984.

Software design—real-time systems

Allworth, S.T., *Introduction to Real-Time Software Design,* Springer-Verlag, 1981.
A monograph on real-time design. Introduces the concept of a real-time virtual machine as a guide to the design process.
Cooling, J.E., *Software Design for Real-Time Systems,* Van Nostrand-Reinhold, 1991.
Another of many books that addresses issues in real-time software engineering. Emphasis is on languages and programming issues.
Foster, R., *Real-Time Programming—Neglected Topics,* Addison-Wesley, 1981.
A pragmatic treatment of "the problems you run into when you try to connect a computer to the real world." Covers interrupts, ports, speed matching, and other important topics.
Glass, R., *Real-Time Software,* Prentice-Hall, 1983.
Covers a broad range of topics relating to real-time software. Methodologies for design, implementation, and test of real-time software are considered.
Δ Hatley, D.J., and I.A. Pirbhai, *Strategies for Real-Time System Specification,* Dorset House, 1987.
This book presents one of two important real-time analysis and specification techniques. (The other is described in Ward and Mellor's volumes described below.) Con-

tains excellent industry examples and a reasonably thorough exposition of the technique.

Heath, W.S., *Real-Time Software Techniques*, Van Nostrand-Reinhold, 1991.
A compact guide for those who must develop real-time software for embedded microprocessor applications.

Leigh, A.W., *Real-Time Software for Small Systems*, Wiley (Sigma), 1988.
Because the focus of this book is small microprocessor-based systems, it should be of particular interest to those readers who develop embedded product software. Covers testing and maintenance issues as well as design. Examples are worthwhile.

Levi, S., and A.K. Agrawal, *Real-Time System Design*, McGraw-Hill, 1990.
One of the more rigorous treatments of the subject, this book takes an object-oriented view and introduces a mathematical perspective missing in other texts. Also contains a discussion of verification techniques for real-time systems.

Mellichamp, D.A. (ed.), *Real-Time Computing*, Van Nostrand-Reinhold, 1983.
A comprehensive treatment of all aspects of real-time systems including hardware, software, and interfacing. Focus is on real-time process control and monitoring and software applications in a laboratory setting.

Siewiork, D.P., et al., *Computer Structures, Principles and Examples*, McGraw-Hill, 1982.
A voluminous treatment of all aspects of computer-based systems design. Although the book has a decided hardware orientation, it should be of interest to real-time system engineers.

Vick, C.R., and C.V. Ramamoorthy, *Handbook of Software Engineering*, chaps. 5–9, Van Nostrand-Reinhold, 1984.
These chapters focus on real-time computing issues and include treatments of real-time control, emulation, hardware–software trade-offs, systems issues, and other topics. Contains an extensive bibliography on real-time software.

Δ **Ward, P.T., and S.J. Mellor, *Structured Development for Real-Time Systems* (3 vols.), Yourdon Press, 1985, 1986.**
This three-volume set presents a worthwhile notation and approach to real-time software design that is adapted from conventional data-flow-oriented methods. Volume 1 introduces the subject, vol. 2 presents analysis methods, and vol. 3 discusses the design approach. Highly recommended.

Software quality assurance

Cho, C.K., *Quality Programming*, Wiley, 1987.
A rigorous treatment of the techniques for developing and testing software with statistical quality control, this book is an important addition to the quality assurance literature. Cho presents a remarkably readable mix of pragmatic guidelines and statistical theory. Discussions of both SQA and testing techniques are presented.

Dunn, R., *Software Quality Assurance*, Prentice-Hall, 1990.
An introduction to SQA with an emphasis on pragmatic management issues. Considers SQA planning and the tasks associated with the activity.

Dunn, R., and R. Ullman, *Quality Assurance for Computer Software*, McGraw-Hill, 1982.
Presents a practical treatment of the procedures and techniques required to institute SQA in an organization.

Evans, M.W., and J.J. Marciniak, *Software Quality Assurance and Management*, Wiley, 1986.
A management-oriented view that contains good information on software quality evaluation, metrics, product issues, and data control. Makes use of the latest IEEE SQA standards.

Δ **Freedman, D., and G. Weinberg, *Handbook of Walkthroughs, Inspections and Technical Reviews*, 3d ed., Dorset House, 1990.**
Written in an unusual question-and-answer format, this book presents a complete introduction to reviews as a quality assurance mechanism for computer software. A wide variety of useful checklists, forms, and guidelines is presented.

Hollecker, C.P., *Software Reviews and Audits Handbook,* Wiley, 1990.
Contains detailed step-by-step guidelines for conducting formal technical reviews and audits.

Δ Musa, J.D., A. Iannino, and K. Okumoto, *Software Reliability,* McGraw-Hill, 1987.
This book is the most thorough treatment of software reliability published to date. A rigorous treatment of the subject, the book also contains an excellent introduction, worthwhile practical examples, and a copious discussion of theory.

Schulmeyer, C.G., *Zero Defect Software,* McGraw-Hill, 1990.
Using concepts derived from quality control techniques from Japanese manufacturing, the author describes an approach for achieving very-high-quality software. Contains a useful overview of existing SQA methods and a detailed dissertation of the "zero defect" approach.

Δ Schulmeyer, C.G., and J.I. McManus (eds.), *Handbook of Software Quality Assurance,* Van Nostrand-Reinhold, 1987.
An excellent anthology of contributed chapters on SQA. Topics include QA management, SQA planning and organization, costs, personnel issues, reviews, software configuration management, and much more. A worthwhile addition to every software engineering library.

Yourdon, E., *Structured Walkthroughs,* 4th ed., Yourdon Press, 1989.
A brief, but worthwhile, discussion of formal technical reviews. Concentrates on mechanics, psychology, and management of walkthroughs.

Software testing

Δ Belzer, B., *Software System Testing and Quality Assurance,* Van Nostrand-Reinhold, 1984.
An excellent treatment of system/software testing strategies and their relationship to SQA. Bezier reproduces worthwhile material from his earlier book on software testing and then extends this with excellent material on system-related issues. Detailed information is presented on each test step.

Δ Belzer, B., *Software Testing Techniques,* 2d ed., Van Nostrand-Reinhold, 1990.
Comprehensive treatment of many important testing techniques. Detailed consideration of path testing and boolean algebraic techniques.

Berg, H.K., et al., *Formal Methods for Program Verification and Specification,* Prentice-Hall, 1982.
For those readers with a theoretical bent, this text presents a detailed treatment of formal verification models for software.

Dunn, R., *Software Defect Removal,* McGraw-Hill, 1984.
Presents methods for static and dynamic testing. Also considers other SQA elements.

Evans, M.W., *Productive Software Test Management,* Wiley, 1984.
One of the few books dedicated to the management issues associated with testing. Presents detailed discussions of test planning, control, scheduling, and other management topics.

Hetzel, W., *The Complete Guide to Software Testing,* QED, 1984.
An introductory survey of all important aspects of testing. Although somewhat superficial, the text presents a useful discussion of testing at each step in the software engineering process.

Howden, W.E., *Functional Program Testing and Analysis,* McGraw-Hill, 1987.
One of the more mathematical of all testing books, Howden's treatment of the subject considers both practical and theoretical issues. Heavy emphasis on function definition and verification distinguishes this book from others.

McCabe, T., *Structured Testing,* IEEE Computer Society, 1982.
A detailed treatment of McCabe's basis path testing technique. Includes discussion of software complexity and its use in test case design.

Δ Myers, G., *The Art of Software Testing,* Wiley, 1979.
Still the most widely referenced and quoted book on software testing. Introduces the reader to a variety of black-box and white-box testing techniques.

Perry, W.E., *How to Test Software Packages,* Wiley, 1986.
Worthwhile because it focuses on how to test software that has been delivered from another source within your company or purchased from the outside, this book describes useful methods for test planning and execution.

Software maintenance

Arthur, L.J., *Software Evolution,* Wiley-Interscience, 1988.
One of the more detailed (but still somewhat superficial) discussions of software maintenance, Arthur's book presents worthwhile discussions of "change management, impact analysis, and reengineering."
Martin, J., and C. McClure, *Software Maintenance,* Prentice-Hall, 1983.
This book is representative of most that are dedicated to software maintenance. Topics include methods for achieving "maintainability," maintenance procedures, new methodologies that may ease the maintenance burden, and other topics.
Parikh, G., *Handbook of Software Maintenance,* Wiley, 1986.
A collection of useful guidelines for maintenance practitioners and managers who must control the process. Presents a useful discussion of how design methods can be applied during maintenance activities.
Zvegintzov, N., and G. Parikh, *Software Maintenance,* IEEE Computer Society, 1983.
This anthology presents many important papers dedicated to software maintenance. Both management and technical topics are presented.

CASE, tools, environments, and other topics

Barstow, D.R., et al., *Interactive Programming Environments,* McGraw-Hill, 1984.
A collection of contributed papers and chapters that describe research efforts in "computer-aided software engineering." Important information for builders of software tools.
Bennett, K.H., *Software Engineering Environments,* Halsted (Wiley), 1989.
A survey of research in software engineering environments. Written in Britain, this book focuses primarily on European work in environments.
***CASE Industry Directory,* CASE Consulting Group, Lake Oswego, OR, 1988.**
A comprehensive survey of existing CASE tools and vendors. An excellent source book for those who are investigating CASE tools.
***CASE: The Potential and the Pitfalls,* QED Information Sciences, Inc., Wellesley, MA, 1989.**
Covers the technology, tools, and environments. Also includes worthwhile case studies from a number of U.S. companies.
Charette, R.N., *Software Engineering Environments,* McGraw-Hill, 1986.
This book presents a detailed treatment of programming environments and associated software tools.
Fisher, A.S., *CASE—Using Software Development Tools,* Wiley, 1988.
One of the best available treatments of the subject. Topics include basic principles, environments, and descriptions of current tools.
Kernighan, B.W., and P.J. Plauger, *Software Tools in Pascal,* Addison-Wesley, 1981.
A pragmatic discussion of generic algorithms (the authors call these "tools") for software development. An earlier version of this book focused on RATFOR (a FORTRAN dialect).
Spurr, K., and P. Layzell (eds.), *CASE on Trial,* Wiley, 1990.
The primary lure of this book is the description of user experiences with CASE technology. Also contains useful discussion of selection and justification of tools.
Towner, L.E., *CASE: Concepts and Implementation,* McGraw-Hill, 1989.
Presents a useful overview of key issues in CASE—tools, environments, and associated methods.

Software Engineering: Other Information Sources

Periodicals—technical content

IEEE Transactions on Software Engineering
Δ   *Computer* (IEEE Computer Society)
Δ   *IEEE Software* (IEEE Computer Society)
Communications of the ACM
Δ   *ACM Software Engineering* (SIGSOFT) *Notes*
IEEE Software Engineering Technical Committee Newsletter

Newsletters—CASE

Δ   *CASE Outlook* (CASE Consulting Group, Lake Oswego, OR, quarterly, fax: 503-245-6935)
CASE Strategies (Cutter Information Corp., Arlington, MA, monthly, fax: 508-544-3779)
Δ   *CASE Trends* (Software Productivity Group, Shrewsbury, MA, monthly, fax: 508-842-7119)
CASE User (CASE Consulting Group, Lake Oswego, OR, monthly, fax: 503-245-6935)
Executive Briefing: CASE (Context Publishing, Portland, OR, bimonthly, fax: 503-232-8057)
Each of the newsletter companies also publishes reports on specific tools and other CASE
    topics.

Directories—CASE

CASEBASE, **an on-line database** (P-Cube Corp., Brea, CA, 714-990-3169)
CASE Locator, **an on-line database** (CASE Associates, Oregon City, OR, 503-656-3207)
CASE Product Guide (*Software Magazine*, Westborough, MA, 800-225-9218)
Tool Finder/Plus (CASE Consulting Group, Lake Oswego, OR, fax: 503-245-6935)
CASE OUTLOOK Guide to Products and Services (CASE Consulting Group, Lake Oswego,
    OR, fax: 503-245-6935)
Testing Tools Reference Guide (Software Quality Engineering, Jacksonville, FL, 904-268-
    8639)

Periodicals—general content

Δ   *American Programmer* (monthly)
Computerworld (weekly)
Software Magazine (monthly)
Datamation (monthly)
BYTE (monthly)

Conference proceedings (held at regular intervals)

Δ   *International Conference on Software Engineering*
COMPSAC, INFOCOM, SOFTCON
Trends and Applications Conference
Design Automation Conference

Standards

Δ   *Software Engineering Standards, 3d ed., IEEE, 1991.*
    Over 500 pages long, this compendium of ANSI and IEEE standards for software en-
    gineering is absolutely essential for any software engineering library. Contains stan-
    dards for documentation, SQA, SCM, testing, reviews, project management, require-
    ments specification, and metrics.

Software Engineering Self-Test[1]

The implementation of software engineering has a high probability of success only when experienced, knowledgeable staff are available to make software engineering happen. In addition, practitioners—the people who will apply the procedures, methods, and tools that are installed—must understand software engineering concepts and methodology.

The following self-test is designed to provide you with an indication of your understanding of important software engineering concepts. Questions span both management and technical topics. Therefore, if you're not technical, you might pass the test along to your technical staff. The self-test is not intended to be a comprehensive examination, but rather a survey of software engineering knowledge.

Go through the questions and indicate the responses that you think are most appropriate. Compare your response with those provided at the end of this section. The results should give you some indication of personal strengths and weaknesses. If your response is incorrect, or agrees with mine, but you still feel uncomfortable with the subject area, further reading and training may be appropriate.

The self-test is composed of multiple-choice questions that have been categorized by subject area. In some cases the differences between responses will be subtle. In fact, it is possible to provide more than one partially correct response. However, the "correct" response provided at the end of this section is felt to be the most appropriate. It is important to note that there is no passing or failing "grade" for the self-test. It is intended solely for your own use in determining areas of strength and weakness.

---

[1]The original version of this self-test was developed by R.S. Pressman & Associates, Inc. and first appeared in *Making Software Engineering Happen* (Prentice-Hall, 1988) by R.S. Pressman.

Important note: The answers to many of the technical questions are not contained in this book. My intent has been to discuss management issues, not the details of the methodology. Refer to R.S. Pressman, *Software Engineering: A Practitioner's Approach* (3d ed., McGraw-Hill, 1992) as well as other books noted in Appendix I, for detailed discussions of software engineering methodology.

Questions for Software Engineering Self-Test

Software project management

1. Progress during a software development effort can be best understood when
   a. Staff report weekly using a percent complete measure for work they are doing.
   b. Dollars expended to date are measured.
   c. A deliverable has been completed and reviewed.
   d. Code is up and running.
2. How should effort be distributed for a typical software development project?
   a. 10 percent definition, 70 percent implementation, 20 percent testing and integration.
   b. 20 percent definition, 50 percent implementation, 30 percent testing and integration.
   c. 50 percent definition, 15 percent implementation, 35 percent testing and integration.
   d. None of the above.
3. Cost and schedule for software projects can be effectively estimated if
   a. Software metrics are collected and used for historical purposes.
   b. Conventional task—effort estimates are made.
   c. Empirical models are calibrated and applied.
   d. All of the above.
4. When a software development project begins to fall behind schedule, the first response should be
   a. Partition the problem and add additional people.
   b. Examine the task network to determine how schedule slippage will affect completion date.
   c. Create a "tiger team" by pulling staff members from areas that are ahead of schedule.
   d. All of the above.
5. A good organizational approach for large-scale software development is
   a. Organize technical staff by specialty (e.g., database, graphics,

operating systems) and assign staff members to specific problems.

    b. Create teams that focus on specific functions and combine necessary skills to accomplish the function.

    c. Assign staff individually to specific, well-defined subfunctions.

    d. All of the above.

6. A project manager's attitude toward documentation should be

    a. Develop detailed documentation for every facet of the project so that future developers will have a roadmap.

    b. Develop as little documentation as possible in that it slows down development progress.

    c. Develop as much documentation as is required to provide a foundation for subsequent development steps and maintenance.

    d. Develop only source-code-level documentation.

7. For many software projects, the best paradigm for software engineering is

    a. The classic life cycle.

    b. Prototyping.

    c. The spiral model.

    d. Some combination of *a, b,* and *c.*

8. Standards and procedures for software development are effective if

    a. A copy is provided for every staff member.

    b. All technical managers have reviewed and approved each standard and procedure.

    c. Automated tools are available to support them.

    d. Staff agree that they make sense and follow them.

    e. All of the above.

    f. None of the above.

Analysis methods

9. As a project manager, your primary role early in the analysis phase is to

    a. Be sure enough time has been allocated to the task.

    b. Be sure that communication between requester and developer is effective and complete.

    c. Be sure that coding of low-level functions has begun.

    d. All of the above.

10. The following techniques are often used as a mechanism for improving user–developer communication and overall specification quality (note all that apply):

    a. JAD

    b. SLIM

    c. The METHOD

    d. Consensus

    e. MASCOT

    f. COCOMO

11. What is the first question that an analyst should ask the user?

    a. What do you want this system to do?

    b. What information do you intend to provide for the system?

    c. What level of efficiency is required?

    d. What information does this system produce?

12. Which of the following analysis methods performs some element of information domain analysis?

    a. Data-structured system development

    b. Structured analysis

    c. Object-oriented analysis

    d. All of the above

13. What information should not be contained in a *Software Requirements Specification?*

    a. Description of important functions

    b. Detailed procedural description of algorithms

    c. Performance criteria

    d. Validation criteria

    e. Top-level description of information flow and content

14. The majority of all analysis techniques can be said to be

    a. Information-driven.

    b. Functionally driven.

    c. Performance-driven.

    d. Constraint-driven.

15. Prototyping is a technique that

    a. Results in faster implementation and precludes the need for conventional analysis methods.

    b. Serves to supplement conventional analysis approaches when requirements are uncertain.

    c. Can be applied to all projects, regardless of application area.

    d. All of the above.

16. Which of the following is not fundamental to requirements analysis?

    a. Problem partitioning

    b. Information domain analysis

    c. Structured programming

    d. Data modeling

17. A *Requirements Specification* (indicate all that apply)

    a. Must always be developed manually and represented using a natural language.

    b. Can be generated automatically and represented in a formal specification language.

    c. Can be created by an analyst who uses computer-based tools that combine graphics and formal representations.

    d. Can be automatically checked for consistency.

18. The primary goal of object-oriented analysis (OOA) is to
    a. Improve customer communication.
    b. Encourage polymorphism.
    c. Create a bridge to structured analysis.
    d. Define messages that must be passed among objects.
    e. Identify classes that may be used to model the system.

Software design

19. The fundamental purpose of software design is to
    a. Develop pictures that enable people to better understand the software.
    b. Enable the developer to apply structured programming.
    c. Develop representations of the software that can be assessed for quality.
    d. Provide management with technical information.
20. There are three fundamental areas of software design. They are
    a. Architectural, data, and procedural.
    b. Language, format, and semantics.
    c. Control flow, decision-based, and syntax-based.
    d. Normalized, procedural, and elemental.
21. A monolithic program is one that
    a. Performs only one function.
    b. Performs only a few functions.
    c. Is not implemented in a high-order language.
    d. None of the above.
22. Abstraction is a mechanism that
    a. Enables a designer to create reusable elements of computer programs.
    b. Enables a designer to define data objects whose internal structure need not be understood by other designers.
    c. Enables a designer to create modules whose internal structure need not be understood by other designers.
    d. All of the above.
23. Effective modularity is achieved by
    a. Keeping all modules smaller than 50 lines of code.
    b. Never using global data structures.
    c. Defining modules with high functional independence.
    d. Avoiding monolithic design.
24. Information hiding is a design concept that
    a. Keeps database size to an absolute minimum.
    b. Results in limited use of global data structures.
    c. Can be implemented with equal facility in any programming language.
    d. Is of academic interest only.

25. Structured programming is a design concept that
    a. Prohibits the use of the "GO TO" in a programming language.
    b. Cannot be implemented when assembler language is used.
    c. Requires the use of flowcharts.
    d. Suggests that good designs can be created using only a limited number of logical constructs.
    e. All of the above.
    f. None of the above.
26. The complexity of a procedural design can be determined
    a. By subjective assessment only.
    b. Mathematically, using McCabe's or Halstead's metrics.
    c. By assessing the design using formal technical review techniques.
    d. Qualitatively at best, given the current state of the art.
27. Program structure provides information that
    a. Indicates the hierarchy of modules in a system.
    b. Provides guidance for the design of integration tests.
    c. Indicates which modules invoke other modules.
    d. All of the above.
    e. None of the above.
28. A procedural design can be represented by (indicate all that apply)
    a. Decision tables.
    b. Flowcharts.
    c. PDL.
    d. State diagrams.
    e. Truth tables.
    f. Box diagrams.
    g. Data flow diagrams.
29. Data design focuses on
    a. The selection of program variable names.
    b. The layout for input and output screens and reports.
    c. The representation of data structures and their contents.
    d. The description of program interfaces through which data flows.
30. Object-oriented design is a relatively new design methodology that
    a. Treats each program statement as an "object."
    b. Models classes and objects that are comprised of data structures and associated processes.
    c. Creates classes and objects that are composed of groups of program modules and their associated interfaces.
    d. Is applicable only for computer graphics applications.

Coding and languages

31. Coding is
    a. A natural outgrowth of good design.
    b. A task that should be initiated as soon as design begins.
    c. The only way that a manager can really determine whether progress is being made.
    d. All of the above.

32. Rank the following languages by the ease with which modern design principles can be implemented (list the most difficult first):
    a. COBOL
    b. Assembly language
    c. Pascal
    d. Ada
    e. Machine language

33. A fourth-generation language (4GL)
    a. Eliminates the need for analysis and design.
    b. Can be used effectively by anyone.
    c. Raises the level of abstraction when a program is represented.
    d. Generally results in more efficient programs when run-time performance is considered.
    e. All of the above.

34. Coding standards should
    a. Define restrictions, limitations, and style for programming.
    b. Define the format for module prologues.
    c. Specify the manner in which internal documentation is represented.
    d. All of the above.

35. A programming language with strong type checking is
    a. Of academic interest, but of no practical use.
    b. An important contributor to software quality.
    c. Difficult to develop given the current state of compiler technology.
    d. All of the above.
    e. None of the above.

36. Abstraction and information hiding are two important design concepts. Which programming languages implement these concepts directly (indicate all that apply)?
    a. FORTRAN
    b. Modula-2
    c. COBOL
    d. Ada
    e. Pascal

37. An object-oriented programming language
    a. Does not enable the specification of abstract data types.
    b. Is similar in many ways to FORTRAN.
    c. Can't be used in production applications.
    d. None of the above.

Testing methods

38. The primary objective of software testing is to
    a. Prove that a program is correct.
    b. Uncover errors.
    c. Exercise each program function.
    d. Provide the only means available for achieving software quality.
39. A large information system, composed of 200 modules, is ready for testing. Indicate the types of testing that would be applicable for this system (indicate all that apply).
    a. Unit testing
    b. Integration testing
    c. Validation testing
    d. Stress testing
    e. Hardness testing
    f. System testing
40. White-box testing is a technique that
    a. Results in the design of test cases based on a knowledge of internal procedural logic of a program.
    b. Includes basis path testing among the specific methods that are applied.
    c. Requires the specification of test cases and expected results.
    d. All of the above.
    e. None of the above.
41. Basis path testing guarantees the following:
    a. That all variables will be defined and tested
    b. That all loops will be executed 1, $n - 1$, n, and $n + 1$ times, where n is the loop limit
    c. That all statements in the program will be executed at least once
    d. None of the above
42. Equivalence partitioning is a
    a. Black-box testing technique.
    b. White-box testing technique.
    c. Testing method that validates FORTRAN EQUIVALENCE statements.
    d. Method for determining the complexity of a test.

43. Which of the following integration strategies is viable for a large information system (indicate all that apply)?
    a. Big-bang testing
    b. Bottom-up testing
    c. Top-down testing
    d. Sandwich testing
    e. Basis path testing
    f. Boundary-value analysis

44. Test documentation should be
    a. Developed as tests are conducted and contain all results.
    b. Developed and reviewed prior to testing and contain detailed descriptions of each test along with expected results.
    c. Developed and reviewed prior to testing and contain general test strategy.
    d. Optional and required only for very large information system projects.

45. Which documents provide information that may be useful for test case design (indicate all that apply)?
    a. Requirements specification
    b. Design specification
    c. Source code listing
    d. Software project plan
    e. User manual

46. Which of the following statements best describes the current state of software tools for testing?
    a. Many useful tools exist but few are widely used.
    b. Few good tools exist.
    c. No testing tools exist.
    d. Testing is inherently a manual task—therefore, tools are superfluous.

Software maintenance

47. The typical information systems organization spends what percentage of all effort on maintenance?
    a. 30 percent
    b. 45 percent
    c. 70 percent
    d. 85 percent

48. Software maintenance can be properly characterized in the following way:
    a. An activity that results in error correction.
    b. An activity that results in adaptations based on external environmental changes.

     c. An activity that results in enhancements based on user requests.

     d. All of the above.

49. It is fair to say that

     a. Many software engineering techniques are not applicable to the software maintenance activity.

     b. Software maintenance procedures must account for special decisions required during the process.

     c. Software maintenance can be reduced dramatically if software engineering practices are followed.

     d. Software maintenance represents a relatively small percentage of a data-processing budget.

50. Which of the following activities are not part of the reengineering paradigm?

     a. Code restructuring

     b. Stabilization

     c. Inventory analysis

     d. Reverse engineering

     e. Statistical analysis

51. If you could magically cause one thing to happen and that thing would achieve the greatest reduction in maintenance costs, it would be

     a. Producing software that is error-free.

     b. Reducing requests for change by 75 percent.

     c. Freezing hardware and operating system characteristics.

     d. Performing better software engineering.

Quality assurance and configuration management

52. The best definition for software quality is

     a. Conformance to user-specified requirements.

     b. Achievement of extremely low defect rates.

     c. Production of software with high reliability.

     d. None of the above.

53. Ideally, the quality assurance function should be

     a. An integral part of the information systems organization.

     b. An ad hoc function performed by programmers.

     c. The responsibility of analysts and designers.

     d. An independent group that is autonomous of information systems management.

54. Which of the following has the strongest influence on software quality?

     a. Applying good programming practice.

    b. Conducting formal technical reviews.

    c. Spending time with the user.

    d. Requiring comprehensive project tracking.

55. The role of software configuration management is

    a. To identify elements of the software configuration.

    b. To control changes that are made on elements of the software configuration.

    c. To ensure that any changes have been properly made.

    d. All of the above.

    e. None of the above.

56. If properly conducted, change control is an activity that

    a. Forces users to delay requests for change.

    b. Forces developers to delay implementation of changes.

    c. Evaluates and prioritizes change requests.

    d. All of the above.

57. Indicate all statements that do not apply to the project database, also called the repository:

    a. Stores personnel information

    b. Enables the impact of changes to be tracked

    c. Acts as a foundation for tools integration

    d. Conforms to well-defined industry standards

    e. Holds project data, technical data, and metadata

58. Software quality can be determined

    a. Only through qualitative assessment of the success of an information system.

    b. Both quantitatively and qualitatively using a combination of metrics and quality criteria.

    c. Both quantitatively and qualitatively using empirical relationships and proven industry models.

    d. Only in the most rudimentary fashion.

59. If SQA or SCM are improperly instituted

    a. The architecture of an information system will suffer.

    b. Serious delays in project completion can occur.

    c. Design strategy will change radically.

    d. All of the above.

    e. None of the above.

60. SCM tools are

    a. Available for source code control, but not available for document control.

    b. Available for source code control and for document control.

    c. Nonexistent.

    d. Not used in conjunction with the CASE repository.

Answers for Software Engineering Self-Test

1. *c*	31. *a*
2. *c*	32. *e, b, a, c, d*
3. *d*	33. *c*
4. *b*	34. *d*
5. *d*	35. *b*
6. *c*	36. *b, d*
7. *d*	37. *d*
8. *d*	38. *b*
9. *b*	39. *a, b, c, d, f*
10. *a, c, d*	40. *d*
11. *d*	41. *c*
12. *d*	42. *a*
13. *b*	43. *b, c, d*
14. *a*	44. *b*
15. *b*	45. *a, b, c, d, e*
16. *c*	46. *a*
17. *b, c, d*	47. *c*
18. *e*	48. *d*
19. *c*	49. *b*
20. *a*	50. *e*
21. *d*	51. *b*
22. *d*	52. *a*
23. *c*	53. *d*
24. *b*	54. *b*
25. *d*	55. *d*
26. *b, c*	56. *c*
27. *d*	57. *a, c*
28. *b, c, d, f*	58. *b*
29. *c*	59. *b*
30. *b*	60. *b*

Interpreting Results of the Self-Assessment Test

Compute the percentage of correct responses for each of the sections of the self-test and enter on the summary sheet below:

Topic	# correct	Total	% correct
Software project management	_____	8	_____
Analysis methods	_____	10	_____
Software design	_____	12	_____
Coding and languages	_____	7	_____
Testing methods	_____	9	_____
Software maintenance	_____	5	_____
SQA & SCM	_____	9	_____
Overall grade:	_____	**60**	_____

If your grade for any section is 60 percent or lower, it is likely that you could benefit from specific education in the topic area indicated. If your overall grade is 60 percent or lower, you should consider a generic course in software engineering that covers all important topics.

III

A Prototype Common Process Framework

A common process framework defines the tasks, milestones, and deliverables that provide a procedural framework for software engineering. This appendix contains a sample process framework that may be of use as you work to assess existing software engineering "methodologies" or to develop your own framework for software engineering practice.

The tasks of the common process framework are presented in outline format. The task hierarchy is as follows:

I. Major Framework Function
    A. Framework task
        1. Subtask
            a. Subtask activity
                (1) Subactivity

The framework task outline follows.

  I. Planning
    A. Business systems planning
      This task is performed only when major systems are to be created or modified. It should be viewed as a complement to the common process framework (CPF), but not a task that is contained within the CPF.
    Document: *Business Systems Plan*
    Tools: business systems planning tools
        1. Create and/or update enterprise model
        2. Define information flows to/from related systems

    3. Develop system architectures

    4. Review business models

B. Customer communication

The intent of this CPF major task is to identify customer requirements and create a team-oriented environment in which the customer and developer work together to specify requirements. The task is iterative; that is, it may be performed a number of times throughout the development/maintenance process. Depending on the size and complexity of the project and whether it is new development or maintenance, one or more of the following subtasks will be initiated.

    1. Receive preliminary SOW (statement of work)

Every project, whether new development or maintenance, begins with a statement of work. For simple, low-complexity projects, the customer's statement may be verbal. For large, complex projects, the SOW must be written and will follow a template developed for the CPF.

Document: SOW template

Tools: no special tools

     a. Conduct informal discussion

        or

     b. Generate written SOW

    2. Conduct customer–developer meeting

The need for a project meeting will depend on project characteristics. In most cases, an informal meeting will be conducted. For large, complex projects, a formal facilitated application specification techniques (FAST) session may be indicated. In such cases, an outside consultant may be used to facilitate the FAST session.

Documents: preliminary list of requirements and other FAST deliverables

Tools: none

     a. Conduct informal meeting

        or

     b. Conduct formal FAST session

    3. Identify key customer requirements

Customer requirements must be documented for all projects, even if only one page is required. These requirements are derived from task B.2 above.

Document: list of requirements

Tools: none

     a. List business requirements

     b. List data requirements

     c. List functional requirements

     d. List interface requirements

4. Prioritize customer requirements

The customer will be asked to group and prioritize requirements.

5. Refine SOW

Requirements are "fleshed out" by software developers and limited by project constraints; both management and technical constraints are listed.

Document: SOW template

Tools: no special tools

a. Develop "minispecs" for requirements

b. List project constraints

6. SQA: review of SOW

The refined SOW is reviewed with the customer to ensure that all requirements have been properly characterized and that inconsistency and/or ambiguity is corrected.

a. Ensure conformance with customer requirements

b. Point out areas of ambiguity or inconsistency

c. Look for possible omissions

C. Develop detailed statement of scope

The intent of this CPF major task is to translate the SOW developed in task B into a statement of software scope for use in project planning. The task is iterative; that is, it may be performed a number of times throughout the development/maintenance process. In most cases, the SOW will simply evolve into the statement of scope (*Scoping Document*). Depending on the size and complexity of the project and whether it is new development or maintenance, one or more of the following subtasks will be initiated.

1. Categorize work request

Using a set of project characteristics defined during task C, each project request is categorized. This task defines the CPF tasks and subtasks that are required, the deliverables and milestones that should be developed, and the overall management approach to the project.

Document: project characterization questionnaire

Tools: no special tools

a. New development

or

b. Defect removal

or

c. Adaptation

or

d. Enhancement

2. Develop bounded scope

The refined statement of work is analyzed from a software development/maintenance perspective. Preliminary data and functional analysis are performed. Behavior is modeled, if required.

Document: preliminary analysis models

Tools: a CASE analysis tool (not essential)

    a. Perform preliminary analysis

        (1) Describe new or modified data to be produced

        (2) Describe new or modified data to be input

        (3) Describe functions to be implemented

        (4) Describe behavior to be modified or implemented

    b. Evaluate existing software to be modified

        (1) List data structures to be affected

        (2) Note program components to be affected

        (3) List other applications or systems to be affected or integrated

        (4) Describe user interaction to be affected

    c. SQA: review scope

D. Project planning

The intent of this CPF major task is to establish a project plan. The task is iterative; that is, it may be performed a number of times throughout the development/maintenance process. Depending on the size and complexity of the project and whether it is new development or maintenance, one or more of the following subtasks will be initiated.

1. Categorize project for common process framework

This activity will be performed by completing a one-page questionnaire that will help a project manager to properly characterize complexity, size, and so on.

Document: project characterization questionnaire

Tools: none

    a. Small

      or

    b. Medium

      or

    c. Large

2. Describe work tasks, deliverables, and milestones

Once task D.1 has been completed, the set of tasks, deliverables, and milestones that is appropriate for the project is selected. Generic task templates may be customized by the project manager to meet special needs of the work to be accomplished.

Document: WBS and deliverables

Tools: project scheduling tool

     a. Use simple task list
     b. Use project scheduling tool
  3. Estimate effort and cost (preliminary)
     Effort and cost are estimated on the basis of information obtained from earlier tasks. For some projects, the function-point value for a project may be estimated at this point.
     Document: effort/cost tables
     Tools: a CASE software estimation tool
     a. Best experience estimate
       and/or
     b. Decompositional estimate
       and/or
     c. Empirical modeling
E. Risk analysis
    The intent of this CPF major task is to delineate the generic and project-specific risks that are likely to be encountered during this project. The task is iterative; that is, it may be performed a number of times throughout the development/maintenance process. Depending on the size and complexity of the project and whether it is new development or maintenance, one or more of the following subtasks will be initiated.
  1. Define project risks
     The project manager creates a list of project risks and then assesses the risks as implied by the subtasks that are shown below.
     Document: description of risks
     Tools: none or a risk management tool
     a. Risk identification
       (1) Use generic project risk checklist
       (2) List project-specific risks
     b. Risk projection (probability)
     c. Impact of risk
       (1) On schedule
       (2) On cost
  2. Develop risk management and monitoring plan
     For larger, high-complexity projects, a written *Risk Management and Monitoring Plan* (RMMP) is developed.
     Document: RMMP
     Tools: none
     a. Medium projects: part of project plan
     b. Large projects: may be a separate document
  3. Conduct maintenance impact analysis

This subtask implements a change control procedure that assesses the impact of a request for change on existing program components, data, and related application systems.

    a. Characterize the types of changes to be made

    b. Review software to be affected by changes

    c. Evaluate potential side effects

F. Management review of project plan

The intent of this CPF major task is to provide software management with a standard approach for the review of the project plan.

G. Customer review of project plan

The intent of this CPF major task is to provide the customer with a standard approach for the review of the project plan. If the customer cannot accept projected delivery dates or budget, the developer will provide alternatives on the basis of the prioritization developed as part of task B.4.

1. Evaluate schedule and/or budget
2. Suggest modifications to plan
3. Negotiate with developer

II. Engineering

A. Prototype development and evaluation

The intent of this CPF major task is to develop a prototype that can assist the customer and developer to refine hazy requirements and demonstrate capability. The task is iterative; that is, it may be performed a number of times throughout the development/maintenance process. Depending on the size and complexity of the project and whether it is new development or maintenance, one or more of the following subtasks will be initiated.

Documents: none

Tools: prototyping tools

1. Select functionality and/or behavior to prototype
2. Create "paper" prototype
   or
3. Create executable prototype
   and/or
4. Create preliminary user guide
5. Customer evaluation
       a. Review the prototype
       b. Suggest changes
       c. Consider impact of changes on plan
       d. Select changes to be implemented

B. Analysis modeling

The intent of this CPF major task is to develop a comprehensive model of the application that describes "what" must be accomplished. The task is iterative; that is, it may be performed a number of times throughout the development/maintenance process. The depth and sophistication of the analysis model will be defined by project characteristics.

Document: analysis models, *Software Specification*

Tool: CASE analysis tool

1. Isolate analysis domain
   a. New application
   b. Maintenance: domain of change
2. Model data
3. Model function
4. Model behavior
5. SQA: review models
   a. For technical content
   b. For requirements traceability
6. Specification
   a. Incorporate models into a document
   b. Define constraints
   c. Establish test criteria
   d. Create software specification
7. SQA: review of specification
   a. Review technical content of models
   b. Review conformance with SOW
8. SQA: begin test planning using test criteria as guide

C. Design

The intent of this CPF major task is to transform the analysis model into a design model that describes how the application is to be built. The task is iterative; that is, it may be performed a number of times throughout the development/maintenance process. The depth and sophistication of the design model will be defined by project characteristics.

Document: *Design Document*

Tool: CASE design tool

1. Data design
   a. Define data structures from data model
      or
   b. Integrate application data into database schema
   c. SQA: review the data design
2. Architectural design
   a. Create design of program architecture
   b. Identify program components to be created or changed

          c. Begin design of component interfaces

          d. Develop cross reference to data design

          e. SQA: review the architectural design

     3. Procedural design

          a. Create algorithms for each new component

          or

          b. Modify algorithms for existing components

          c. SQA: review procedural design at the component level

     4. Interface design

          a. Design new or modified screen layout and special displays

          b. Integrate interface with other components

          c. SQA: review the interface design

     5. Design documentation

          a. Create design overview

          or

          b. Create design specification

          c. SQA: design review

             (1) Conduct informal peer review

             (2) Conduct formal walkthrough

                (a) Schedule walkthrough meeting

                (b) Hold meeting

                (c) Complete summary report

D. Code generation

    The intent of this CPF major task is to transform the design model into executable code.

    Document: source code

    Tools: compilers, editors, 4GT tools

    1. Use conventional programming language

      or

    2. Use 4GL

      or

    3. Use database query language

    4. SQA: code review

          a. Check conformance to design

          b. Check conformance to coding standards

E. Testing

    The intent of this CPF major task is to provide a plan and procedure for software testing.

    Document: *Test Plan and Procedure*

    Tools: CASE testing tools

    1. Revise test plan based on "as built" design

  2. Unit testing
    a. Design white-box tests for program components
    b. Execute the tests
    c. Record results
  3. System testing
    a. Use test plan as a guide for testing
    b. Execute the tests
    c. Record results
    d. SQA: review results
  4. Regression testing
  5. User acceptance testing
F. User acceptance
    The intent of this CPF major task is to establish a set of SQA tasks that will be invoked whenever an application is released to an end user.
  1. SQA: conduct final review of all requirements
  2. SQA: review readiness for "cutover"
  3. SQA: review user documentation

III. Installation
  A. Production update
      The intent of this CPF major task is to create an SCM procedure that ensures that change control and version control have been properly implemented.
    1. Use SCM environment for version control
    2. SQA: review all system documentation
  B. Postinstallation review
      The intent of this CPF major task is to establish a debriefing activity that will be used to improve the CPF.
    1. Review project plan versus actuals
    2. Identify what worked and what didn't
    3. Review metrics collected during project
    4. Solicit customer feedback
  C. System support plan
      The intent of this CPF major task is to define a plan for ongoing support of a production application.
      Document: *System Support Plan*
    1. Evaluate status of production system
      a. Users
      b. Changing needs
      c. Related systems
    2. Define approach for user support
      a. User training

Index

ABOUT THE AUTHOR

Roger S. Pressman is president of R. S. Pressman and
Associates, Inc. He serves as principal consultant, helping
companies establish effective software engineering
practices. As an engineer and manager, a professor, and an
internationally recognized consultant, Dr. Pressman brings
more than two decades of experience to his work. He is the
author of six books, including *Software Engineering: A
Practitioner's Approach*, Third Edition.